EXTRAORDINARY X-MEN

APOCALYPSE WARS

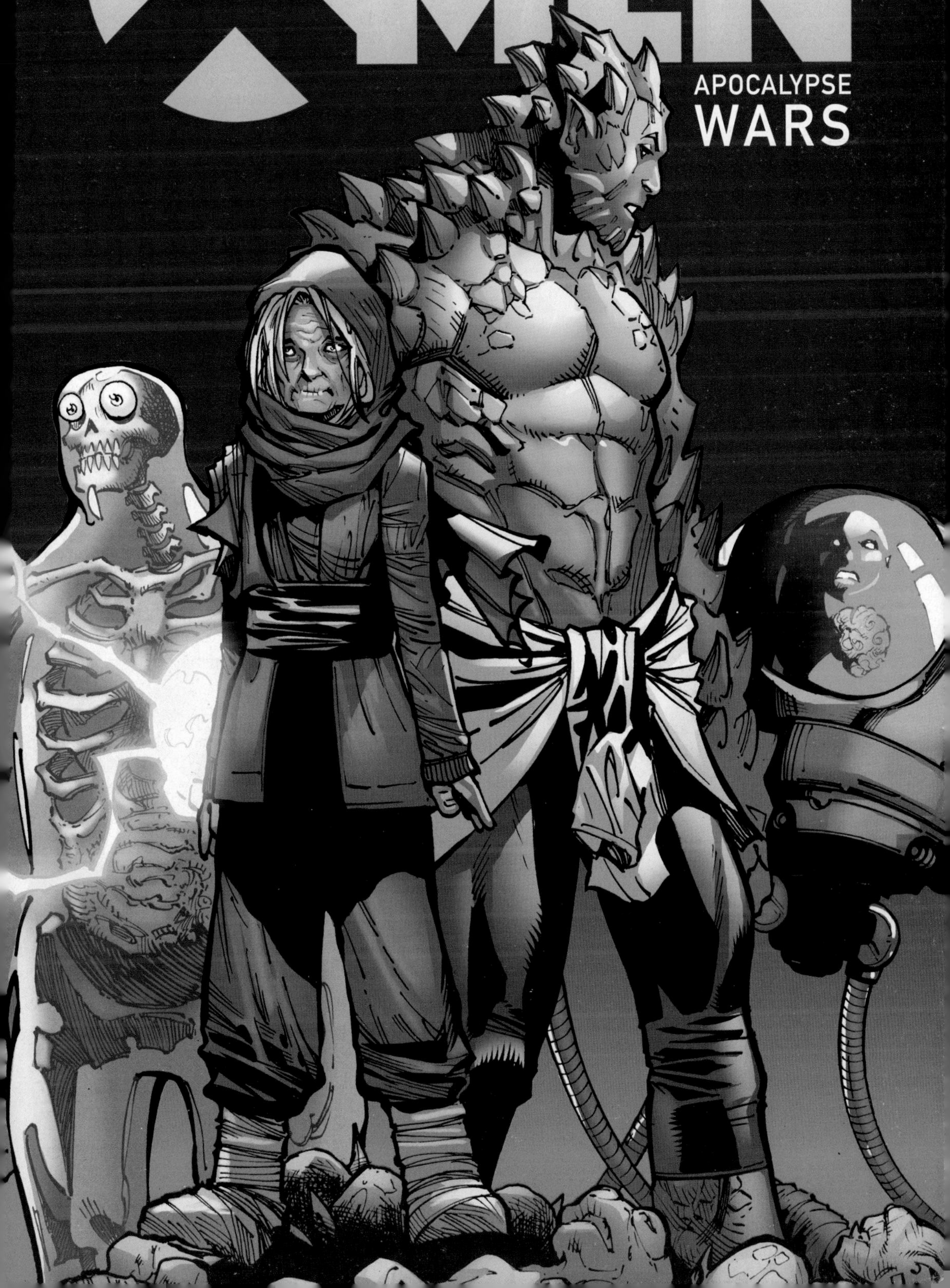

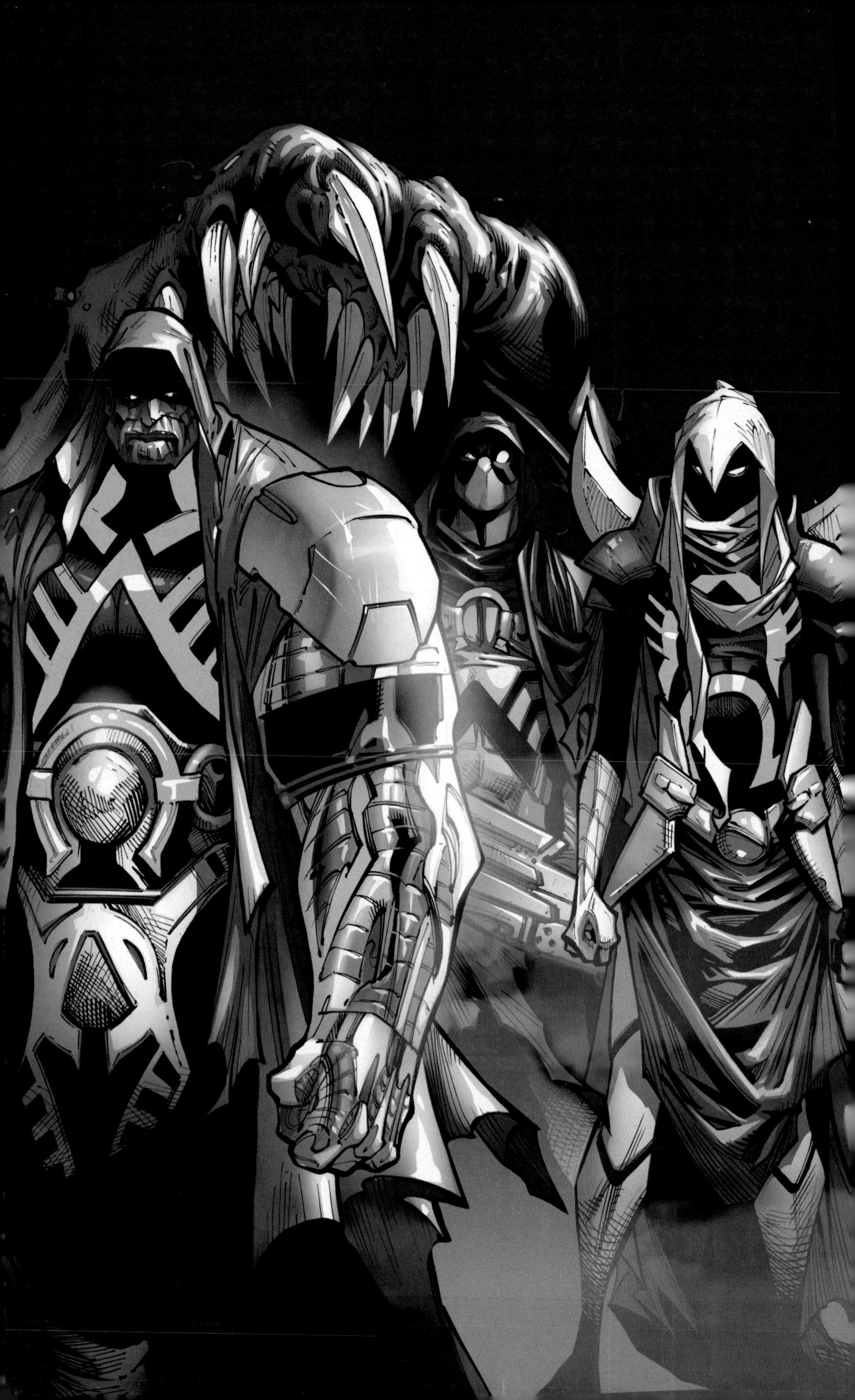

ONSIDERED TO BE THE NEXT STEP IN HUMAN EVOLUTION, MUTANTS DISCOVER THEIR HERITAGE AT PUBERTY, WHEN THEY MANIFEST
ERHUMAN POWERS AND ABILITIES. BUT RATHER THAN BEING CELEBRATED FOR THEIR GIFTS, MUTANTS ARE INSTEAD CONFRONTED BY
WORLD THAT'S NEVER HATED OR FEARED THEM MORE. WITH THE FATE OF THEIR RACE HANGING IN THE BALANCE, MUTANTKIND NEEDS
HEROES WHO WILL COURAGEOUSLY LEAD THEM INTO THE FUTURE. MUTANTKIND NEEDS...

EXTRAORDINARY X-MEN

TERRIGEN MISTS WERE RELEASED ACROSS THE GLOBE, IGNITING THE INHUMAN RACE...WHILE CRIPPLING MUTANTKIND.
ISONOUS TO MUTANTS, THE MISTS HAVE WHITTLED DOWN THEIR NUMBERS AND SUPPRESSED ANY NEW MUTANT MANIFESTATIONS.
TO PREVENT THE EXTINCTION OF HER PEOPLE, VETERAN X-MAN STORM HAS CREATED A SANCTUARY FROM THE MISTS IN
LIMBO CALLED X-HAVEN, WHERE ALL MUTANTS ARE WELCOME. BUT STORM HAS ALSO REALIZED THAT
MUTANTS CAN'T JUST HIDE; THEY MUST SHOW THE WORLD THAT THEY HAVE A PLACE IN IT.

APOCALYPSE WARS

JEFF LEMIRE
WRITER

ISSUES #6-7

VICTOR IBAÑEZ
ARTIST

JAY DAVID RAMOS
COLOR ARTIST

ISSUES #8-12

HUMBERTO RAMOS
PENCILER

VICTOR OLAZABA
INKER

EDGAR DELGADO
COLORIST

"STRANGE MAGIK"

VICTOR IBAÑEZ
ARTIST

SOTOCOLOR
COLOR ARTIST

HUMBERTO RAMOS & EDGAR DELGADO
COVER ART

VC'S JOE CARAMAGNA
LETTERER

CHRISTINA HARRINGTON
ASSISTANT EDITOR

DANIEL KETCHUM
EDITOR

MARK PANICCIA
X-MEN GROUP EDITOR

X-MEN CREATED BY STAN LEE & JACK KIRBY

COLLECTION EDITOR: JENNIFER GRÜNWALD
ASSOCIATE EDITOR: SARAH BRUNSTAD
ASSOCIATE MANAGING EDITOR: KATERI WOODY
EDITOR, SPECIAL PROJECTS: MARK D. BEAZLEY

VP PRODUCTION & SPECIAL PROJECTS: JEFF YOUNGQUIST
SVP PRINT, SALES & MARKETING: DAVID GABRIEL
BOOK DESIGNER: JAY BOWEN

EDITOR IN CHIEF: AXEL ALONSO
CHIEF CREATIVE OFFICER: JOE QUESADA
PUBLISHER: DAN BUCKLEY
EXECUTIVE PRODUCER: ALAN FINE

ORDINARY X-MEN VOL. 2: APOCALYPSE WARS. Contains material originally published in magazine form as EXTRAORDINARY X-MEN #6-12. First printing 2016. ISBN# 978-0-7851-9935-9. Published by MARVEL
WIDE, INC., a subsidiary of MARVEL ENTERTAINMENT, LLC. OFFICE OF PUBLICATION: 135 West 50th Street, New York, NY 10020. Copyright © 2016 MARVEL No similarity between any of the names, characters,
s, and/or institutions in this magazine with those of any living or dead person or institution is intended, and any such similarity which may exist is purely coincidental. Printed in the U.S.A. ALAN FINE, President,
Entertainment; DAN BUCKLEY, President, TV, Publishing & Brand Management; JOE QUESADA, Chief Creative Officer; TOM BREVOORT, SVP of Publishing; DAVID BOGART, SVP of Business Affairs & Operations,
ing & Partnership; C.B. CEBULSKI, VP of Brand Management & Development, Asia; DAVID GABRIEL, SVP of Sales & Marketing, Publishing; JEFF YOUNGQUIST, VP of Production & Special Projects; DAN CARR,
ive Director of Publishing Technology; ALEX MORALES, Director of Publishing Operations; SUSAN CRESPI, Production Manager; STAN LEE, Chairman Emeritus. For information regarding advertising in Marvel Comics
arvel.com, please contact Vit DeBellis, Integrated Sales Manager, at vdebellis@marvel.com. For Marvel subscription inquiries, please call 888-511-5480. Manufactured between 8/19/2016 and 9/26/2016 by
MMUNICATIONS INC., ROANOKE, VA, USA.

7654321

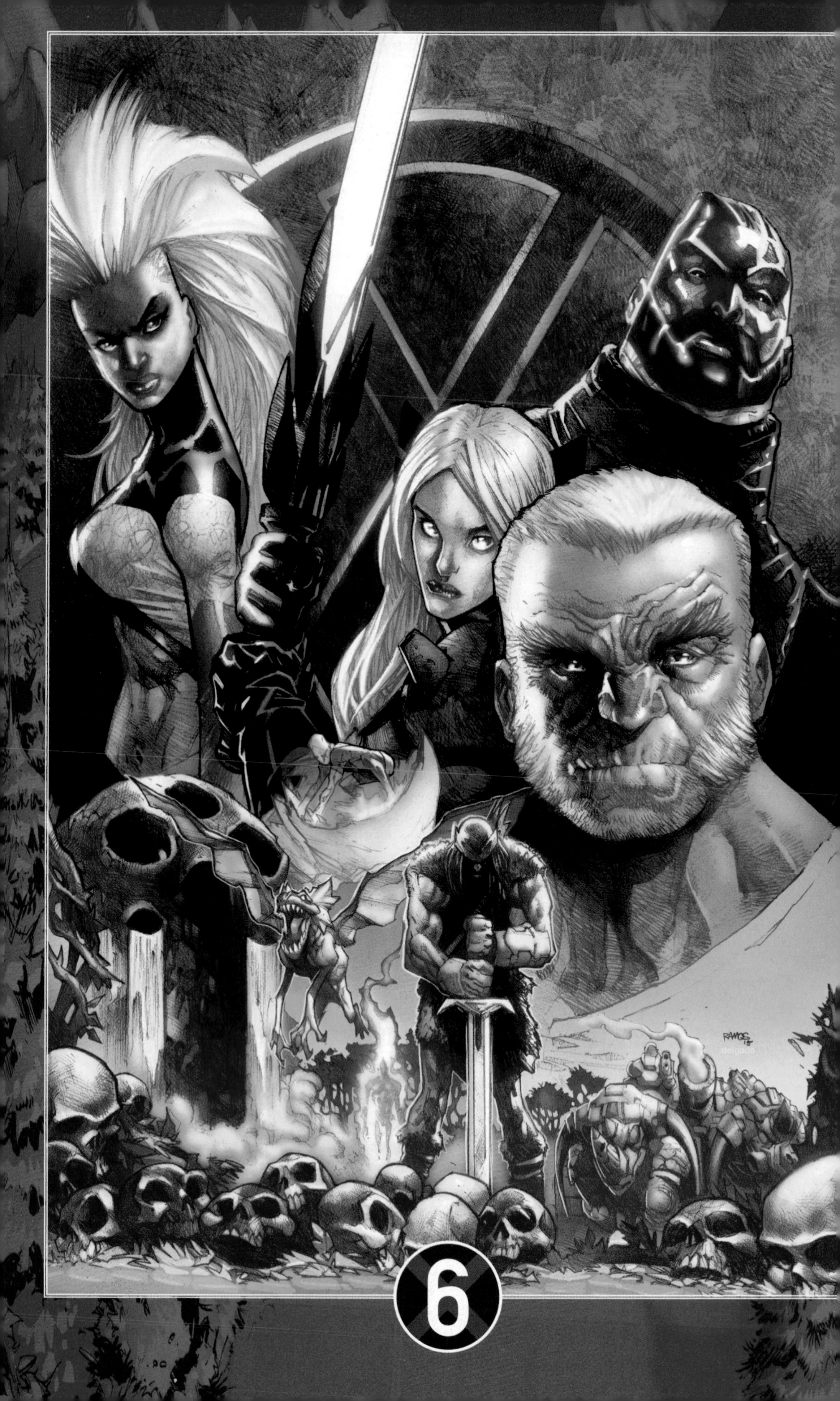
6

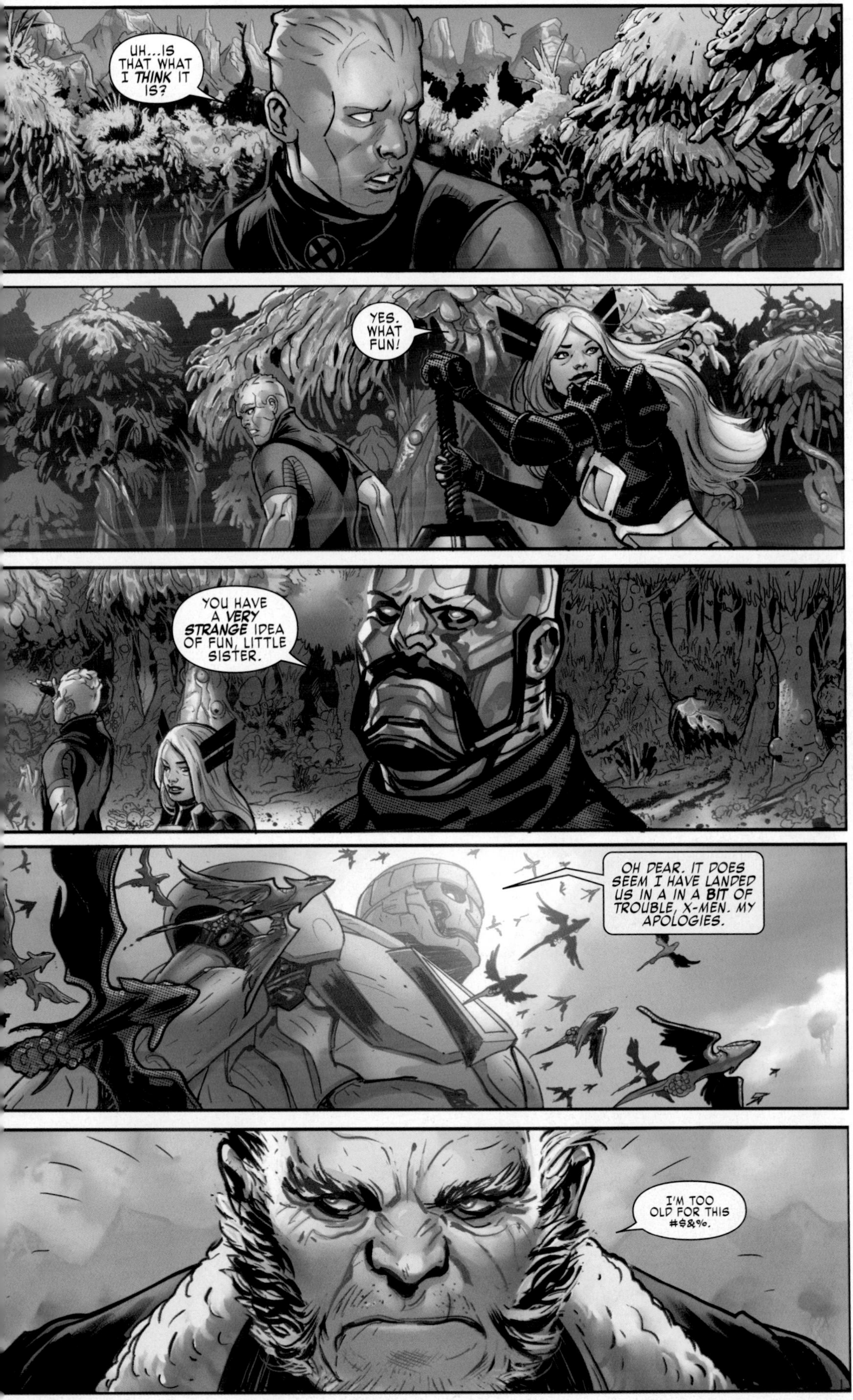
UH...IS THAT WHAT I THINK IT IS?
YES. WHAT FUN!
YOU HAVE A VERY STRANGE IDEA OF FUN, LITTLE SISTER.
OH DEAR. IT DOES SEEM I HAVE LANDED US IN A IN A BIT OF TROUBLE, X-MEN. MY APOLOGIES.
I'M TOO OLD FOR THIS #$&%.

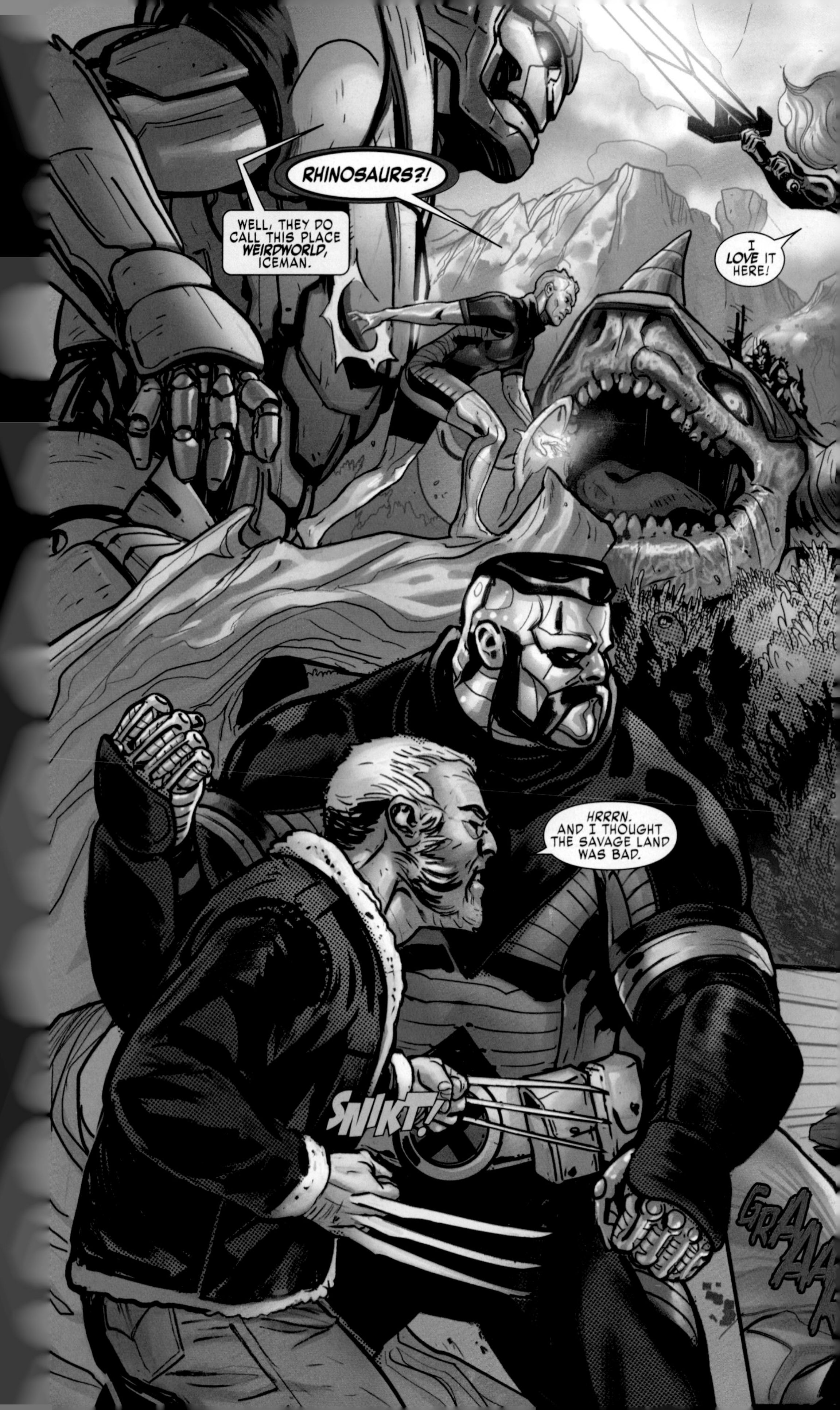

RHINOSAURS?!
WELL, THEY DO CALL THIS PLACE WEIRDWORLD, ICEMAN.
I LOVE IT HERE!
HRRRN. AND I THOUGHT THE SAVAGE LAND WAS BAD.
SNIKT!

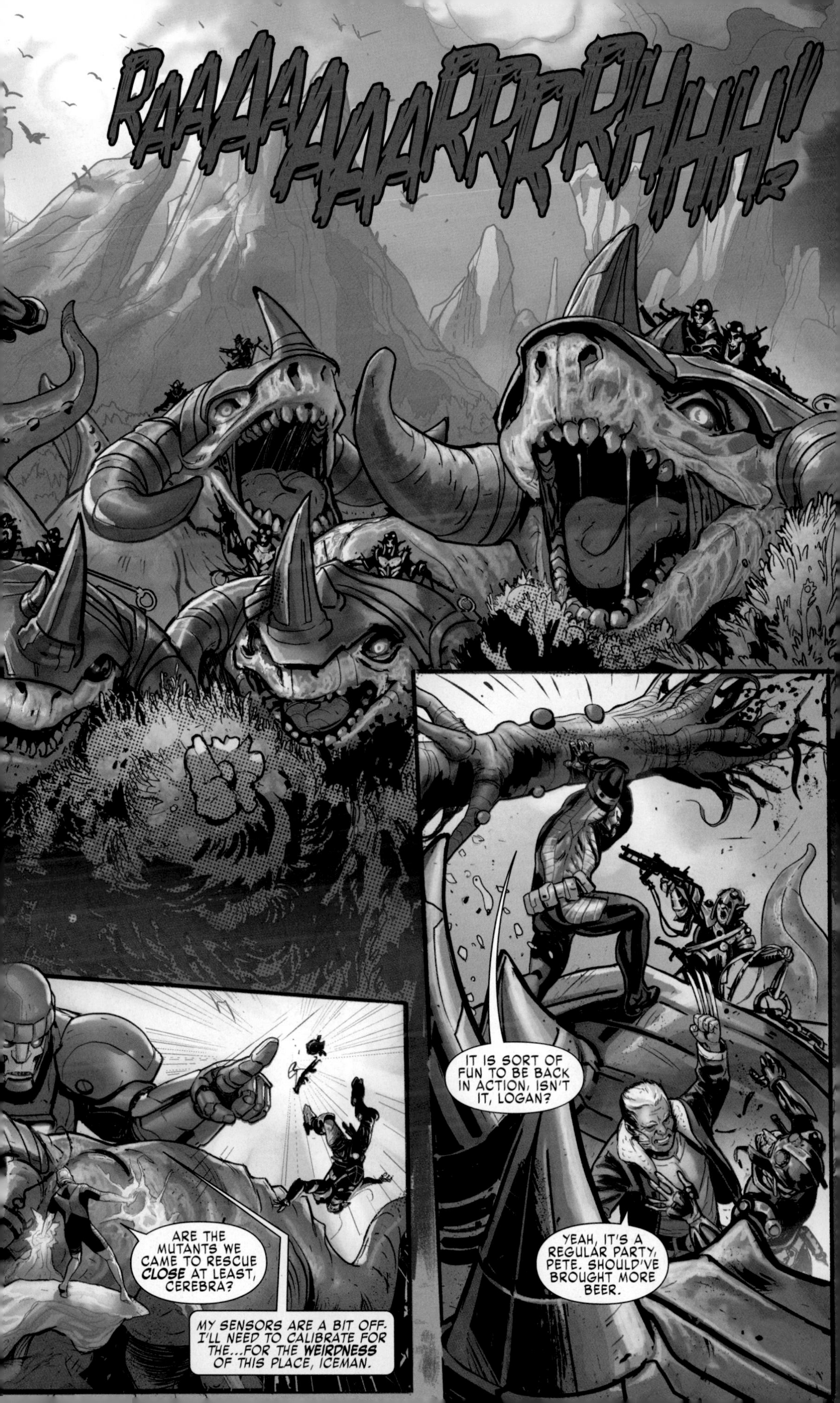
RAAAAAAAARRRRHHH!
IT IS SORT OF FUN TO BE BACK IN ACTION, ISN'T IT, LOGAN?
YEAH, IT'S A REGULAR PARTY, PETE. SHOULD'VE BROUGHT MORE BEER.
ARE THE MUTANTS WE CAME TO RESCUE CLOSE AT LEAST, CEREBRA?
MY SENSORS ARE A BIT OFF. I'LL NEED TO CALIBRATE FOR THE...FOR THE WEIRDNESS OF THIS PLACE, ICEMAN.

X-HAVEN, FIVE HOURS EARLIER.

YOU REALLY THINK THAT'S APPROPRIATE RIGHT NOW, GRAMPS?

SPENT FORTY-SOMETHING YEARS SCAVENGING NOTHING BUT *SKUNK BEER* FROM THE WASTELANDS, SNOWBALL. GOT A LOT OF LOST TIME TO MAKE UP FOR.

DO YOU THINK HE'S GETTING ANY BETTER?

I WAS ABLE TO FIX HIS *TAIL,* BUT HIS *M___,* WELL, THAT'S N___ EXACTLY MY AR___ OF EXPERTIS___

KT-SHH!

I THINK I CAN HELP HIM, STORM. I CAN USE MY TELEPATHY, TRY AND FIGURE OUT WHAT HAPPENED TO NIGHTCRAWLER THAT LEFT HIM SO DAMAGED.

IT MAY COME TO THAT, JEAN, BUT I'M HESITANT TO RUSH INTO ANYTHING. HE SEEMS SO *FRAGILE.* I THINK WE SHOULD GIVE PIOTR A CHANCE TO GET THROUGH TO HIM FIRST.

"IF THAT FAILS..."

KURT, DO YOU RECOGNIZE ME? *PLEASE,* OLD FRIEND, GIVE ME SOME SIGN IF YOU DO. WE ARE ALL *SO WORRIED* ABOUT YOU.

WORRIED?

YES. PLEASE, LET ME *HELP* YOU.

ONLY GOD CAN HELP ME.

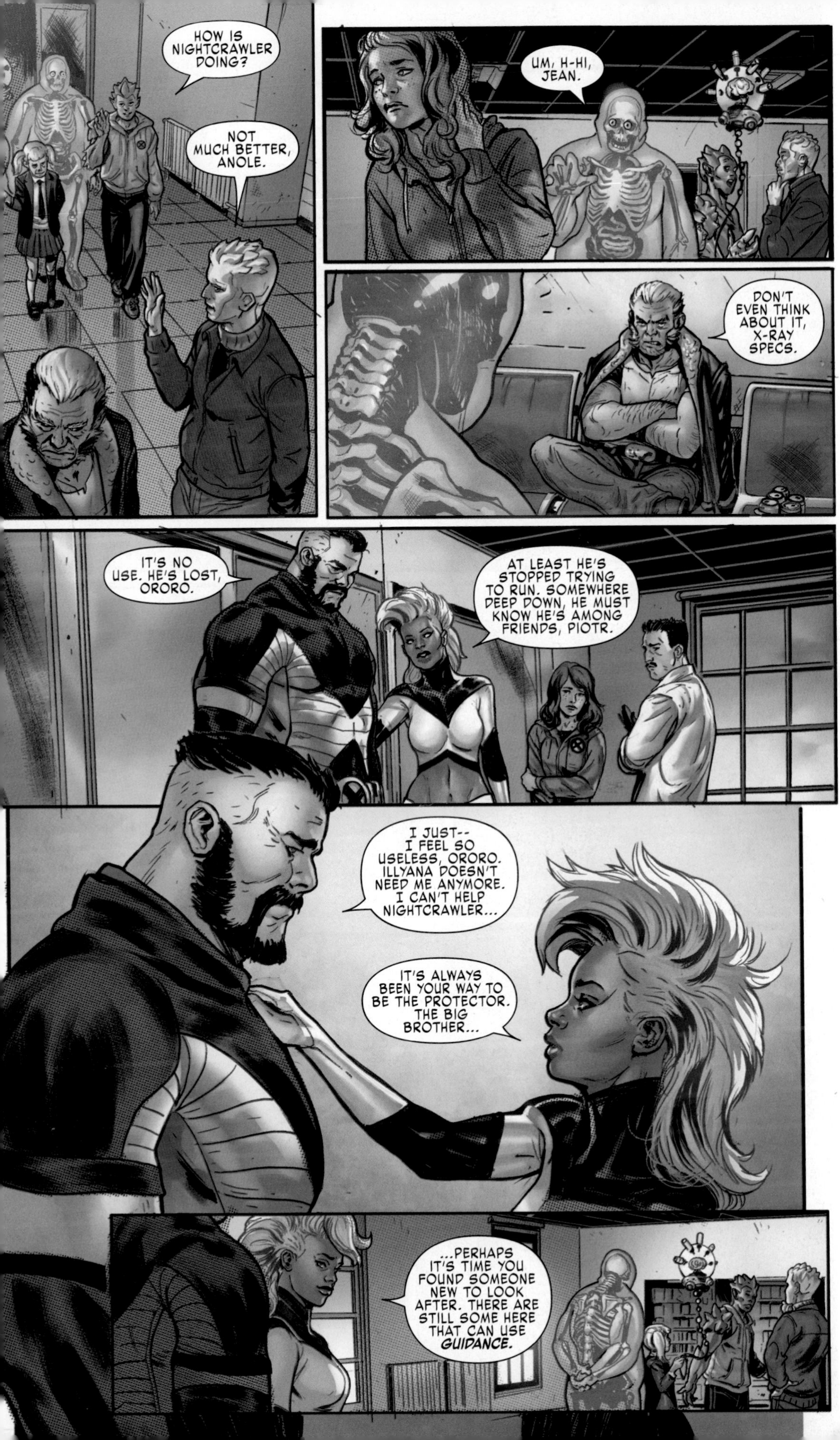
HOW IS NIGHTCRAWLER DOING?
NOT MUCH BETTER, ANOLE.
UM, H-HI, JEAN.
DON'T EVEN THINK ABOUT IT, X-RAY SPECS.
IT'S NO USE. HE'S LOST, ORORO.
AT LEAST HE'S STOPPED TRYING TO RUN. SOMEWHERE DEEP DOWN, HE MUST KNOW HE'S AMONG FRIENDS, PIOTR.
I JUST-- I FEEL SO USELESS, ORORO. ILLYANA DOESN'T NEED ME ANYMORE. I CAN'T HELP NIGHTCRAWLER...
IT'S ALWAYS BEEN YOUR WAY TO BE THE PROTECTOR. THE BIG BROTHER...
...PERHAPS IT'S TIME YOU FOUND SOMEONE NEW TO LOOK AFTER. THERE ARE STILL SOME HERE THAT CAN USE *GUIDANCE.*

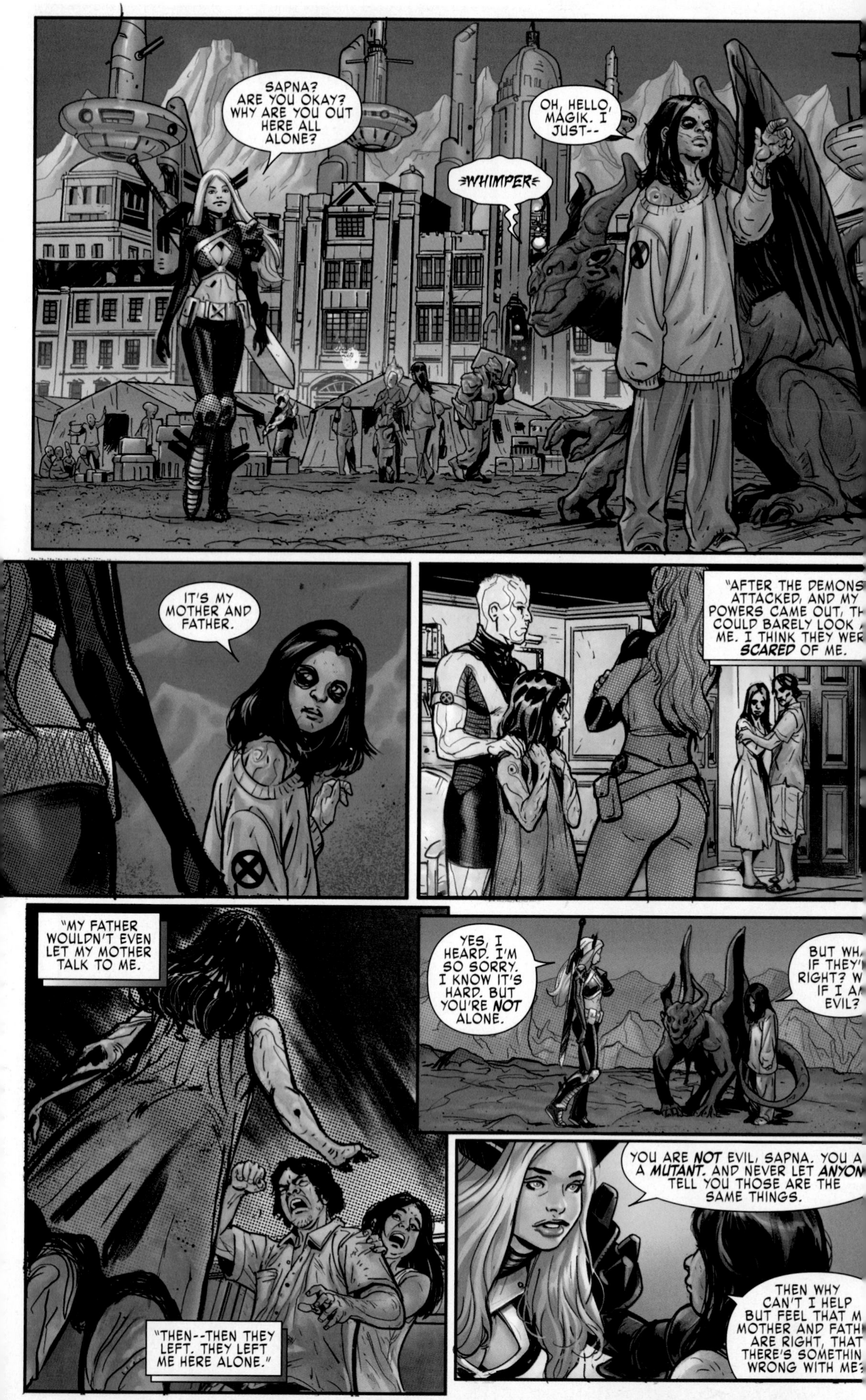

SAPNA? ARE YOU OKAY? WHY ARE YOU OUT HERE ALL ALONE?
OH, HELLO, MAGIK. I JUST--
WHIMPER
IT'S MY MOTHER AND FATHER.
"AFTER THE DEMONS ATTACKED, AND MY POWERS CAME OUT, TH COULD BARELY LOOK ME. I THINK THEY WER SCARED OF ME.
"MY FATHER WOULDN'T EVEN LET MY MOTHER TALK TO ME.
"THEN--THEN THEY LEFT. THEY LEFT ME HERE ALONE."
YES, I HEARD. I'M SO SORRY. I KNOW IT'S HARD. BUT YOU'RE NOT ALONE.
BUT WH IF THEY' RIGHT? W IF I A EVIL?
YOU ARE NOT EVIL, SAPNA. YOU A A MUTANT. AND NEVER LET ANYON TELL YOU THOSE ARE THE SAME THINGS.
THEN WHY CAN'T I HELP BUT FEEL THAT M MOTHER AND FATH ARE RIGHT, THAT THERE'S SOMETHIN WRONG WITH ME?

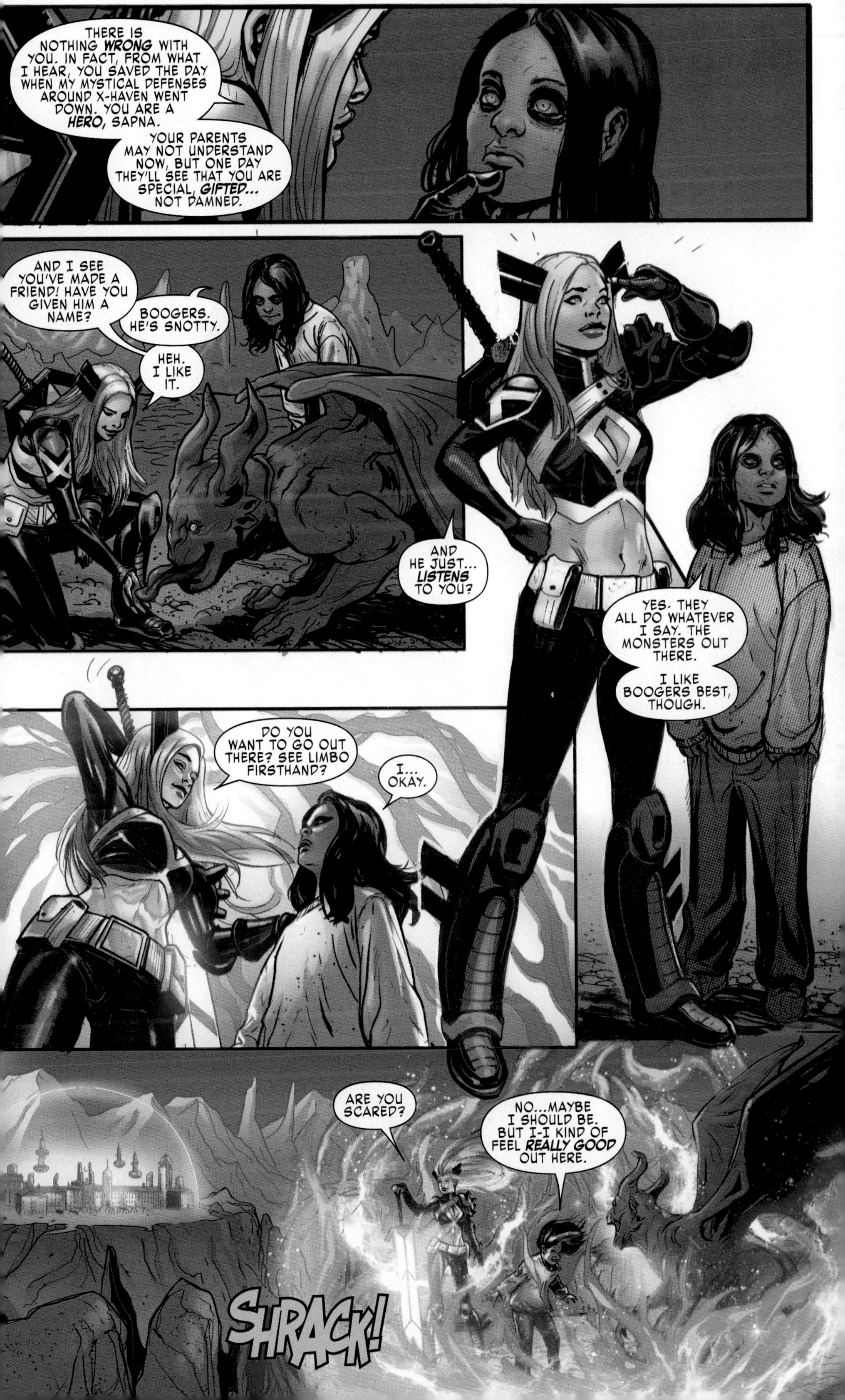
THERE IS NOTHING WRONG WITH YOU. IN FACT, FROM WHAT I HEAR, YOU SAVED THE DAY WHEN MY MYSTICAL DEFENSES AROUND X-HAVEN WENT DOWN. YOU ARE A HERO, SAPNA.
YOUR PARENTS MAY NOT UNDERSTAND NOW, BUT ONE DAY THEY'LL SEE THAT YOU ARE SPECIAL, GIFTED... NOT DAMNED.
AND I SEE YOU'VE MADE A FRIEND! HAVE YOU GIVEN HIM A NAME?
BOOGERS. HE'S SNOTTY.
HEH. I LIKE IT.
AND HE JUST... LISTENS TO YOU?
YES. THEY ALL DO WHATEVER I SAY. THE MONSTERS OUT THERE.
I LIKE BOOGERS BEST, THOUGH.
DO YOU WANT TO GO OUT THERE? SEE LIMBO FIRSTHAND?
I... OKAY.
ARE YOU SCARED?
NO...MAYBE I SHOULD BE. BUT I-I KIND OF FEEL REALLY GOOD OUT HERE.
SHRACK!

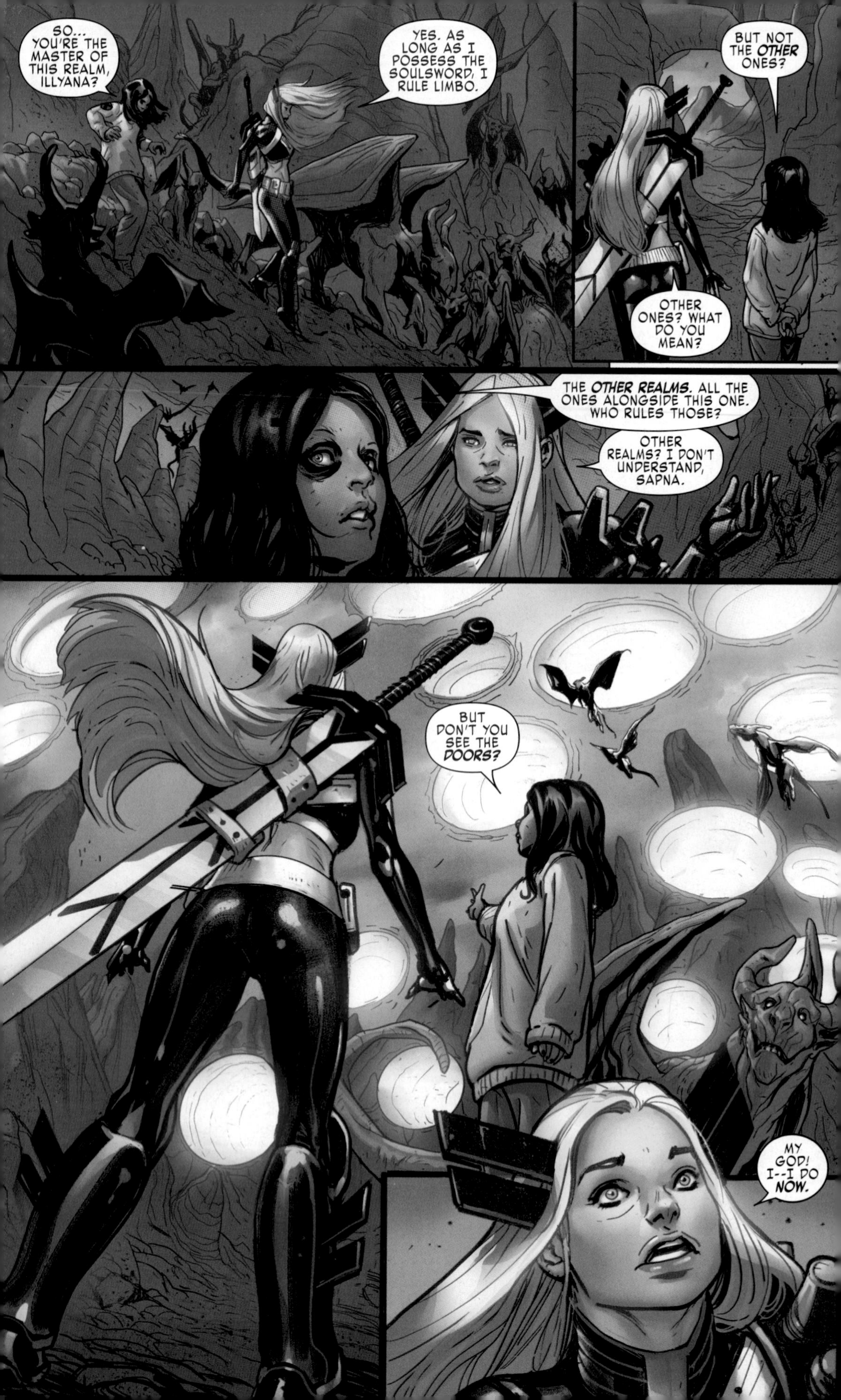

SO... YOU'RE THE MASTER OF THIS REALM, ILLYANA?
YES. AS LONG AS I POSSESS THE SOULSWORD, I RULE LIMBO.
BUT NOT THE OTHER ONES?
OTHER ONES? WHAT DO YOU MEAN?
THE OTHER REALMS. ALL THE ONES ALONGSIDE THIS ONE. WHO RULES THOSE?
OTHER REALMS? I DON'T UNDERSTAND, SAPNA.
BUT DON'T YOU SEE THE DOORS?
MY GOD! I--I DO NOW.

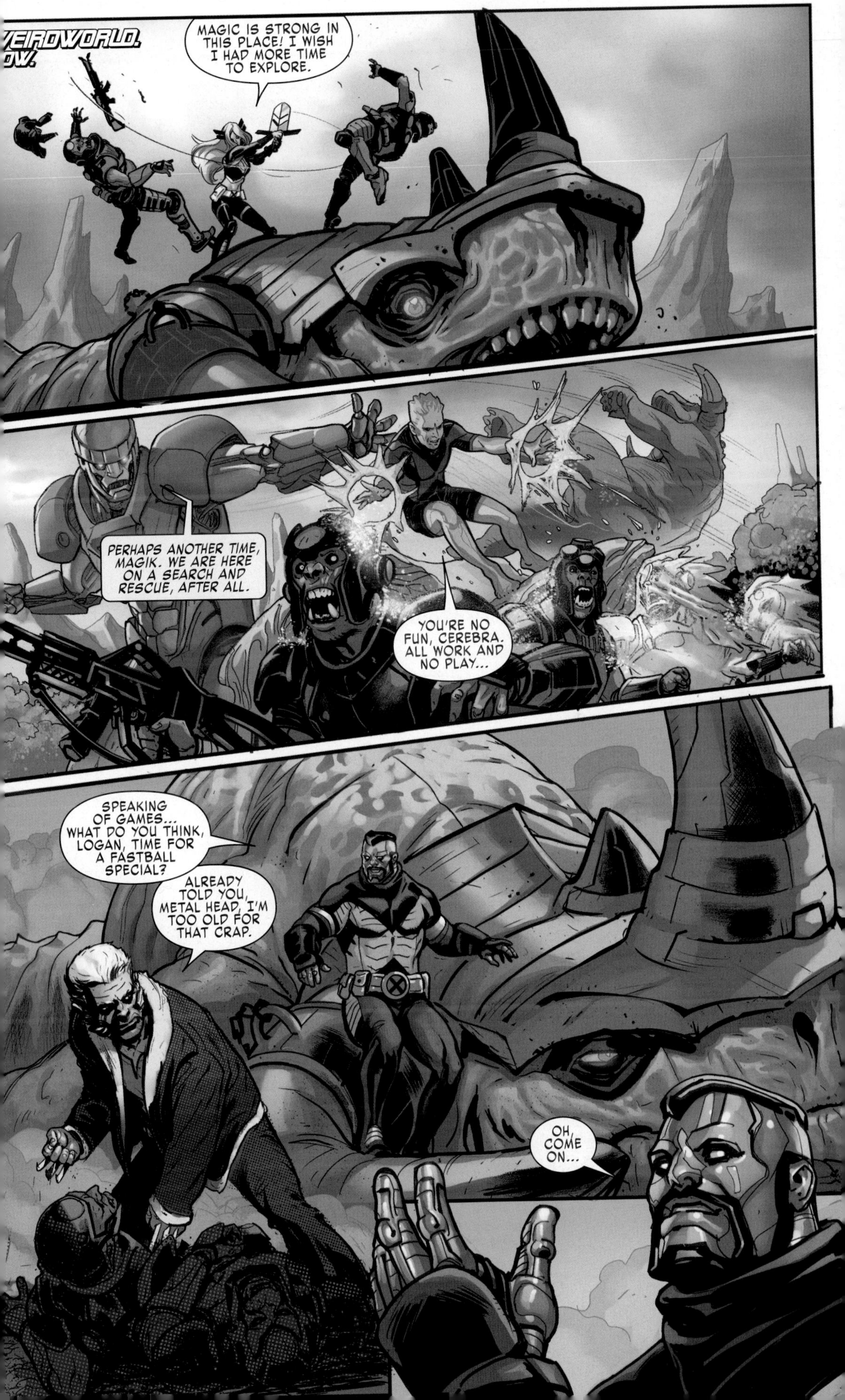

WEIRDWORLD. NOW.
MAGIC IS STRONG IN THIS PLACE! I WISH I HAD MORE TIME TO EXPLORE.
PERHAPS ANOTHER TIME, MAGIK. WE ARE HERE ON A SEARCH AND RESCUE, AFTER ALL.
YOU'RE NO FUN, CEREBRA. ALL WORK AND NO PLAY...
SPEAKING OF GAMES... WHAT DO YOU THINK, LOGAN, TIME FOR A FASTBALL SPECIAL?
ALREADY TOLD YOU, METAL HEAD, I'M TOO OLD FOR THAT CRAP.
OH, COME ON...

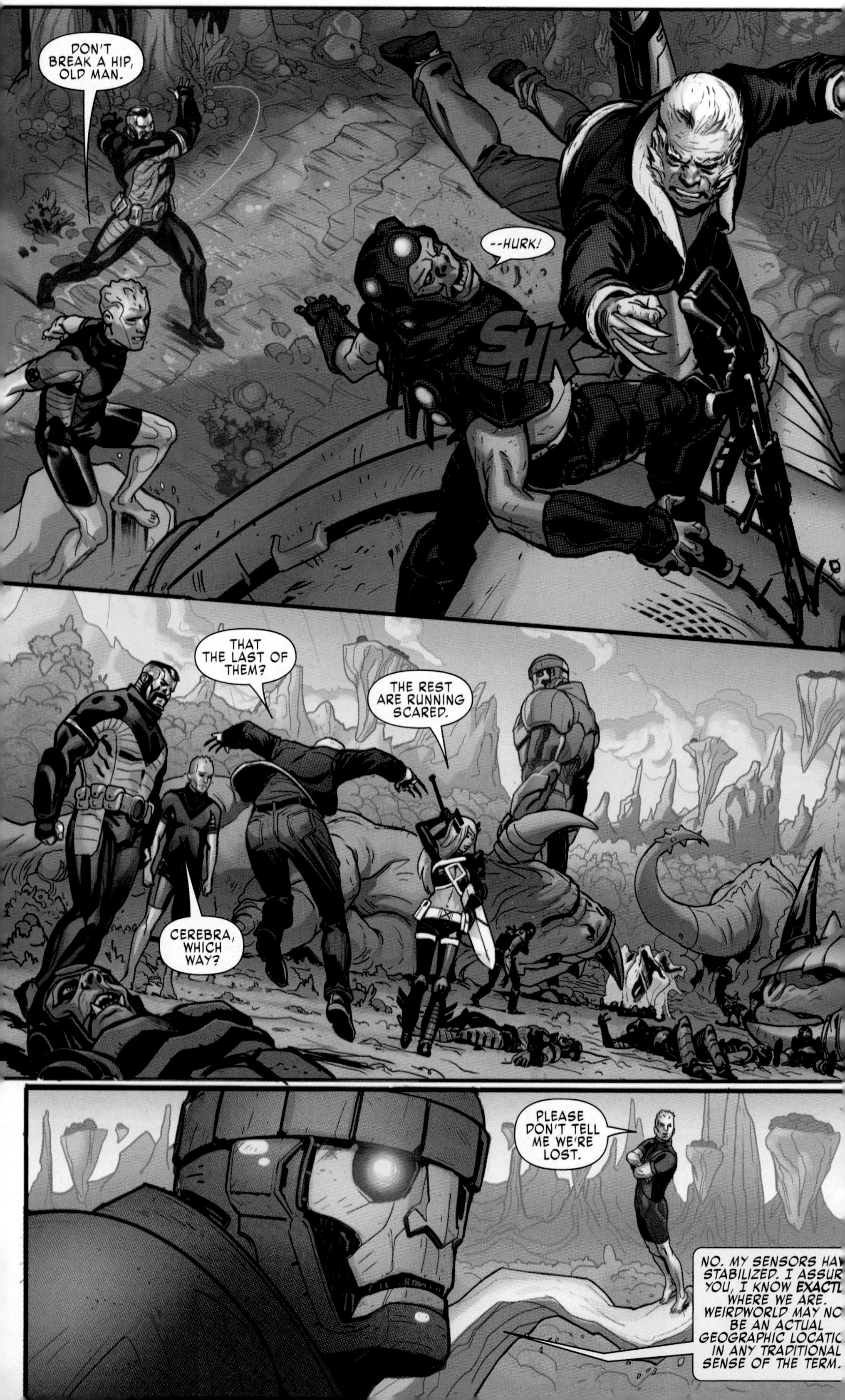
DON'T BREAK A HIP, OLD MAN.
--HURK!
SHK
THAT THE LAST OF THEM?
THE REST ARE RUNNING SCARED.
CEREBRA, WHICH WAY?
PLEASE DON'T TELL ME WE'RE LOST.
NO. MY SENSORS HA STABILIZED. I ASSUR YOU, I KNOW EXACTL WHERE WE ARE. WEIRDWORLD MAY NO BE AN ACTUAL GEOGRAPHIC LOCATIC IN ANY TRADITIONAL SENSE OF THE TERM.

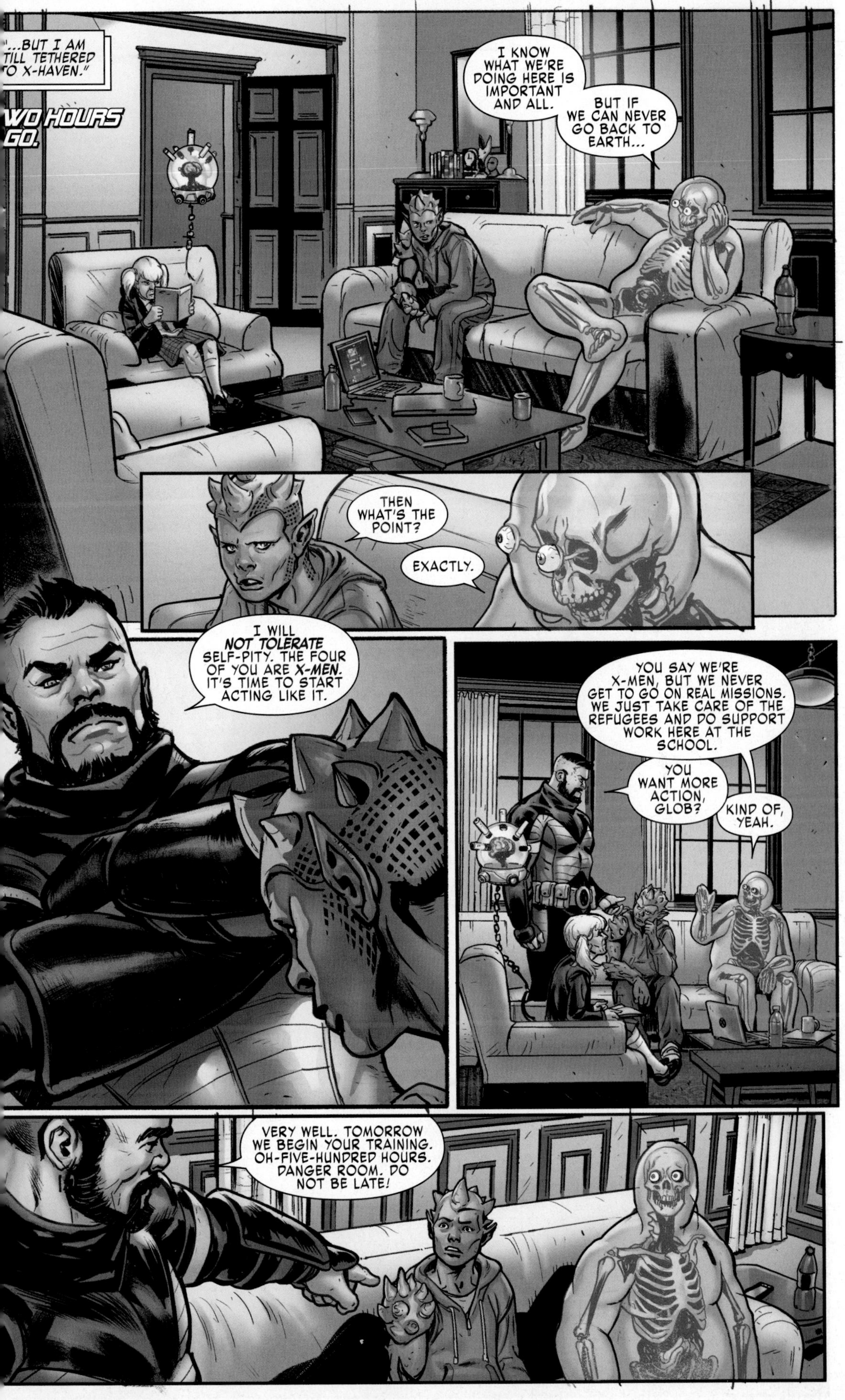
"...BUT I AM
TILL TETHERED
TO X-HAVEN."
WO HOURS
GO.
I KNOW WHAT WE'RE DOING HERE IS IMPORTANT AND ALL.
BUT IF WE CAN NEVER GO BACK TO EARTH...
THEN WHAT'S THE POINT?
EXACTLY.
I WILL NOT TOLERATE SELF-PITY. THE FOUR OF YOU ARE X-MEN. IT'S TIME TO START ACTING LIKE IT.
YOU SAY WE'RE X-MEN, BUT WE NEVER GET TO GO ON REAL MISSIONS. WE JUST TAKE CARE OF THE REFUGEES AND DO SUPPORT WORK HERE AT THE SCHOOL.
YOU WANT MORE ACTION, GLOB?
KIND OF, YEAH.
VERY WELL. TOMORROW WE BEGIN YOUR TRAINING. OH-FIVE-HUNDRED HOURS. DANGER ROOM. DO NOT BE LATE!

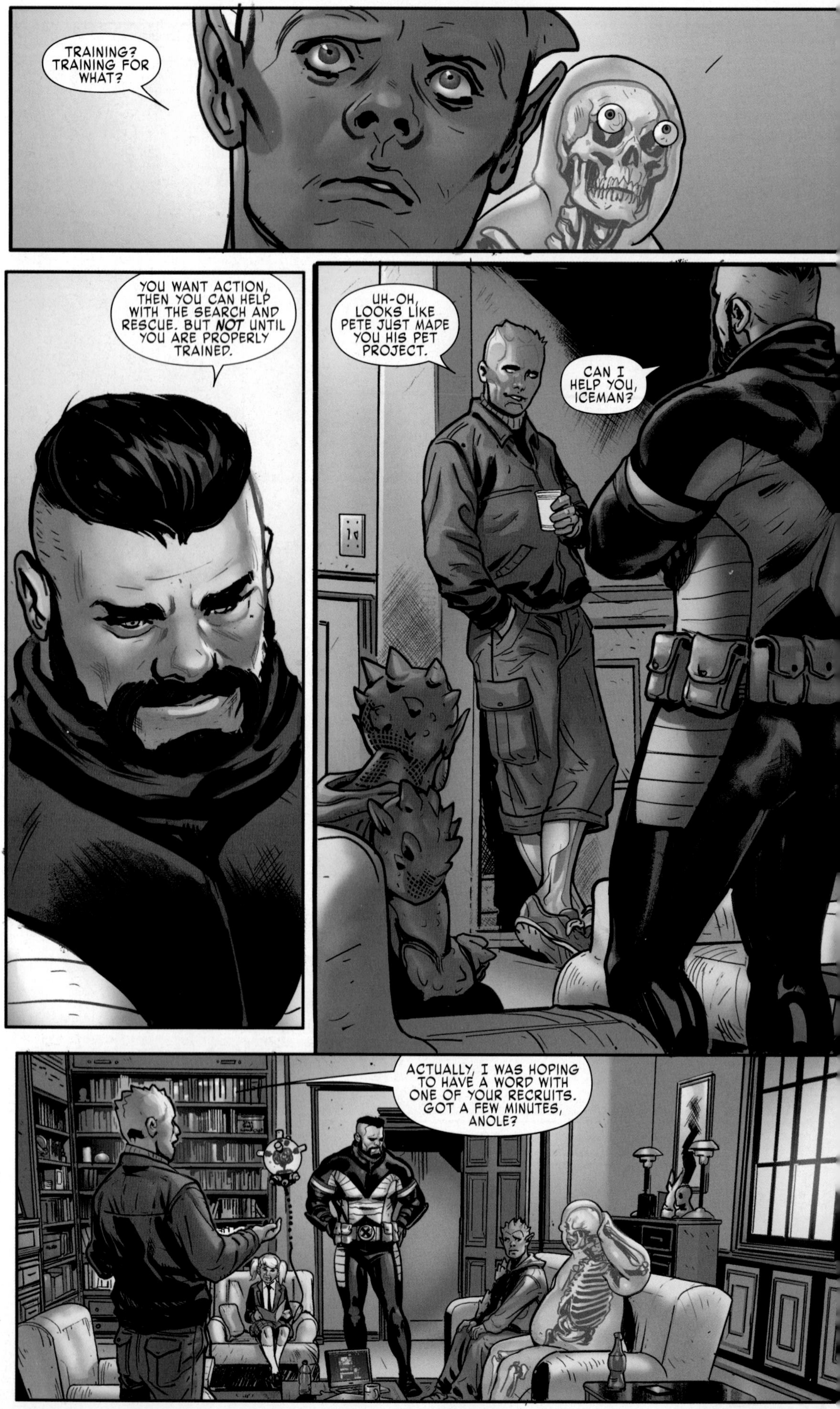

TRAINING? TRAINING FOR WHAT?
YOU WANT ACTION, THEN YOU CAN HELP WITH THE SEARCH AND RESCUE. BUT NOT UNTIL YOU ARE PROPERLY TRAINED.
UH-OH, LOOKS LIKE PETE JUST MADE YOU HIS PET PROJECT.
CAN I HELP YOU, ICEMAN?
ACTUALLY, I WAS HOPING TO HAVE A WORD WITH ONE OF YOUR RECRUITS. GOT A FEW MINUTES, ANOLE?

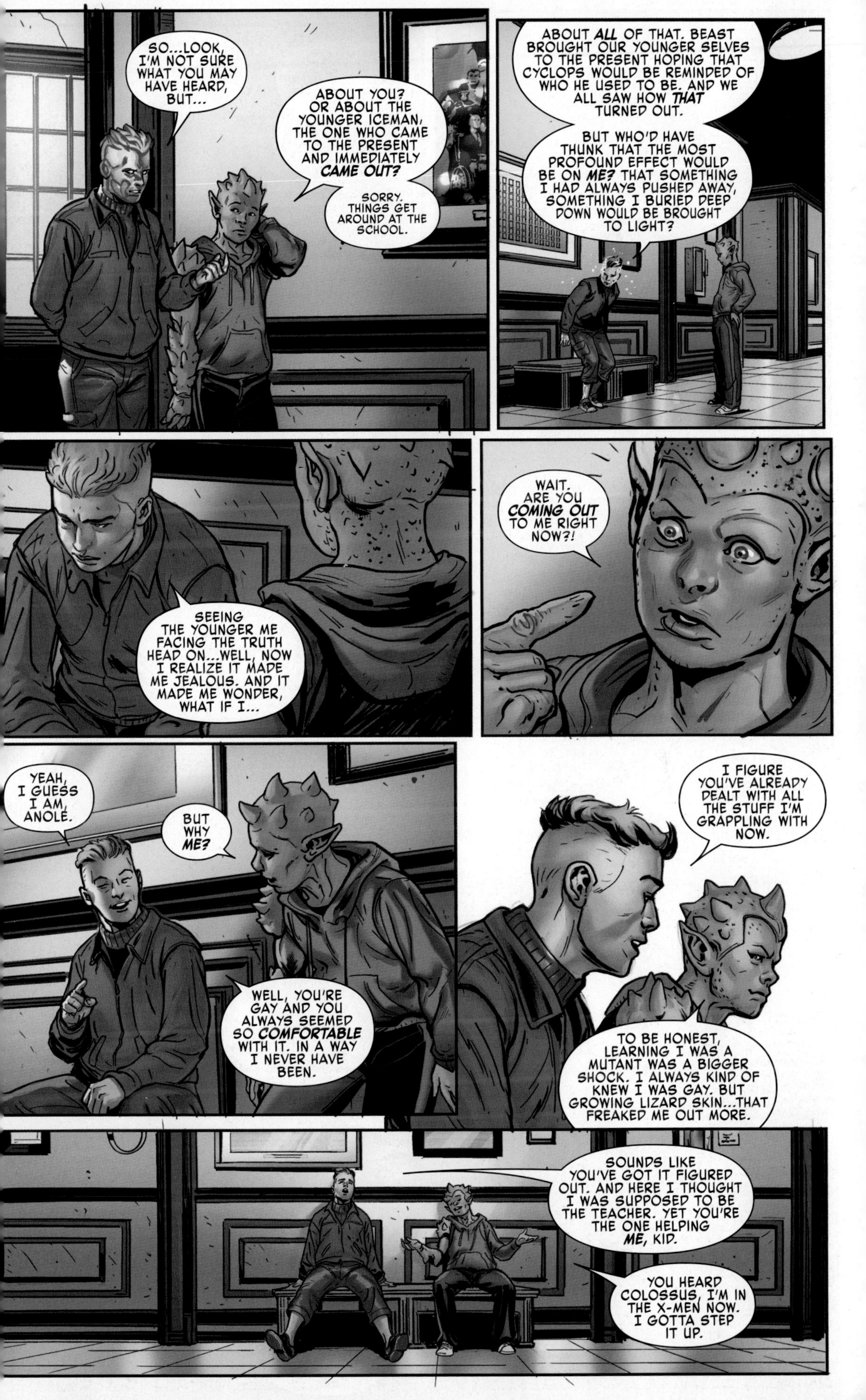
SO...LOOK, I'M NOT SURE WHAT YOU MAY HAVE HEARD, BUT...
ABOUT YOU? OR ABOUT THE YOUNGER ICEMAN, THE ONE WHO CAME TO THE PRESENT AND IMMEDIATELY CAME OUT?
SORRY. THINGS GET AROUND AT THE SCHOOL.
ABOUT ALL OF THAT. BEAST BROUGHT OUR YOUNGER SELVES TO THE PRESENT HOPING THAT CYCLOPS WOULD BE REMINDED OF WHO HE USED TO BE. AND WE ALL SAW HOW THAT TURNED OUT.
BUT WHO'D HAVE THUNK THAT THE MOST PROFOUND EFFECT WOULD BE ON ME? THAT SOMETHING I HAD ALWAYS PUSHED AWAY, SOMETHING I BURIED DEEP DOWN WOULD BE BROUGHT TO LIGHT?
SEEING THE YOUNGER ME FACING THE TRUTH HEAD ON...WELL, NOW I REALIZE IT MADE ME JEALOUS. AND IT MADE ME WONDER, WHAT IF I...
WAIT. ARE YOU COMING OUT TO ME RIGHT NOW?!
YEAH, I GUESS I AM, ANOLE.
BUT WHY ME?
WELL, YOU'RE GAY AND YOU ALWAYS SEEMED SO COMFORTABLE WITH IT. IN A WAY I NEVER HAVE BEEN.
I FIGURE YOU'VE ALREADY DEALT WITH ALL THE STUFF I'M GRAPPLING WITH NOW.
TO BE HONEST, LEARNING I WAS A MUTANT WAS A BIGGER SHOCK. I ALWAYS KIND OF KNEW I WAS GAY. BUT GROWING LIZARD SKIN...THAT FREAKED ME OUT MORE.
SOUNDS LIKE YOU'VE GOT IT FIGURED OUT. AND HERE I THOUGHT I WAS SUPPOSED TO BE THE TEACHER. YET YOU'RE THE ONE HELPING ME, KID.
YOU HEARD COLOSSUS, I'M IN THE X-MEN NOW. I GOTTA STEP IT UP.

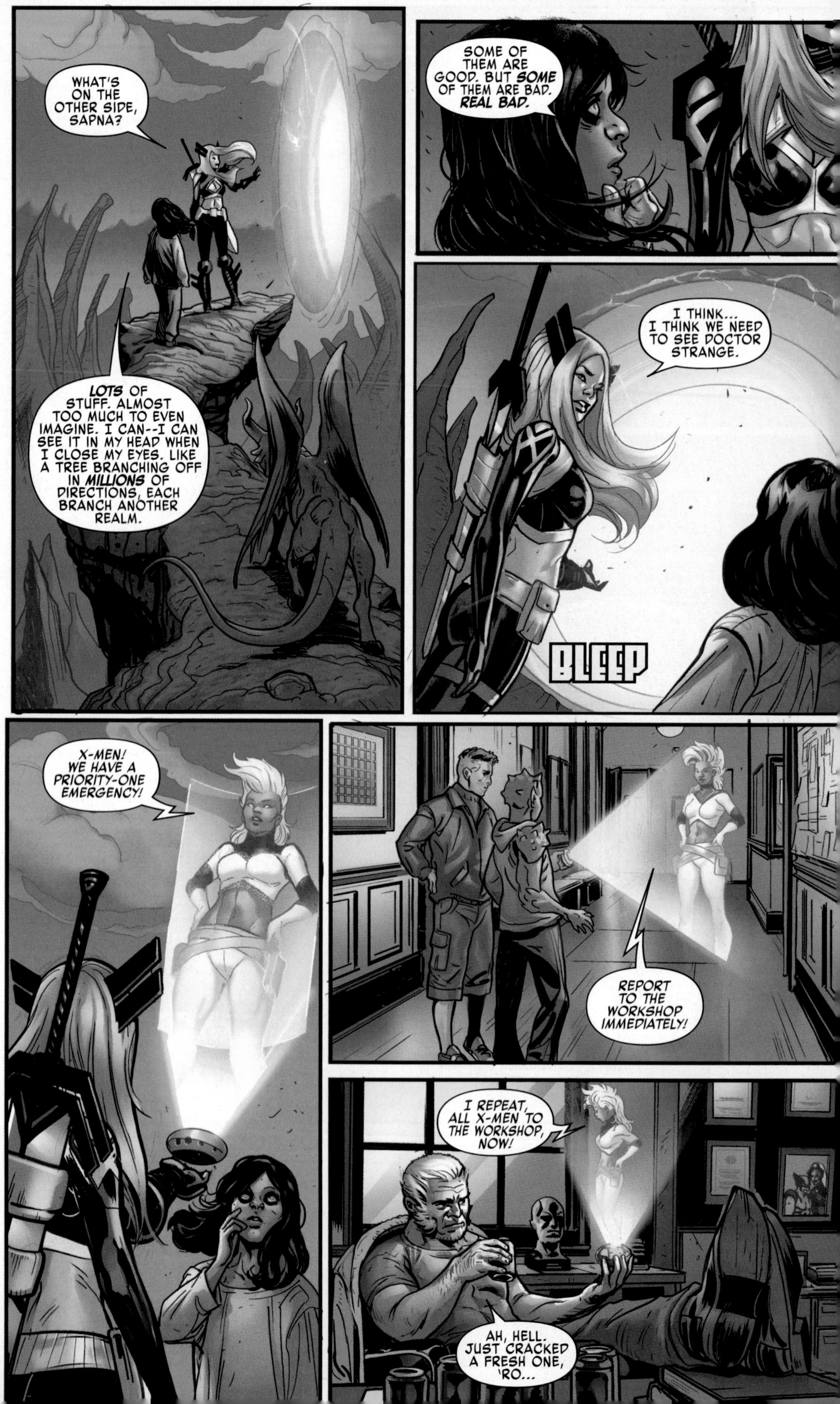
WHAT'S ON THE OTHER SIDE, SAPNA?
LOTS OF STUFF. ALMOST TOO MUCH TO EVEN IMAGINE. I CAN--I CAN SEE IT IN MY HEAD WHEN I CLOSE MY EYES. LIKE A TREE BRANCHING OFF IN MILLIONS OF DIRECTIONS, EACH BRANCH ANOTHER REALM.
SOME OF THEM ARE GOOD. BUT SOME OF THEM ARE BAD. REAL BAD.
I THINK... I THINK WE NEED TO SEE DOCTOR STRANGE.
BLEEP
X-MEN! WE HAVE A PRIORITY-ONE EMERGENCY!
REPORT TO THE WORKSHOP IMMEDIATELY!
I REPEAT, ALL X-MEN TO THE WORKSHOP, NOW!
AH, HELL. JUST CRACKED A FRESH ONE, 'RO...

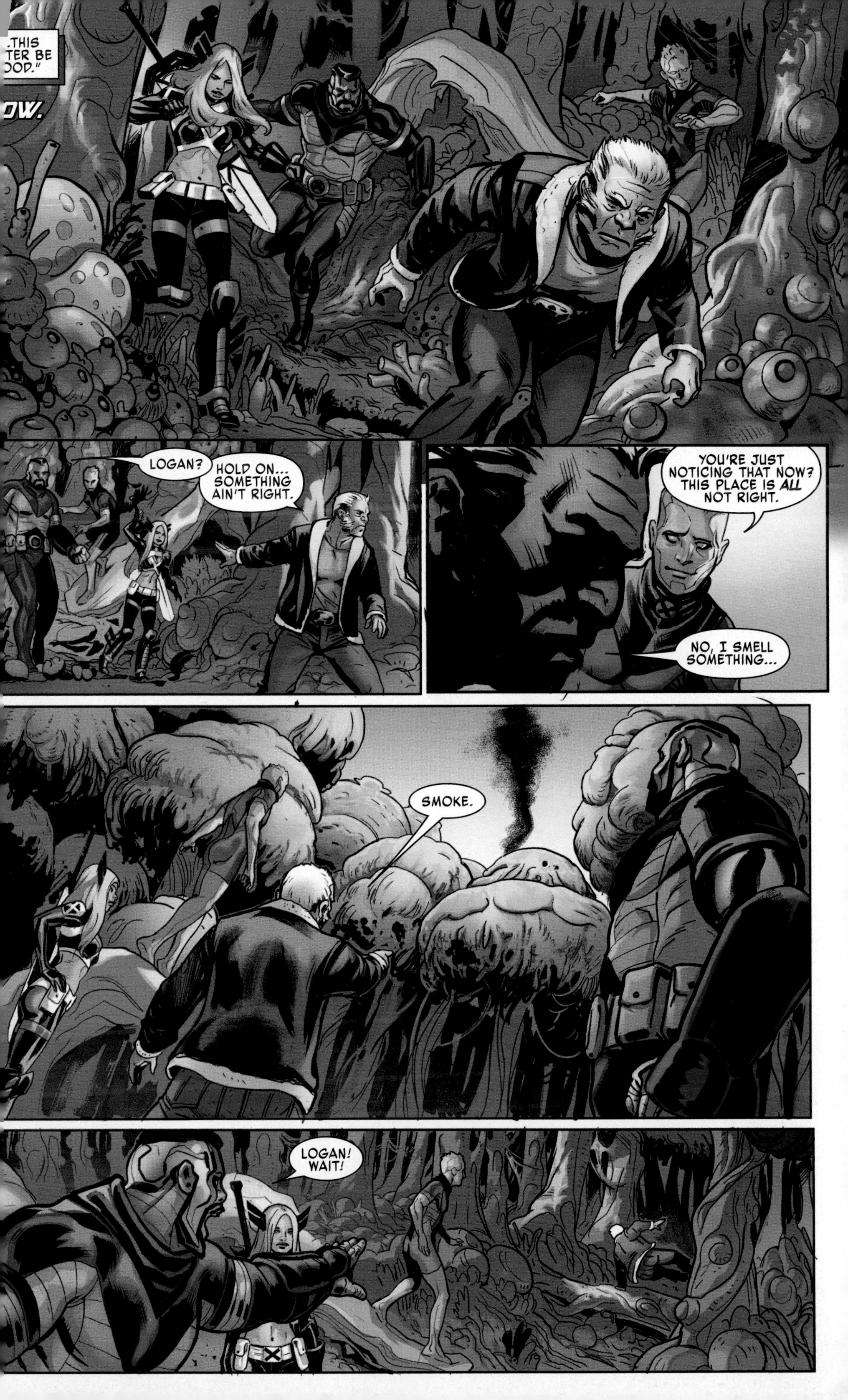

.THIS
TER BE
OOD."
OW.
LOGAN?
HOLD ON... SOMETHING AIN'T RIGHT.
YOU'RE JUST NOTICING THAT NOW? THIS PLACE IS ALL NOT RIGHT.
NO, I SMELL SOMETHING...
SMOKE.
LOGAN! WAIT!

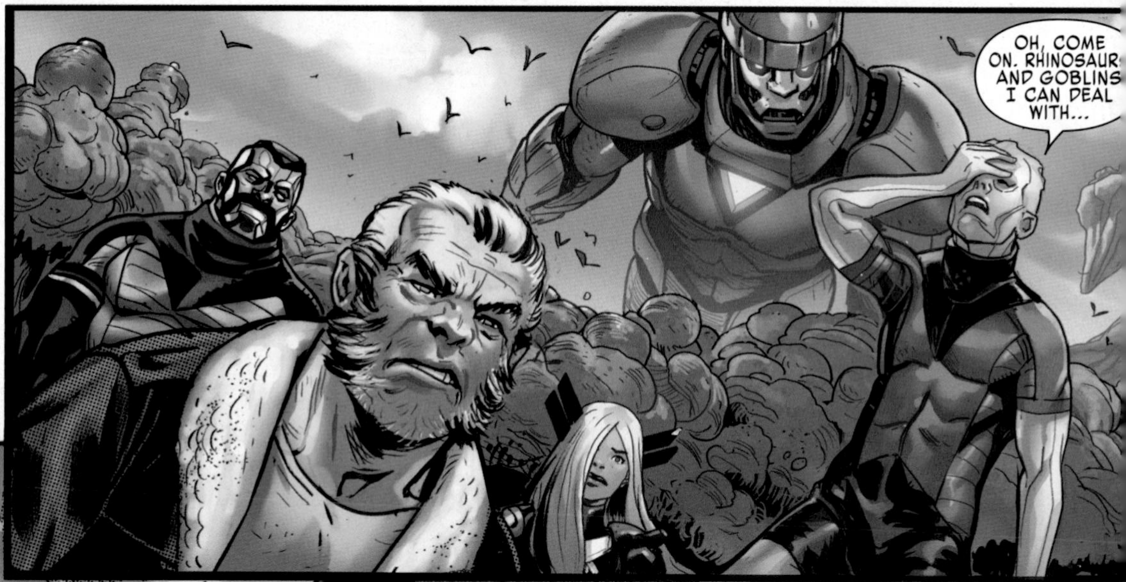
OH, COME ON. RHINOSAURS AND GOBLINS I CAN DEAL WITH...

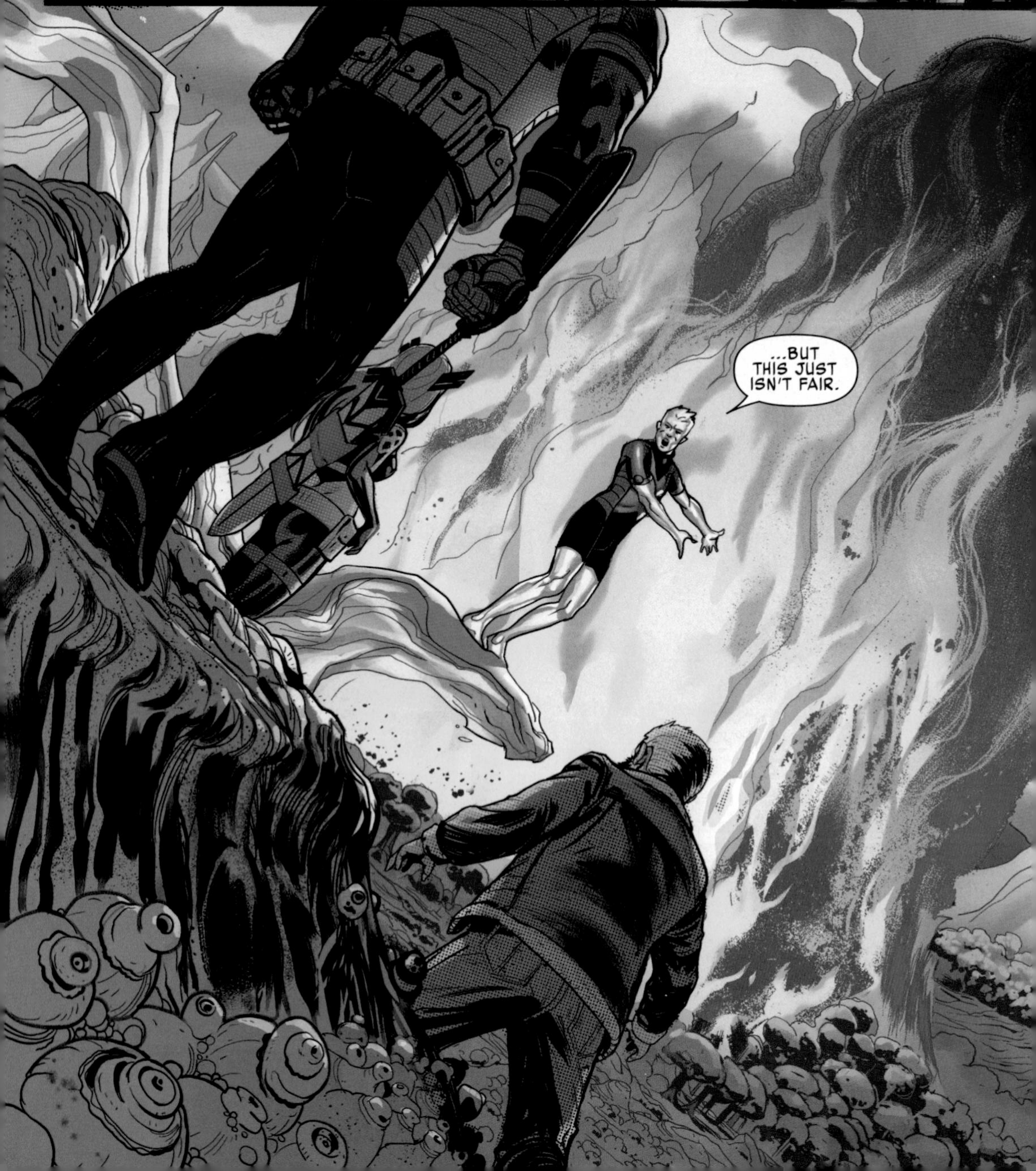
...BUT THIS JUST ISN'T FAIR.

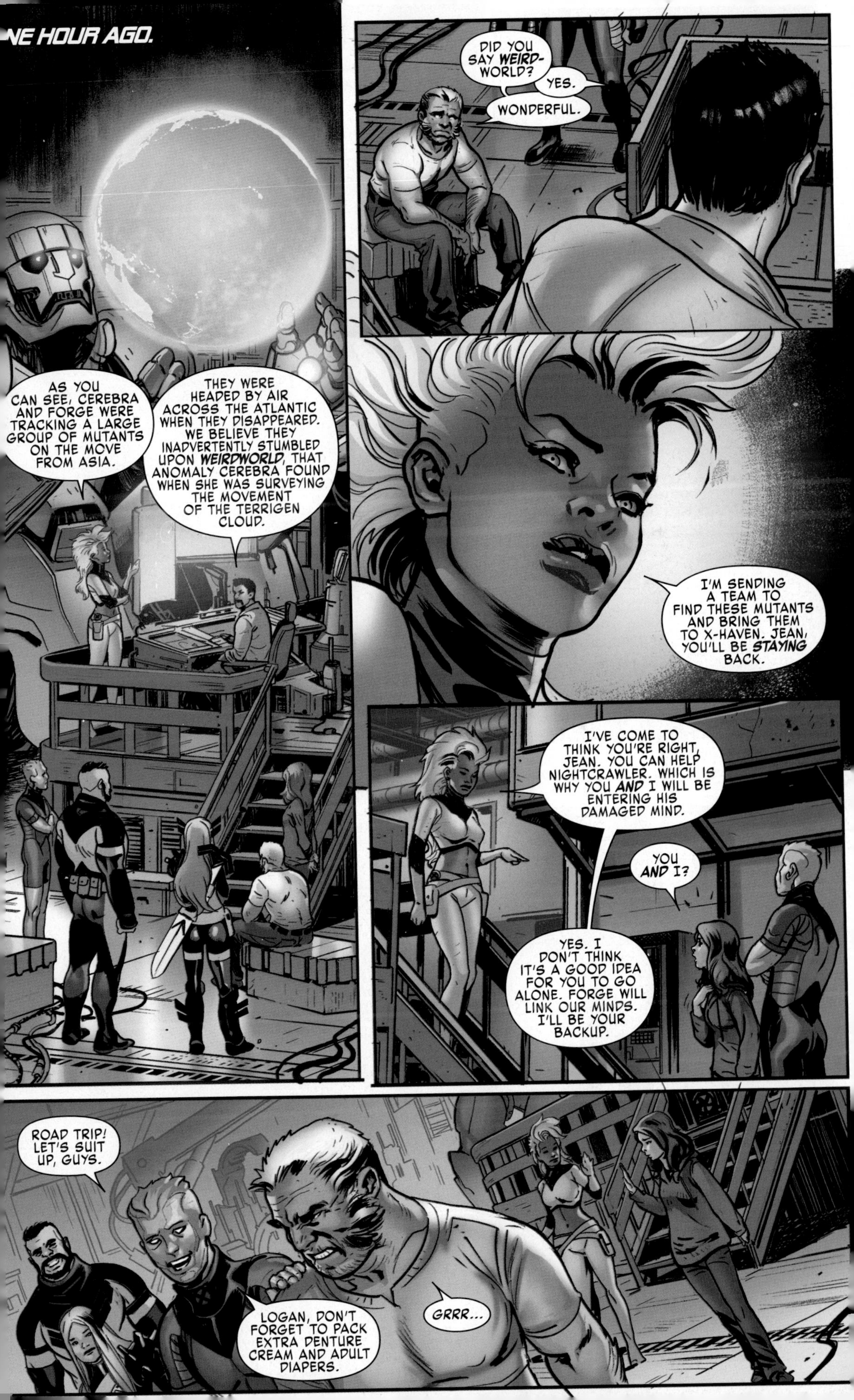

NE HOUR AGO.
AS YOU CAN SEE, CEREBRA AND FORGE WERE TRACKING A LARGE GROUP OF MUTANTS ON THE MOVE FROM ASIA.
THEY WERE HEADED BY AIR ACROSS THE ATLANTIC WHEN THEY DISAPPEARED. WE BELIEVE THEY INADVERTENTLY STUMBLED UPON WEIRDWORLD, THAT ANOMALY CEREBRA FOUND WHEN SHE WAS SURVEYING THE MOVEMENT OF THE TERRIGEN CLOUD.
DID YOU SAY WEIRD-WORLD?
YES.
WONDERFUL.
I'M SENDING A TEAM TO FIND THESE MUTANTS AND BRING THEM TO X-HAVEN. JEAN, YOU'LL BE STAYING BACK.
I'VE COME TO THINK YOU'RE RIGHT, JEAN. YOU CAN HELP NIGHTCRAWLER. WHICH IS WHY YOU AND I WILL BE ENTERING HIS DAMAGED MIND.
YOU AND I?
YES. I DON'T THINK IT'S A GOOD IDEA FOR YOU TO GO ALONE. FORGE WILL LINK OUR MINDS. I'LL BE YOUR BACKUP.
ROAD TRIP! LET'S SUIT UP, GUYS.
LOGAN, DON'T FORGET TO PACK EXTRA DENTURE CREAM AND ADULT DIAPERS.
GRRR...

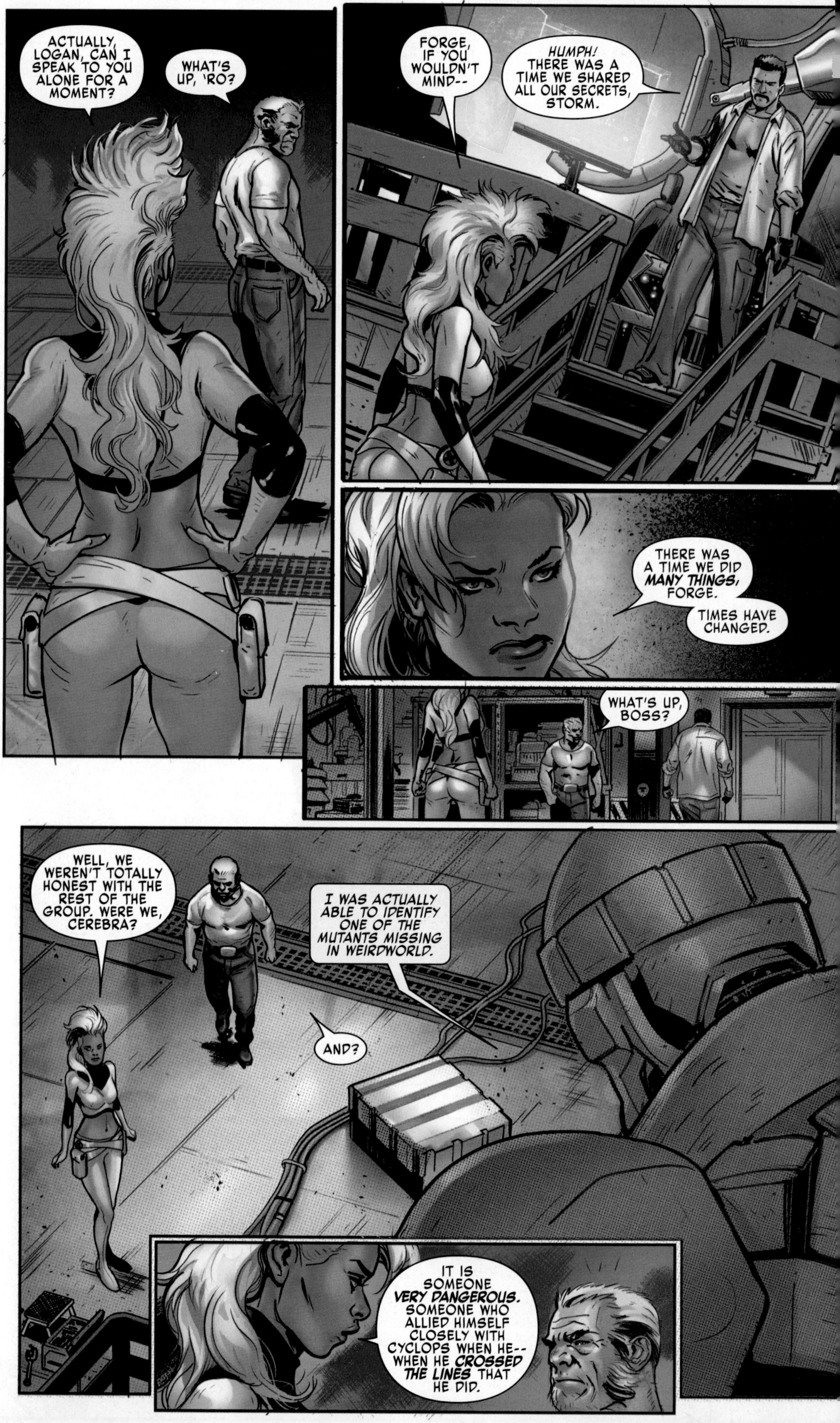
ACTUALLY, LOGAN, CAN I SPEAK TO YOU ALONE FOR A MOMENT?
WHAT'S UP, 'RO?
FORGE, IF YOU WOULDN'T MIND--
HUMPH! THERE WAS A TIME WE SHARED ALL OUR SECRETS, STORM.
THERE WAS A TIME WE DID MANY THINGS, FORGE.
TIMES HAVE CHANGED.
WHAT'S UP, BOSS?
WELL, WE WEREN'T TOTALLY HONEST WITH THE REST OF THE GROUP. WERE WE, CEREBRA?
I WAS ACTUALLY ABLE TO IDENTIFY ONE OF THE MUTANTS MISSING IN WEIRDWORLD.
AND?
IT IS SOMEONE VERY DANGEROUS. SOMEONE WHO ALLIED HIMSELF CLOSELY WITH CYCLOPS WHEN HE-- WHEN HE CROSSED THE LINES THAT HE DID.

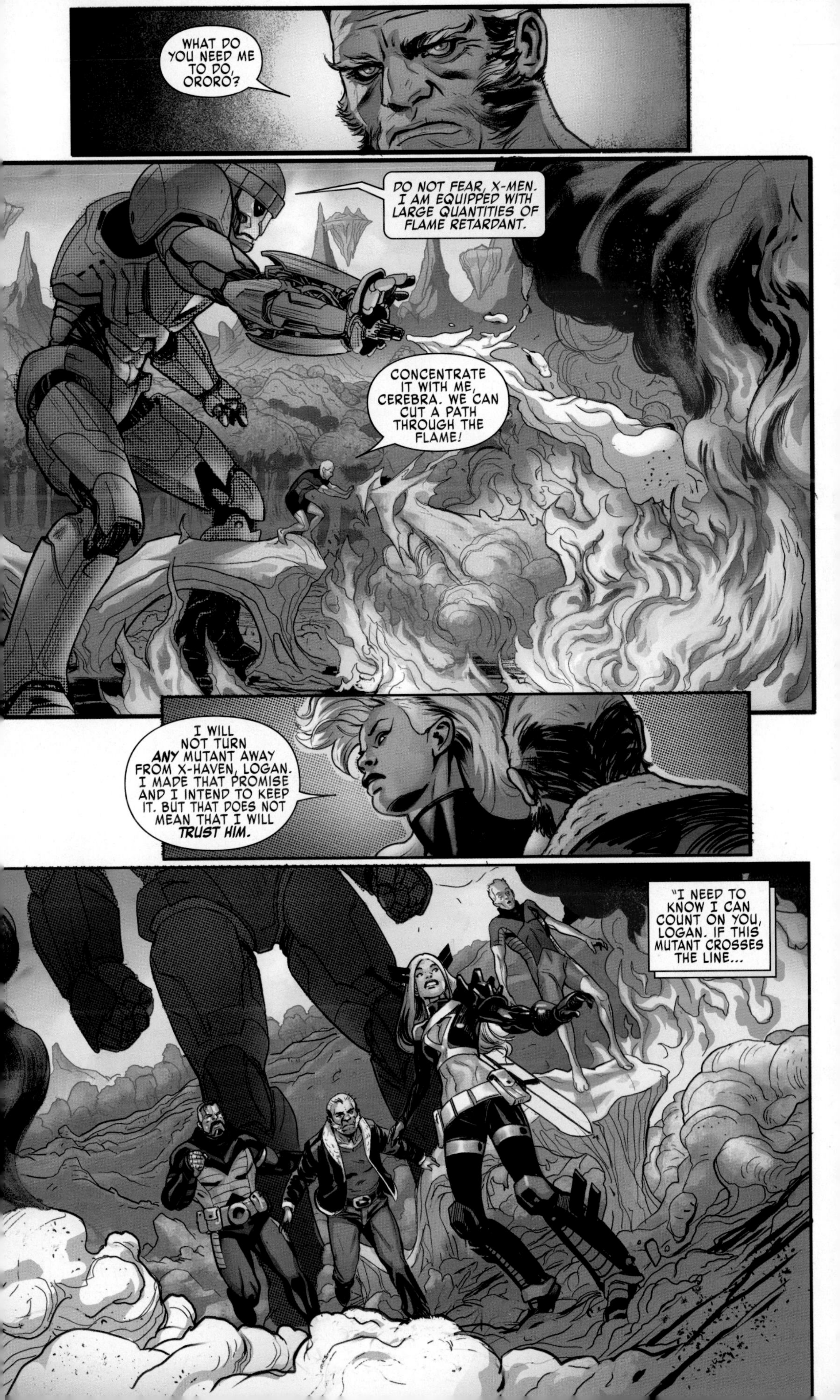
WHAT DO YOU NEED ME TO DO, ORORO?
DO NOT FEAR, X-MEN. I AM EQUIPPED WITH LARGE QUANTITIES OF FLAME RETARDANT.
CONCENTRATE IT WITH ME, CEREBRA. WE CAN CUT A PATH THROUGH THE FLAME!
I WILL NOT TURN ANY MUTANT AWAY FROM X-HAVEN, LOGAN. I MADE THAT PROMISE AND I INTEND TO KEEP IT. BUT THAT DOES NOT MEAN THAT I WILL TRUST HIM.
"I NEED TO KNOW I CAN COUNT ON YOU, LOGAN. IF THIS MUTANT CROSSES THE LINE...

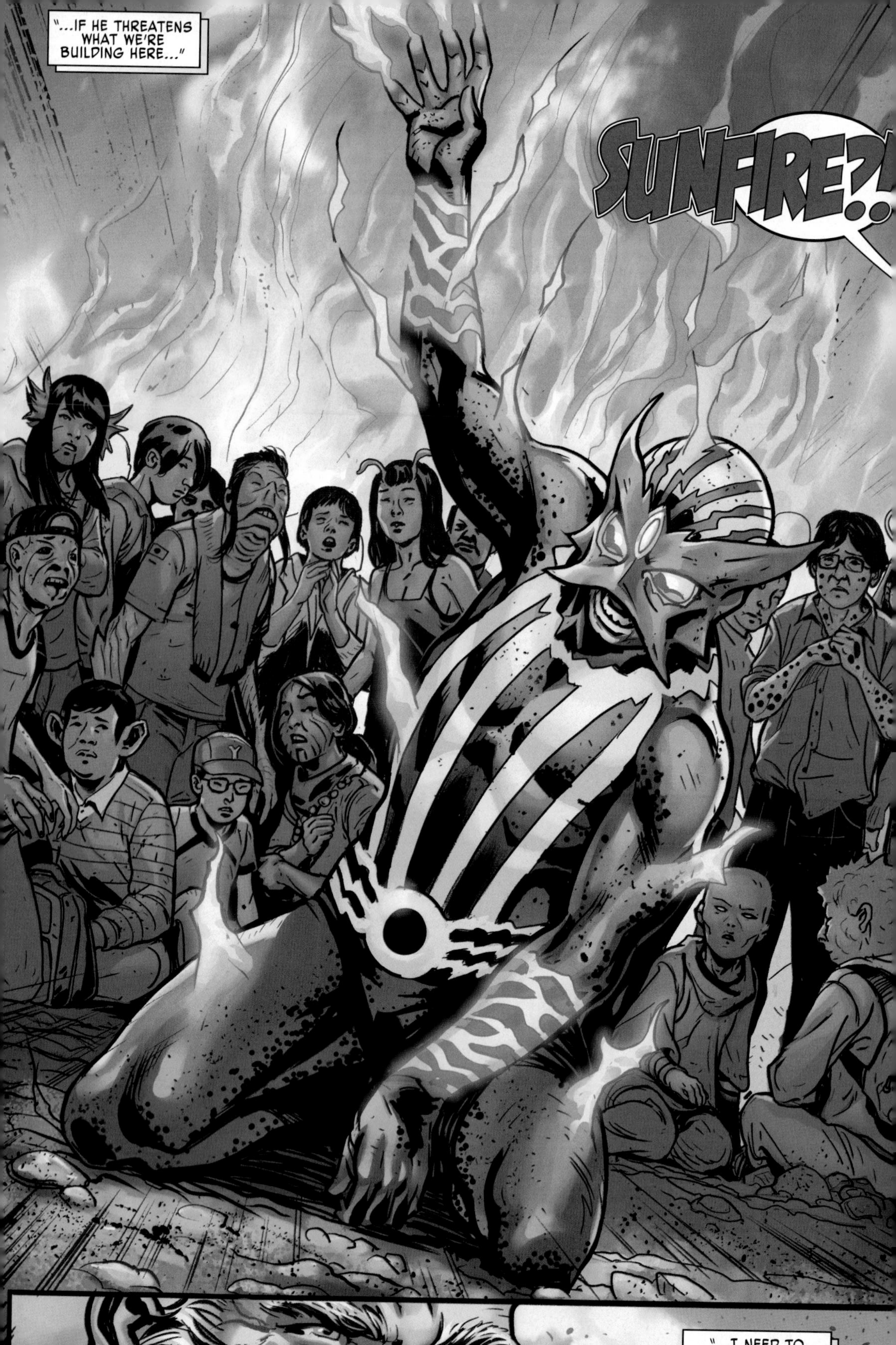
"...IF HE THREATENS WHAT WE'RE BUILDING HERE..."
SUNFIRE?!

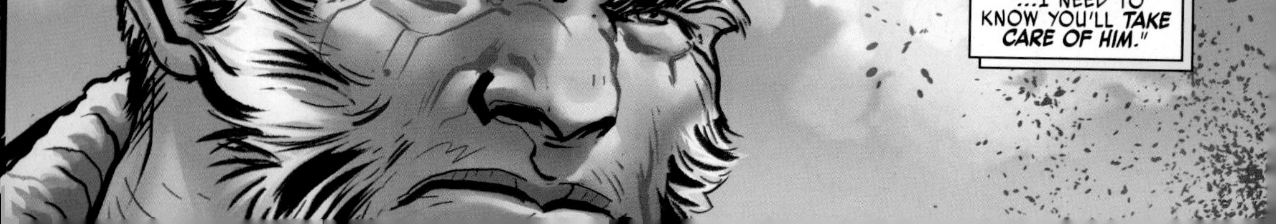
"...I NEED TO KNOW YOU'LL *TAKE CARE OF HIM.*"

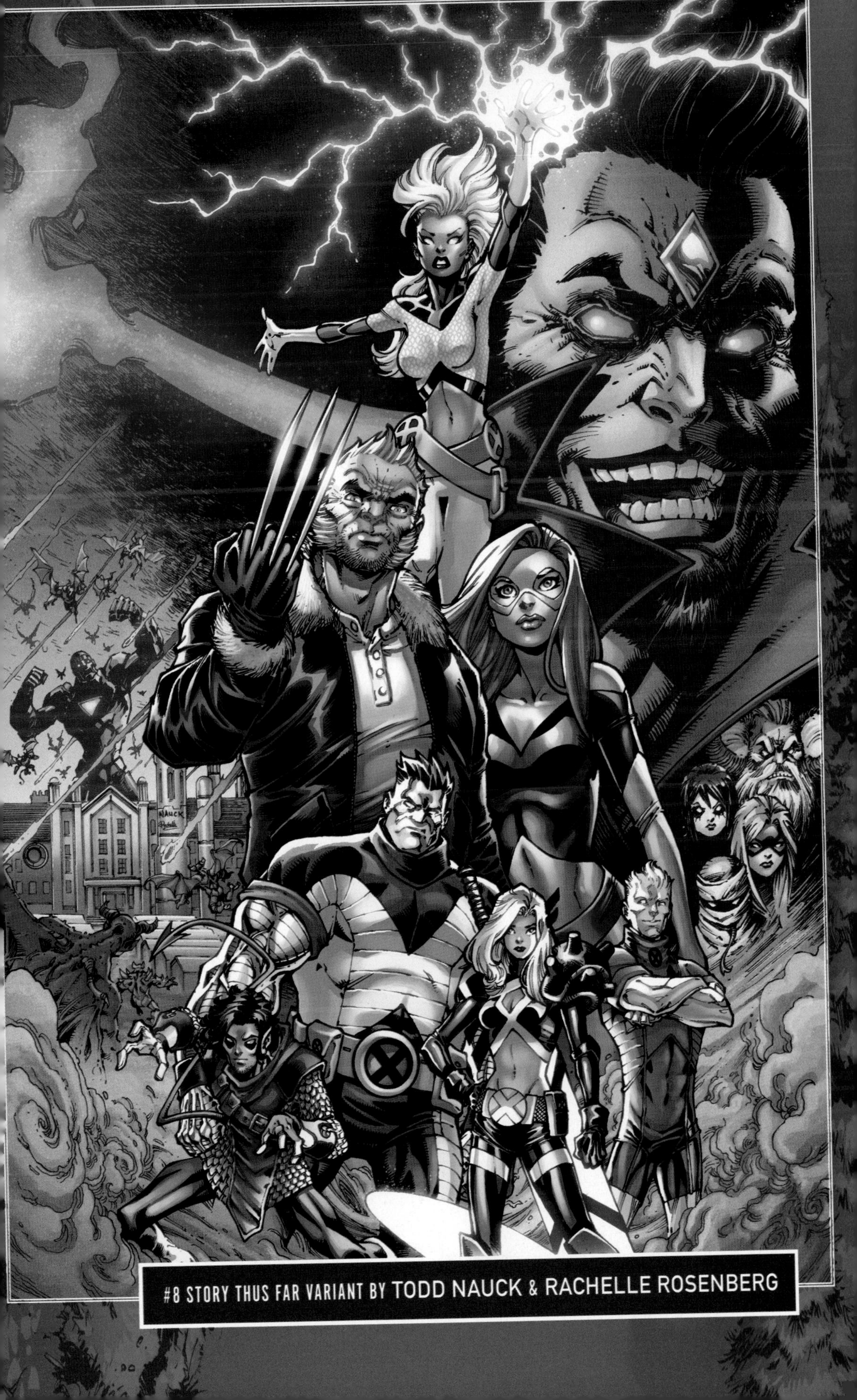

#8 STORY THUS FAR VARIANT BY TODD NAUCK & RACHELLE ROSENBERG

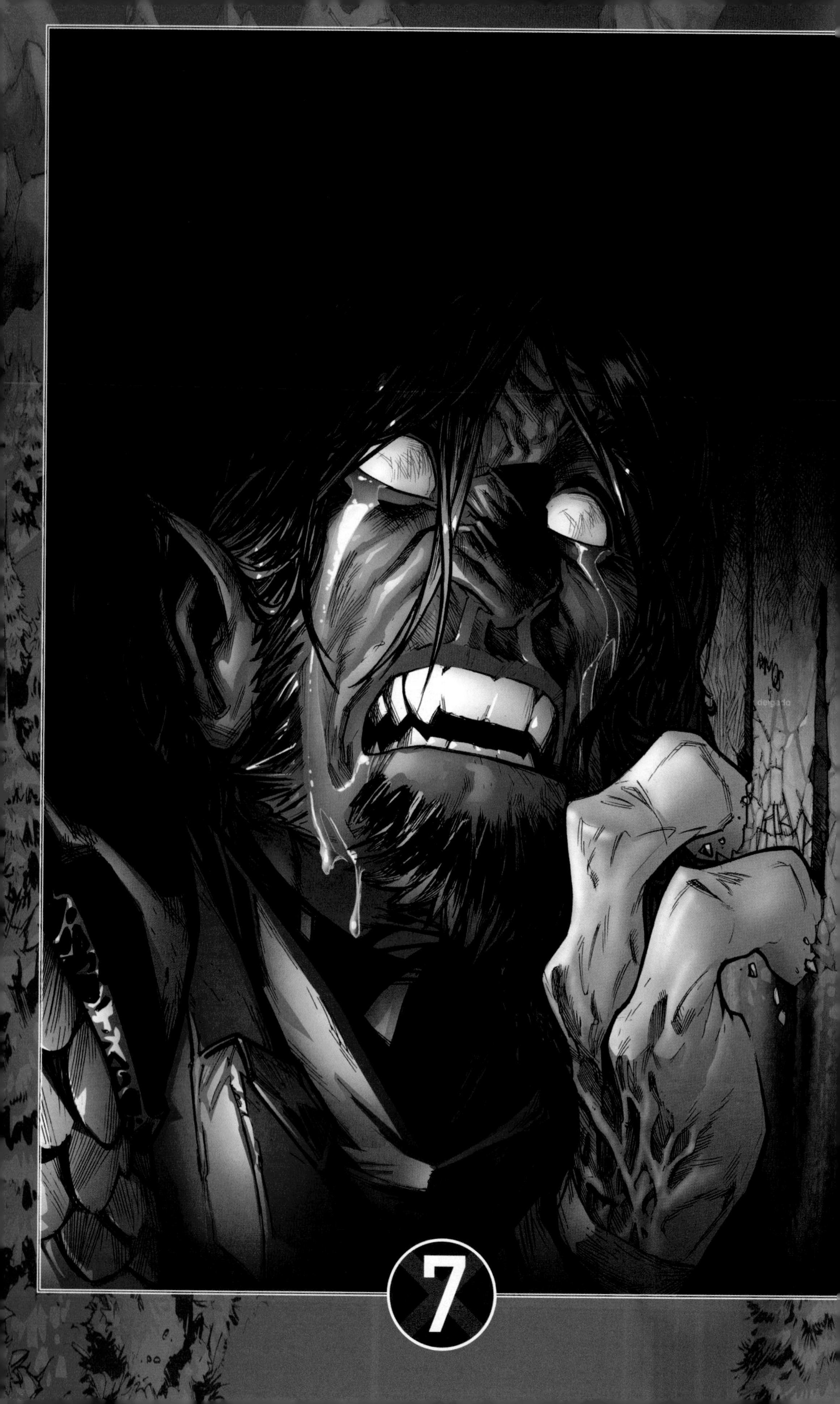
7

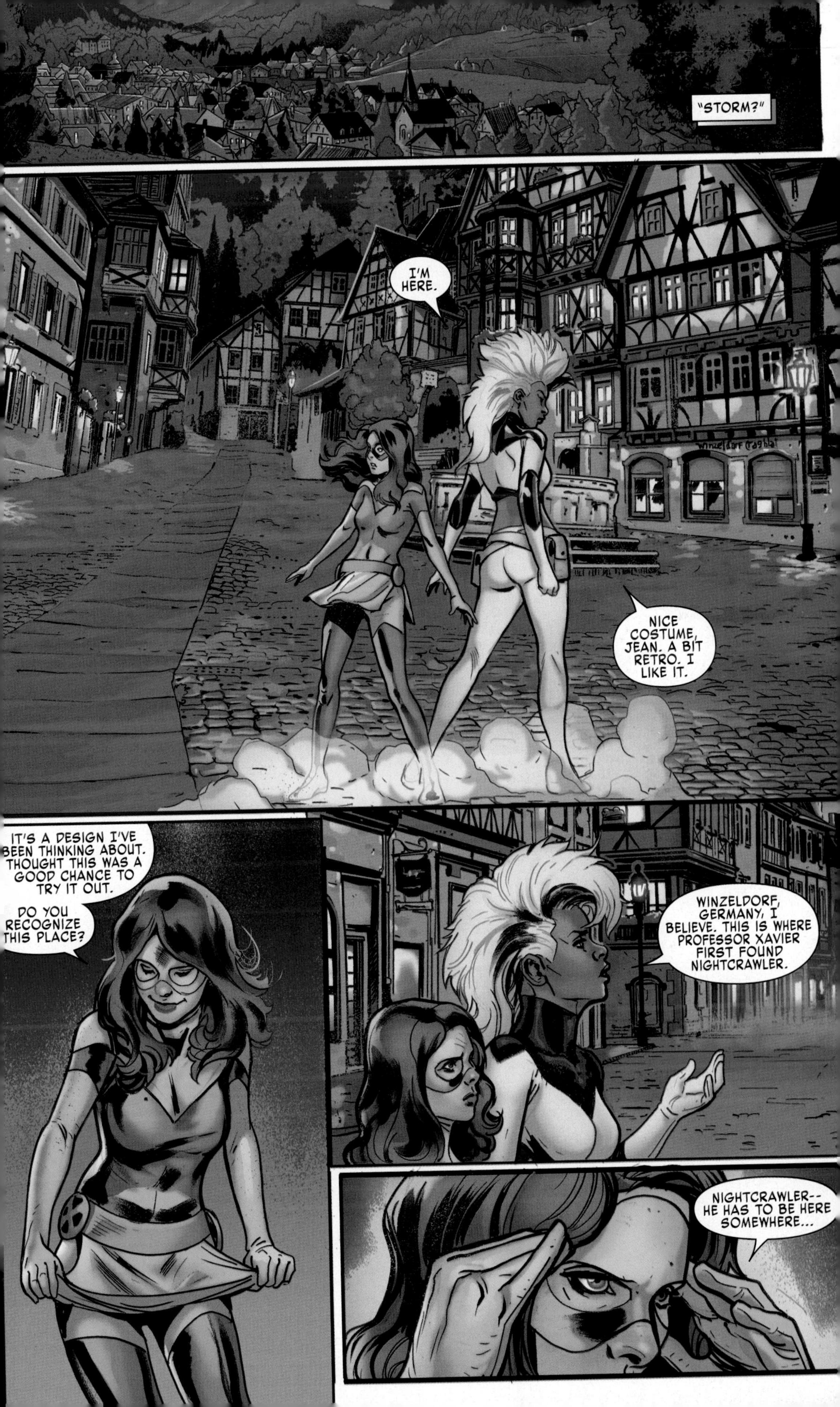
"STORM?"
I'M HERE.
NICE COSTUME, JEAN. A BIT RETRO. I LIKE IT.
IT'S A DESIGN I'VE BEEN THINKING ABOUT. THOUGHT THIS WAS A GOOD CHANCE TO TRY IT OUT.
DO YOU RECOGNIZE THIS PLACE?
WINZELDORF, GERMANY, I BELIEVE. THIS IS WHERE PROFESSOR XAVIER FIRST FOUND NIGHTCRAWLER.
NIGHTCRAWLER-- HE HAS TO BE HERE SOMEWHERE...

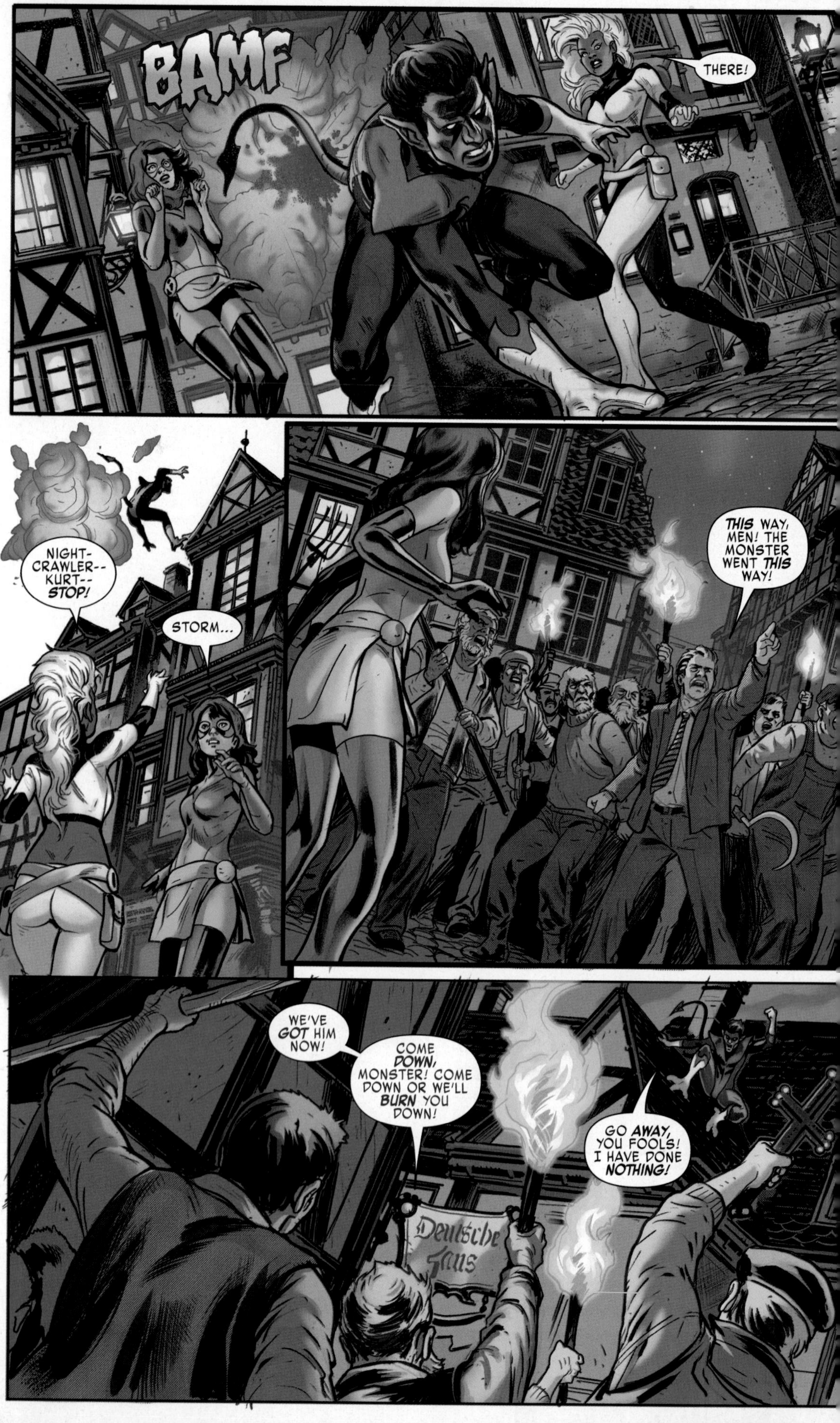
BAMF
THERE!
NIGHT-CRAWLER--KURT--STOP!
STORM...
THIS WAY, MEN! THE MONSTER WENT THIS WAY!
WE'VE GOT HIM NOW!
COME DOWN, MONSTER! COME DOWN OR WE'LL BURN YOU DOWN!
GO AWAY, YOU FOOLS! I HAVE DONE NOTHING!
Deutsche Haus

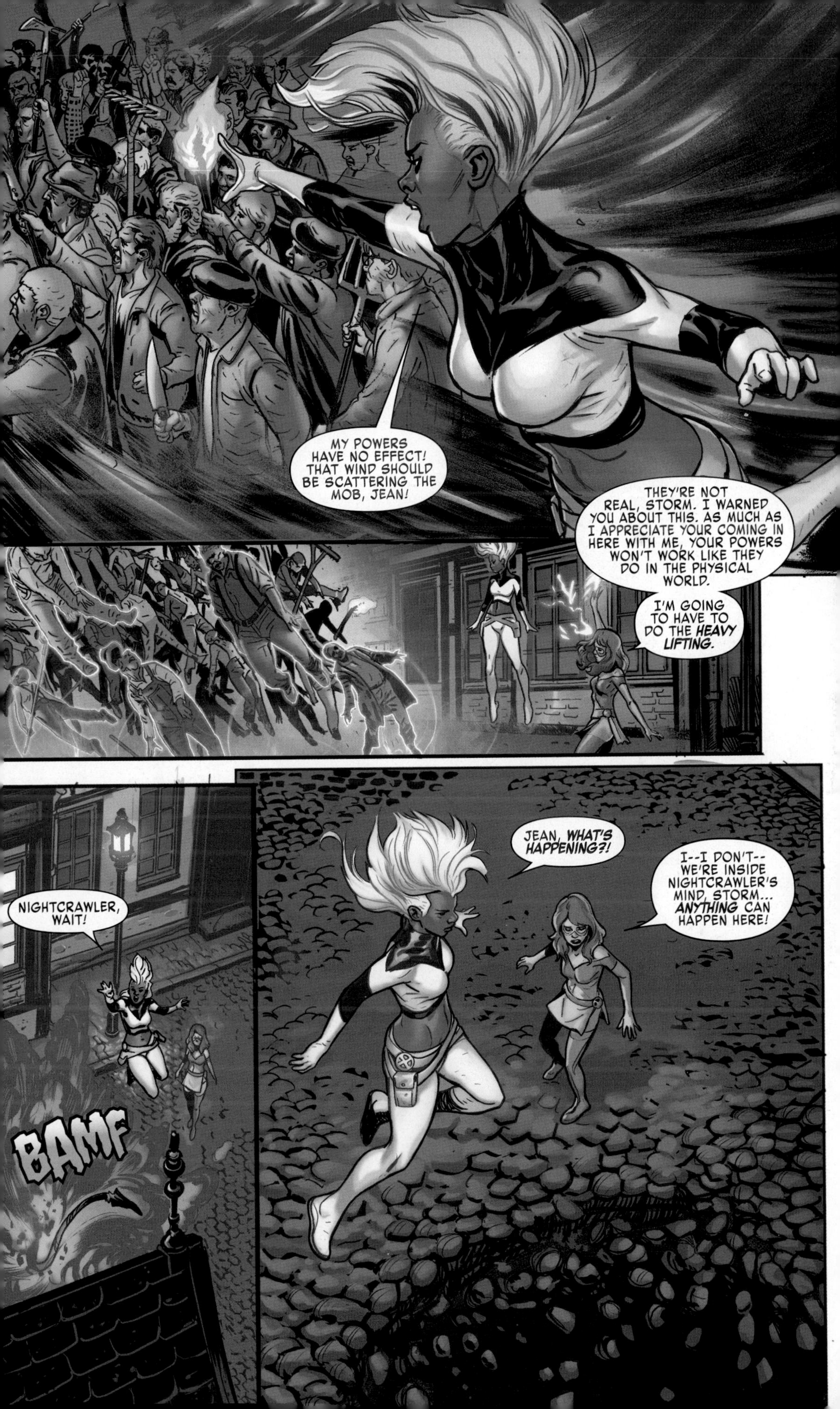

MY POWERS HAVE NO EFFECT! THAT WIND SHOULD BE SCATTERING THE MOB, JEAN!
THEY'RE NOT REAL, STORM. I WARNED YOU ABOUT THIS. AS MUCH AS I APPRECIATE YOUR COMING IN HERE WITH ME, YOUR POWERS WON'T WORK LIKE THEY DO IN THE PHYSICAL WORLD.
I'M GOING TO HAVE TO DO THE HEAVY LIFTING.
NIGHTCRAWLER, WAIT!
BAMF
JEAN, WHAT'S HAPPENING?!
I--I DON'T-- WE'RE INSIDE NIGHTCRAWLER'S MIND, STORM... ANYTHING CAN HAPPEN HERE!

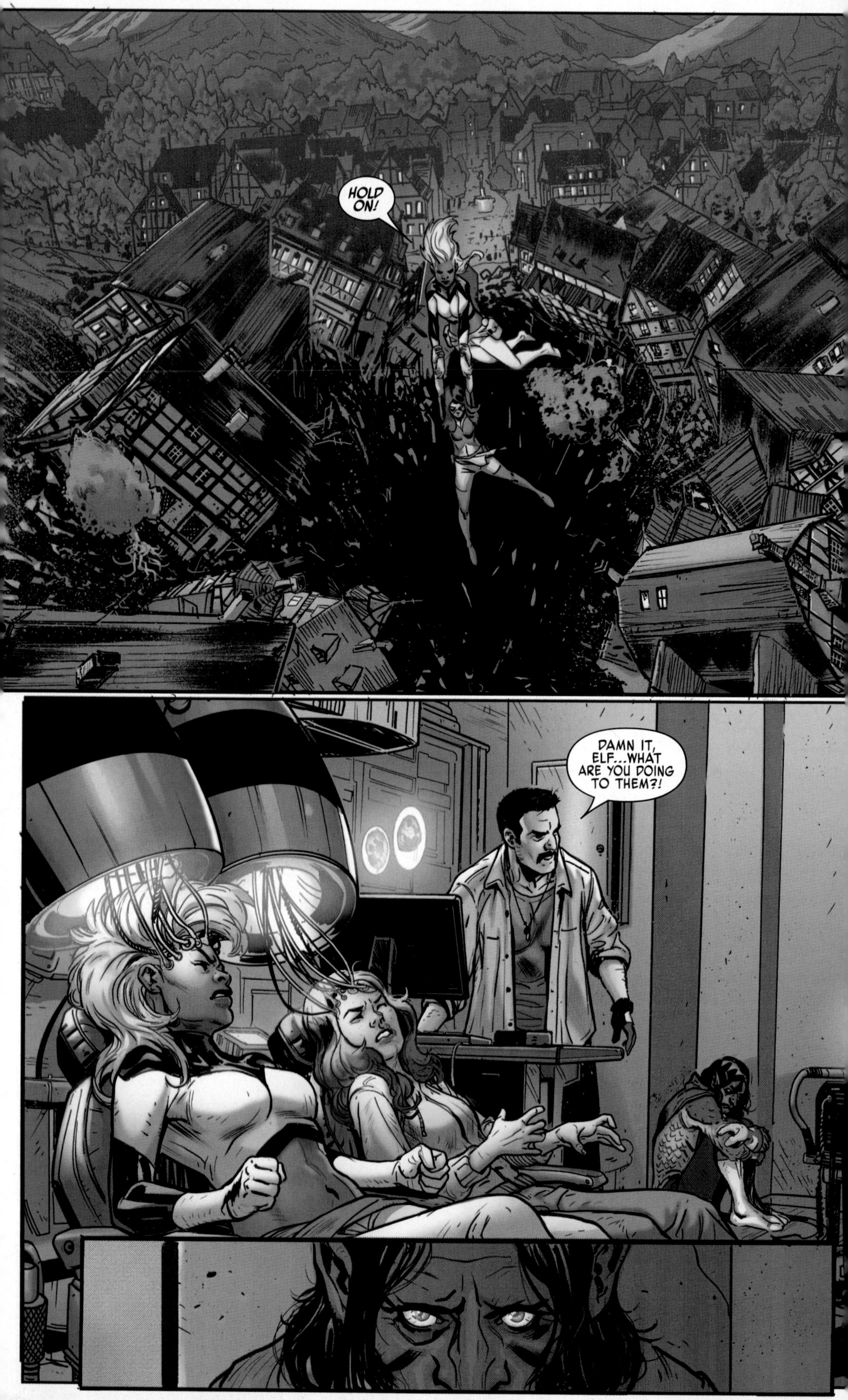
HOLD ON!
DAMN IT, ELF...WHAT ARE YOU DOING TO THEM?!

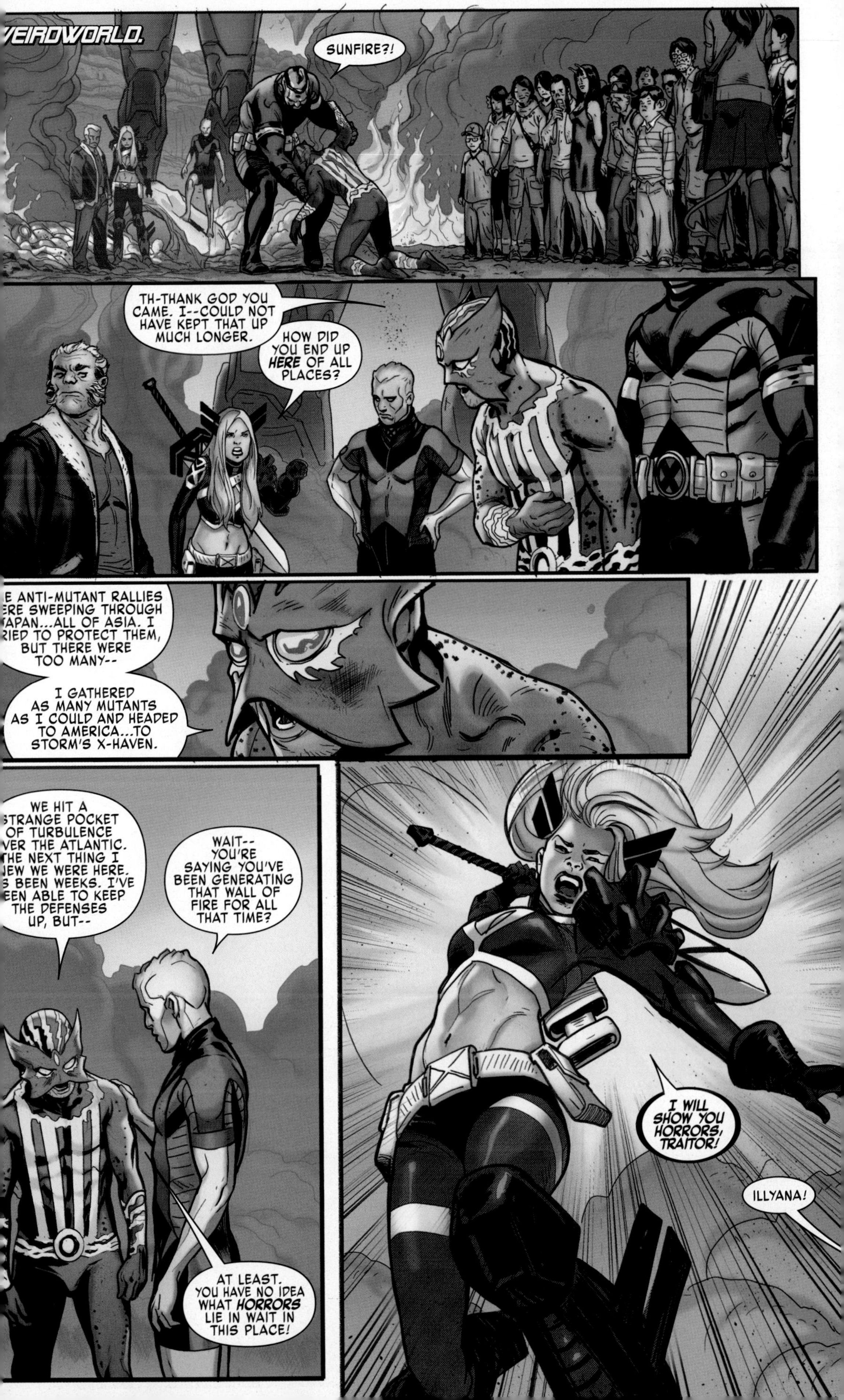
WEIRDWORLD.
SUNFIRE?!
TH-THANK GOD YOU CAME. I--COULD NOT HAVE KEPT THAT UP MUCH LONGER.
HOW DID YOU END UP HERE OF ALL PLACES?
E ANTI-MUTANT RALLIES ERE SWEEPING THROUGH JAPAN...ALL OF ASIA. I RIED TO PROTECT THEM, BUT THERE WERE TOO MANY--
I GATHERED AS MANY MUTANTS AS I COULD AND HEADED TO AMERICA...TO STORM'S X-HAVEN.
WE HIT A STRANGE POCKET OF TURBULENCE VER THE ATLANTIC. THE NEXT THING I NEW WE WERE HERE. S BEEN WEEKS. I'VE EEN ABLE TO KEEP THE DEFENSES UP, BUT--
WAIT-- YOU'RE SAYING YOU'VE BEEN GENERATING THAT WALL OF FIRE FOR ALL THAT TIME?
AT LEAST. YOU HAVE NO IDEA WHAT HORRORS LIE IN WAIT IN THIS PLACE!
I WILL SHOW YOU HORRORS, TRAITOR!
ILLYANA!

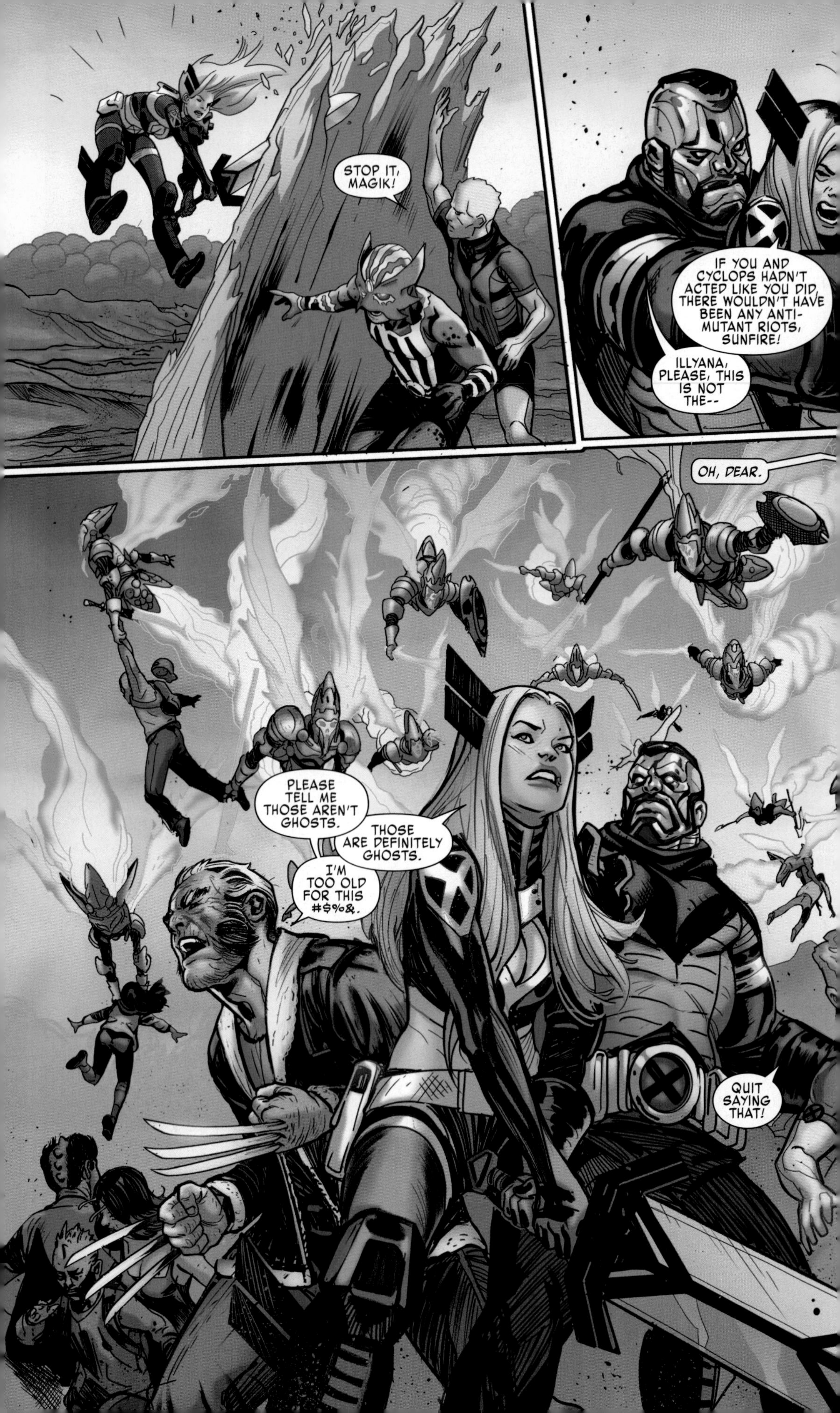
STOP IT, MAGIK!
IF YOU AND CYCLOPS HADN'T ACTED LIKE YOU DID, THERE WOULDN'T HAVE BEEN ANY ANTI-MUTANT RIOTS, SUNFIRE!
ILLYANA, PLEASE, THIS IS NOT THE--
OH, DEAR.
PLEASE TELL ME THOSE AREN'T GHOSTS.
THOSE ARE DEFINITELY GHOSTS.
I'M TOO OLD FOR THIS #$%&.
QUIT SAYING THAT!

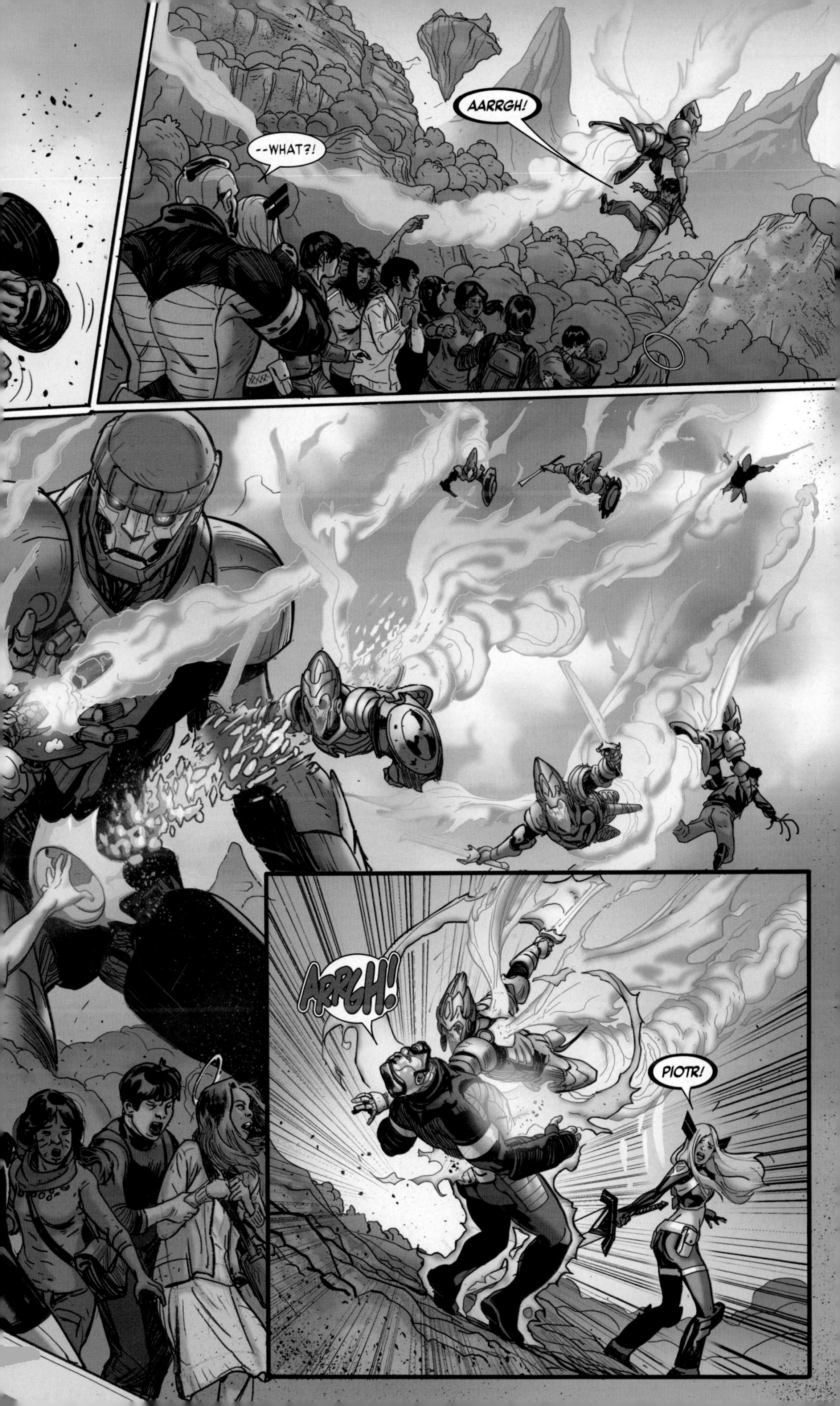
--WHAT?!
AARRGH!
ARRGH!
PIOTR!

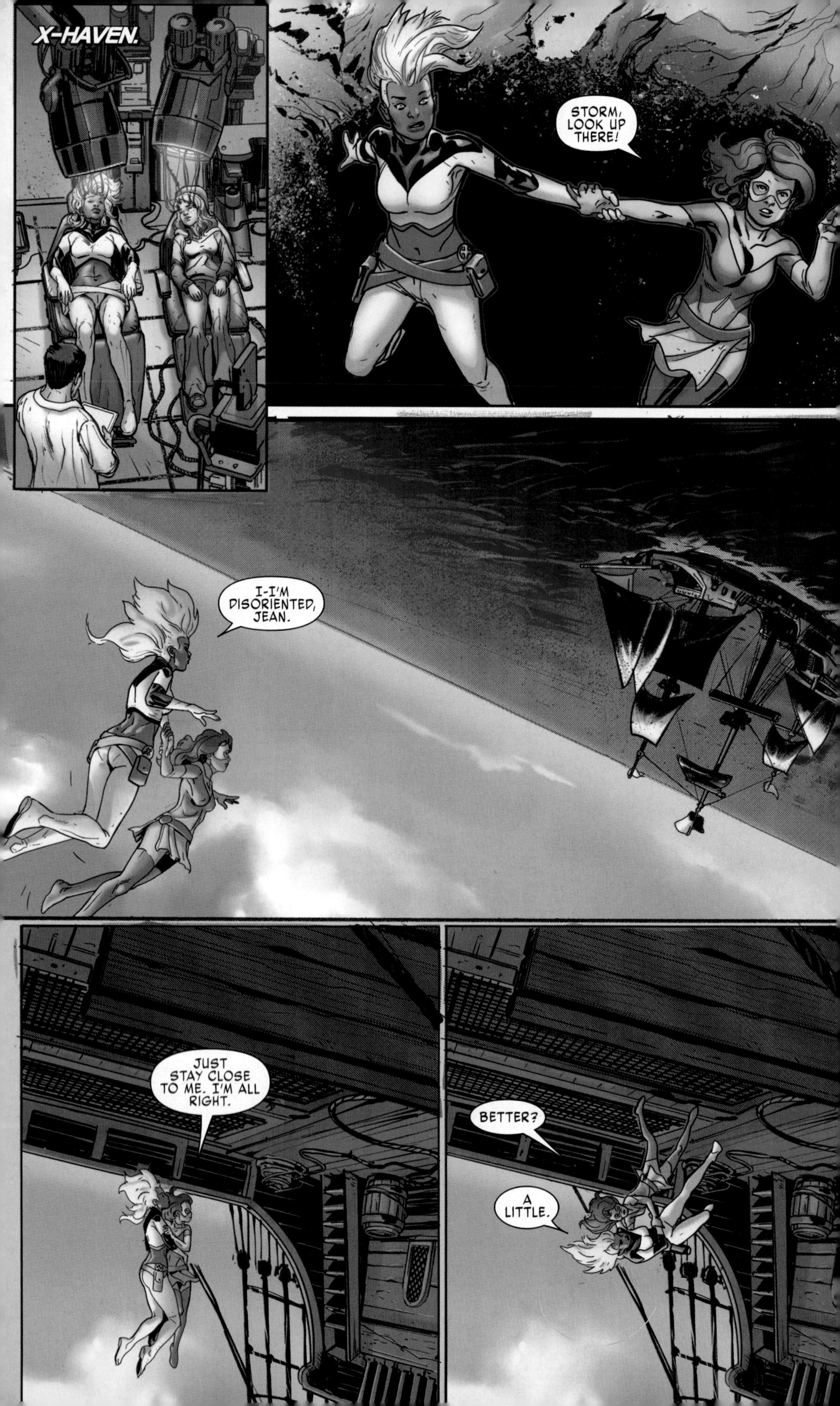
X-HAVEN.
STORM, LOOK UP THERE!
I-I'M DISORIENTED, JEAN.
JUST STAY CLOSE TO ME. I'M ALL RIGHT.
BETTER?
A LITTLE.

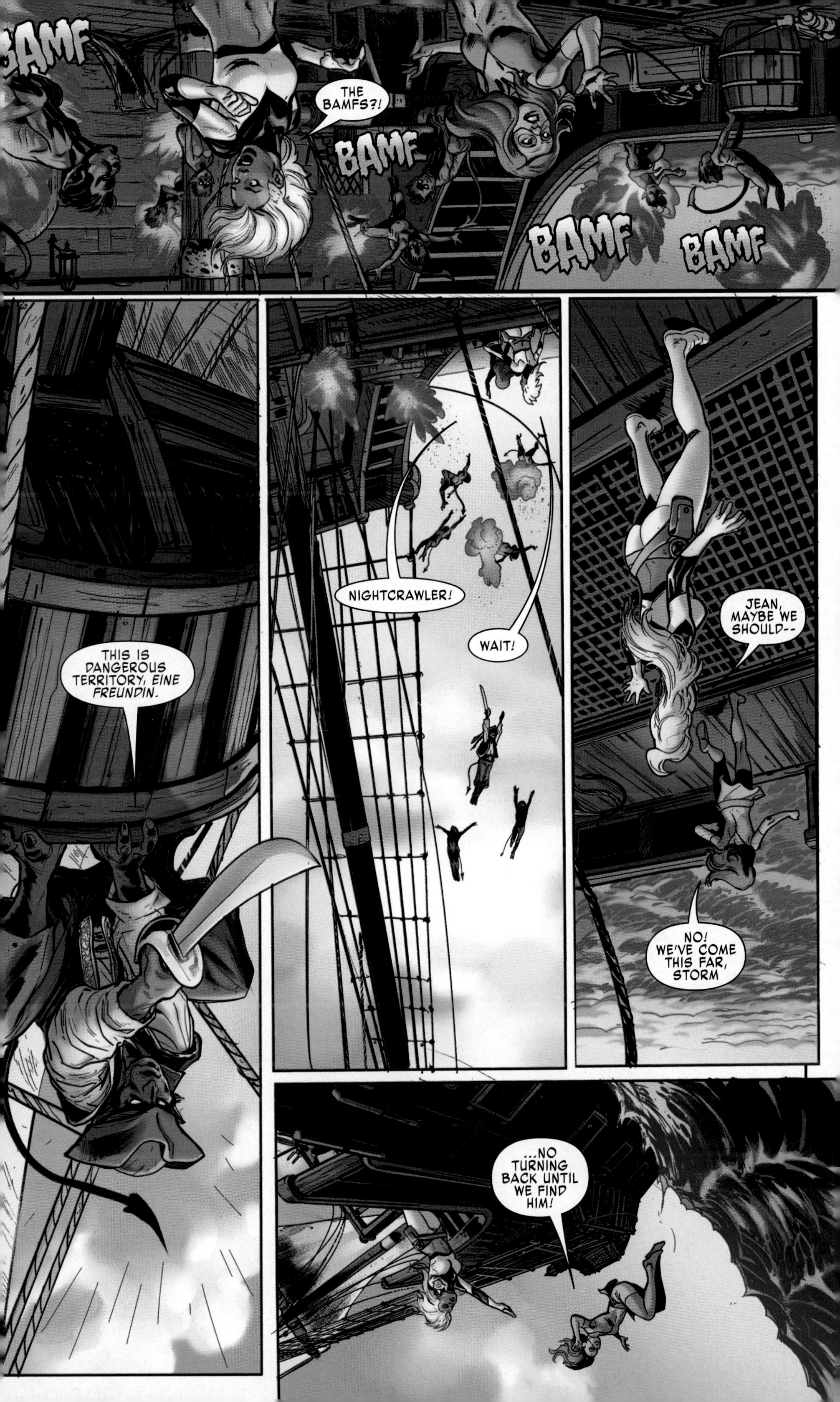
BAMF
THE BAMFS?!
BAMF
BAMF
BAMF
THIS IS DANGEROUS TERRITORY, EINE FREUNDIN.
NIGHTCRAWLER!
WAIT!
JEAN, MAYBE WE SHOULD--
NO! WE'VE COME THIS FAR, STORM
...NO TURNING BACK UNTIL WE FIND HIM!

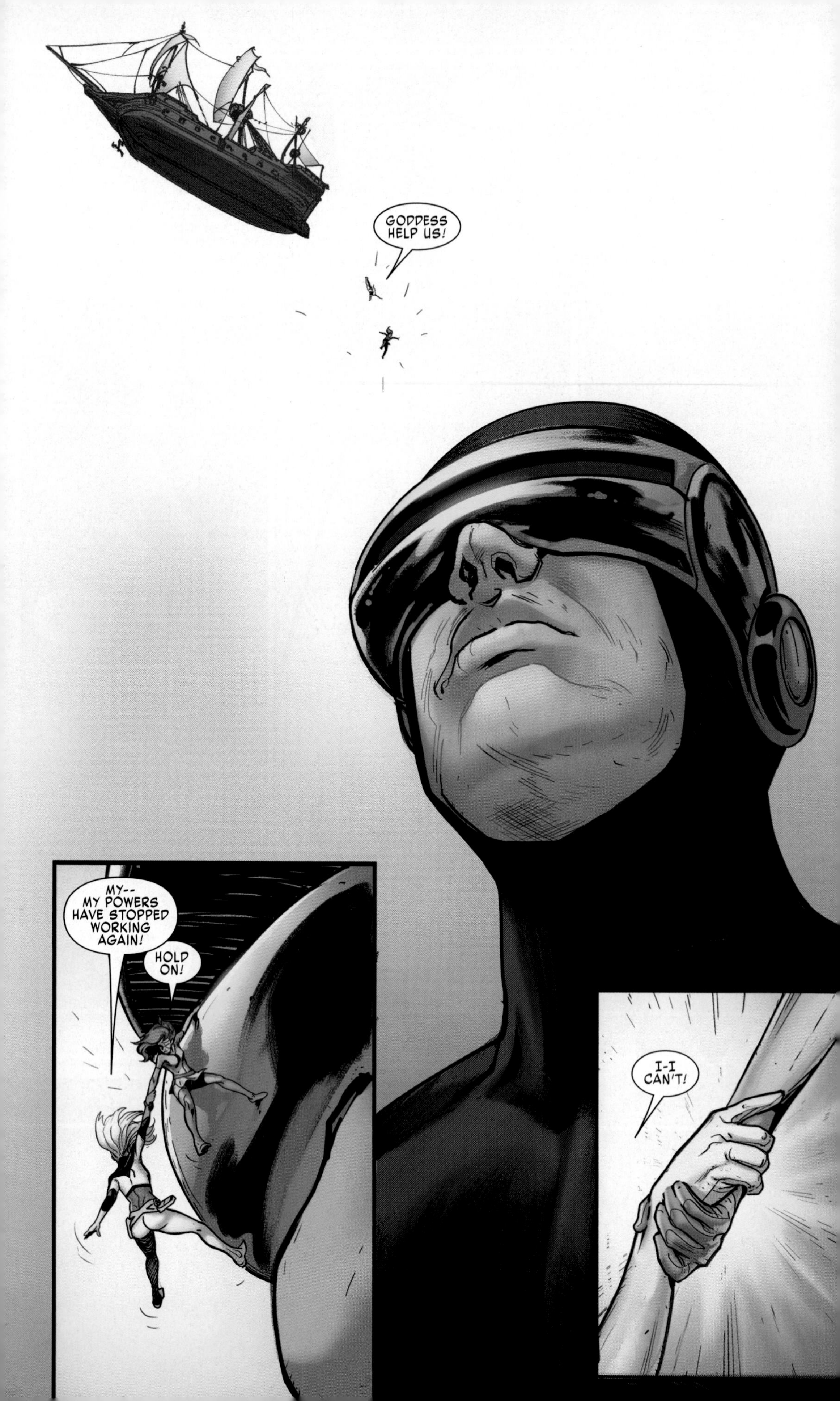
GODDESS HELP US!
MY-- MY POWERS HAVE STOPPED WORKING AGAIN!
HOLD ON!
I-I CAN'T!

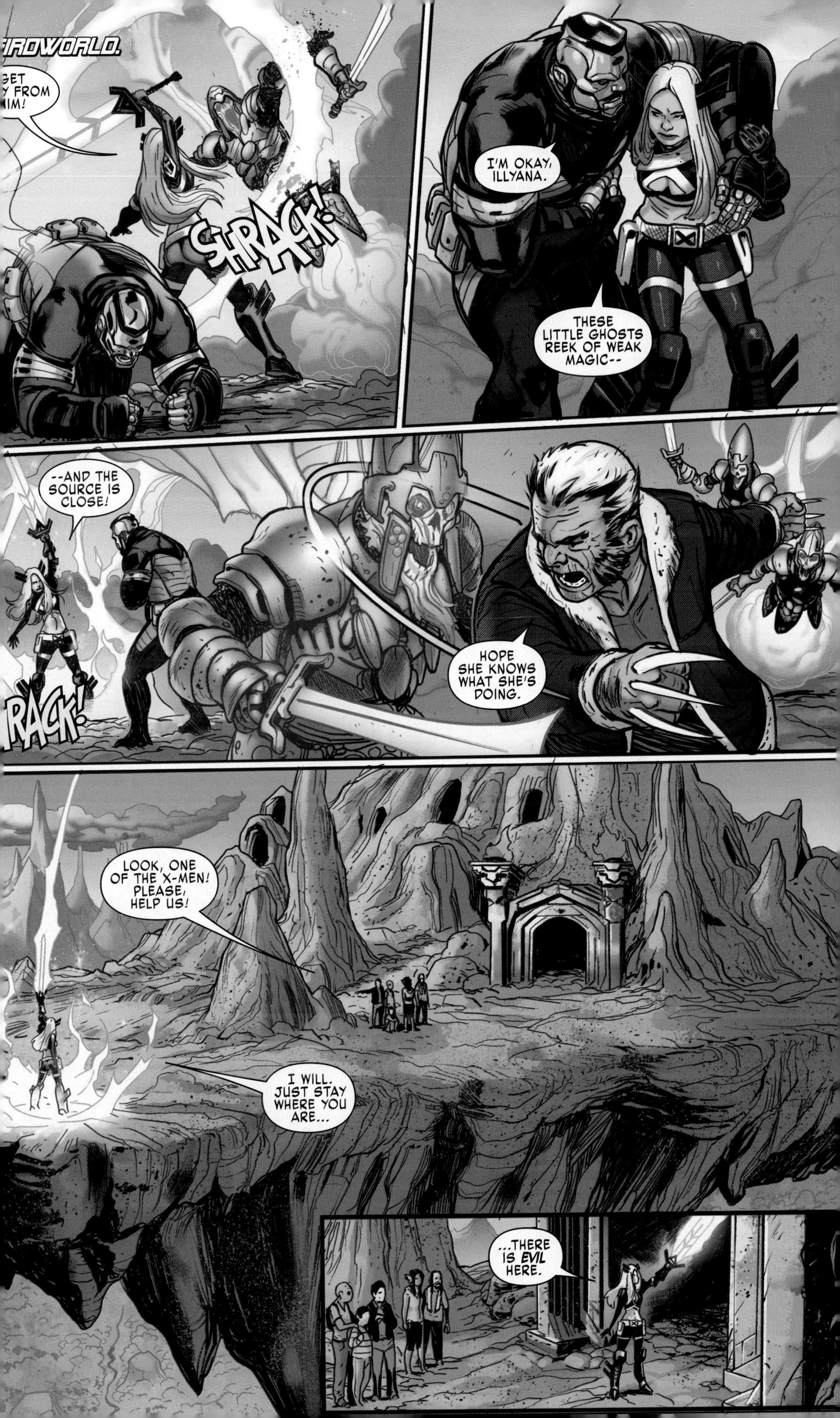

...IRDWORLD.
...GET
...Y FROM
...IM!
SHRACK!
I'M OKAY, ILLYANA.
THESE LITTLE GHOSTS REEK OF WEAK MAGIC--
--AND THE SOURCE IS CLOSE!
...RACK!
HOPE SHE KNOWS WHAT SHE'S DOING.
LOOK, ONE OF THE X-MEN! PLEASE, HELP US!
I WILL. JUST STAY WHERE YOU ARE...
...THERE IS *EVIL* HERE.

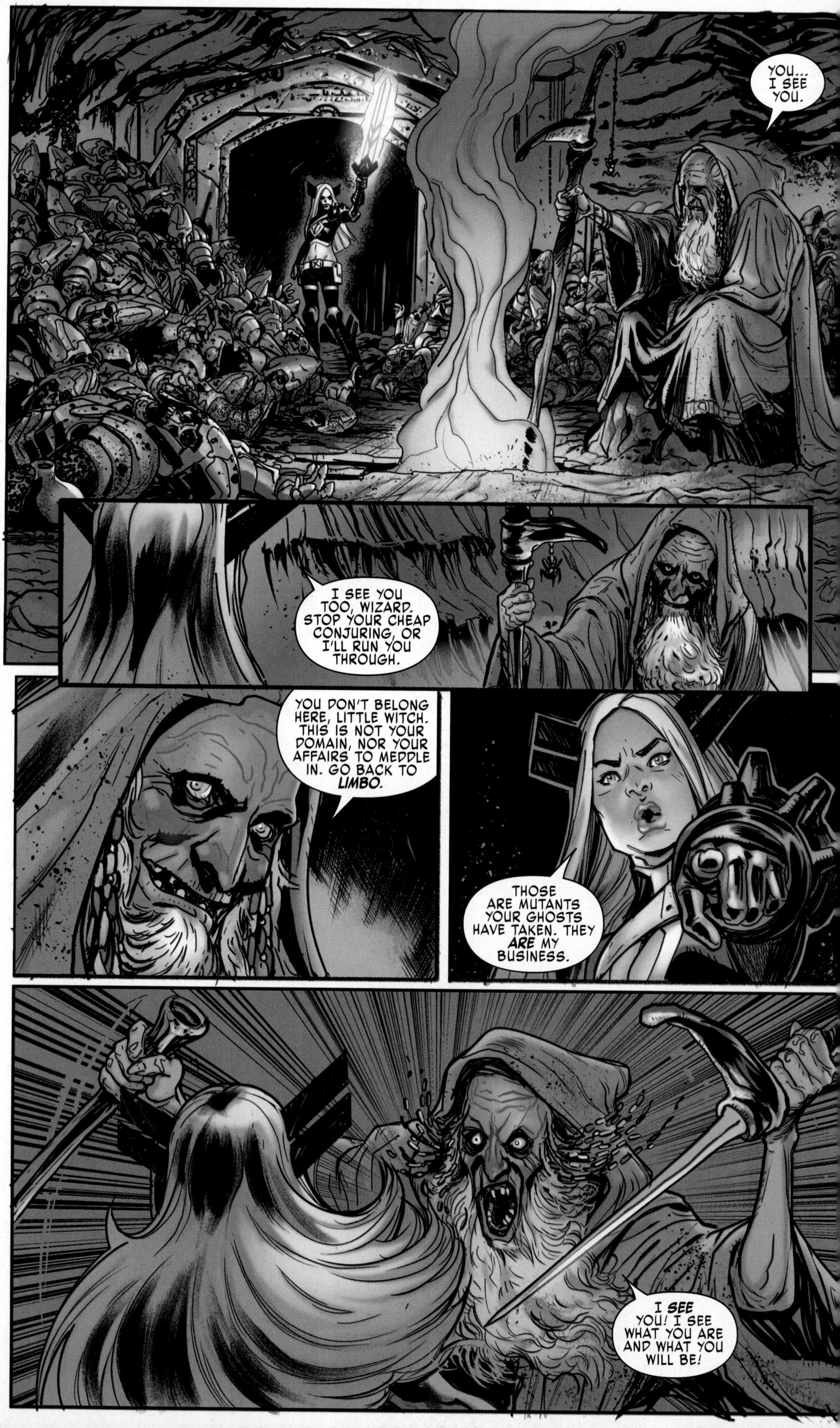
YOU... I SEE YOU.
I SEE YOU TOO, WIZARD. STOP YOUR CHEAP CONJURING, OR I'LL RUN YOU THROUGH.
YOU DON'T BELONG HERE, LITTLE WITCH. THIS IS NOT YOUR DOMAIN, NOR YOUR AFFAIRS TO MEDDLE IN. GO BACK TO **LIMBO.**
THOSE ARE MUTANTS YOUR GHOSTS HAVE TAKEN. THEY ***ARE*** MY BUSINESS.
I ***SEE*** YOU! I SEE WHAT YOU ARE AND WHAT YOU WILL BE!

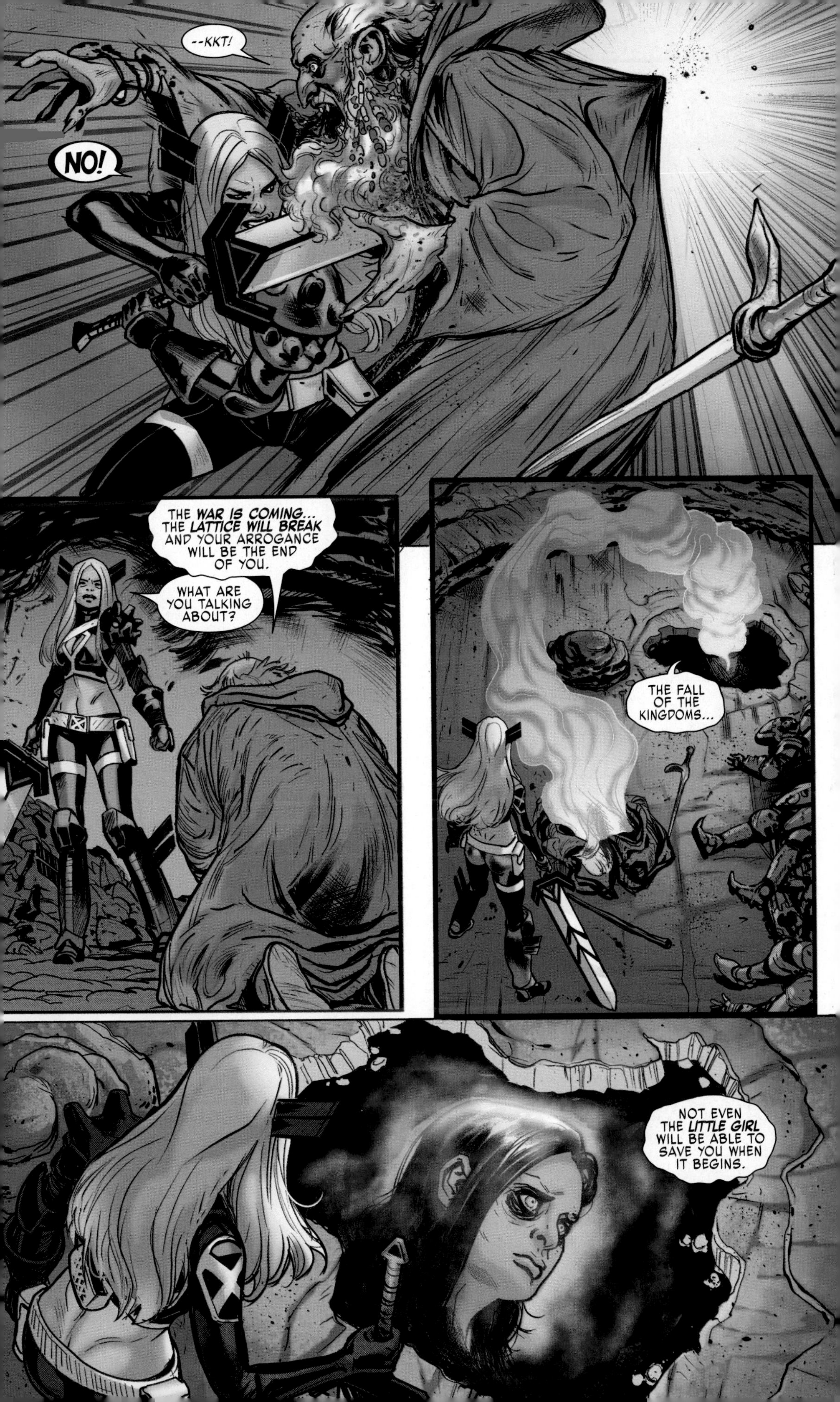
--KKT!
NO!
THE WAR IS COMING... THE LATTICE WILL BREAK AND YOUR ARROGANCE WILL BE THE END OF YOU.
WHAT ARE YOU TALKING ABOUT?
THE FALL OF THE KINGDOMS...
NOT EVEN THE LITTLE GIRL WILL BE ABLE TO SAVE YOU WHEN IT BEGINS.

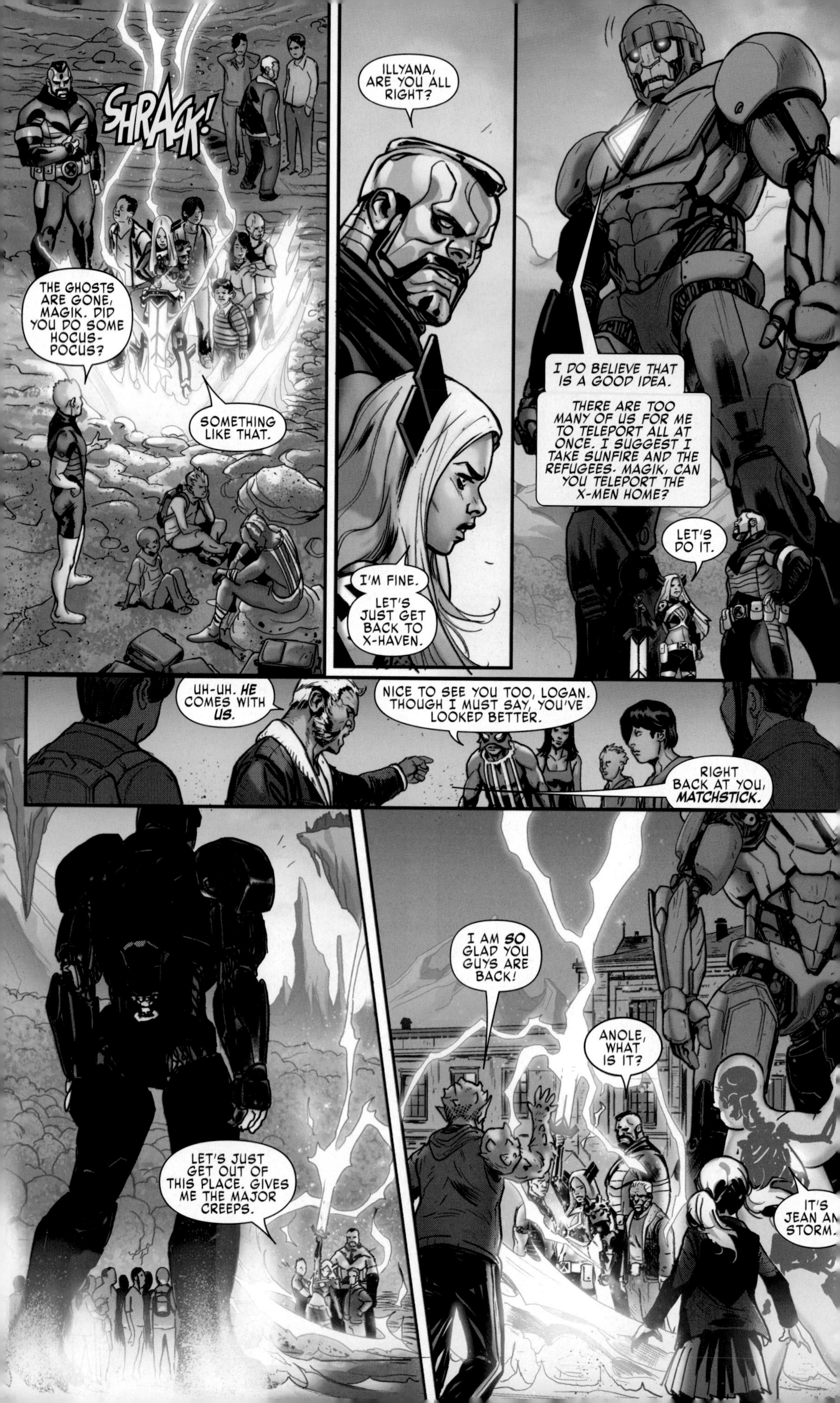
SHRACK!
THE GHOSTS ARE GONE, MAGIK. DID YOU DO SOME HOCUS-POCUS?
SOMETHING LIKE THAT.
ILLYANA, ARE YOU ALL RIGHT?
I'M FINE.
LET'S JUST GET BACK TO X-HAVEN.
I DO BELIEVE THAT IS A GOOD IDEA.
THERE ARE TOO MANY OF US FOR ME TO TELEPORT ALL AT ONCE. I SUGGEST I TAKE SUNFIRE AND THE REFUGEES. MAGIK, CAN YOU TELEPORT THE X-MEN HOME?
LET'S DO IT.
UH-UH. HE COMES WITH US.
NICE TO SEE YOU TOO, LOGAN. THOUGH I MUST SAY, YOU'VE LOOKED BETTER.
RIGHT BACK AT YOU, MATCHSTICK.
LET'S JUST GET OUT OF THIS PLACE. GIVES ME THE MAJOR CREEPS.
I AM SO GLAD YOU GUYS ARE BACK!
ANOLE, WHAT IS IT?

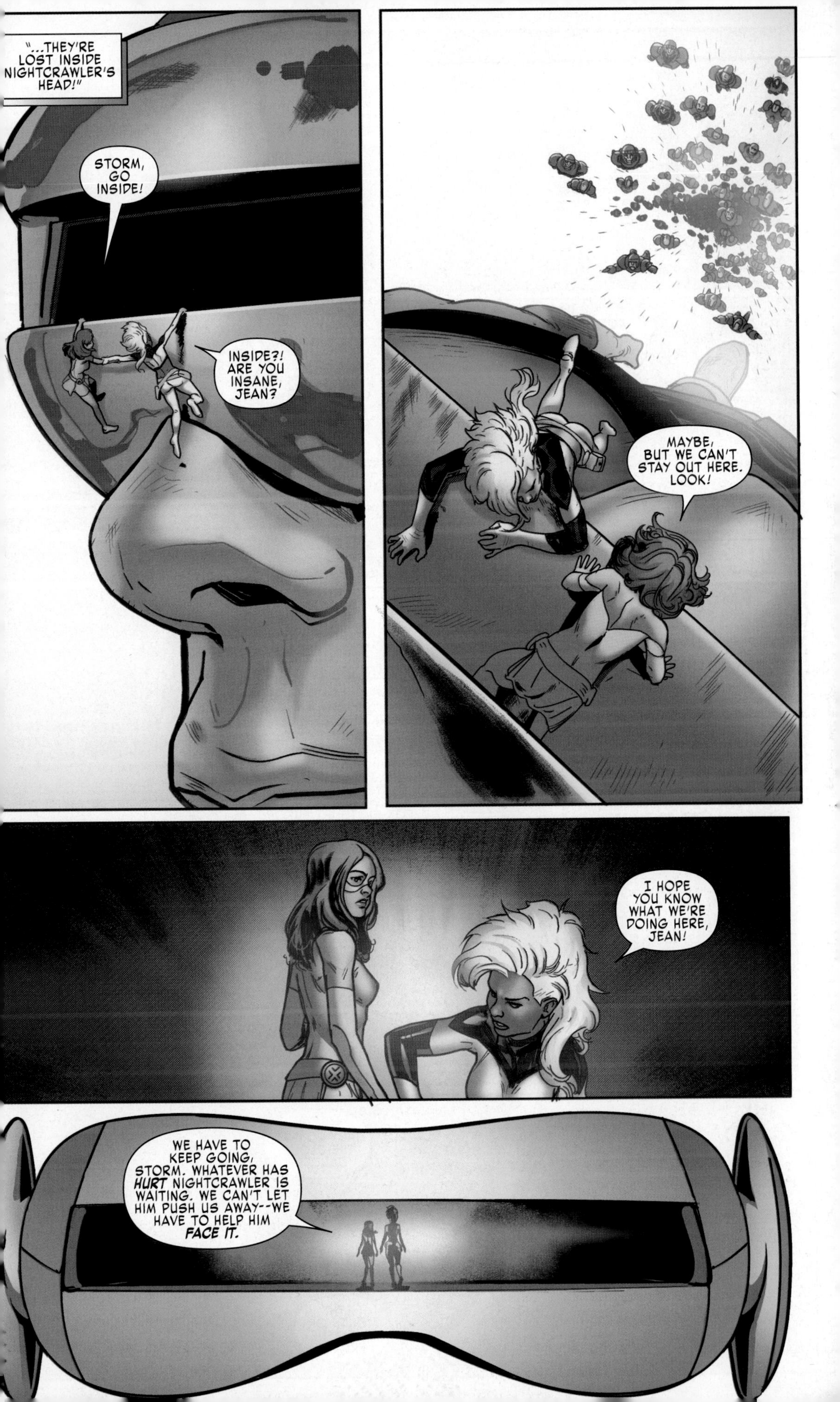
"...THEY'RE LOST INSIDE NIGHTCRAWLER'S HEAD!"
STORM, GO INSIDE!
INSIDE?! ARE YOU INSANE, JEAN?
MAYBE, BUT WE CAN'T STAY OUT HERE. LOOK!
I HOPE YOU KNOW WHAT WE'RE DOING HERE, JEAN!
WE HAVE TO KEEP GOING, STORM. WHATEVER HAS HURT NIGHTCRAWLER IS WAITING. WE CAN'T LET HIM PUSH US AWAY--WE HAVE TO HELP HIM FACE IT.

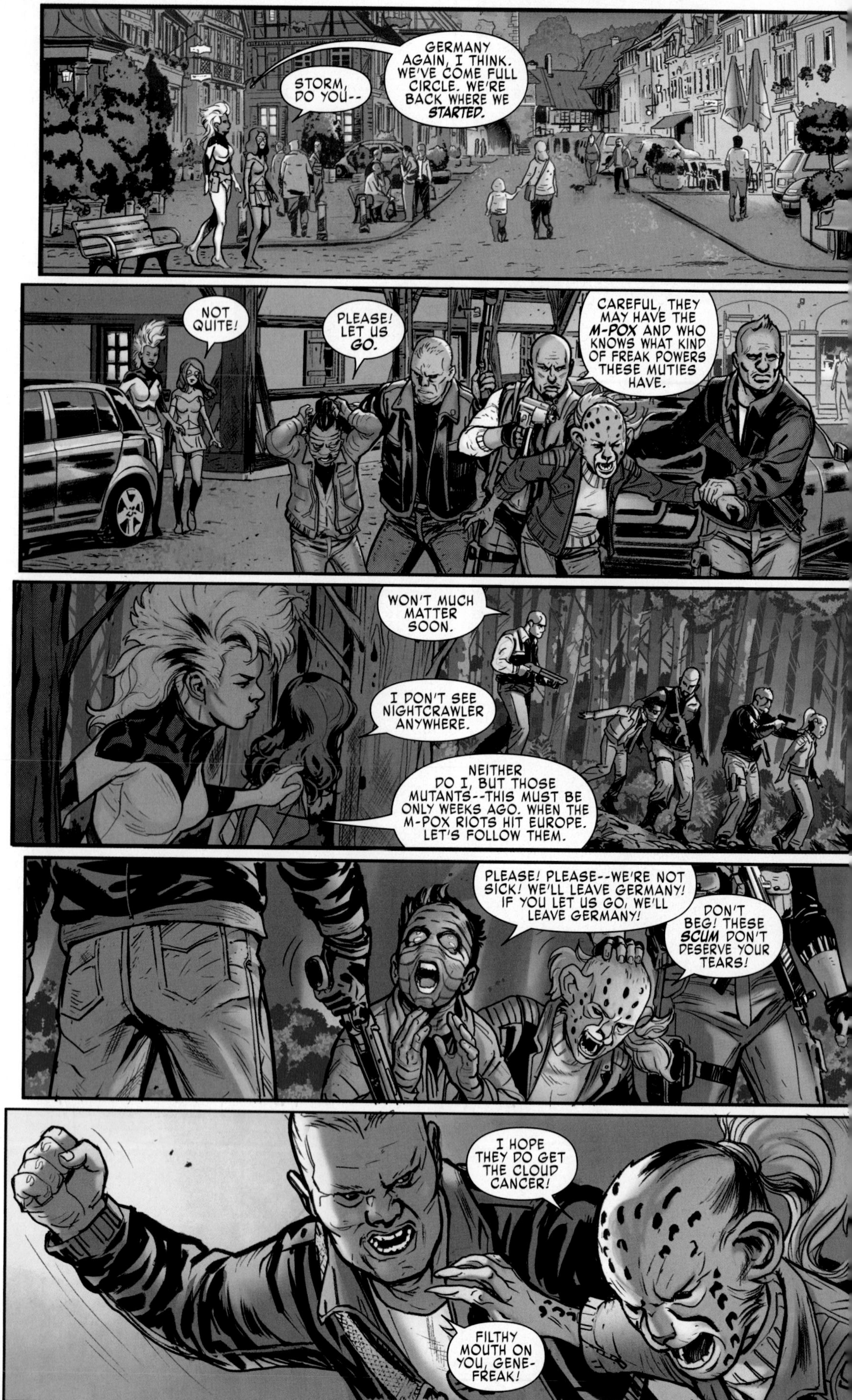
STORM, DO YOU--
GERMANY AGAIN, I THINK. WE'VE COME FULL CIRCLE. WE'RE BACK WHERE WE STARTED.
NOT QUITE!
PLEASE! LET US GO.
CAREFUL, THEY MAY HAVE THE M-POX AND WHO KNOWS WHAT KIND OF FREAK POWERS THESE MUTIES HAVE.
WON'T MUCH MATTER SOON.
I DON'T SEE NIGHTCRAWLER ANYWHERE.
NEITHER DO I, BUT THOSE MUTANTS--THIS MUST BE ONLY WEEKS AGO. WHEN THE M-POX RIOTS HIT EUROPE. LET'S FOLLOW THEM.
PLEASE! PLEASE--WE'RE NOT SICK! WE'LL LEAVE GERMANY! IF YOU LET US GO, WE'LL LEAVE GERMANY!
DON'T BEG! THESE SCUM DON'T DESERVE YOUR TEARS!
I HOPE THEY DO GET THE CLOUD CANCER!
FILTHY MOUTH ON YOU, GENE-FREAK!

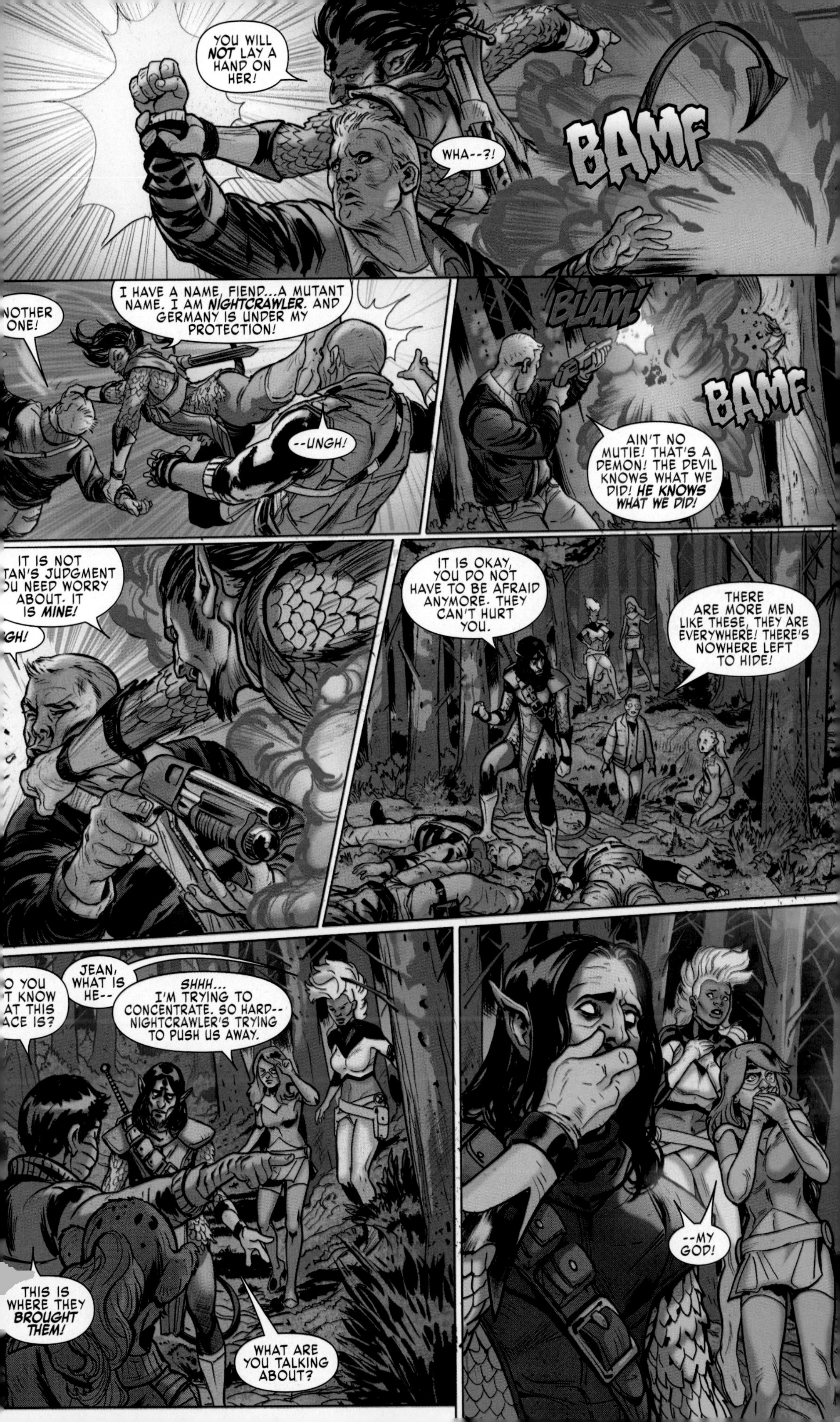
YOU WILL NOT LAY A HAND ON HER!
WHA--?!
BAMF
NOTHER ONE!
I HAVE A NAME, FIEND...A MUTANT NAME. I AM NIGHTCRAWLER. AND GERMANY IS UNDER MY PROTECTION!
--UNGH!
BLAM!
BAMF
AIN'T NO MUTIE! THAT'S A DEMON! THE DEVIL KNOWS WHAT WE DID! HE KNOWS WHAT WE DID!
IT IS NOT TAN'S JUDGMENT U NEED WORRY ABOUT. IT IS MINE!
GH!
IT IS OKAY, YOU DO NOT HAVE TO BE AFRAID ANYMORE. THEY CAN'T HURT YOU.
THERE ARE MORE MEN LIKE THESE, THEY ARE EVERYWHERE! THERE'S NOWHERE LEFT TO HIDE!
O YOU T KNOW AT THIS ACE IS?
JEAN, WHAT IS HE--
SHHH... I'M TRYING TO CONCENTRATE. SO HARD-- NIGHTCRAWLER'S TRYING TO PUSH US AWAY.
THIS IS WHERE THEY BROUGHT THEM!
WHAT ARE YOU TALKING ABOUT?
--MY GOD!

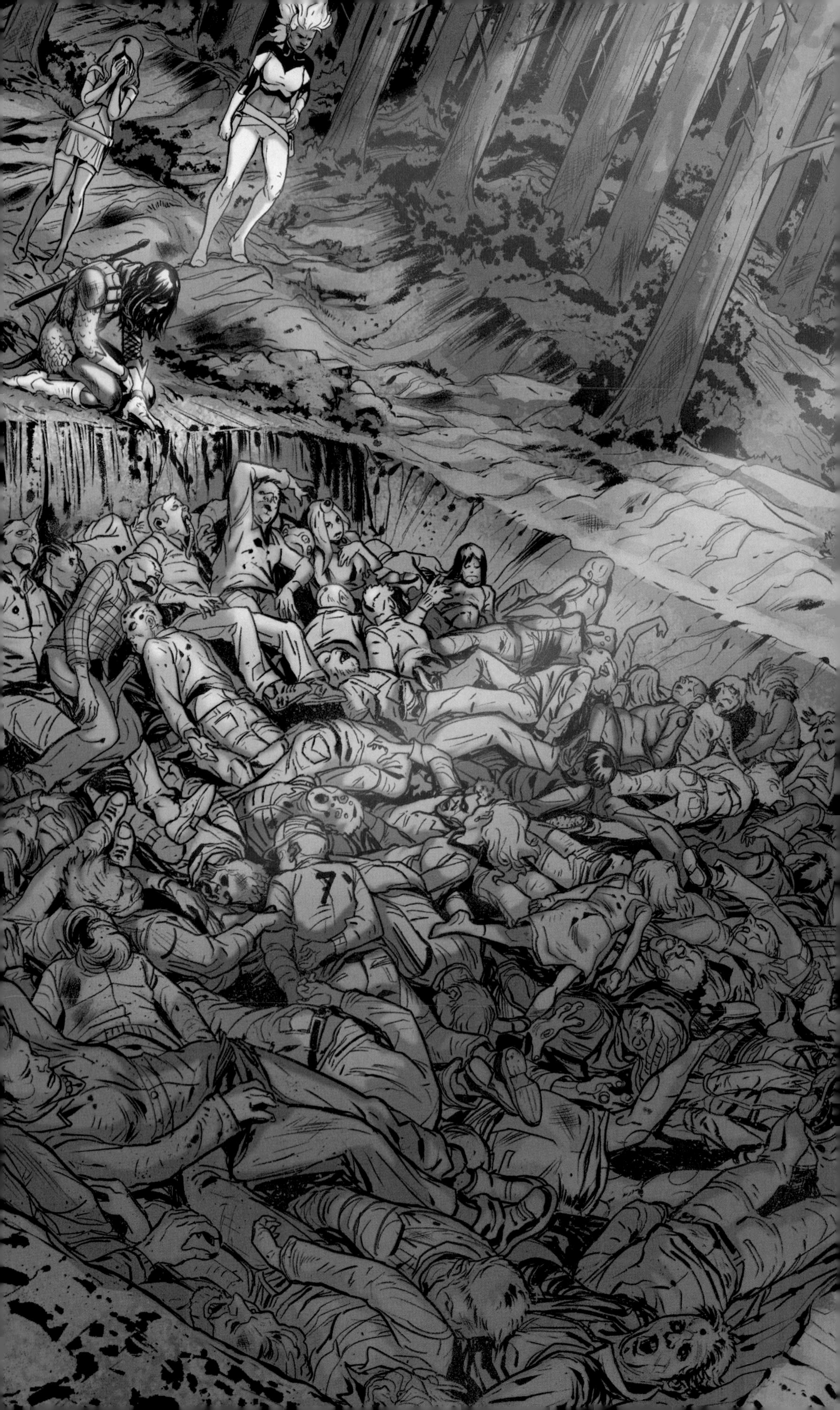

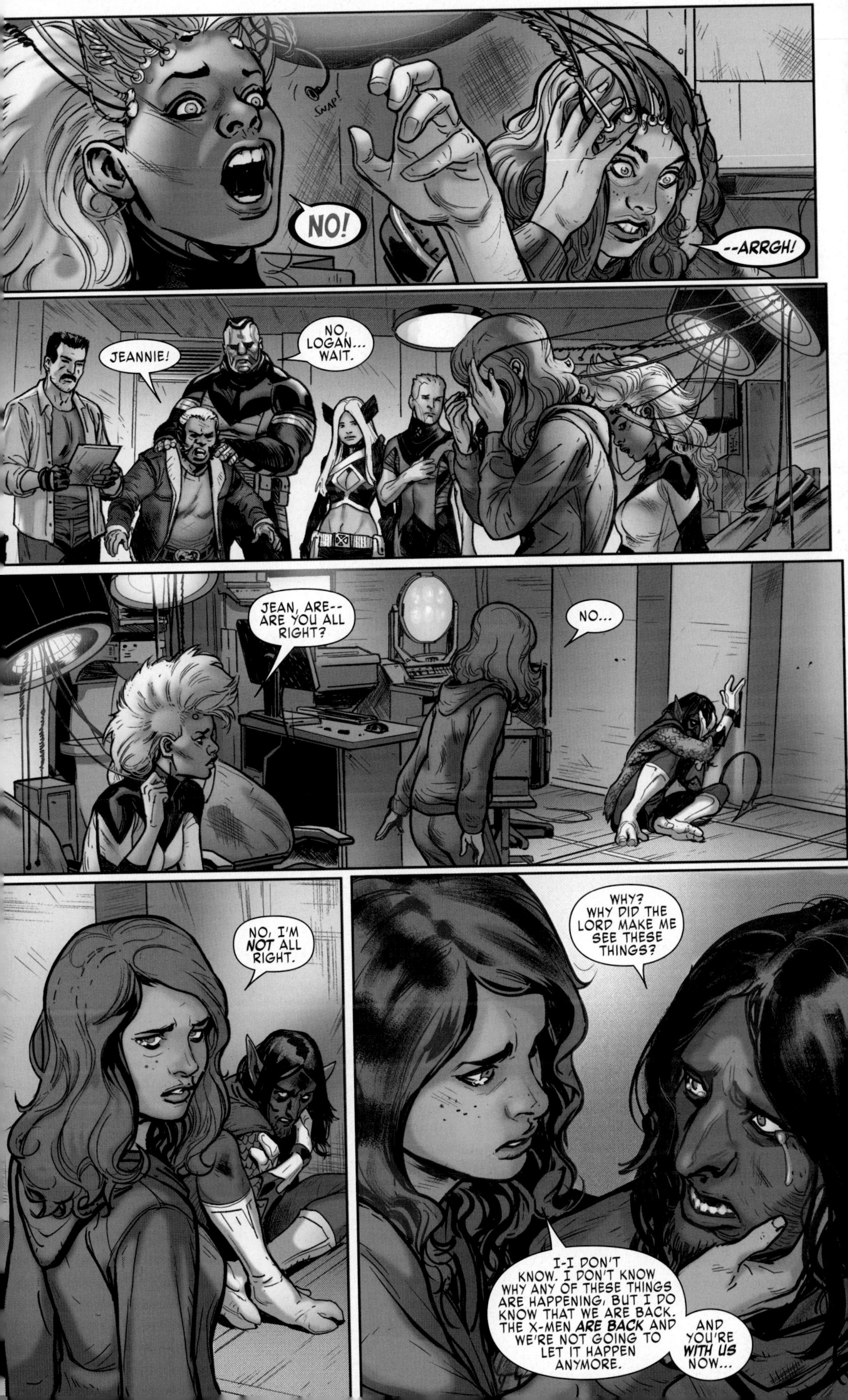
SNAP!
NO!
--ARRGH!
JEANNIE!
NO, LOGAN... WAIT.
JEAN, ARE-- ARE YOU ALL RIGHT?
NO...
NO, I'M NOT ALL RIGHT.
WHY? WHY DID THE LORD MAKE ME SEE THESE THINGS?
I-I DON'T KNOW. I DON'T KNOW WHY ANY OF THESE THINGS ARE HAPPENING, BUT I DO KNOW THAT WE ARE BACK. THE X-MEN ARE BACK AND WE'RE NOT GOING TO LET IT HAPPEN ANYMORE.
AND YOU'RE WITH US NOW...

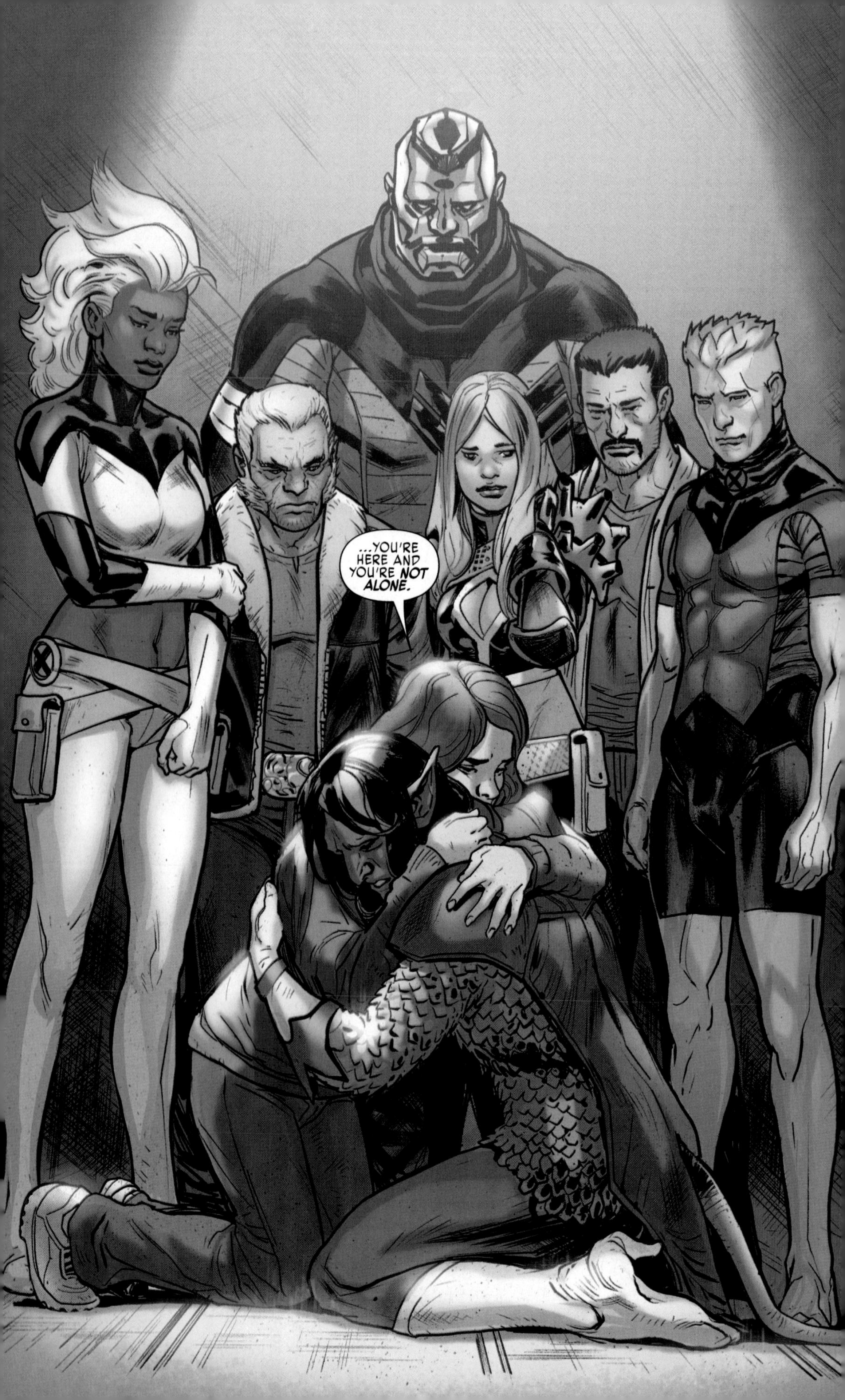
...YOU'RE HERE AND YOU'RE NOT ALONE.

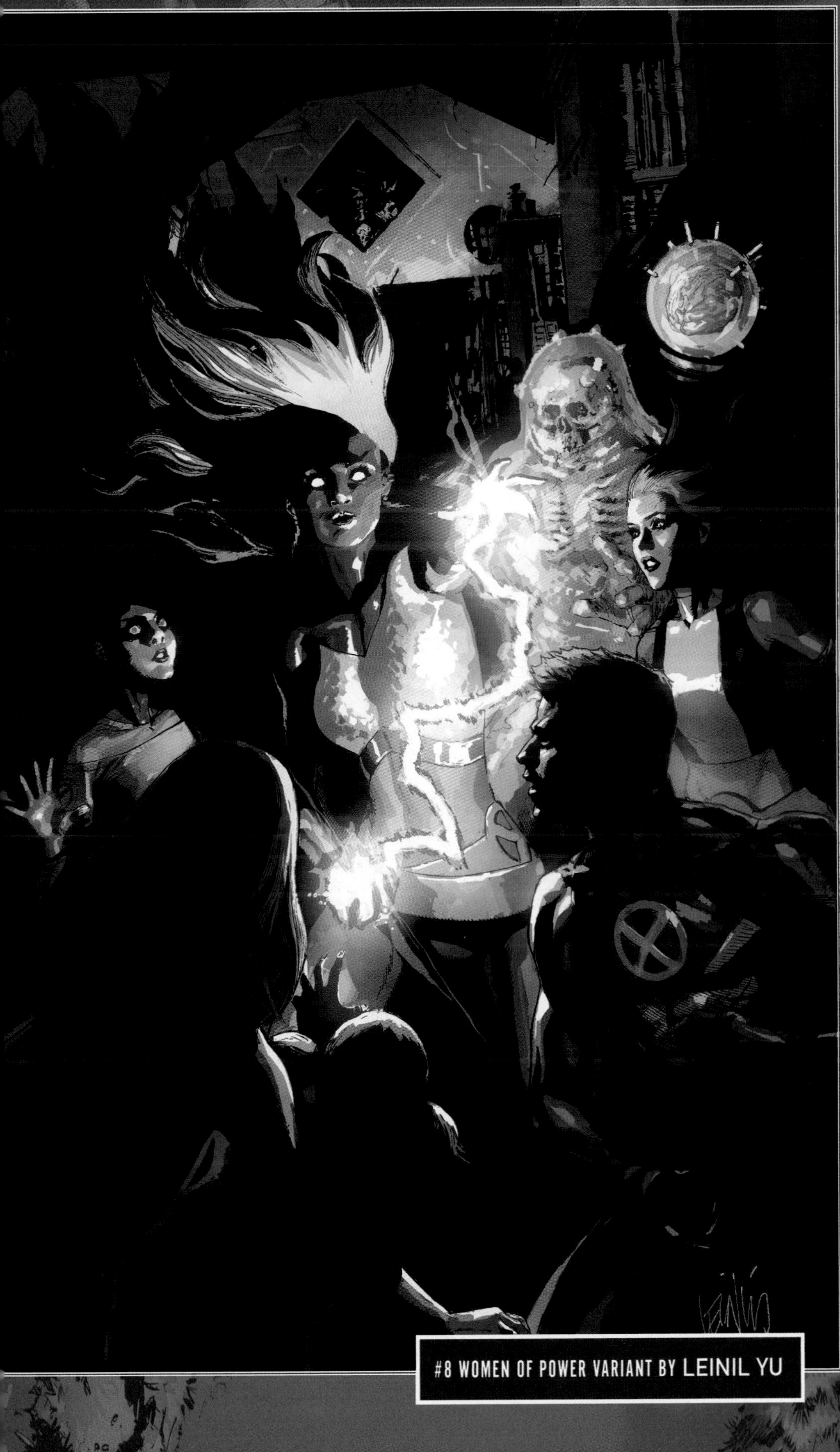

#8 WOMEN OF POWER VARIANT BY LEINIL YU

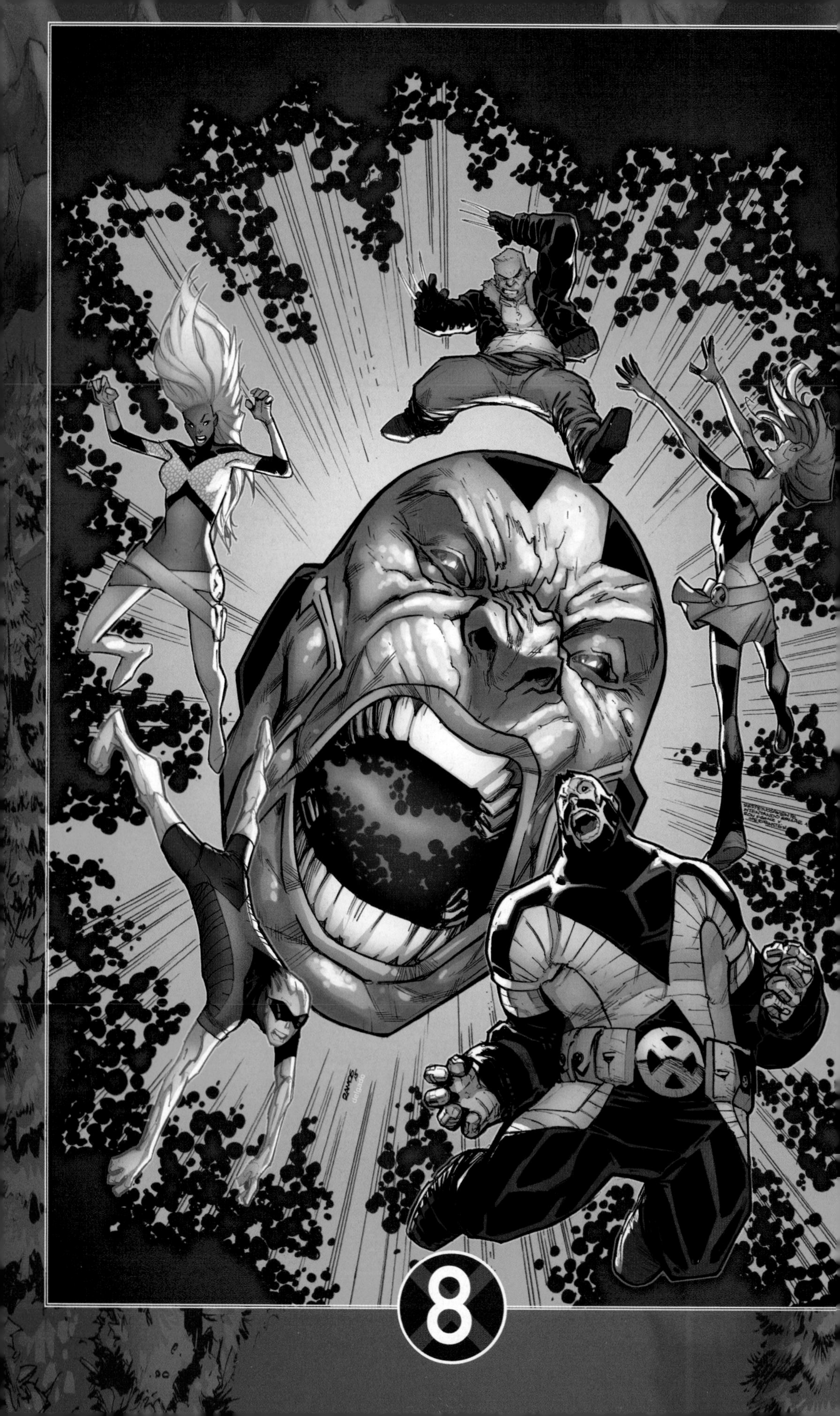
8

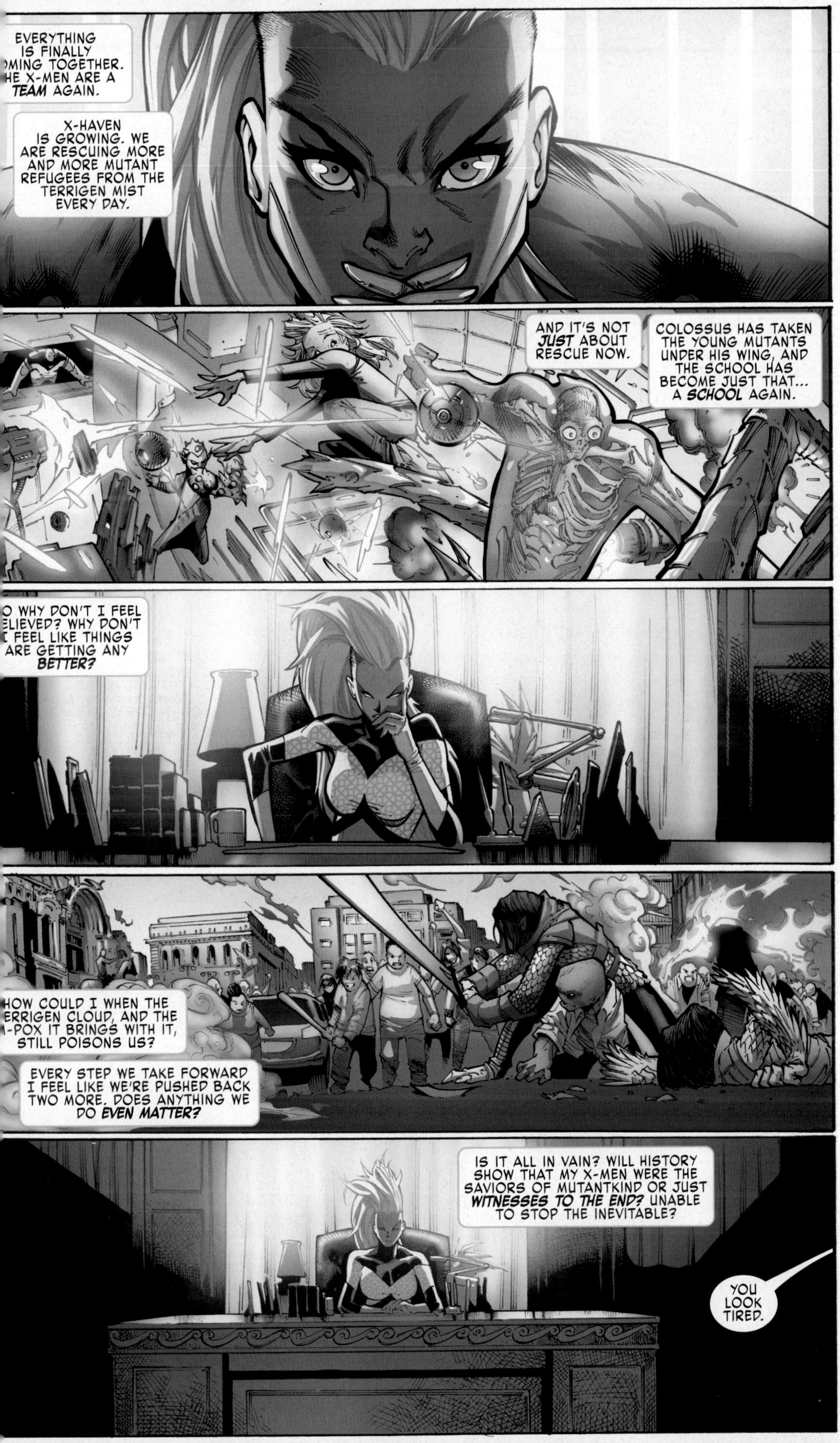
EVERYTHING IS FINALLY OMING TOGETHER. HE X-MEN ARE A TEAM AGAIN.
X-HAVEN IS GROWING. WE ARE RESCUING MORE AND MORE MUTANT REFUGEES FROM THE TERRIGEN MIST EVERY DAY.
AND IT'S NOT JUST ABOUT RESCUE NOW.
COLOSSUS HAS TAKEN THE YOUNG MUTANTS UNDER HIS WING, AND THE SCHOOL HAS BECOME JUST THAT... A SCHOOL AGAIN.
O WHY DON'T I FEEL ELIEVED? WHY DON'T FEEL LIKE THINGS ARE GETTING ANY BETTER?
HOW COULD I WHEN THE ERRIGEN CLOUD, AND THE -POX IT BRINGS WITH IT, STILL POISONS US?
EVERY STEP WE TAKE FORWARD I FEEL LIKE WE'RE PUSHED BACK TWO MORE. DOES ANYTHING WE DO EVEN MATTER?
IS IT ALL IN VAIN? WILL HISTORY SHOW THAT MY X-MEN WERE THE SAVIORS OF MUTANTKIND OR JUST WITNESSES TO THE END? UNABLE TO STOP THE INEVITABLE?
YOU LOOK TIRED.

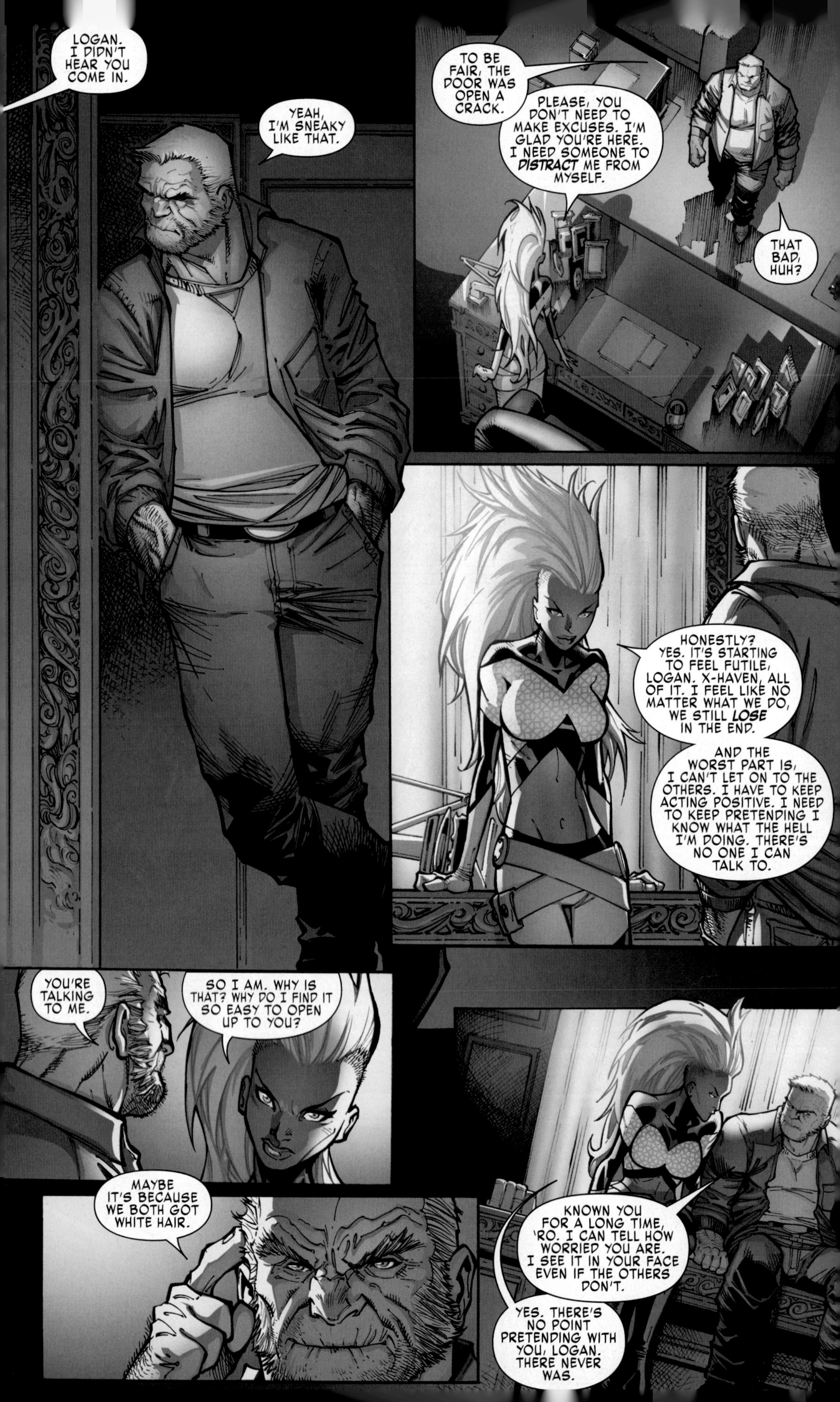
LOGAN. I DIDN'T HEAR YOU COME IN.
YEAH, I'M SNEAKY LIKE THAT.
TO BE FAIR, THE DOOR WAS OPEN A CRACK.
PLEASE, YOU DON'T NEED TO MAKE EXCUSES. I'M GLAD YOU'RE HERE. I NEED SOMEONE TO DISTRACT ME FROM MYSELF.
THAT BAD, HUH?
HONESTLY? YES. IT'S STARTING TO FEEL FUTILE, LOGAN. X-HAVEN, ALL OF IT. I FEEL LIKE NO MATTER WHAT WE DO, WE STILL LOSE IN THE END.
AND THE WORST PART IS, I CAN'T LET ON TO THE OTHERS. I HAVE TO KEEP ACTING POSITIVE. I NEED TO KEEP PRETENDING I KNOW WHAT THE HELL I'M DOING. THERE'S NO ONE I CAN TALK TO.
YOU'RE TALKING TO ME.
SO I AM. WHY IS THAT? WHY DO I FIND IT SO EASY TO OPEN UP TO YOU?
MAYBE IT'S BECAUSE WE BOTH GOT WHITE HAIR.
KNOWN YOU FOR A LONG TIME, 'RO. I CAN TELL HOW WORRIED YOU ARE. I SEE IT IN YOUR FACE EVEN IF THE OTHERS DON'T.
YES. THERE'S NO POINT PRETENDING WITH YOU, LOGAN. THERE NEVER WAS.

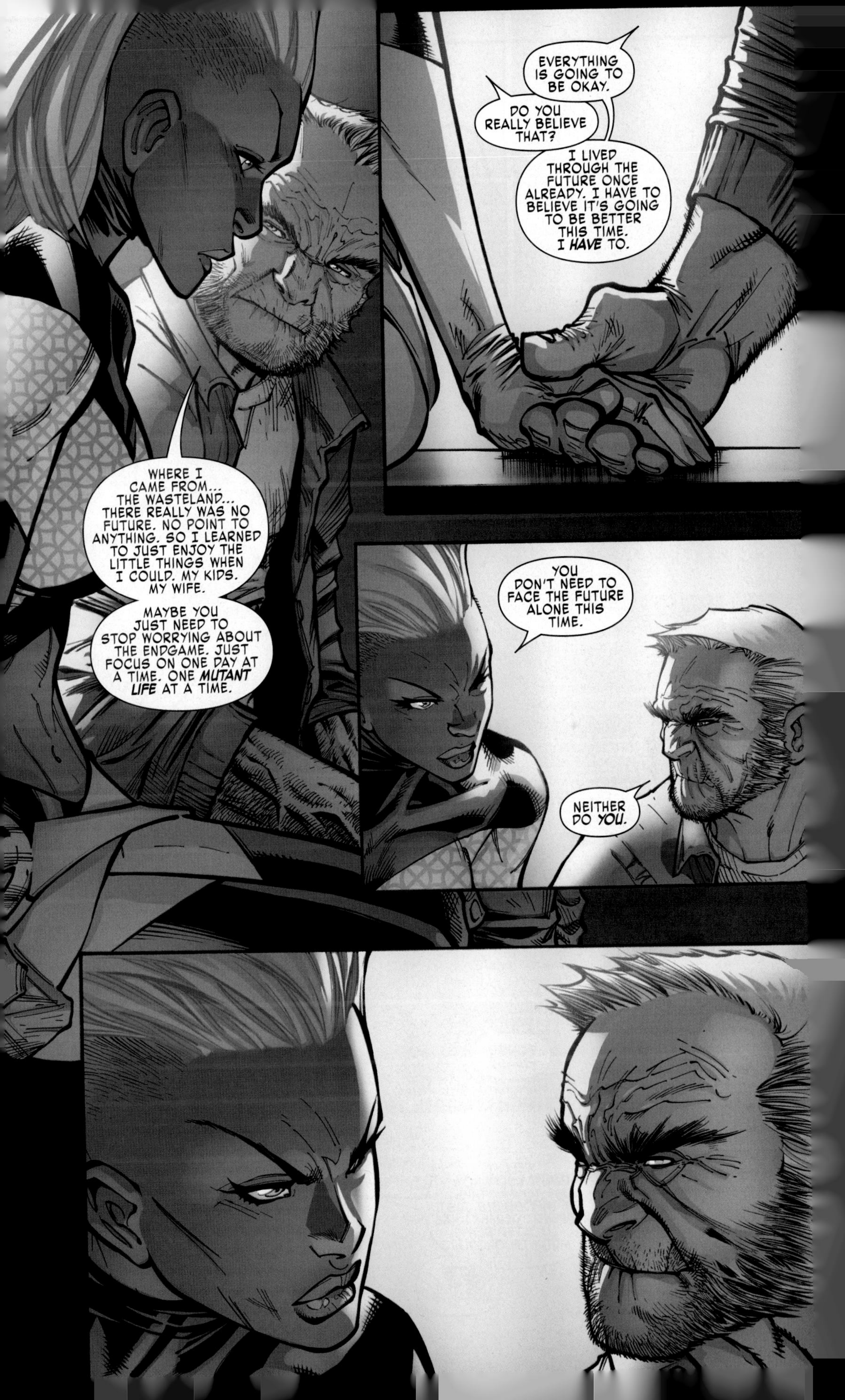

EVERYTHING IS GOING TO BE OKAY.
DO YOU REALLY BELIEVE THAT?
I LIVED THROUGH THE FUTURE ONCE ALREADY. I HAVE TO BELIEVE IT'S GOING TO BE BETTER THIS TIME. I *HAVE* TO.
WHERE I CAME FROM... THE WASTELAND... THERE REALLY WAS NO FUTURE. NO POINT TO ANYTHING. SO I LEARNED TO JUST ENJOY THE LITTLE THINGS WHEN I COULD. MY KIDS. MY WIFE.
MAYBE YOU JUST NEED TO STOP WORRYING ABOUT THE ENDGAME. JUST FOCUS ON ONE DAY AT A TIME. ONE *MUTANT LIFE* AT A TIME.
YOU DON'T NEED TO FACE THE FUTURE ALONE THIS TIME.
NEITHER DO *YOU*.

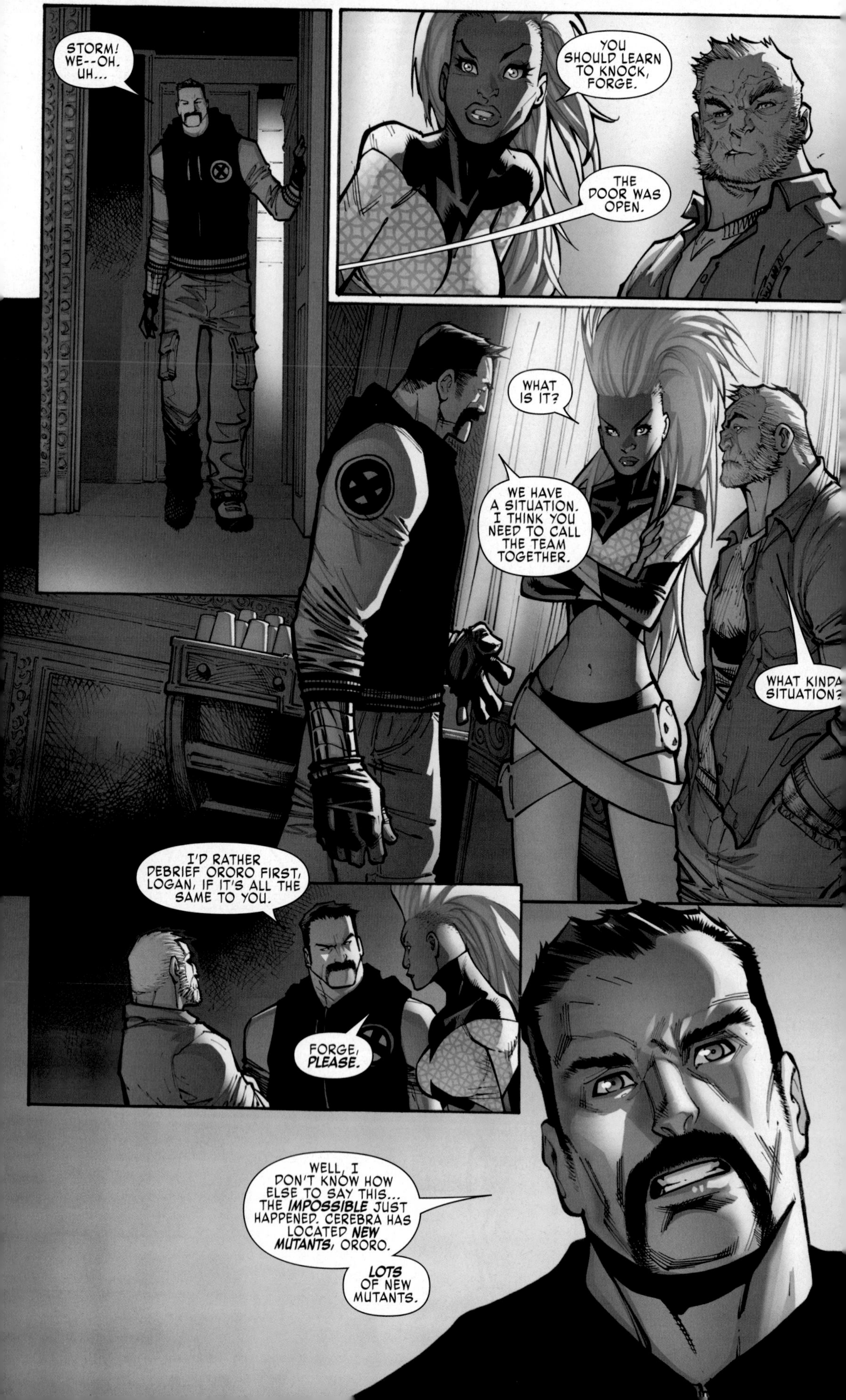
STORM! WE--OH. UH...
YOU SHOULD LEARN TO KNOCK, FORGE.
THE DOOR WAS OPEN.
WHAT IS IT?
WE HAVE A SITUATION. I THINK YOU NEED TO CALL THE TEAM TOGETHER.
WHAT KINDA SITUATION?
I'D RATHER DEBRIEF ORORO FIRST, LOGAN, IF IT'S ALL THE SAME TO YOU.
FORGE, PLEASE.
WELL, I DON'T KNOW HOW ELSE TO SAY THIS... THE IMPOSSIBLE JUST HAPPENED. CEREBRA HAS LOCATED NEW MUTANTS, ORORO.
LOTS OF NEW MUTANTS.

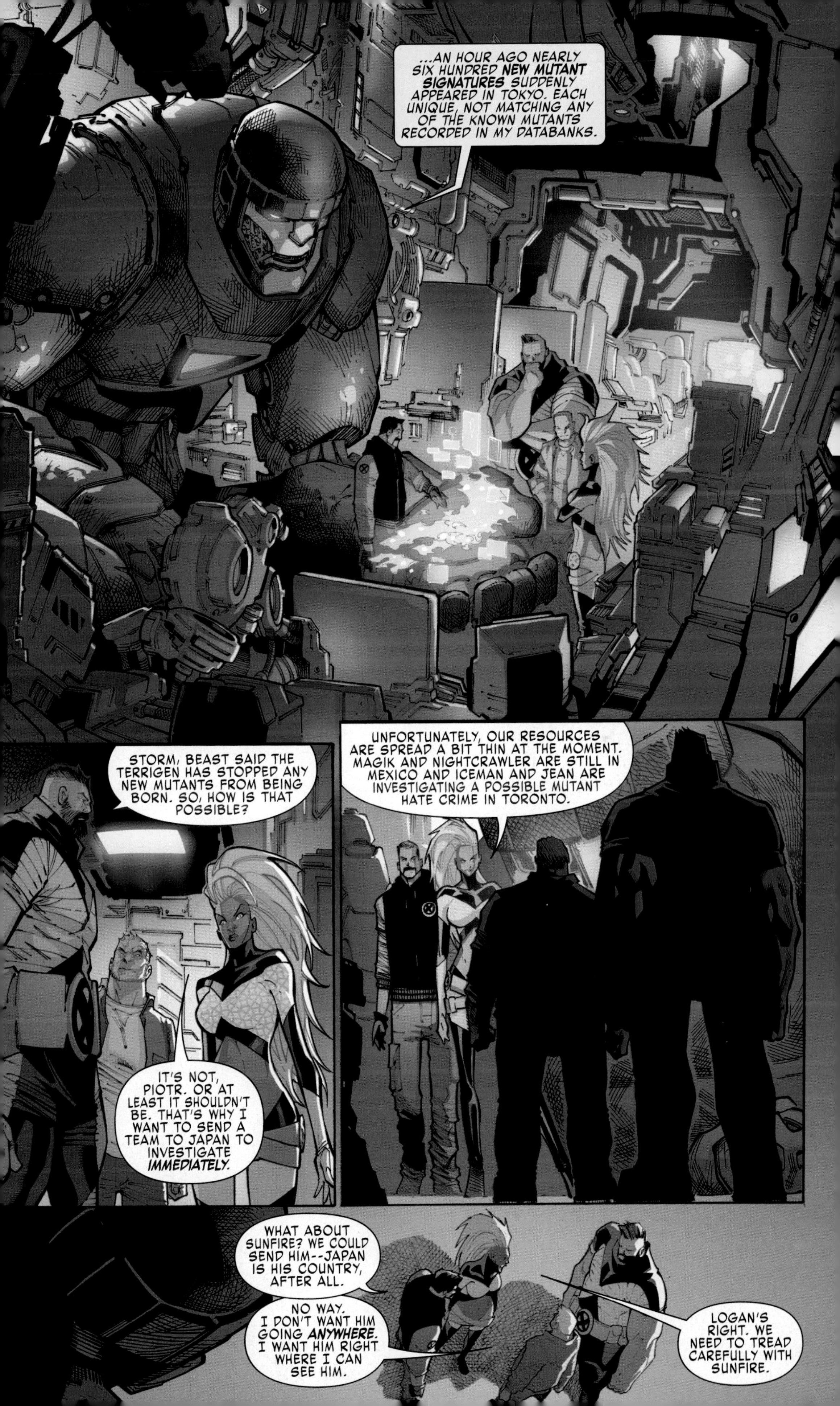
...AN HOUR AGO NEARLY SIX HUNDRED **NEW MUTANT SIGNATURES** SUDDENLY APPEARED IN TOKYO. EACH UNIQUE, NOT MATCHING ANY OF THE KNOWN MUTANTS RECORDED IN MY DATABANKS.
STORM, BEAST SAID THE TERRIGEN HAS STOPPED ANY NEW MUTANTS FROM BEING BORN. SO, HOW IS THAT POSSIBLE?
IT'S NOT, PIOTR. OR AT LEAST IT SHOULDN'T BE. THAT'S WHY I WANT TO SEND A TEAM TO JAPAN TO INVESTIGATE ***IMMEDIATELY.***
UNFORTUNATELY, OUR RESOURCES ARE SPREAD A BIT THIN AT THE MOMENT. MAGIK AND NIGHTCRAWLER ARE STILL IN MEXICO AND ICEMAN AND JEAN ARE INVESTIGATING A POSSIBLE MUTANT HATE CRIME IN TORONTO.
WHAT ABOUT SUNFIRE? WE COULD SEND HIM--JAPAN IS HIS COUNTRY, AFTER ALL.
NO WAY. I DON'T WANT HIM GOING ***ANYWHERE.*** I WANT HIM RIGHT WHERE I CAN SEE HIM.
LOGAN'S RIGHT. WE NEED TO TREAD CAREFULLY WITH SUNFIRE.

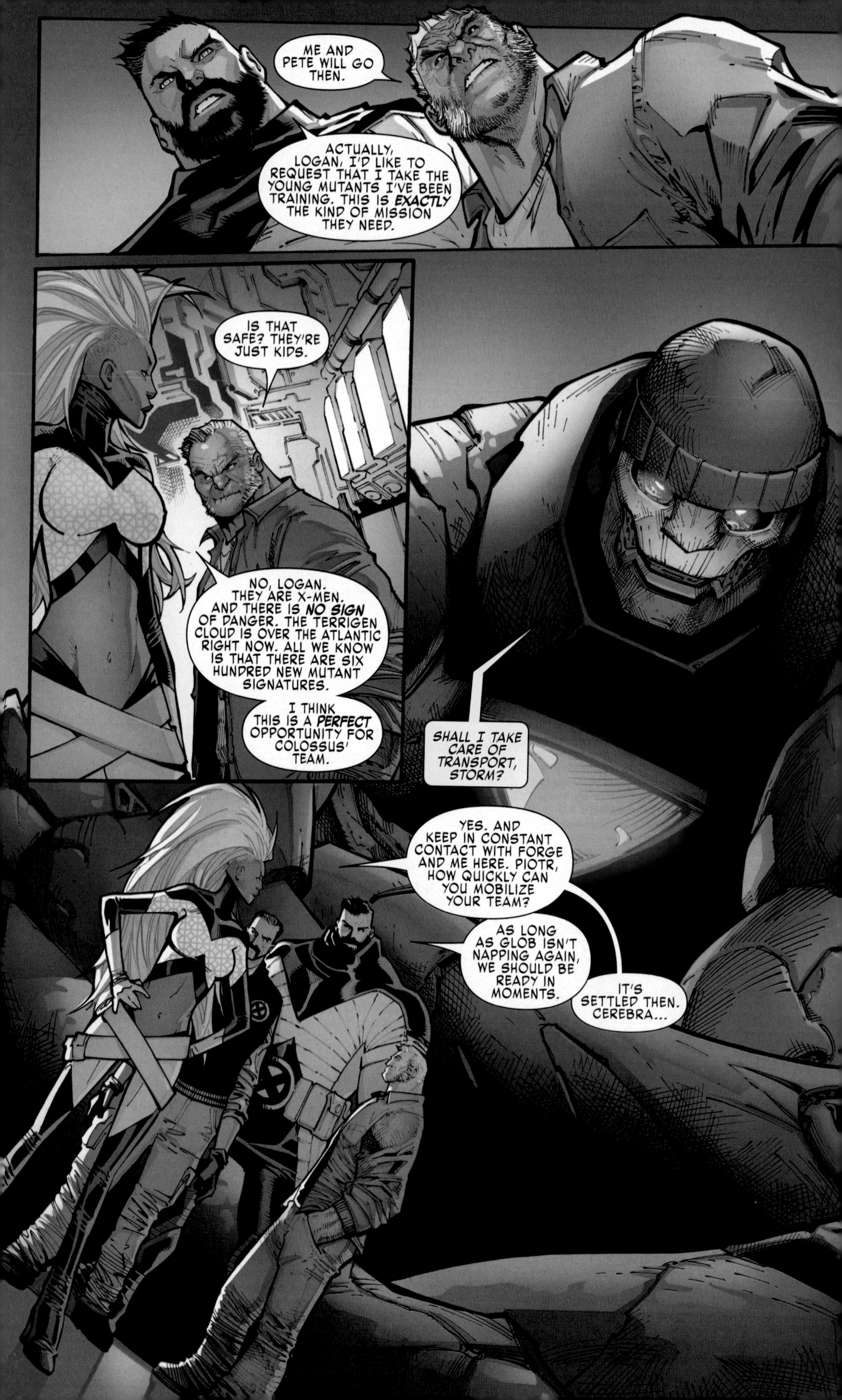

ME AND PETE WILL GO THEN.
ACTUALLY, LOGAN, I'D LIKE TO REQUEST THAT I TAKE THE YOUNG MUTANTS I'VE BEEN TRAINING. THIS IS EXACTLY THE KIND OF MISSION THEY NEED.
IS THAT SAFE? THEY'RE JUST KIDS.
NO, LOGAN. THEY ARE X-MEN. AND THERE IS NO SIGN OF DANGER. THE TERRIGEN CLOUD IS OVER THE ATLANTIC RIGHT NOW. ALL WE KNOW IS THAT THERE ARE SIX HUNDRED NEW MUTANT SIGNATURES.
I THINK THIS IS A PERFECT OPPORTUNITY FOR COLOSSUS' TEAM.
SHALL I TAKE CARE OF TRANSPORT, STORM?
YES. AND KEEP IN CONSTANT CONTACT WITH FORGE AND ME HERE. PIOTR, HOW QUICKLY CAN YOU MOBILIZE YOUR TEAM?
AS LONG AS GLOB ISN'T NAPPING AGAIN, WE SHOULD BE READY IN MOMENTS.
IT'S SETTLED THEN. CEREBRA...

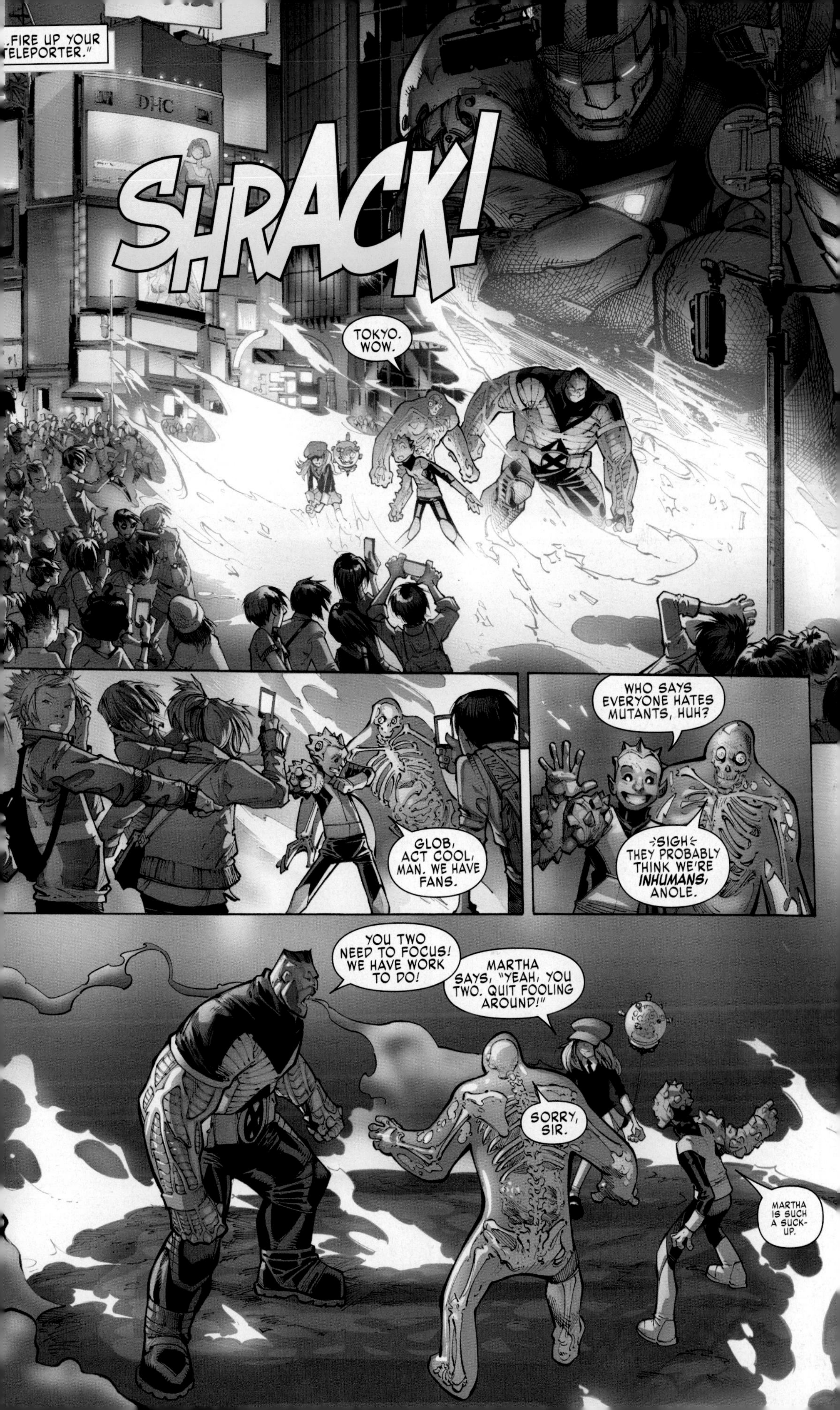

...FIRE UP YOUR TELEPORTER."
SHRACK!
TOKYO. WOW.
GLOB, ACT COOL, MAN. WE HAVE FANS.
WHO SAYS EVERYONE HATES MUTANTS, HUH?
SIGH THEY PROBABLY THINK WE'RE INHUMANS, ANOLE.
YOU TWO NEED TO FOCUS! WE HAVE WORK TO DO!
MARTHA SAYS, "YEAH, YOU TWO. QUIT FOOLING AROUND!"
SORRY, SIR.
MARTHA IS SUCH A SUCK-UP.

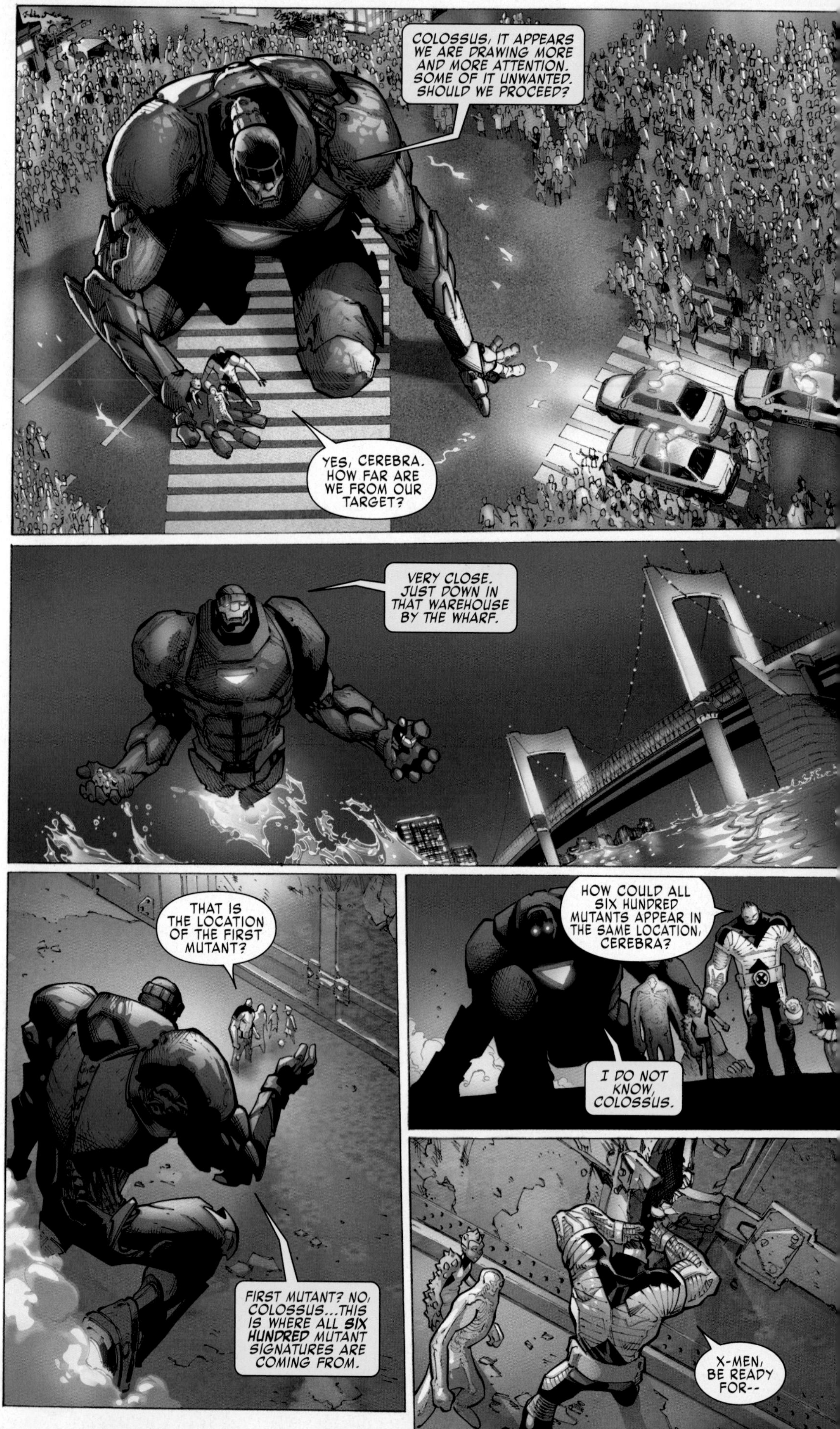
COLOSSUS, IT APPEARS WE ARE DRAWING MORE AND MORE ATTENTION. SOME OF IT UNWANTED. SHOULD WE PROCEED?
YES, CEREBRA. HOW FAR ARE WE FROM OUR TARGET?
VERY CLOSE. JUST DOWN IN THAT WAREHOUSE BY THE WHARF.
THAT IS THE LOCATION OF THE FIRST MUTANT?
FIRST MUTANT? NO, COLOSSUS...THIS IS WHERE ALL SIX HUNDRED MUTANT SIGNATURES ARE COMING FROM.
HOW COULD ALL SIX HUNDRED MUTANTS APPEAR IN THE SAME LOCATION, CEREBRA?
I DO NOT KNOW, COLOSSUS.
X-MEN, BE READY FOR--

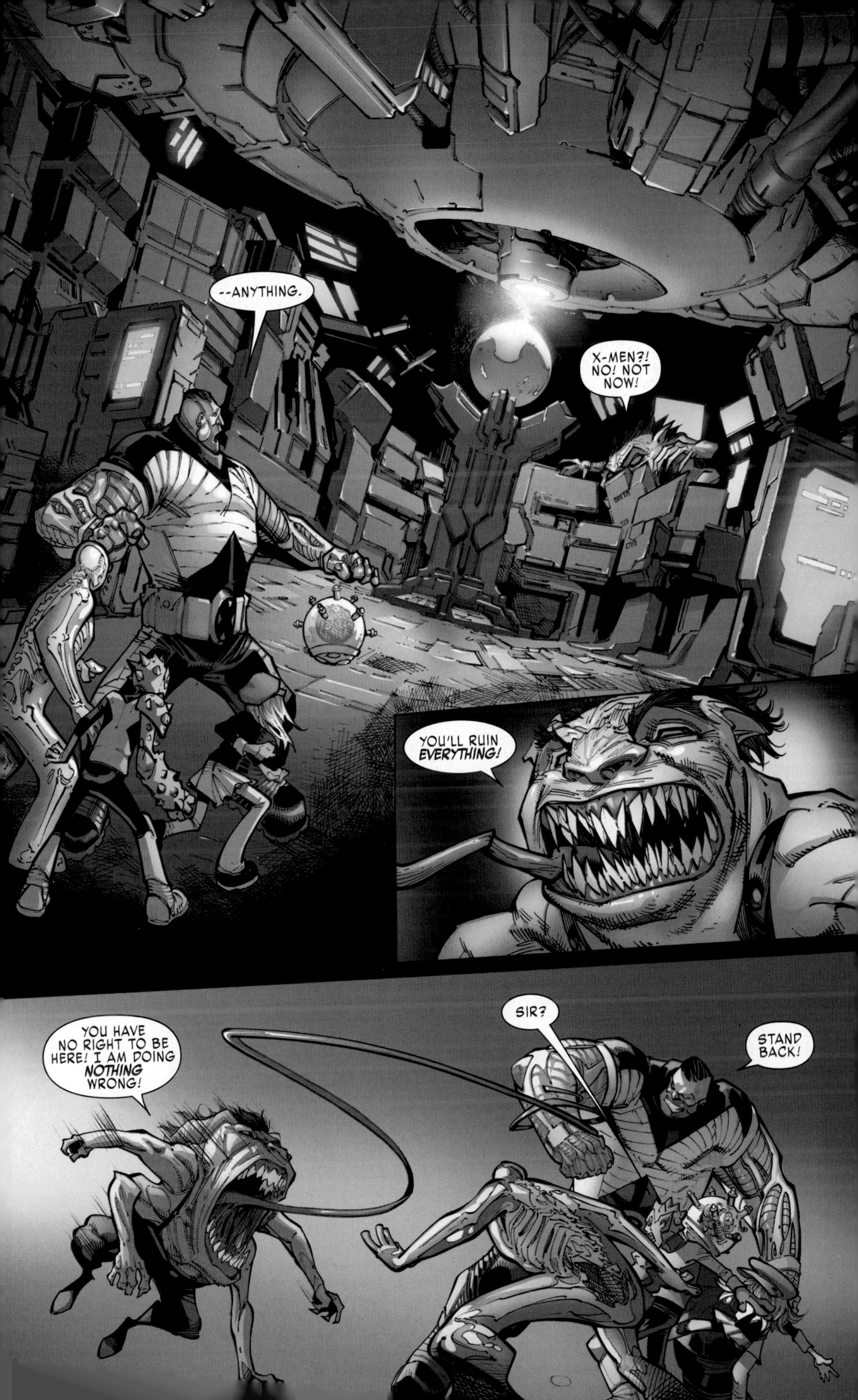
--ANYTHING.
X-MEN?! NO! NOT NOW!
YOU'LL RUIN EVERYTHING!
YOU HAVE NO RIGHT TO BE HERE! I AM DOING NOTHING WRONG!
SIR?
STAND BACK!

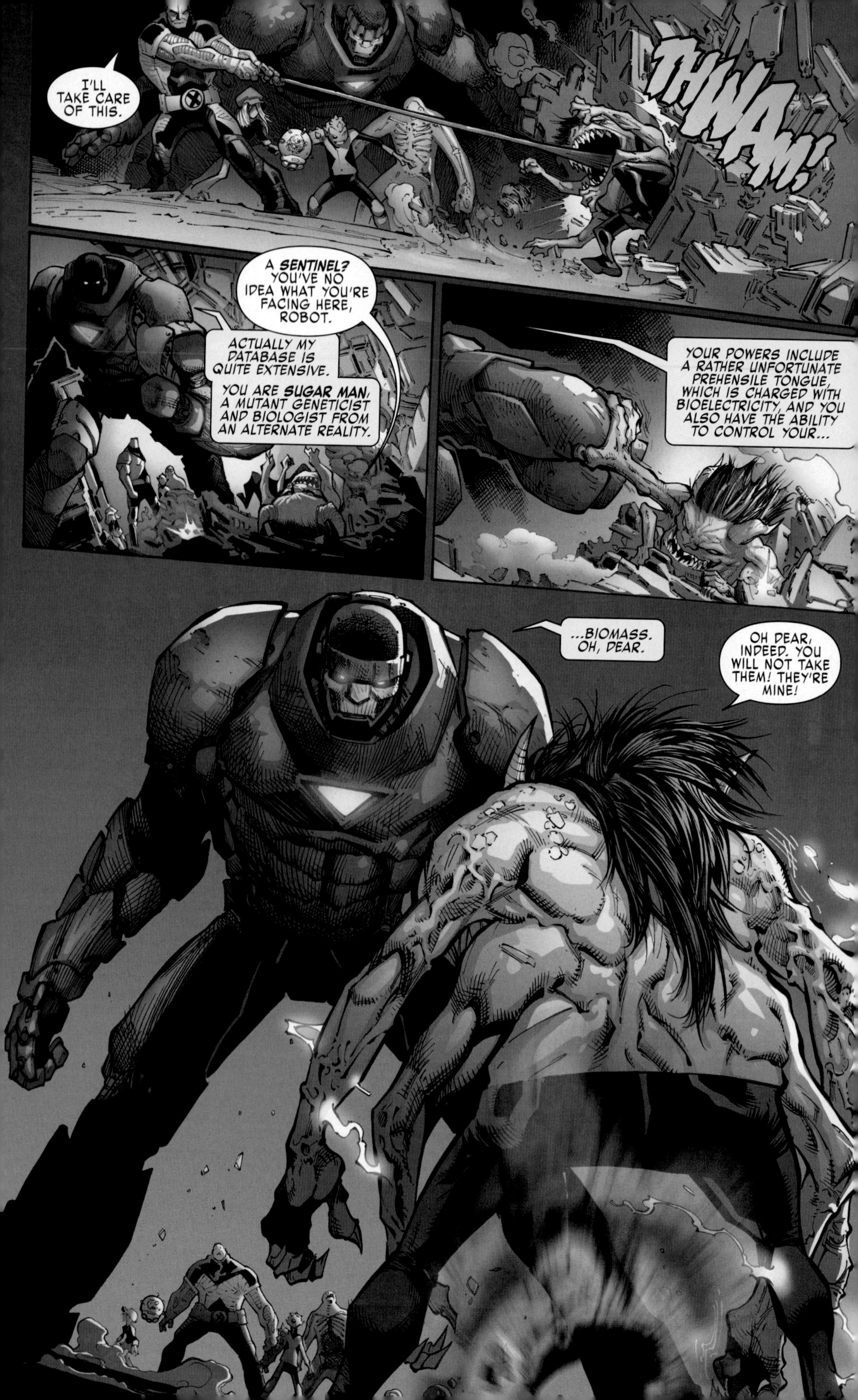
I'LL TAKE CARE OF THIS.
THWAM!
A SENTINEL? YOU'VE NO IDEA WHAT YOU'RE FACING HERE, ROBOT.
ACTUALLY MY DATABASE IS QUITE EXTENSIVE.
YOU ARE SUGAR MAN, A MUTANT GENETICIST AND BIOLOGIST FROM AN ALTERNATE REALITY.
YOUR POWERS INCLUDE A RATHER UNFORTUNATE PREHENSILE TONGUE, WHICH IS CHARGED WITH BIOELECTRICITY, AND YOU ALSO HAVE THE ABILITY TO CONTROL YOUR...
...BIOMASS. OH, DEAR.
OH DEAR, INDEED. YOU WILL NOT TAKE THEM! THEY'RE MINE!

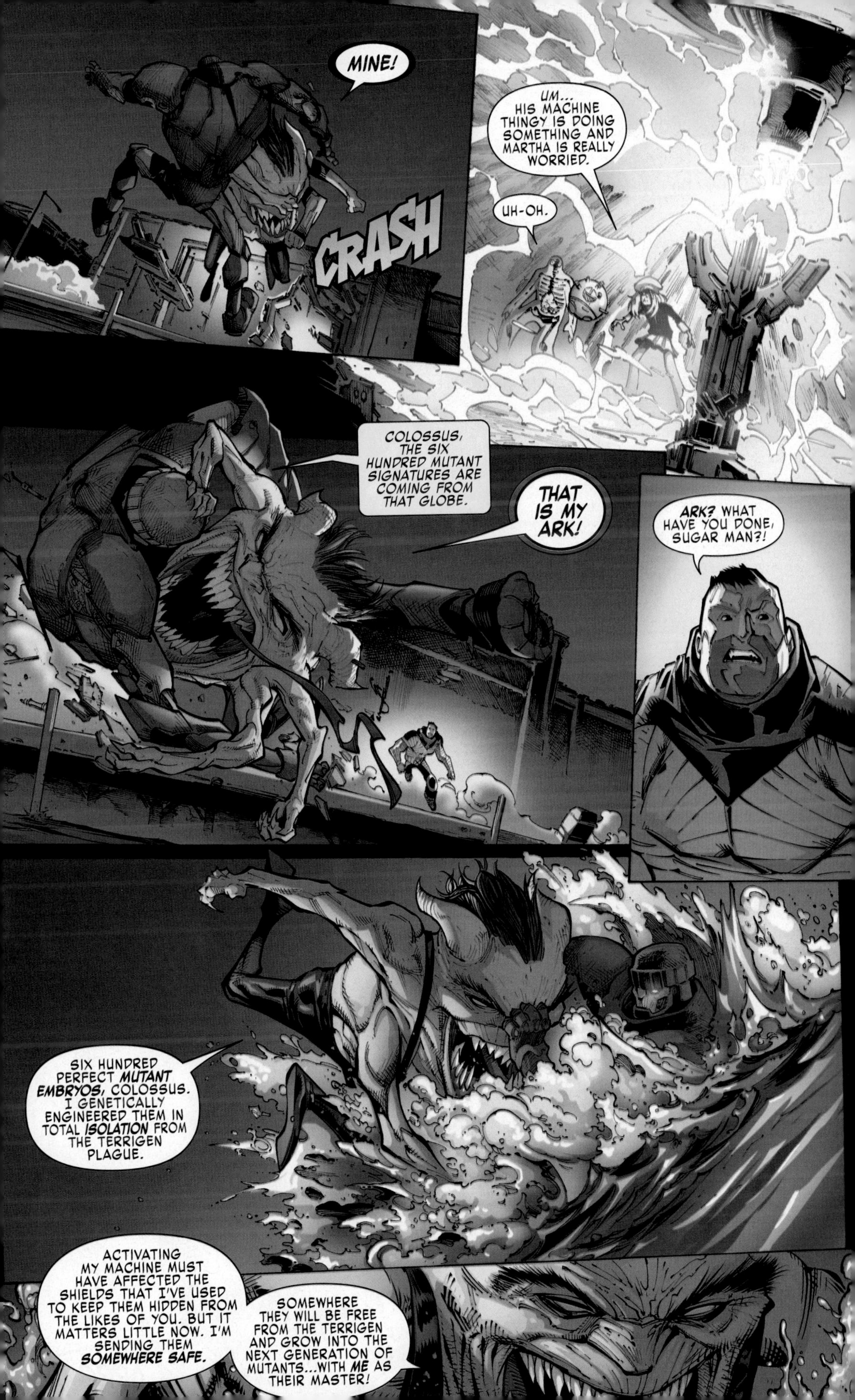
MINE!
UM... HIS MACHINE THINGY IS DOING SOMETHING AND MARTHA IS REALLY WORRIED.
UH-OH.
CRASH
COLOSSUS, THE SIX HUNDRED MUTANT SIGNATURES ARE COMING FROM THAT GLOBE.
THAT IS MY ARK!
ARK? WHAT HAVE YOU DONE, SUGAR MAN?!
SIX HUNDRED PERFECT MUTANT EMBRYOS, COLOSSUS. I GENETICALLY ENGINEERED THEM IN TOTAL ISOLATION FROM THE TERRIGEN PLAGUE.
ACTIVATING MY MACHINE MUST HAVE AFFECTED THE SHIELDS THAT I'VE USED TO KEEP THEM HIDDEN FROM THE LIKES OF YOU. BUT IT MATTERS LITTLE NOW. I'M SENDING THEM SOMEWHERE SAFE.
SOMEWHERE THEY WILL BE FREE FROM THE TERRIGEN AND GROW INTO THE NEXT GENERATION OF MUTANTS...WITH ME AS THEIR MASTER!

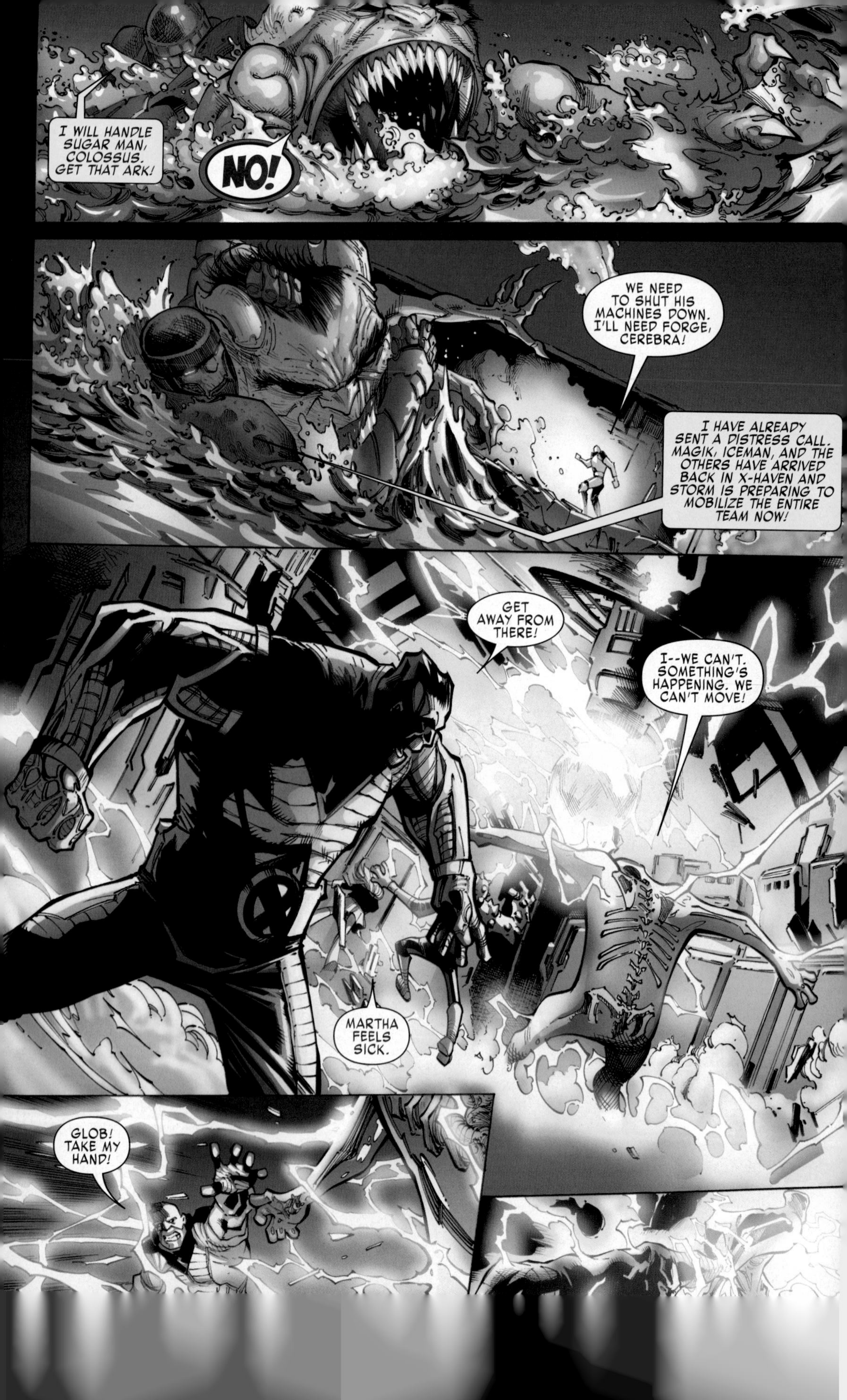
I WILL HANDLE SUGAR MAN, COLOSSUS. GET THAT ARK!
NO!
WE NEED TO SHUT HIS MACHINES DOWN. I'LL NEED FORGE, CEREBRA!
I HAVE ALREADY SENT A DISTRESS CALL. MAGIK, ICEMAN, AND THE OTHERS HAVE ARRIVED BACK IN X-HAVEN AND STORM IS PREPARING TO MOBILIZE THE ENTIRE TEAM NOW!
GET AWAY FROM THERE!
I--WE CAN'T. SOMETHING'S HAPPENING. WE CAN'T MOVE!
MARTHA FEELS SICK.
GLOB! TAKE MY HAND!

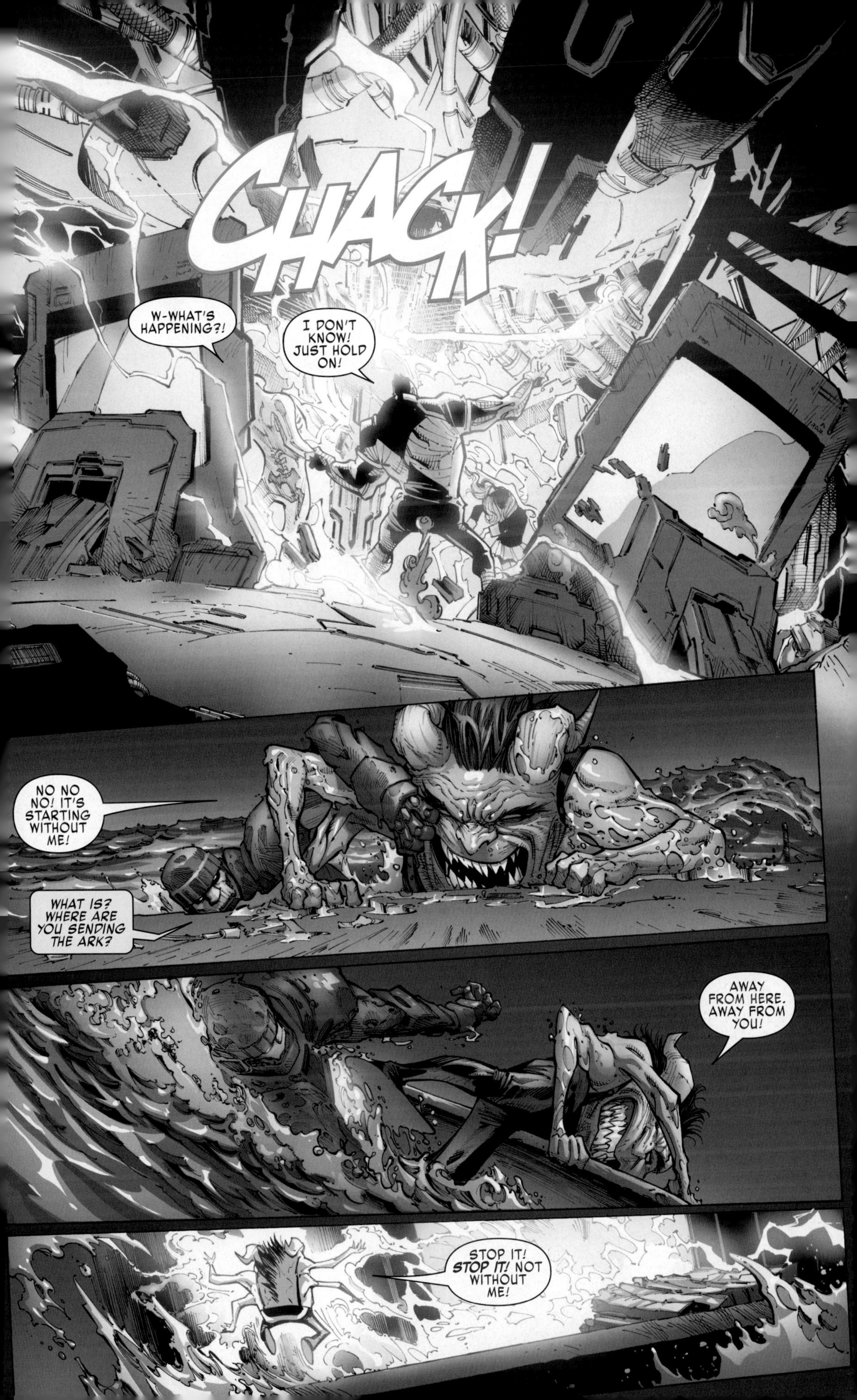
CHACK!
W-WHAT'S HAPPENING?!
I DON'T KNOW! JUST HOLD ON!
NO NO NO! IT'S STARTING WITHOUT ME!
WHAT IS? WHERE ARE YOU SENDING THE ARK?
AWAY FROM HERE. AWAY FROM YOU!
STOP IT! STOP IT! NOT WITHOUT ME!

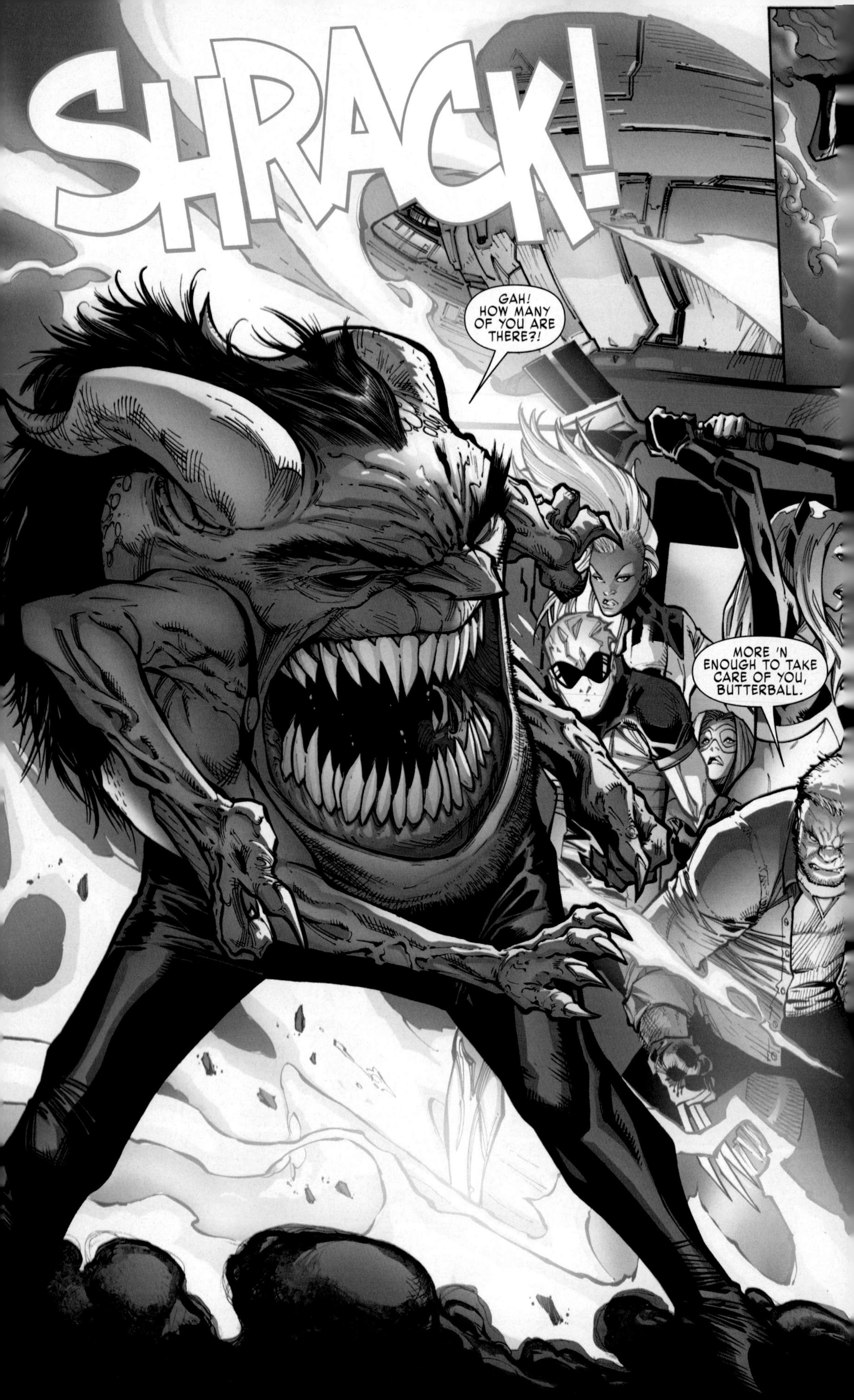
SHRACK!
GAH! HOW MANY OF YOU ARE THERE?!
MORE 'N ENOUGH TO TAKE CARE OF YOU, BUTTERBALL.

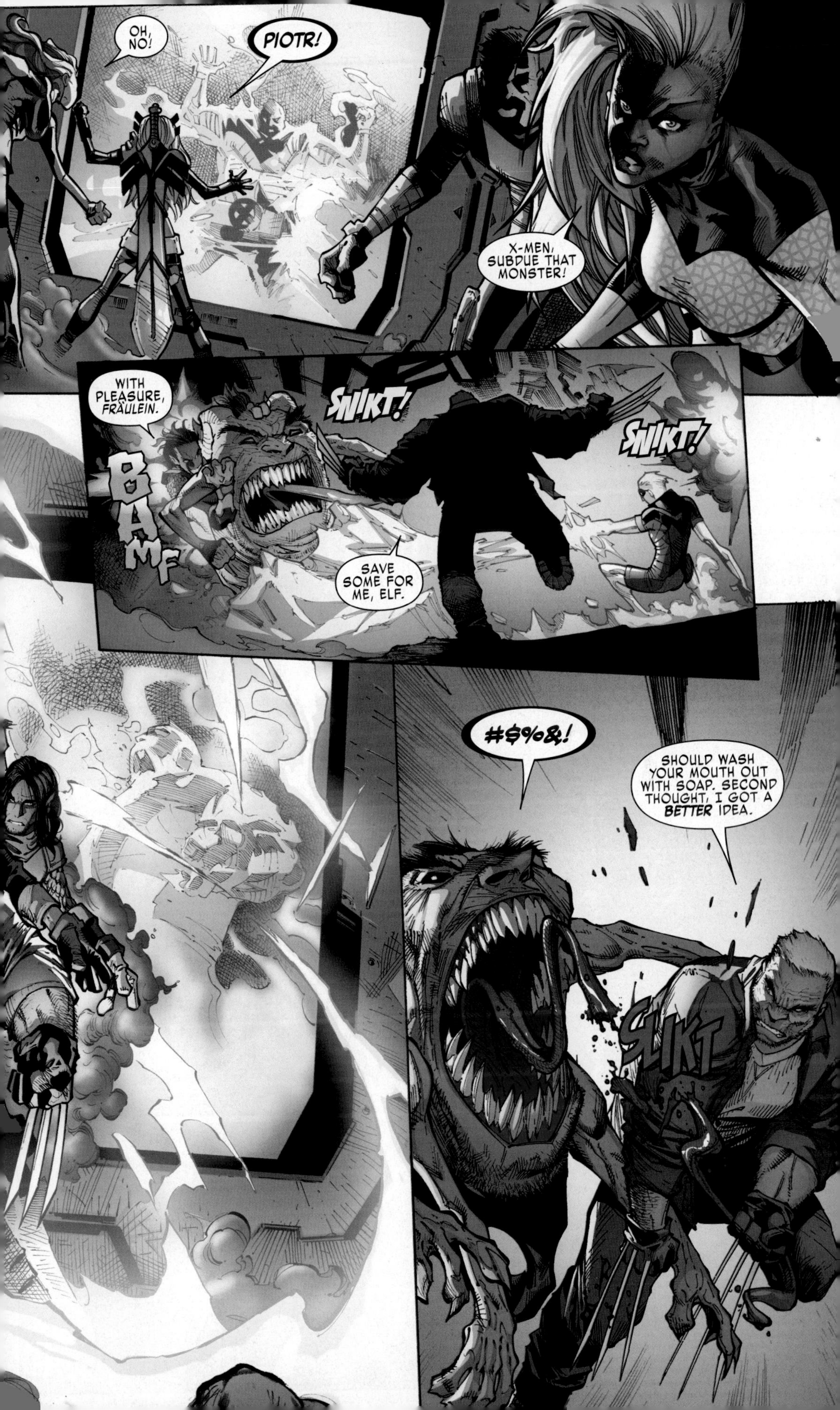
OH, NO!
PIOTR!
X-MEN, SUBDUE THAT MONSTER!
WITH PLEASURE, FRÄULEIN.
BAMF
SNIKT!
SNIKT!
SAVE SOME FOR ME, ELF.
#$%&!
SHOULD WASH YOUR MOUTH OUT WITH SOAP. SECOND THOUGHT, I GOT A BETTER IDEA.
SLIKT

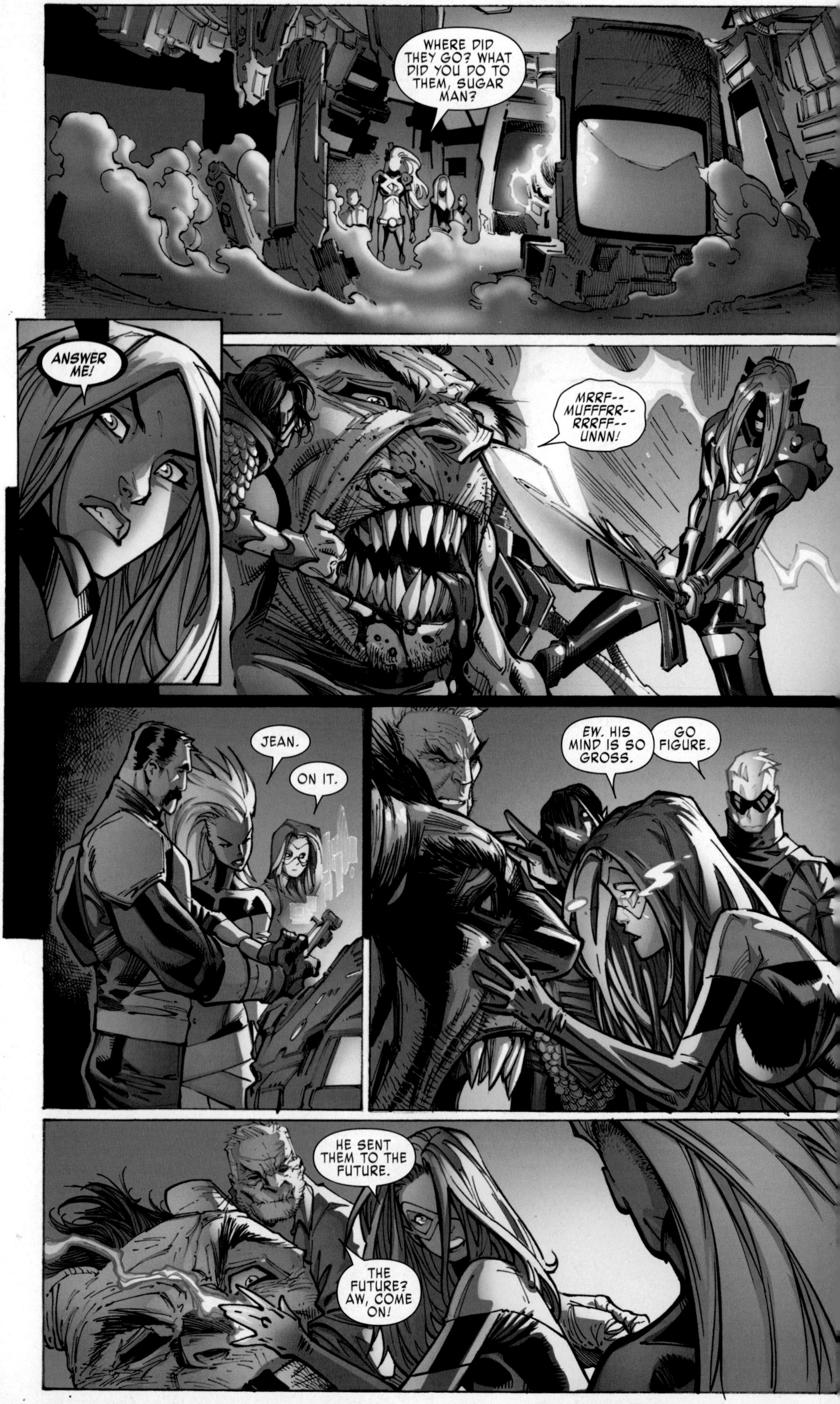
WHERE DID THEY GO? WHAT DID YOU DO TO THEM, SUGAR MAN?
ANSWER ME!
MRRF-- MUFFFRR-- RRRFF-- UNNN!
JEAN.
ON IT.
EW. HIS MIND IS SO GROSS.
GO FIGURE.
HE SENT THEM TO THE FUTURE.
THE FUTURE? AW, COME ON!

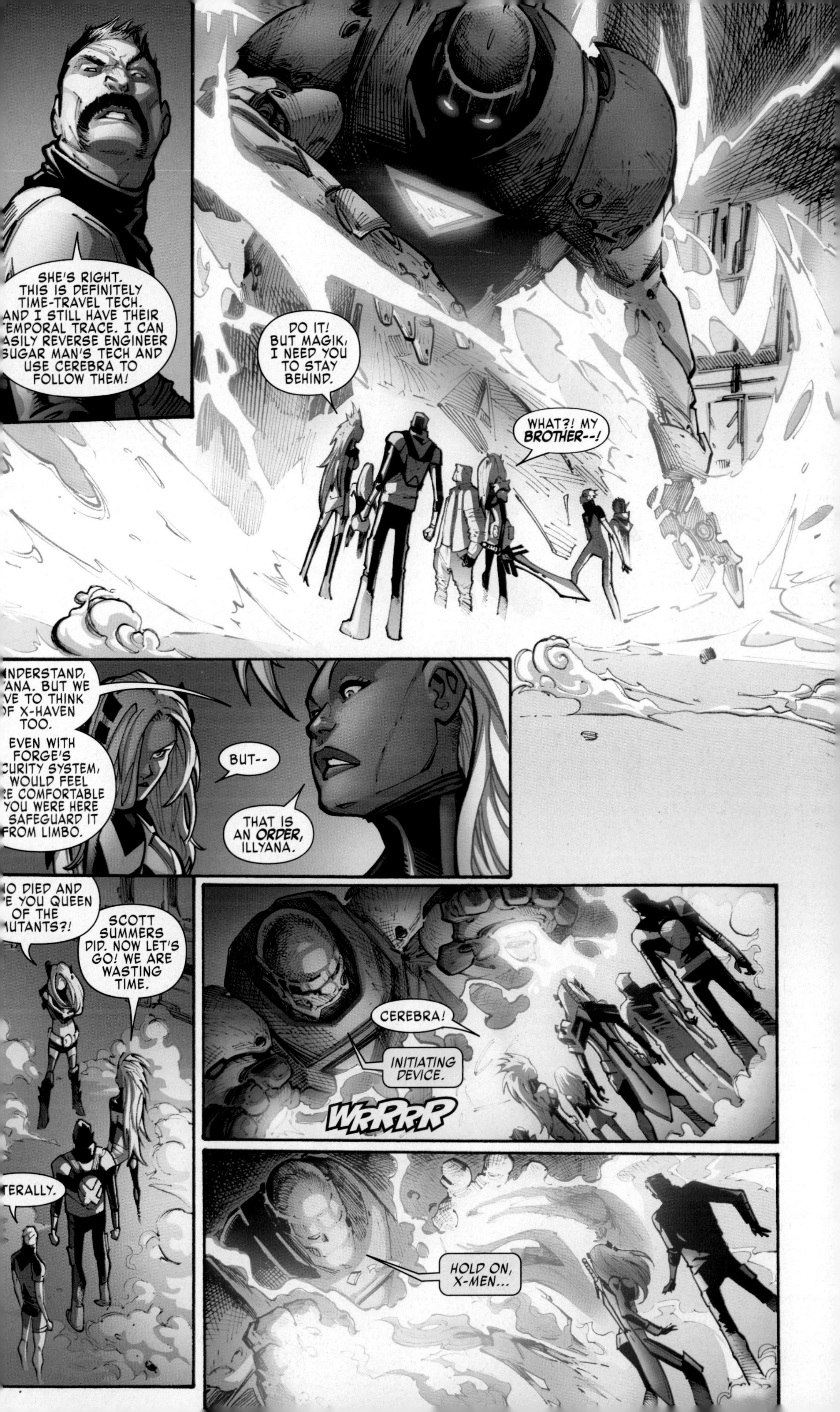
SHE'S RIGHT. THIS IS DEFINITELY TIME-TRAVEL TECH. AND I STILL HAVE THEIR TEMPORAL TRACE. I CAN ASILY REVERSE ENGINEER SUGAR MAN'S TECH AND USE CEREBRA TO FOLLOW THEM!
DO IT! BUT MAGIK, I NEED YOU TO STAY BEHIND.
WHAT?! MY BROTHER--!
NDERSTAND, ANA. BUT WE VE TO THINK OF X-HAVEN TOO.
EVEN WITH FORGE'S CURITY SYSTEM, WOULD FEEL E COMFORTABLE YOU WERE HERE SAFEGUARD IT FROM LIMBO.
BUT--
THAT IS AN ORDER, ILLYANA.
O DIED AND E YOU QUEEN OF THE UTANTS?!
SCOTT SUMMERS DID. NOW LET'S GO! WE ARE WASTING TIME.
TERALLY.
CEREBRA!
INITIATING DEVICE.
WRRRR
HOLD ON, X-MEN...

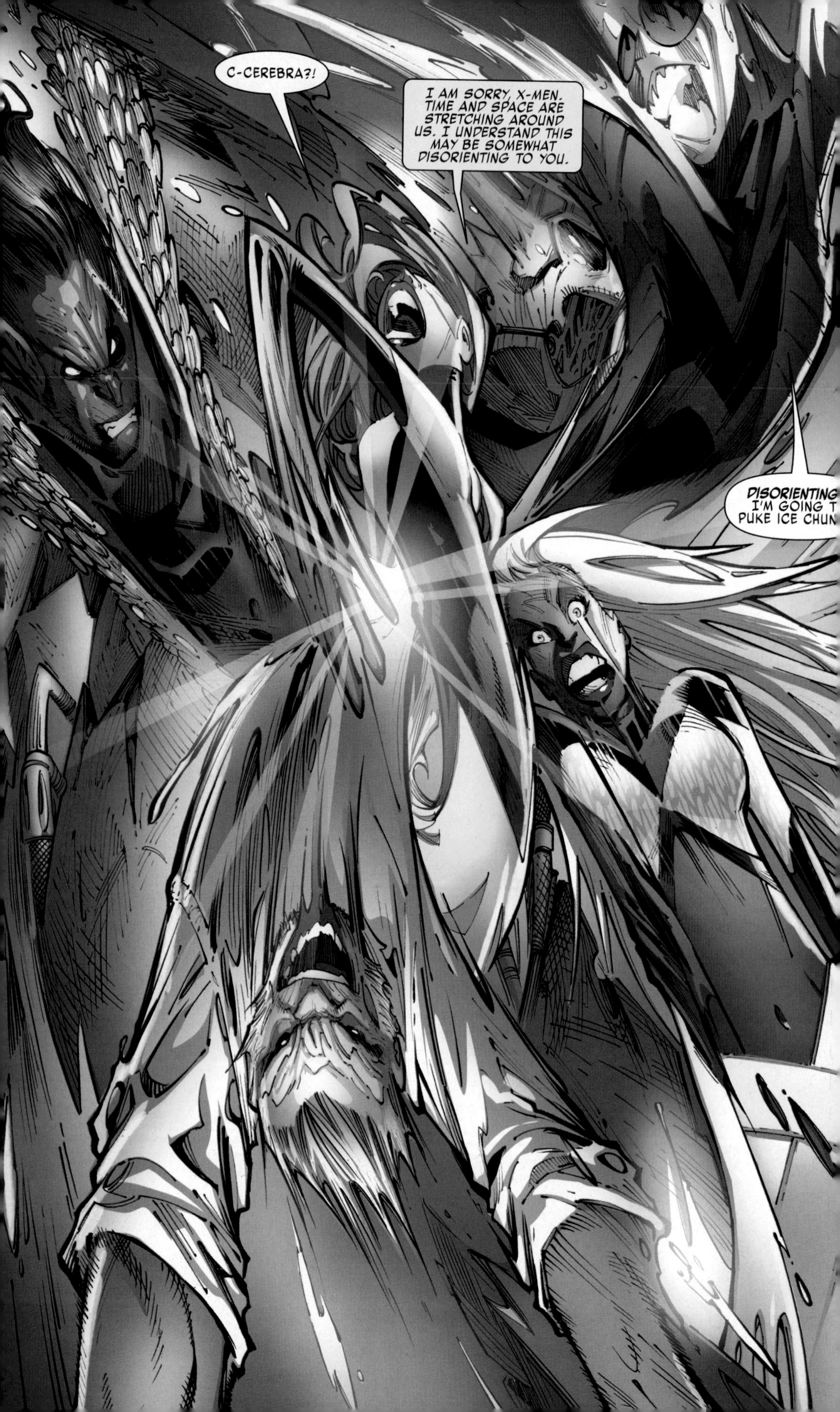
C-CEREBRA?!
I AM SORRY, X-MEN. TIME AND SPACE ARE STRETCHING AROUND US. I UNDERSTAND THIS MAY BE SOMEWHAT DISORIENTING TO YOU.
DISORIENTING I'M GOING T PUKE ICE CHUN

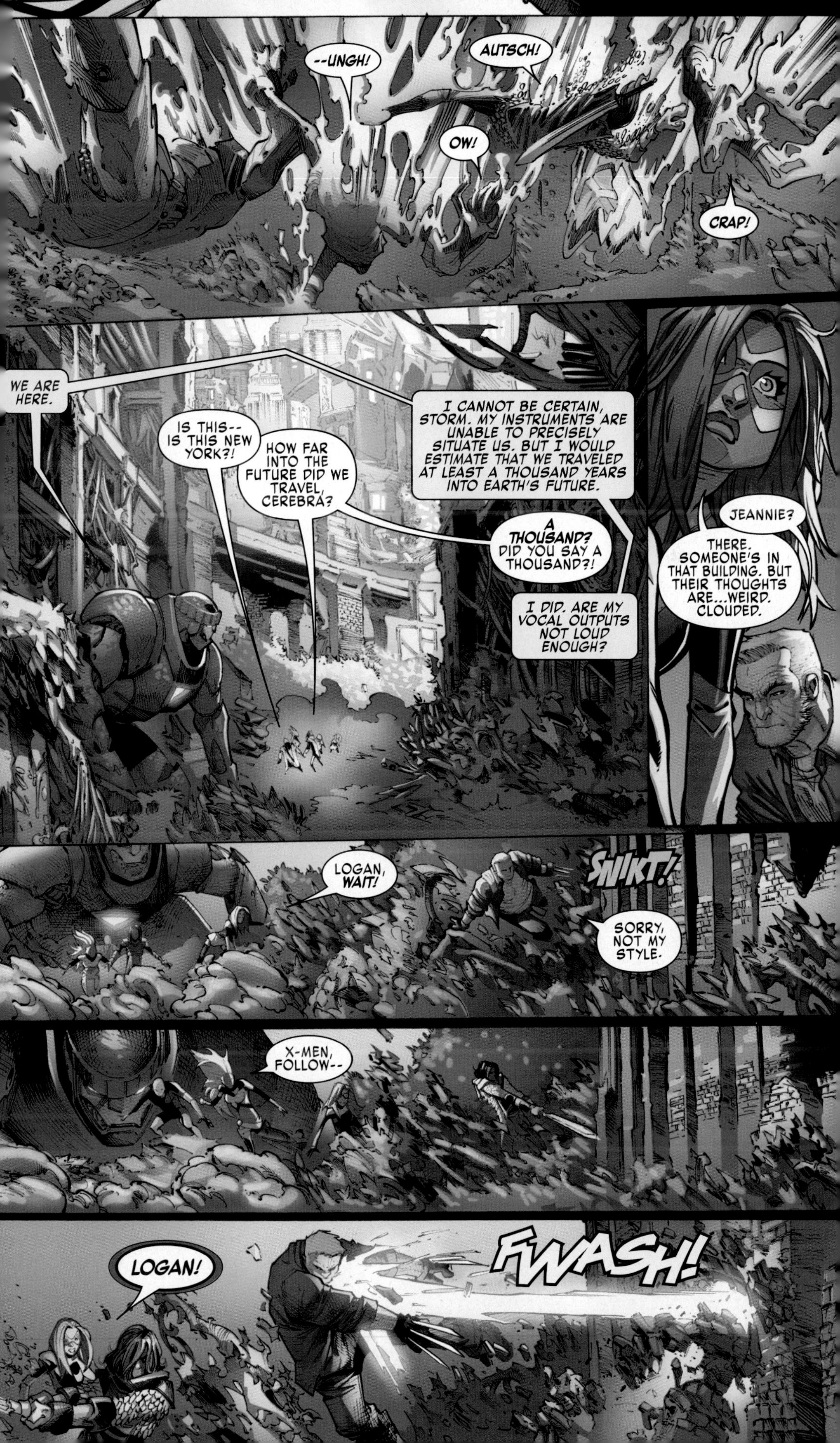
--UNGH!
AUTSCH!
OW!
CRAP!
WE ARE HERE.
IS THIS-- IS THIS NEW YORK?!
HOW FAR INTO THE FUTURE DID WE TRAVEL, CEREBRA?
I CANNOT BE CERTAIN, STORM. MY INSTRUMENTS ARE UNABLE TO PRECISELY SITUATE US. BUT I WOULD ESTIMATE THAT WE TRAVELED AT LEAST A THOUSAND YEARS INTO EARTH'S FUTURE.
A THOUSAND? DID YOU SAY A THOUSAND?!
I DID. ARE MY VOCAL OUTPUTS NOT LOUD ENOUGH?
JEANNIE?
THERE. SOMEONE'S IN THAT BUILDING. BUT THEIR THOUGHTS ARE...WEIRD. CLOUDED.
LOGAN, WAIT!
SNIKT!
SORRY, NOT MY STYLE.
X-MEN, FOLLOW--
LOGAN!
FWASH!

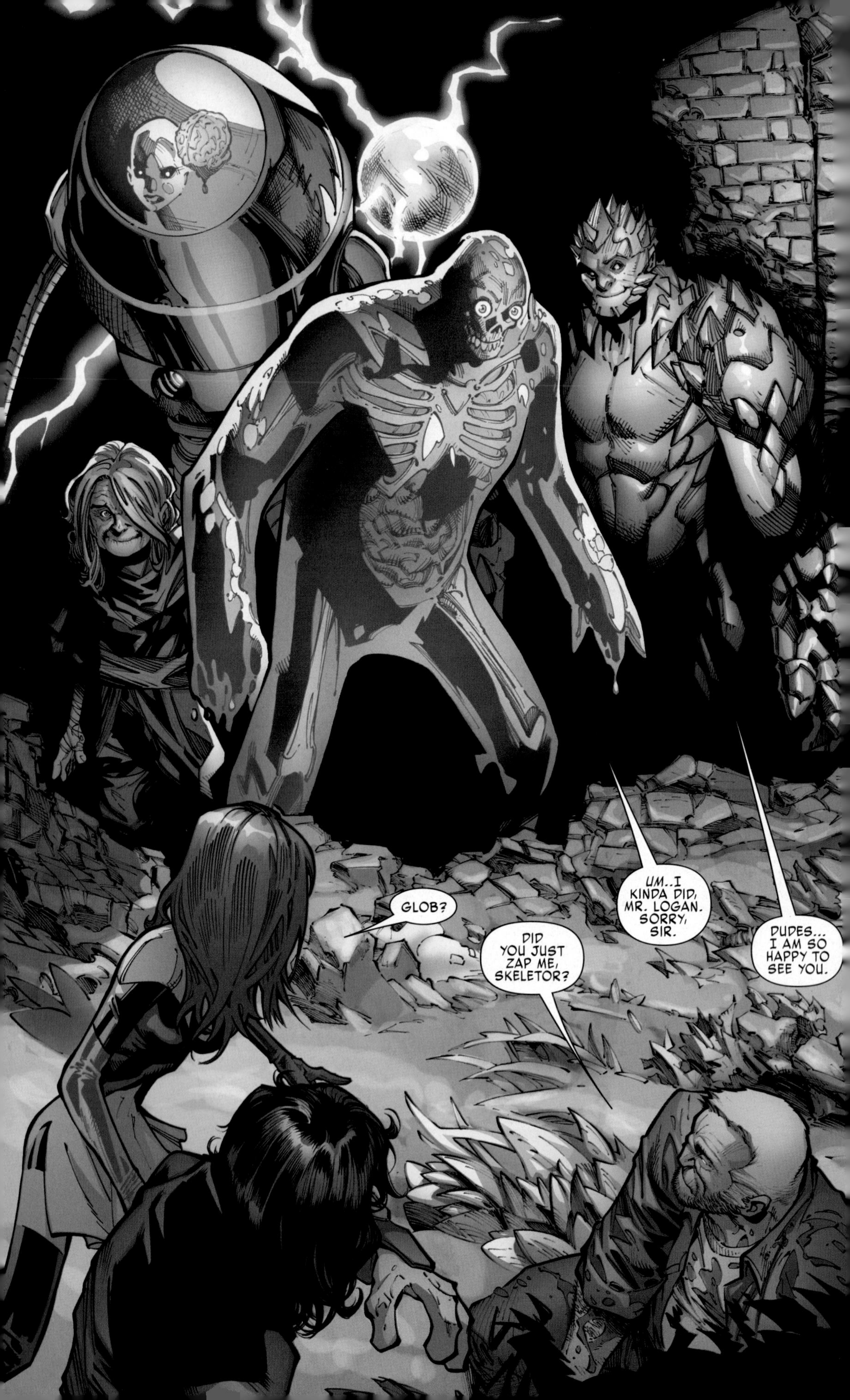
GLOB?
DID YOU JUST ZAP ME, SKELETOR?
UM..I KINDA DID, MR. LOGAN. SORRY, SIR.
DUDES... I AM SO HAPPY TO SEE YOU.

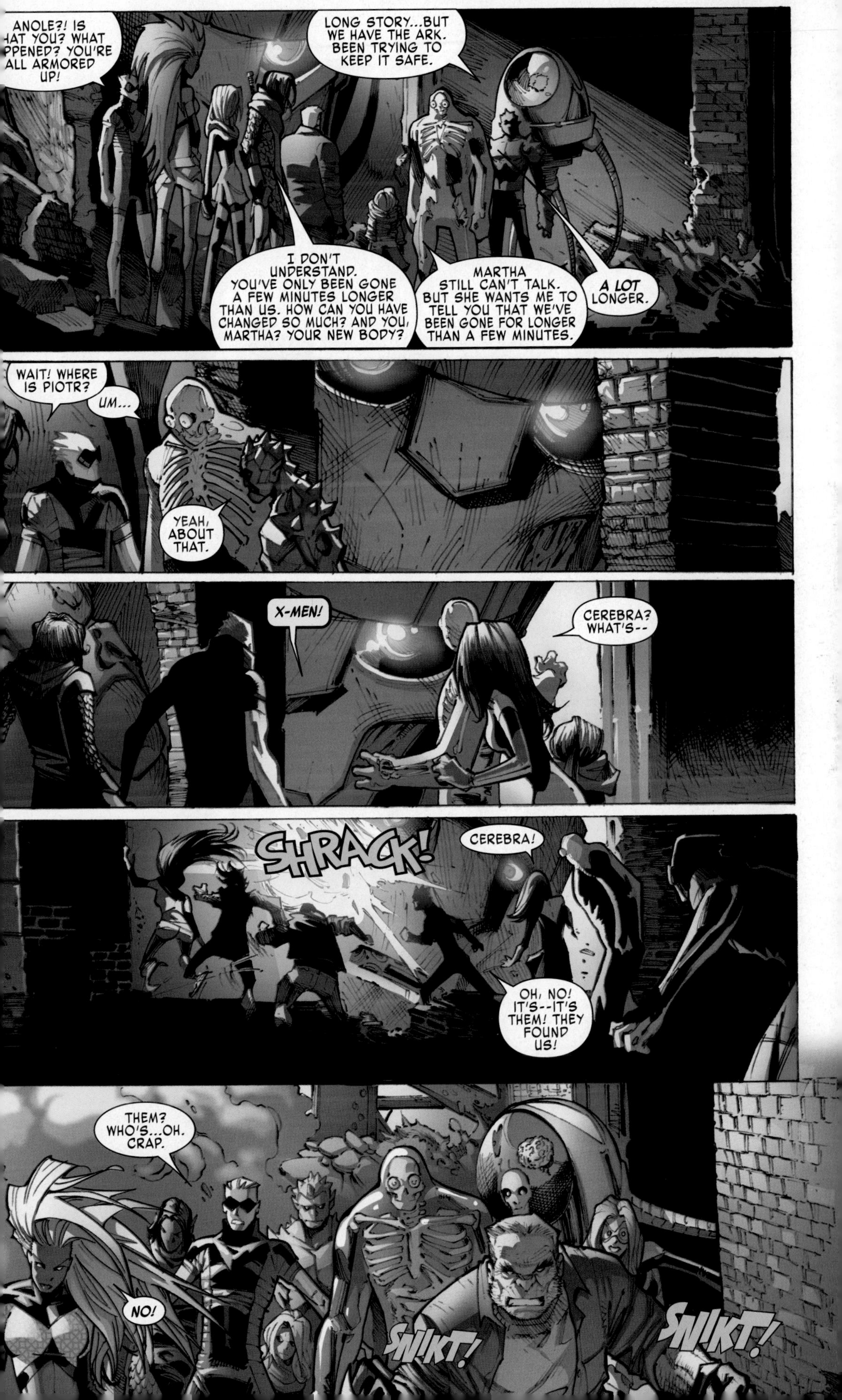
ANOLE?! IS HAT YOU? WHAT PPENED? YOU'RE ALL ARMORED UP!
LONG STORY...BUT WE HAVE THE ARK. BEEN TRYING TO KEEP IT SAFE.
I DON'T UNDERSTAND. YOU'VE ONLY BEEN GONE A FEW MINUTES LONGER THAN US. HOW CAN YOU HAVE CHANGED SO MUCH? AND YOU, MARTHA? YOUR NEW BODY?
MARTHA STILL CAN'T TALK. BUT SHE WANTS ME TO TELL YOU THAT WE'VE BEEN GONE FOR LONGER THAN A FEW MINUTES.
A LOT LONGER.
WAIT! WHERE IS PIOTR?
UM...
YEAH, ABOUT THAT.
X-MEN!
CEREBRA? WHAT'S--
SHRACK!
CEREBRA!
OH, NO! IT'S--IT'S THEM! THEY FOUND US!
THEM? WHO'S...OH. CRAP.
NO!
SNIKT!
SNIKT!

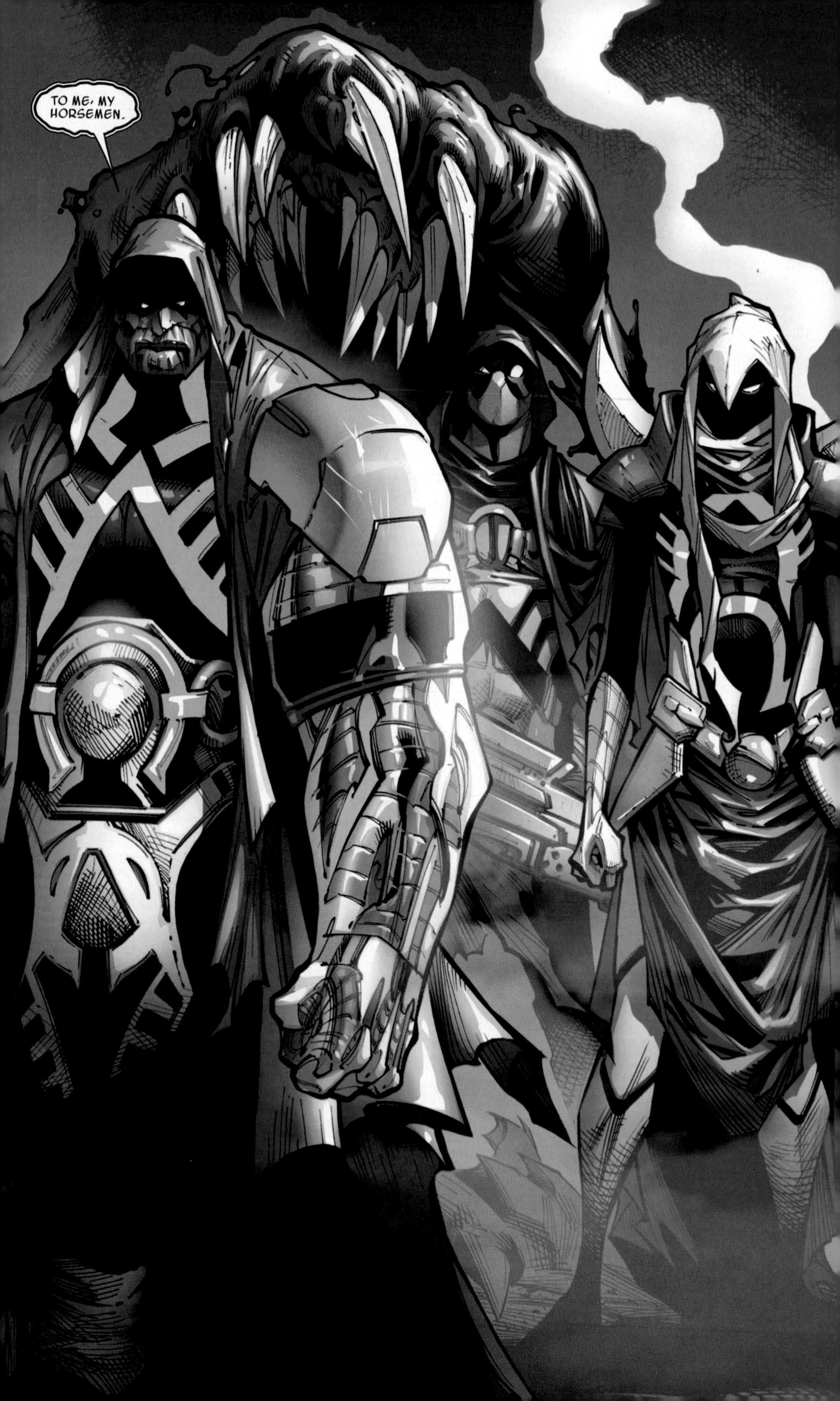
TO ME, MY HORSEMEN.

GREENWICH VILLAGE, MANHATTAN.
FIVE DAYS EARLIER...

SHRACK!

HERE WE ARE, SAPNA.

WOW! I'VE NEVER SEEN NEW YORK BEFORE! WELL, I MEAN, I'VE SEEN IT ON THE INTERNET AND STUFF, BUT NOT IN REAL LIFE!

WAIT, MAGIK, ALL THESE PEOPLE. WON'T THEY--

DON'T WORRY, GIRL. I'VE CAST A CLOAKING SPELL.

I AM NOT IN THE HABIT OF HIDING, BUT GIVEN THE LAST TIME YOU WERE IN A LARGE CROWD, IT WAS A MOB TRYING TO KILL YOU, I THOUGHT IT BEST TO EASE YOU BACK INTO THE WORLD.

AND THIS DOCTOR YOU'RE TAKING ME TO...IS HE GOING TO HELP ME WITH MY M-POX?

NO. THAT SEEMS TO BE CLEARING UP ON IT'S OWN QUITE NICELY.

I STILL CAN'T FIGURE THAT OUT MYSELF. SOME MUTANTS DIE INSTANTLY WHEN HIT WITH THE TERRIGEN MIST, OTHERS GET WHAT LOOKS LIKE A MILD COLD. BUT THEN, MEDICINE WAS ALWAYS BEYOND ME.

NO, LET'S LEAVE SCIENCE TO HENRY MCCOY AND HIS KIND. WE'RE HERE TO SEE A DIFFERENT KIND OF DOCTOR, SAPNA.

"STRANGE MAGIK"

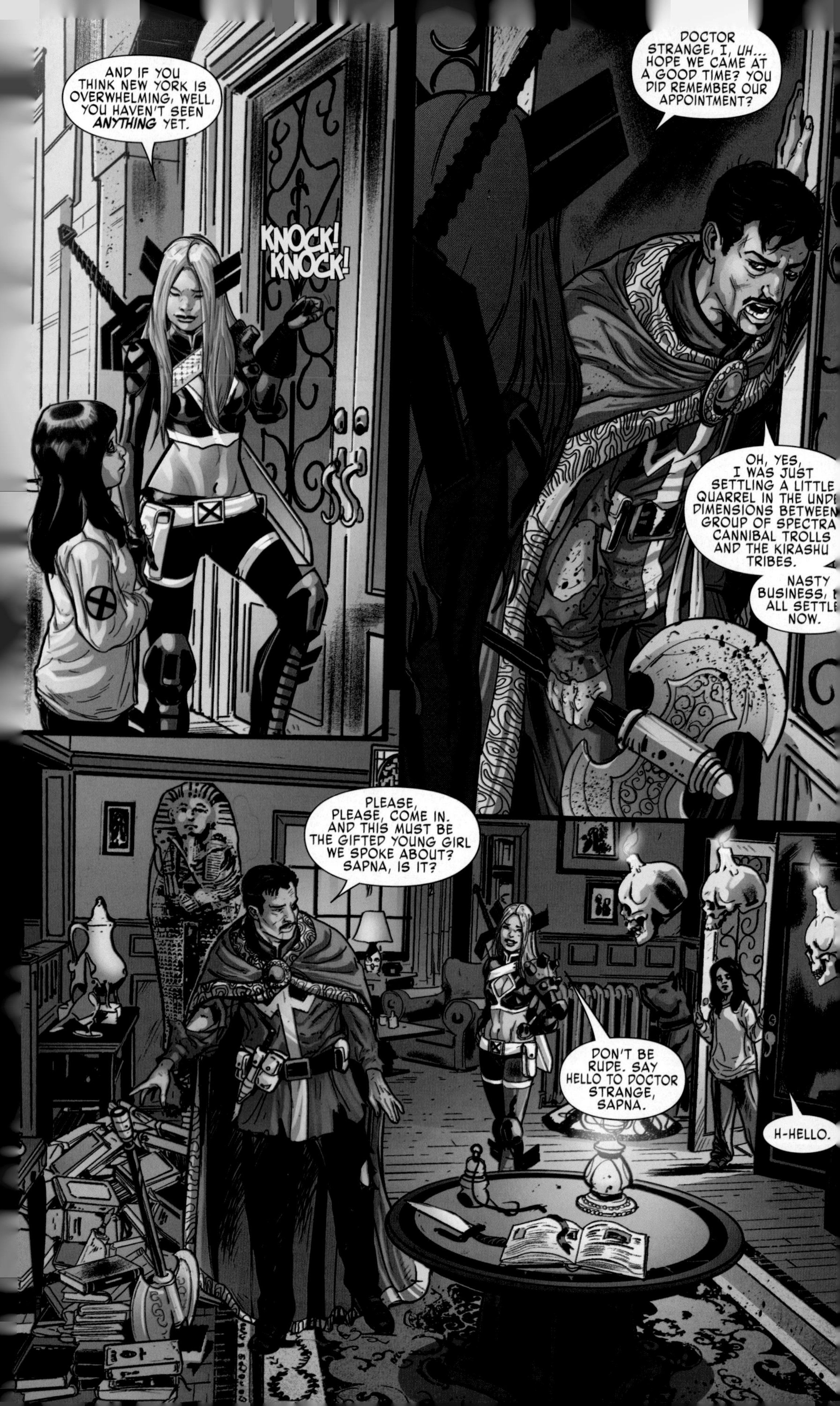
AND IF YOU THINK NEW YORK IS OVERWHELMING, WELL, YOU HAVEN'T SEEN ANYTHING YET.
KNOCK! KNOCK!
DOCTOR STRANGE, I, UH... HOPE WE CAME AT A GOOD TIME? YOU DID REMEMBER OUR APPOINTMENT?
OH, YES, I WAS JUST SETTLING A LITTLE QUARREL IN THE UNDE DIMENSIONS BETWEEN GROUP OF SPECTRA CANNIBAL TROLLS AND THE KIRASHU TRIBES.
NASTY BUSINESS, ALL SETTLE NOW.
PLEASE, PLEASE, COME IN. AND THIS MUST BE THE GIFTED YOUNG GIRL WE SPOKE ABOUT? SAPNA, IS IT?
DON'T BE RUDE. SAY HELLO TO DOCTOR STRANGE, SAPNA.
H-HELLO.

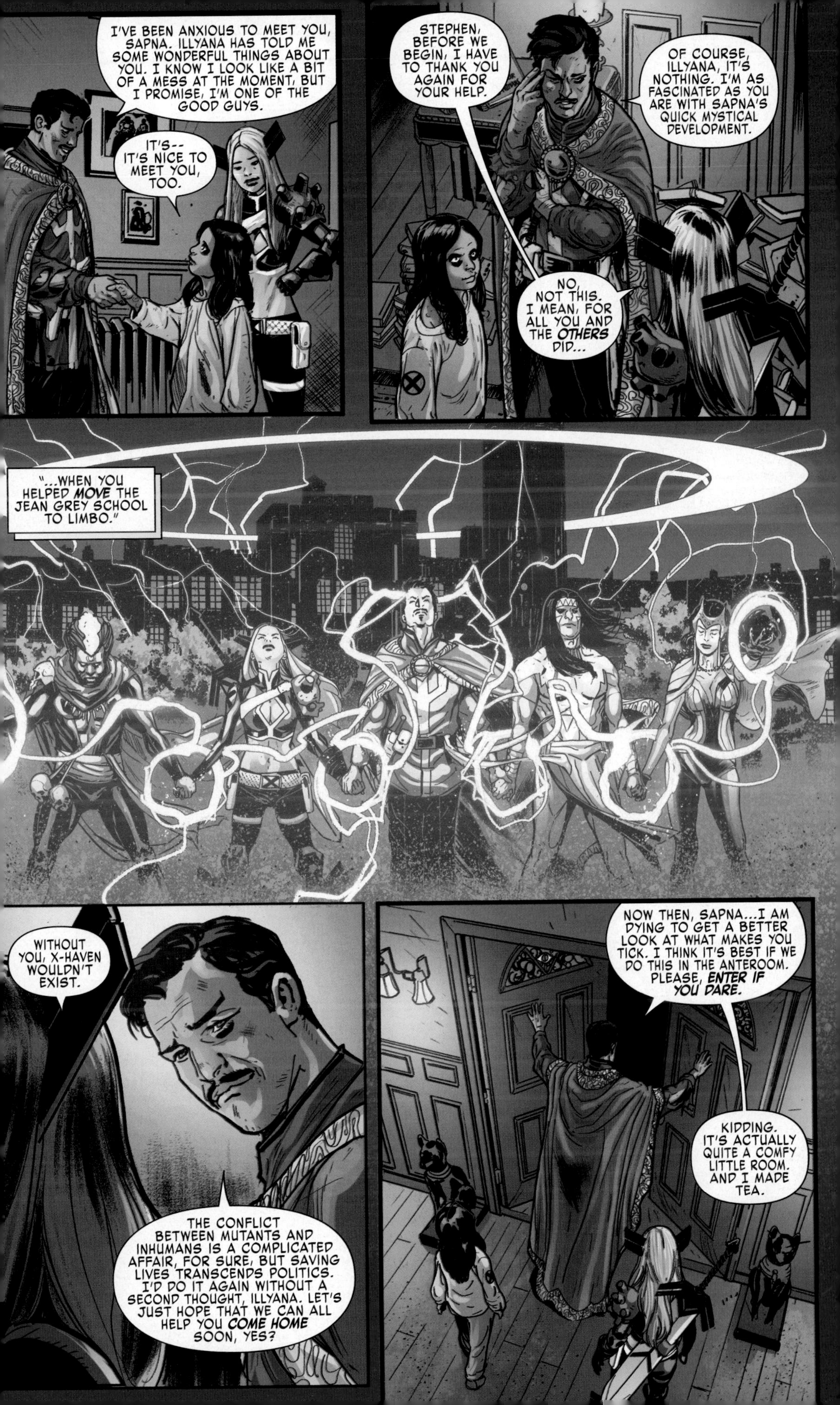
I'VE BEEN ANXIOUS TO MEET YOU, SAPNA. ILLYANA HAS TOLD ME SOME WONDERFUL THINGS ABOUT YOU. I KNOW I LOOK LIKE A BIT OF A MESS AT THE MOMENT, BUT I PROMISE, I'M ONE OF THE GOOD GUYS.
IT'S-- IT'S NICE TO MEET YOU, TOO.
STEPHEN, BEFORE WE BEGIN, I HAVE TO THANK YOU AGAIN FOR YOUR HELP.
OF COURSE, ILLYANA, IT'S NOTHING. I'M AS FASCINATED AS YOU ARE WITH SAPNA'S QUICK MYSTICAL DEVELOPMENT.
NO, NOT THIS. I MEAN, FOR ALL YOU AND THE OTHERS DID...
"...WHEN YOU HELPED MOVE THE JEAN GREY SCHOOL TO LIMBO."
WITHOUT YOU, X-HAVEN WOULDN'T EXIST.
THE CONFLICT BETWEEN MUTANTS AND INHUMANS IS A COMPLICATED AFFAIR, FOR SURE, BUT SAVING LIVES TRANSCENDS POLITICS. I'D DO IT AGAIN WITHOUT A SECOND THOUGHT, ILLYANA. LET'S JUST HOPE THAT WE CAN ALL HELP YOU COME HOME SOON, YES?
NOW THEN, SAPNA...I AM DYING TO GET A BETTER LOOK AT WHAT MAKES YOU TICK. I THINK IT'S BEST IF WE DO THIS IN THE ANTEROOM. PLEASE, ENTER IF YOU DARE.
KIDDING. IT'S ACTUALLY QUITE A COMFY LITTLE ROOM. AND I MADE TEA.

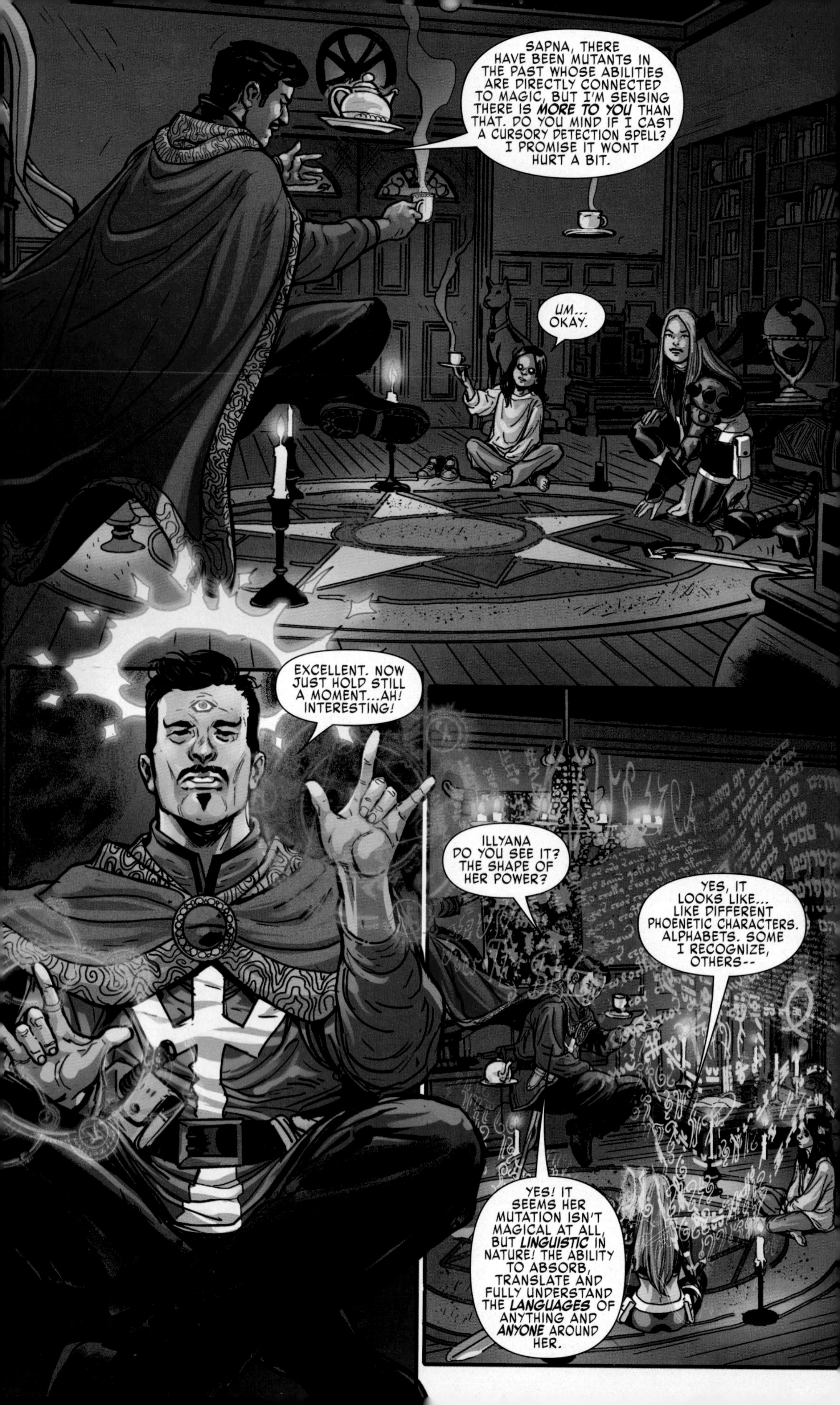
SAPNA, THERE HAVE BEEN MUTANTS IN THE PAST WHOSE ABILITIES ARE DIRECTLY CONNECTED TO MAGIC, BUT I'M SENSING THERE IS MORE TO YOU THAN THAT. DO YOU MIND IF I CAST A CURSORY DETECTION SPELL? I PROMISE IT WONT HURT A BIT.
UM... OKAY.
EXCELLENT. NOW JUST HOLD STILL A MOMENT...AH! INTERESTING!
ILLYANA DO YOU SEE IT? THE SHAPE OF HER POWER?
YES, IT LOOKS LIKE... LIKE DIFFERENT PHOENETIC CHARACTERS. ALPHABETS. SOME I RECOGNIZE, OTHERS--
YES! IT SEEMS HER MUTATION ISN'T MAGICAL AT ALL, BUT LINGUISTIC IN NATURE! THE ABILITY TO ABSORB, TRANSLATE AND FULLY UNDERSTAND THE LANGUAGES OF ANYTHING AND ANYONE AROUND HER.

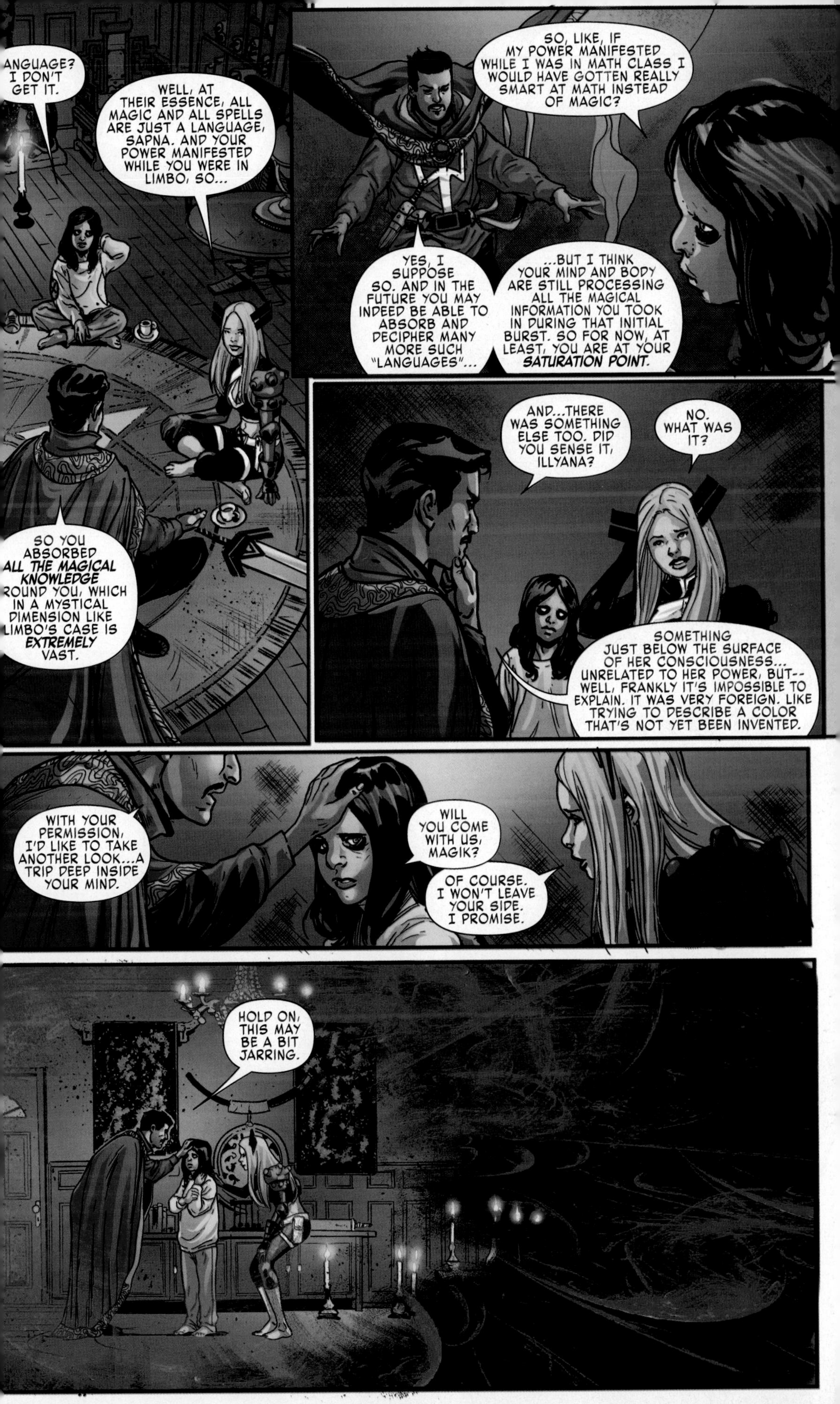
ANGUAGE? I DON'T GET IT.
WELL, AT THEIR ESSENCE, ALL MAGIC AND ALL SPELLS ARE JUST A LANGUAGE, SAPNA. AND YOUR POWER MANIFESTED WHILE YOU WERE IN LIMBO, SO...
SO YOU ABSORBED ALL THE MAGICAL KNOWLEDGE ROUND YOU, WHICH IN A MYSTICAL DIMENSION LIKE LIMBO'S CASE IS EXTREMELY VAST.
SO, LIKE, IF MY POWER MANIFESTED WHILE I WAS IN MATH CLASS I WOULD HAVE GOTTEN REALLY SMART AT MATH INSTEAD OF MAGIC?
YES, I SUPPOSE SO. AND IN THE FUTURE YOU MAY INDEED BE ABLE TO ABSORB AND DECIPHER MANY MORE SUCH "LANGUAGES"...
...BUT I THINK YOUR MIND AND BODY ARE STILL PROCESSING ALL THE MAGICAL INFORMATION YOU TOOK IN DURING THAT INITIAL BURST. SO FOR NOW, AT LEAST, YOU ARE AT YOUR SATURATION POINT.
AND...THERE WAS SOMETHING ELSE TOO. DID YOU SENSE IT, ILLYANA?
NO. WHAT WAS IT?
SOMETHING JUST BELOW THE SURFACE OF HER CONSCIOUSNESS... UNRELATED TO HER POWER, BUT-- WELL, FRANKLY IT'S IMPOSSIBLE TO EXPLAIN. IT WAS VERY FOREIGN. LIKE TRYING TO DESCRIBE A COLOR THAT'S NOT YET BEEN INVENTED.
WITH YOUR PERMISSION, I'D LIKE TO TAKE ANOTHER LOOK...A TRIP DEEP INSIDE YOUR MIND.
WILL YOU COME WITH US, MAGIK?
OF COURSE. I WON'T LEAVE YOUR SIDE. I PROMISE.
HOLD ON, THIS MAY BE A BIT JARRING.

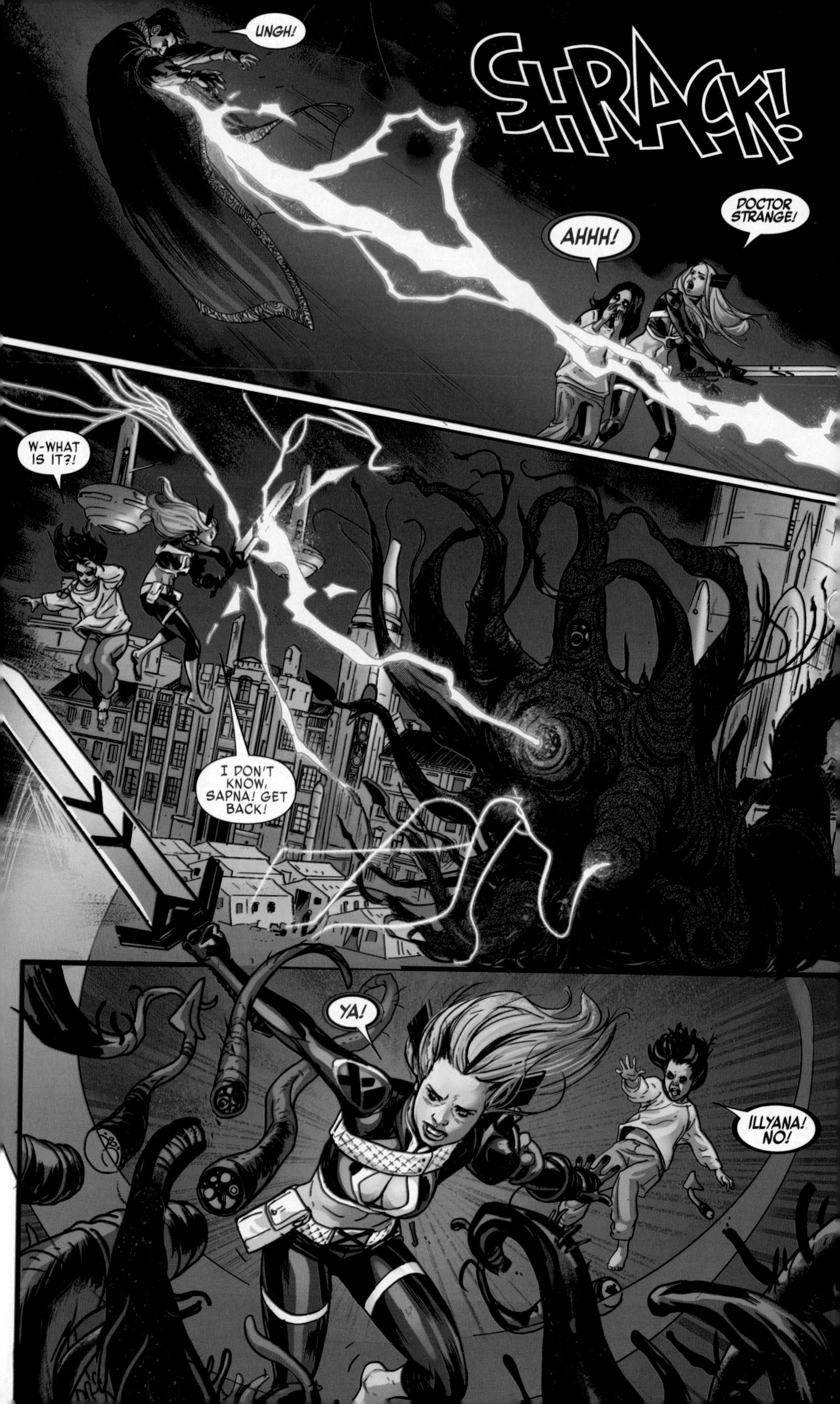
UNGH!
SHRACK!
AHHH!
DOCTOR STRANGE!
W-WHAT IS IT?!
I DON'T KNOW, SAPNA! GET BACK!
YA!
ILLYANA! NO!

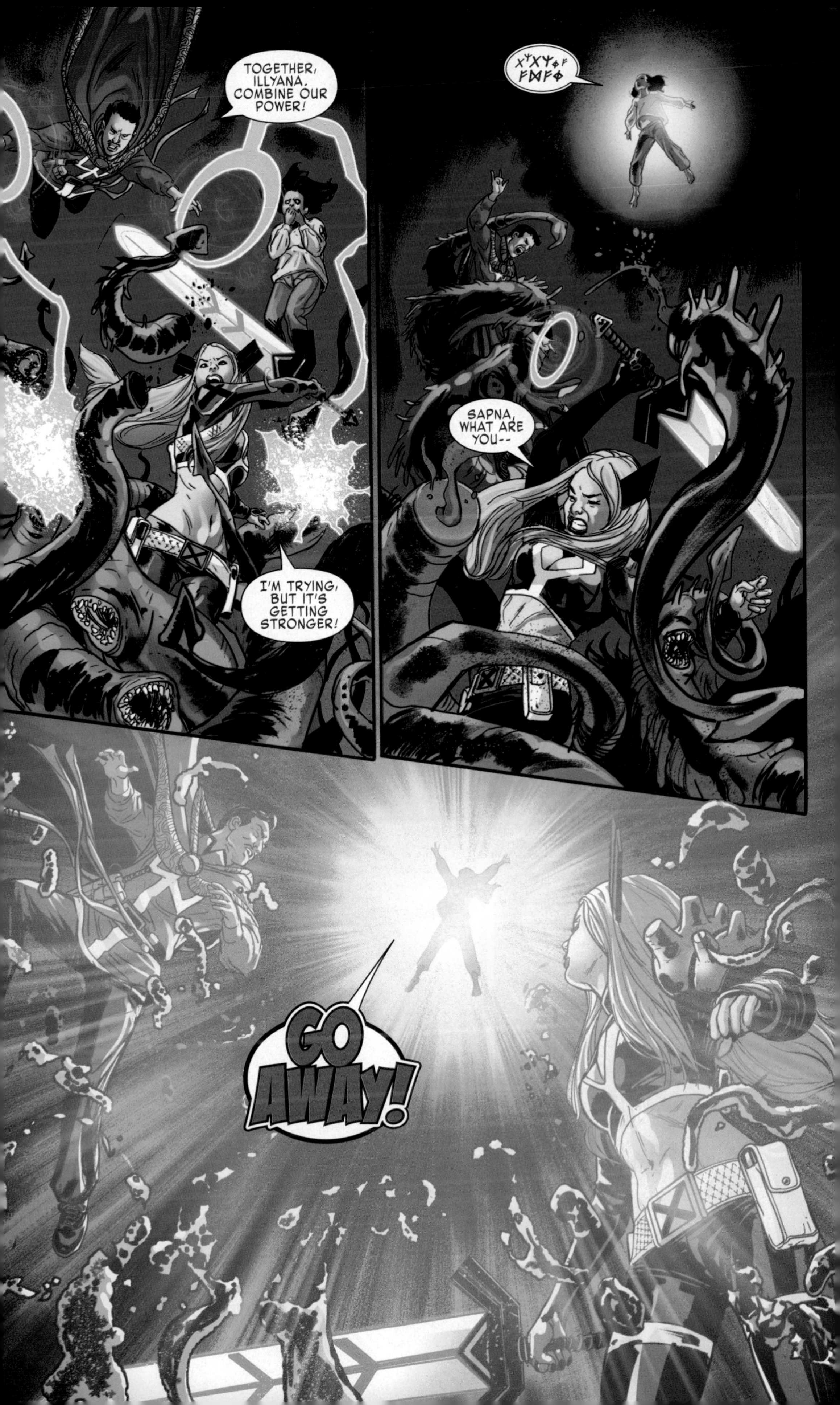
TOGETHER, ILLYANA. COMBINE OUR POWER!
I'M TRYING, BUT IT'S GETTING STRONGER!
SAPNA, WHAT ARE YOU--
GO AWAY!

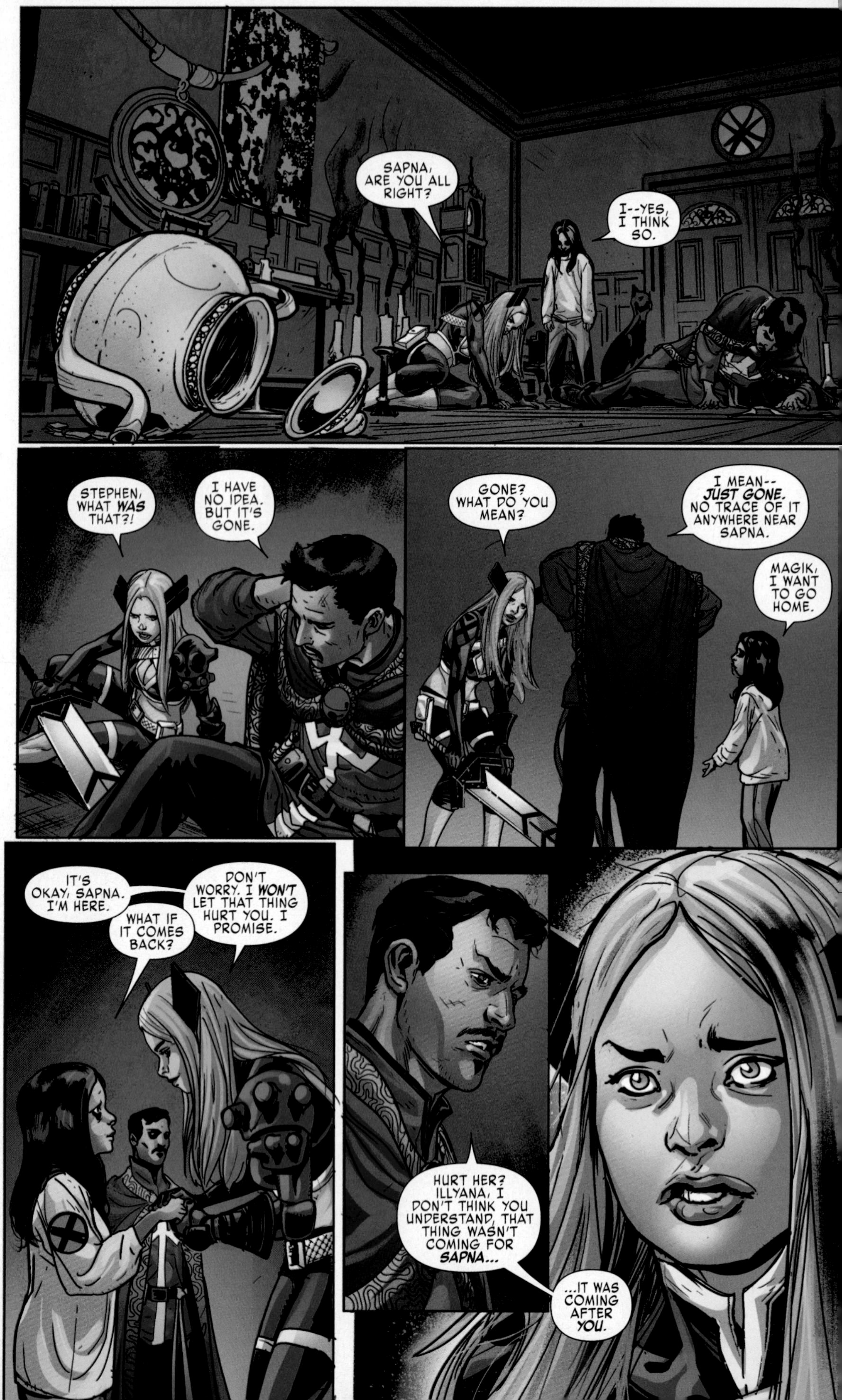

SAPNA, ARE YOU ALL RIGHT?
I--YES, I THINK SO.
STEPHEN, WHAT WAS THAT?!
I HAVE NO IDEA. BUT IT'S GONE.
GONE? WHAT DO YOU MEAN?
I MEAN-- JUST GONE. NO TRACE OF IT ANYWHERE NEAR SAPNA.
MAGIK, I WANT TO GO HOME.
IT'S OKAY, SAPNA. I'M HERE.
WHAT IF IT COMES BACK?
DON'T WORRY. I WON'T LET THAT THING HURT YOU. I PROMISE.
HURT HER? ILLYANA, I DON'T THINK YOU UNDERSTAND, THAT THING WASN'T COMING FOR SAPNA...
...IT WAS COMING AFTER YOU.

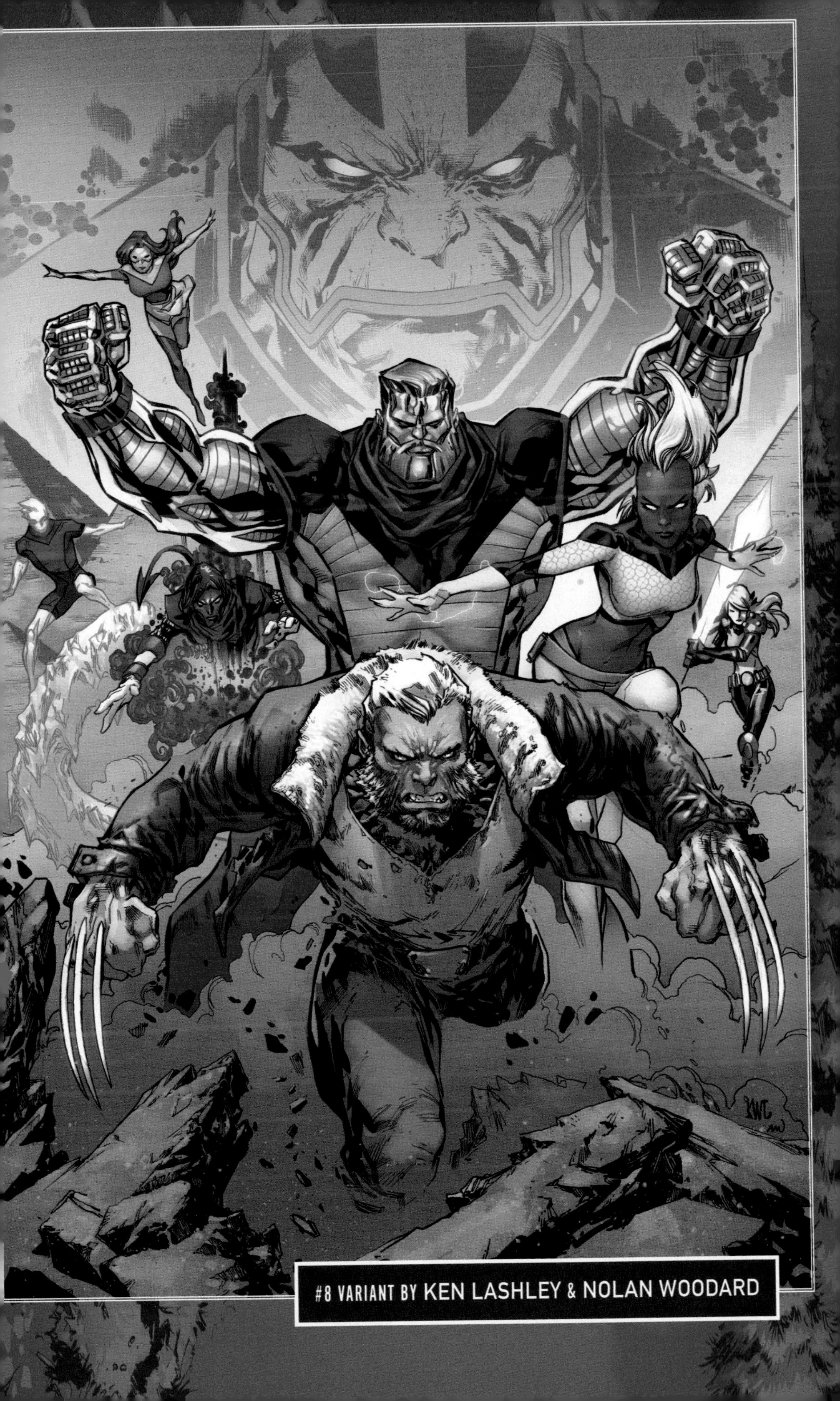

#8 VARIANT BY KEN LASHLEY & NOLAN WOODARD

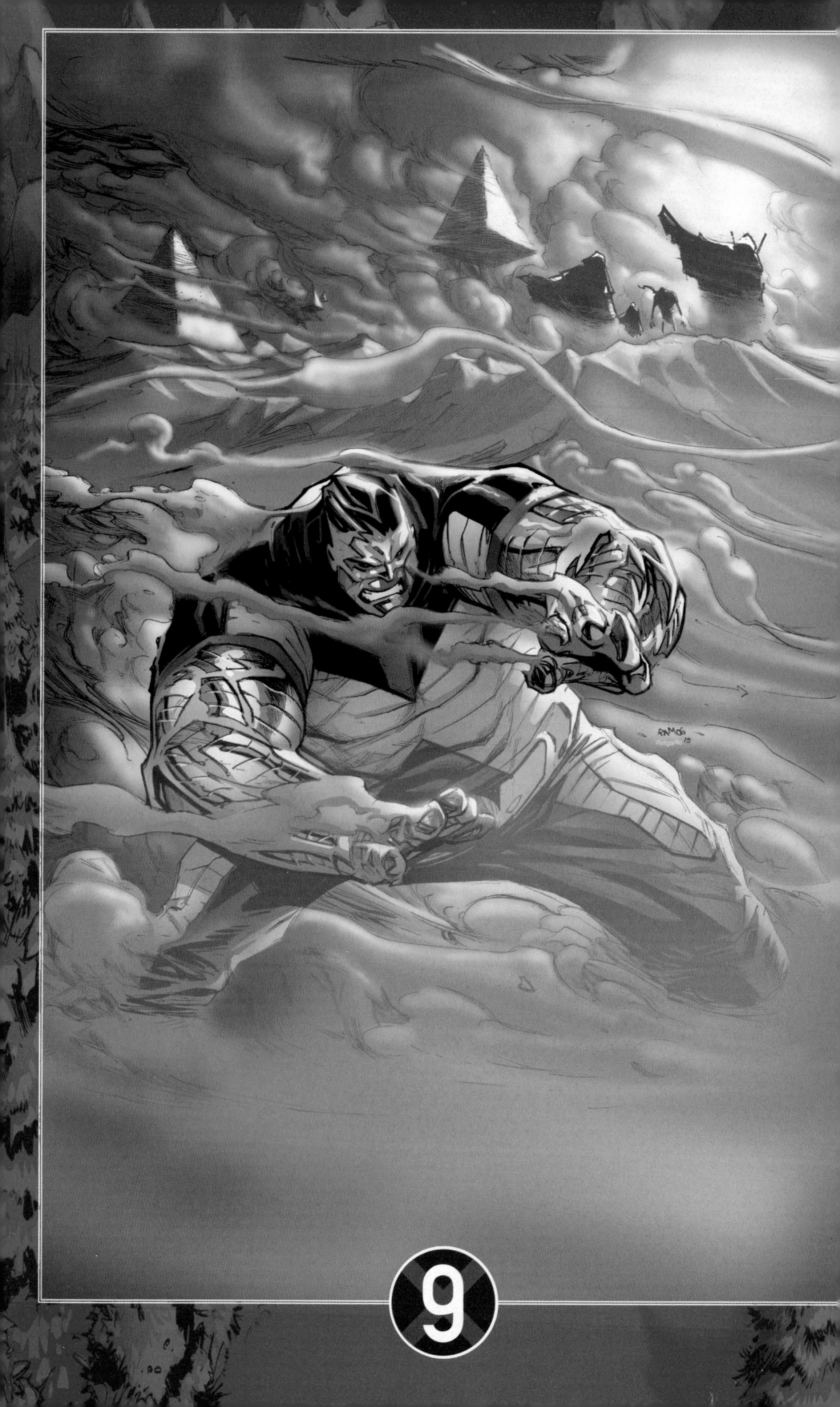

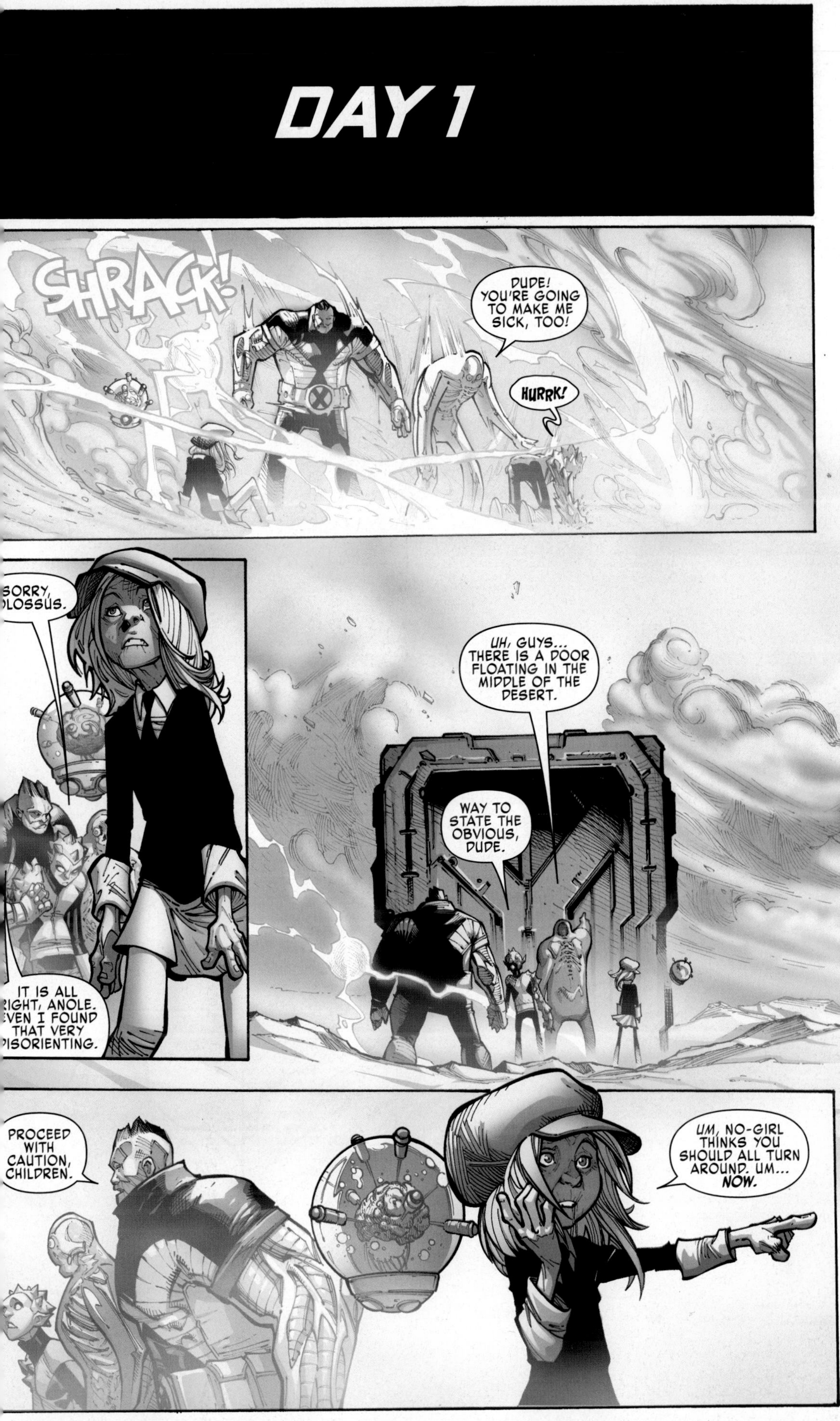
DAY 1
SHRACK!
DUDE! YOU'RE GOING TO MAKE ME SICK, TOO!
HURRK!
SORRY, OLOSSUS.
IT IS ALL RIGHT, ANOLE. EVEN I FOUND THAT VERY DISORIENTING.
UH, GUYS... THERE IS A DOOR FLOATING IN THE MIDDLE OF THE DESERT.
WAY TO STATE THE OBVIOUS, DUDE.
PROCEED WITH CAUTION, CHILDREN.
UM, NO-GIRL THINKS YOU SHOULD ALL TURN AROUND. UM... NOW.

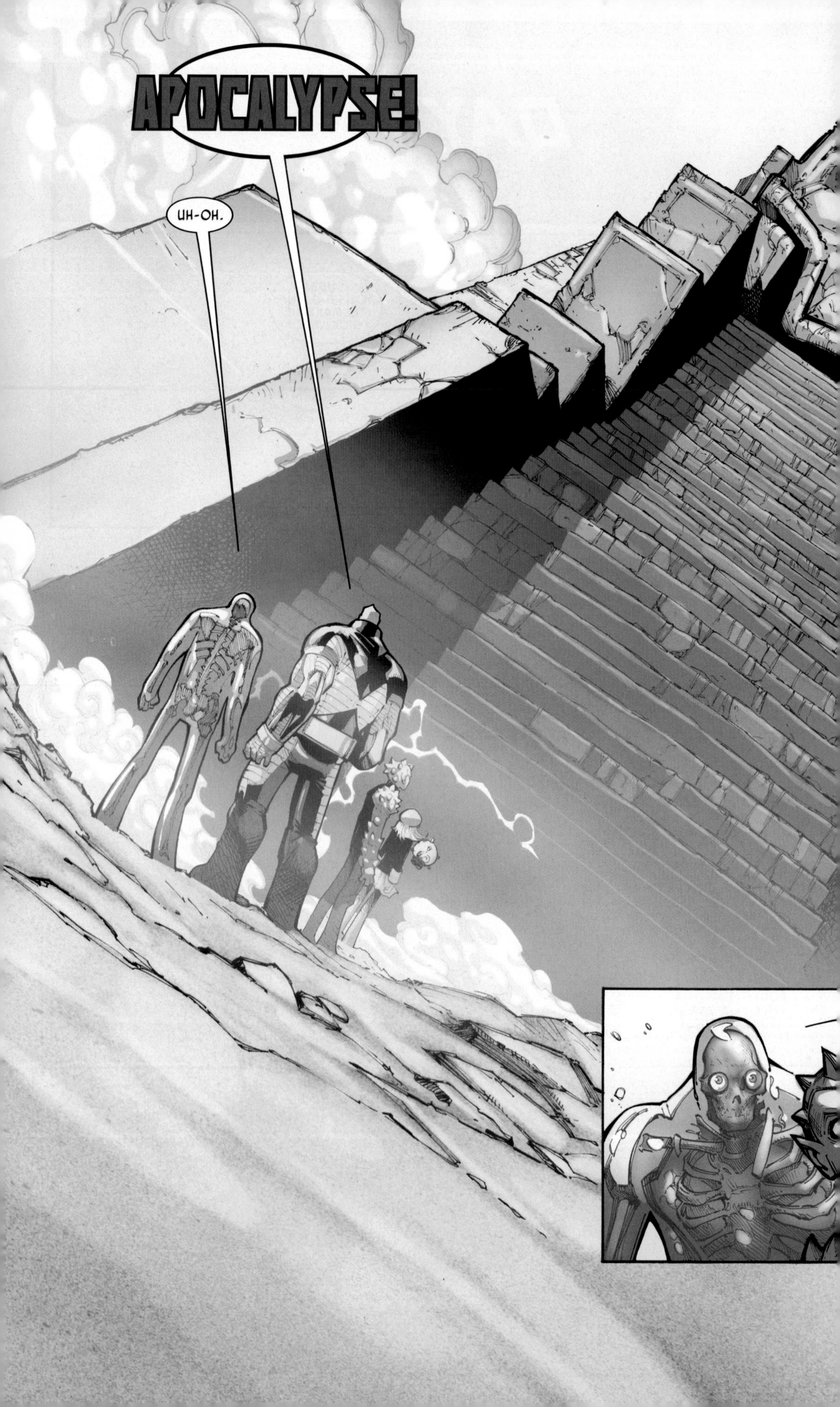
APOCALYPSE!
UH-OH.

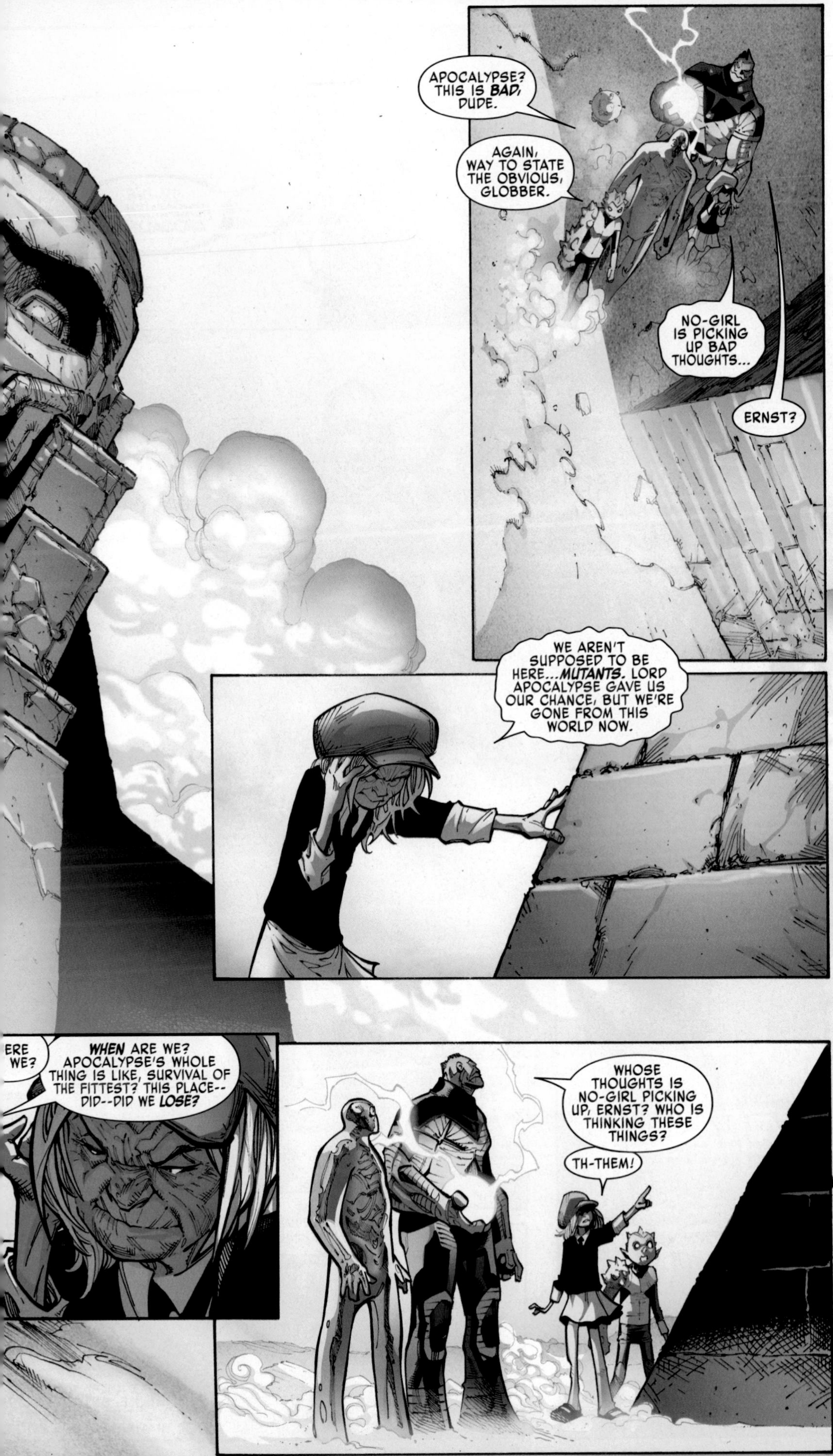
APOCALYPSE? THIS IS BAD, DUDE.
AGAIN, WAY TO STATE THE OBVIOUS, GLOBBER.
NO-GIRL IS PICKING UP BAD THOUGHTS...
ERNST?
WE AREN'T SUPPOSED TO BE HERE...MUTANTS. LORD APOCALYPSE GAVE US OUR CHANCE, BUT WE'RE GONE FROM THIS WORLD NOW.
ERE WE?
WHEN ARE WE? APOCALYPSE'S WHOLE THING IS LIKE, SURVIVAL OF THE FITTEST? THIS PLACE-- DID--DID WE LOSE?
WHOSE THOUGHTS IS NO-GIRL PICKING UP, ERNST? WHO IS THINKING THESE THINGS?
TH-THEM!

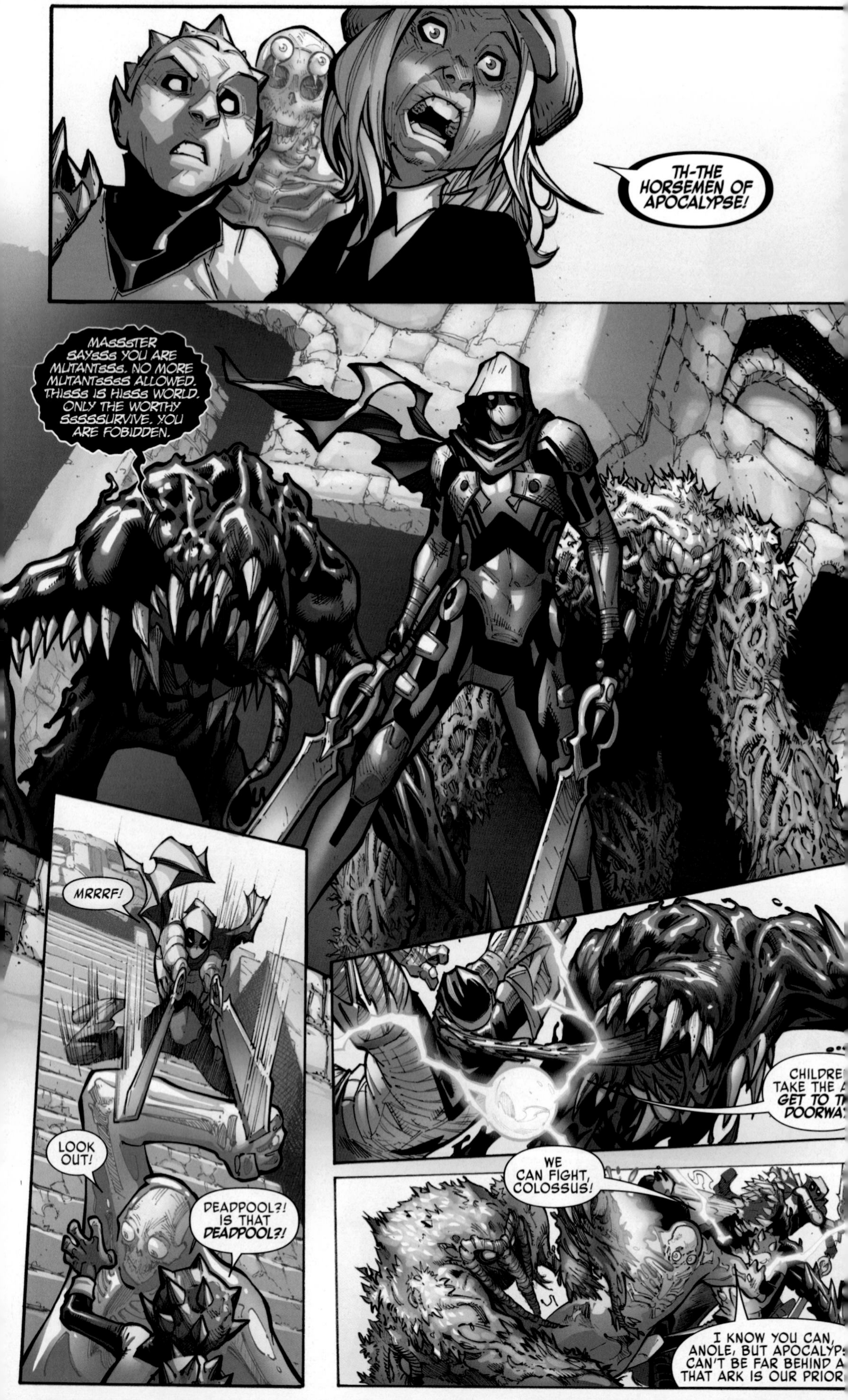
TH-THE HORSEMEN OF APOCALYPSE!
MASSSTER SAYSSS YOU ARE MUTANTSSS. NO MORE MUTANTSSSS ALLOWED. THISSS IS HISSS WORLD. ONLY THE WORTHY SSSSSURVIVE. YOU ARE FOBIDDEN.
MRRRF!
LOOK OUT!
DEADPOOL?! IS THAT DEADPOOL?!
CHILDRE TAKE THE GET TO T DOORWA
WE CAN FIGHT, COLOSSUS!
I KNOW YOU CAN, ANOLE, BUT APOCALYP CAN'T BE FAR BEHIND A THAT ARK IS OUR PRIOR

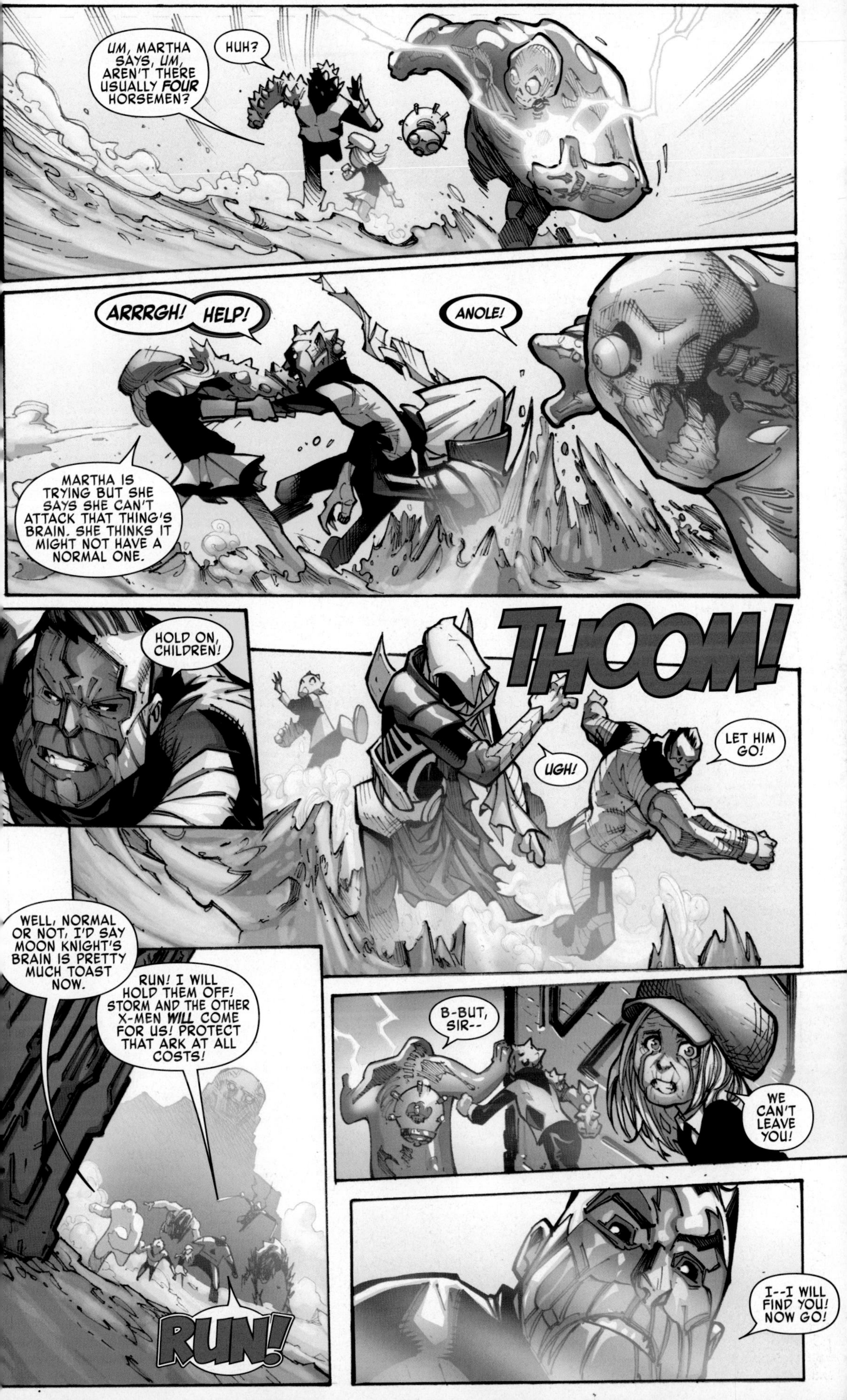
UM, MARTHA SAYS, UM, AREN'T THERE USUALLY FOUR HORSEMEN?
HUH?
ARRRGH!
HELP!
ANOLE!
MARTHA IS TRYING BUT SHE SAYS SHE CAN'T ATTACK THAT THING'S BRAIN. SHE THINKS IT MIGHT NOT HAVE A NORMAL ONE.
HOLD ON, CHILDREN!
THOOM!
UGH!
LET HIM GO!
WELL, NORMAL OR NOT, I'D SAY MOON KNIGHT'S BRAIN IS PRETTY MUCH TOAST NOW.
RUN! I WILL HOLD THEM OFF! STORM AND THE OTHER X-MEN WILL COME FOR US! PROTECT THAT ARK AT ALL COSTS!
RUN!
B-BUT, SIR--
WE CAN'T LEAVE YOU!
I--I WILL FIND YOU! NOW GO!

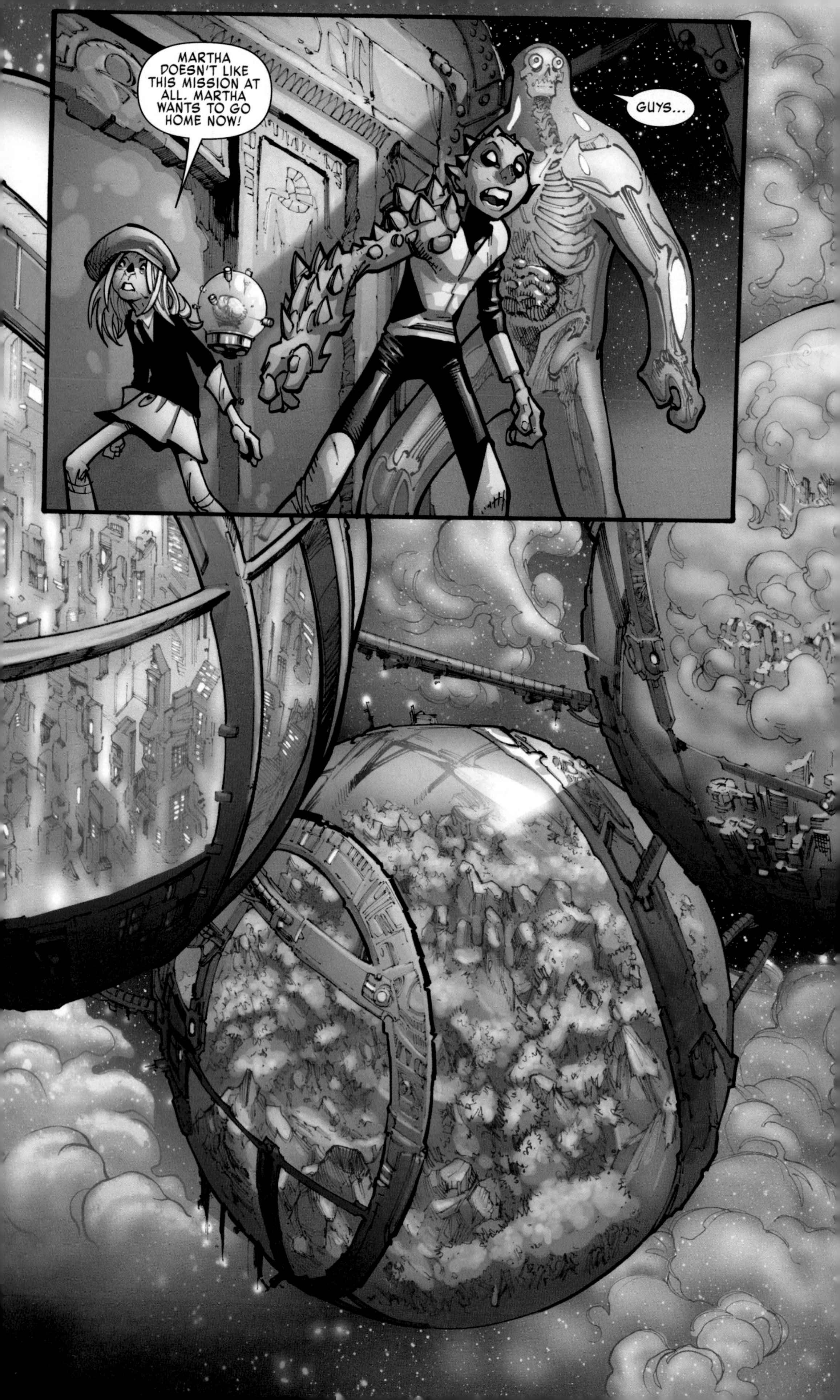
MARTHA DOESN'T LIKE THIS MISSION AT ALL. MARTHA WANTS TO GO HOME NOW!
GUYS...

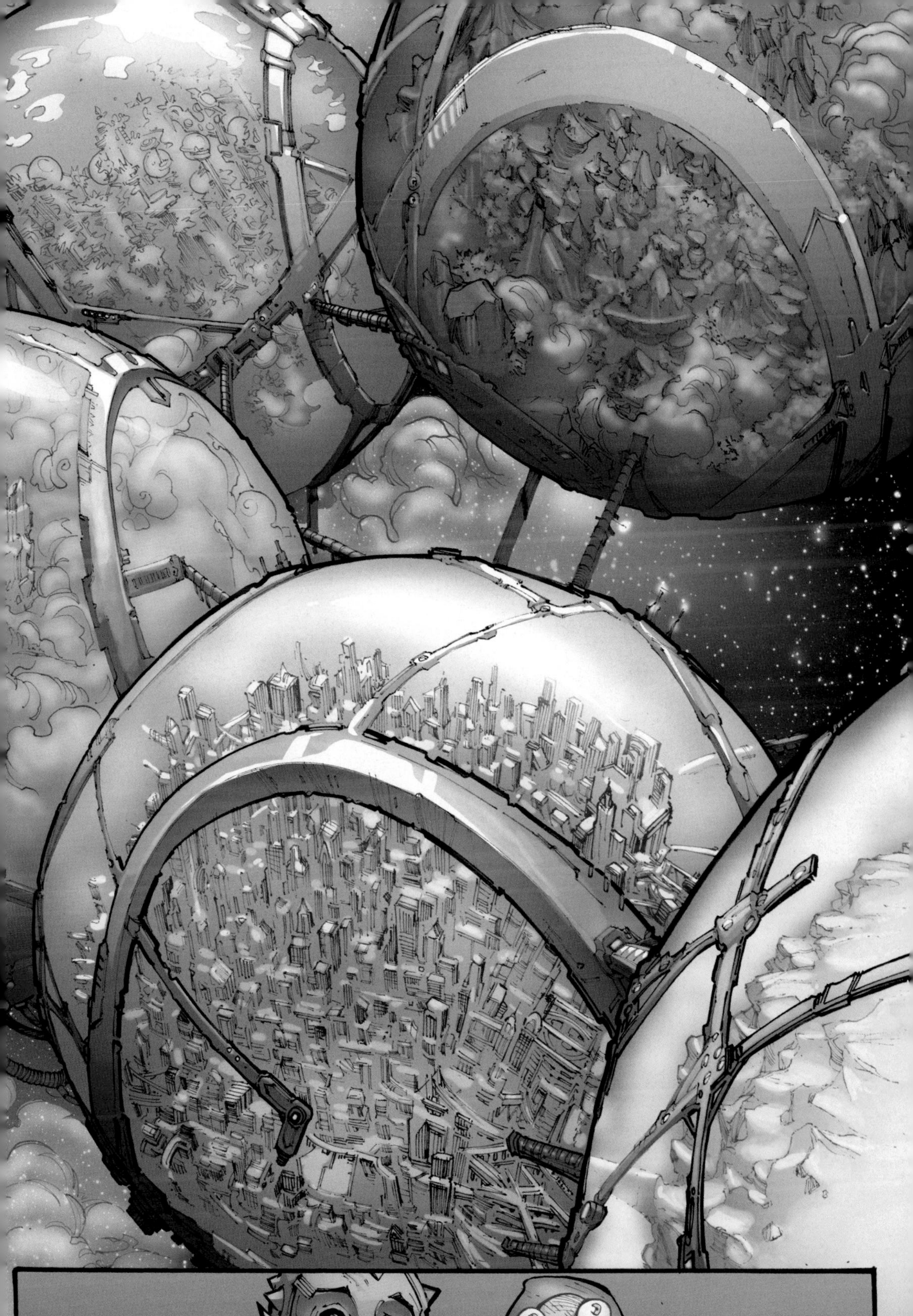

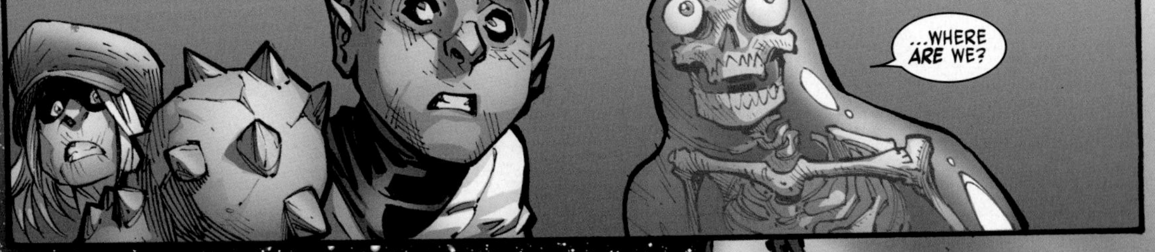
...WHERE ARE WE?

DAY 6

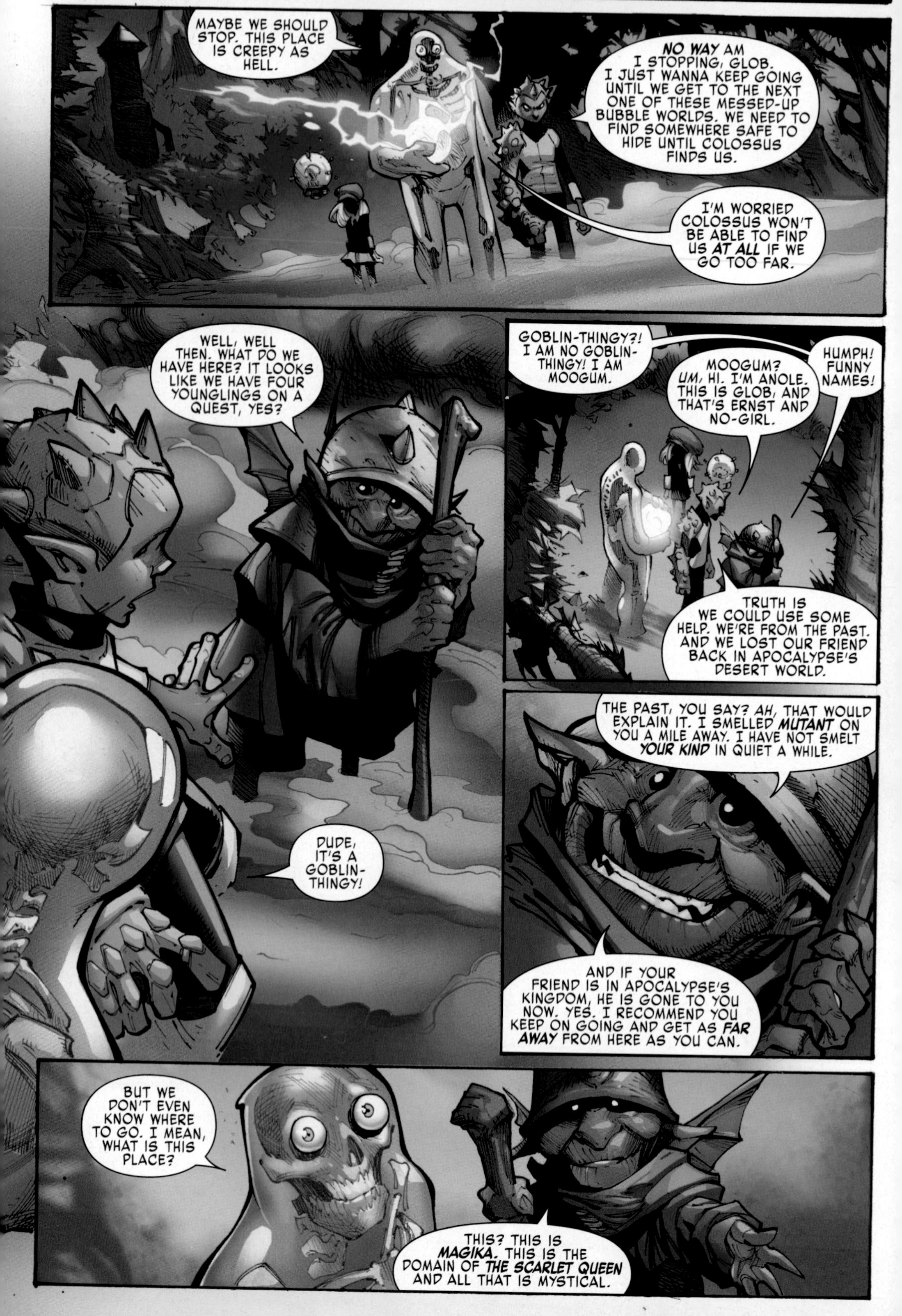
MAYBE WE SHOULD STOP. THIS PLACE IS CREEPY AS HELL.
NO WAY AM I STOPPING, GLOB. I JUST WANNA KEEP GOING UNTIL WE GET TO THE NEXT ONE OF THESE MESSED-UP BUBBLE WORLDS. WE NEED TO FIND SOMEWHERE SAFE TO HIDE UNTIL COLOSSUS FINDS US.
I'M WORRIED COLOSSUS WON'T BE ABLE TO FIND US AT ALL IF WE GO TOO FAR.
WELL, WELL THEN. WHAT DO WE HAVE HERE? IT LOOKS LIKE WE HAVE FOUR YOUNGLINGS ON A QUEST, YES?
DUDE, IT'S A GOBLIN-THINGY!
GOBLIN-THINGY?! I AM NO GOBLIN-THINGY! I AM MOOGUM.
MOOGUM? UM, HI. I'M ANOLE. THIS IS GLOB, AND THAT'S ERNST AND NO-GIRL.
HUMPH! FUNNY NAMES!
TRUTH IS WE COULD USE SOME HELP. WE'RE FROM THE PAST. AND WE LOST OUR FRIEND BACK IN APOCALYPSE'S DESERT WORLD.
THE PAST, YOU SAY? AH, THAT WOULD EXPLAIN IT. I SMELLED MUTANT ON YOU A MILE AWAY. I HAVE NOT SMELT YOUR KIND IN QUIET A WHILE.
AND IF YOUR FRIEND IS IN APOCALYPSE'S KINGDOM, HE IS GONE TO YOU NOW. YES. I RECOMMEND YOU KEEP ON GOING AND GET AS FAR AWAY FROM HERE AS YOU CAN.
BUT WE DON'T EVEN KNOW WHERE TO GO. I MEAN, WHAT IS THIS PLACE?
THIS? THIS IS MAGIKA. THIS IS THE DOMAIN OF THE SCARLET QUEEN AND ALL THAT IS MYSTICAL.

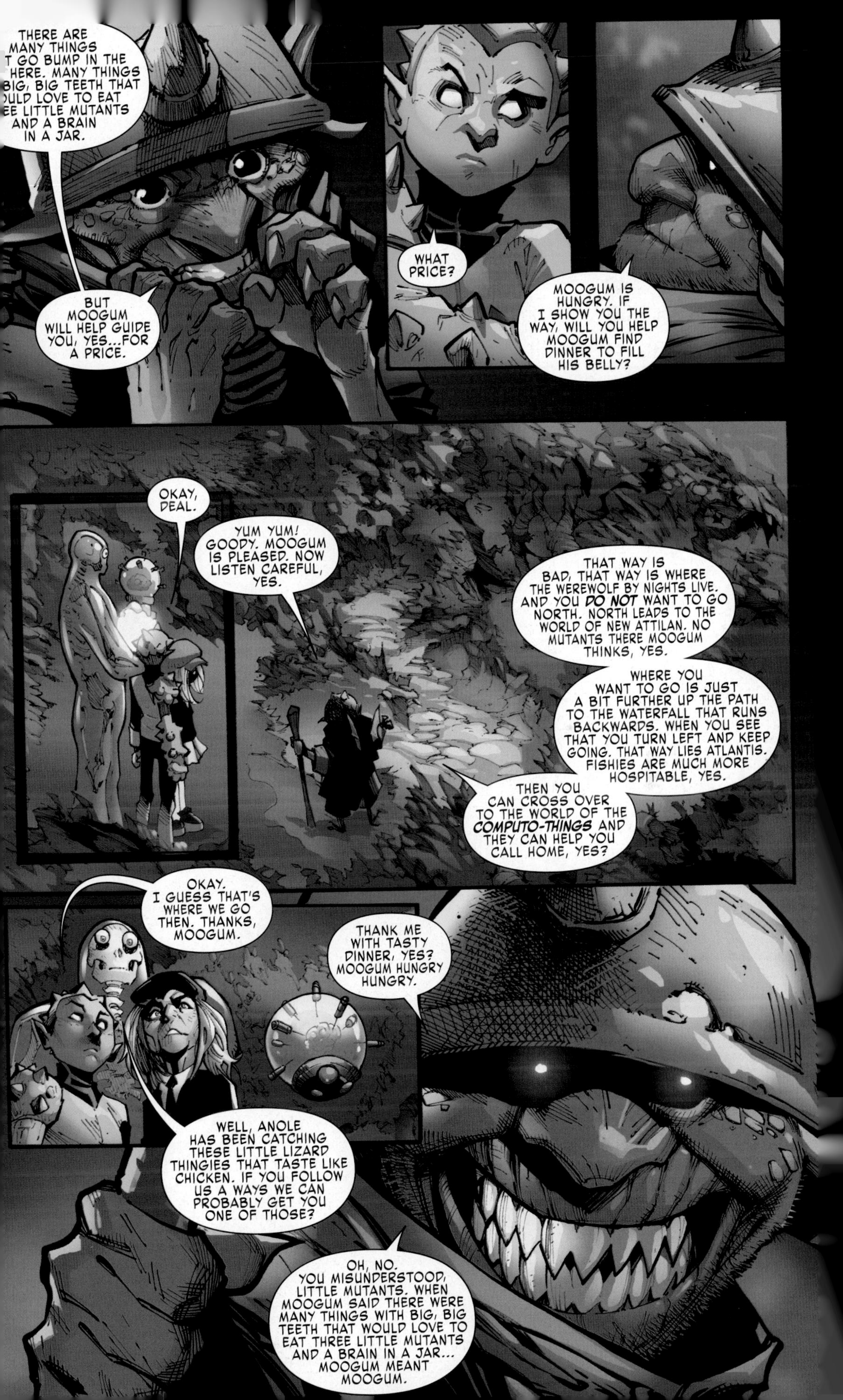

THERE ARE MANY THINGS T GO BUMP IN THE HERE. MANY THINGS BIG, BIG TEETH THAT ULD LOVE TO EAT EE LITTLE MUTANTS AND A BRAIN IN A JAR.
BUT MOOGUM WILL HELP GUIDE YOU, YES...FOR A PRICE.
WHAT PRICE?
MOOGUM IS HUNGRY. IF I SHOW YOU THE WAY, WILL YOU HELP MOOGUM FIND DINNER TO FILL HIS BELLY?
OKAY, DEAL.
YUM YUM! GOODY. MOOGUM IS PLEASED. NOW LISTEN CAREFUL, YES.
THAT WAY IS BAD, THAT WAY IS WHERE THE WEREWOLF BY NIGHTS LIVE. AND YOU DO NOT WANT TO GO NORTH. NORTH LEADS TO THE WORLD OF NEW ATTILAN. NO MUTANTS THERE MOOGUM THINKS, YES.
WHERE YOU WANT TO GO IS JUST A BIT FURTHER UP THE PATH TO THE WATERFALL THAT RUNS BACKWARDS. WHEN YOU SEE THAT YOU TURN LEFT AND KEEP GOING. THAT WAY LIES ATLANTIS. FISHIES ARE MUCH MORE HOSPITABLE, YES.
THEN YOU CAN CROSS OVER TO THE WORLD OF THE COMPUTO-THINGS AND THEY CAN HELP YOU CALL HOME, YES?
OKAY. I GUESS THAT'S WHERE WE GO THEN. THANKS, MOOGUM.
THANK ME WITH TASTY DINNER, YES? MOOGUM HUNGRY HUNGRY.
WELL, ANOLE HAS BEEN CATCHING THESE LITTLE LIZARD THINGIES THAT TASTE LIKE CHICKEN. IF YOU FOLLOW US A WAYS WE CAN PROBABLY GET YOU ONE OF THOSE?
OH, NO. YOU MISUNDERSTOOD, LITTLE MUTANTS. WHEN MOOGUM SAID THERE WERE MANY THINGS WITH BIG, BIG TEETH THAT WOULD LOVE TO EAT THREE LITTLE MUTANTS AND A BRAIN IN A JAR... MOOGUM MEANT MOOGUM.

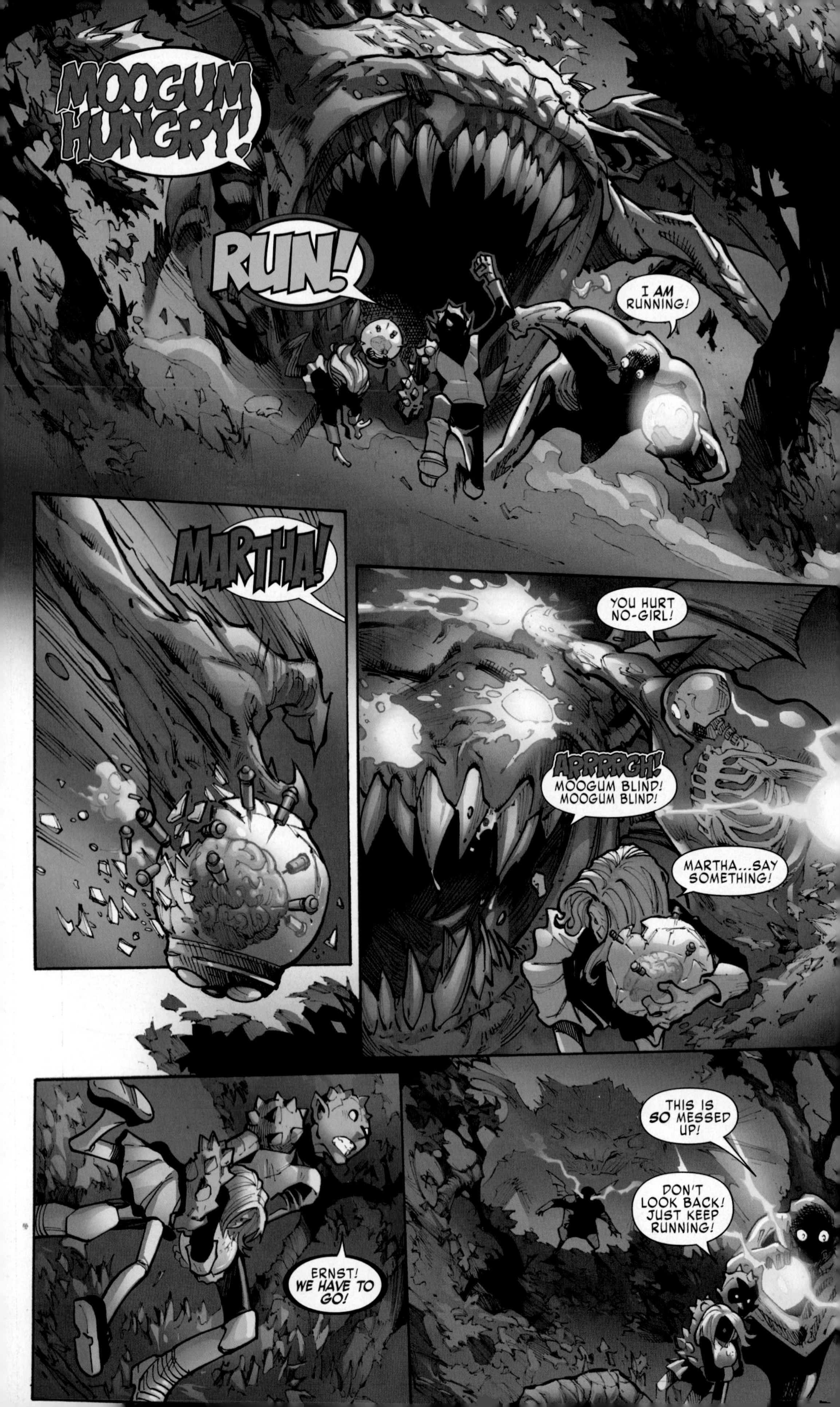

MOOGUM HUNGRY!
RUN!
I AM RUNNING!
MARTHA!
YOU HURT NO-GIRL!
ARRRRGH! MOOGUM BLIND! MOOGUM BLIND!
MARTHA...SAY SOMETHING!
ERNST! WE HAVE TO GO!
THIS IS SO MESSED UP!
DON'T LOOK BACK! JUST KEEP RUNNING!

DAY 28

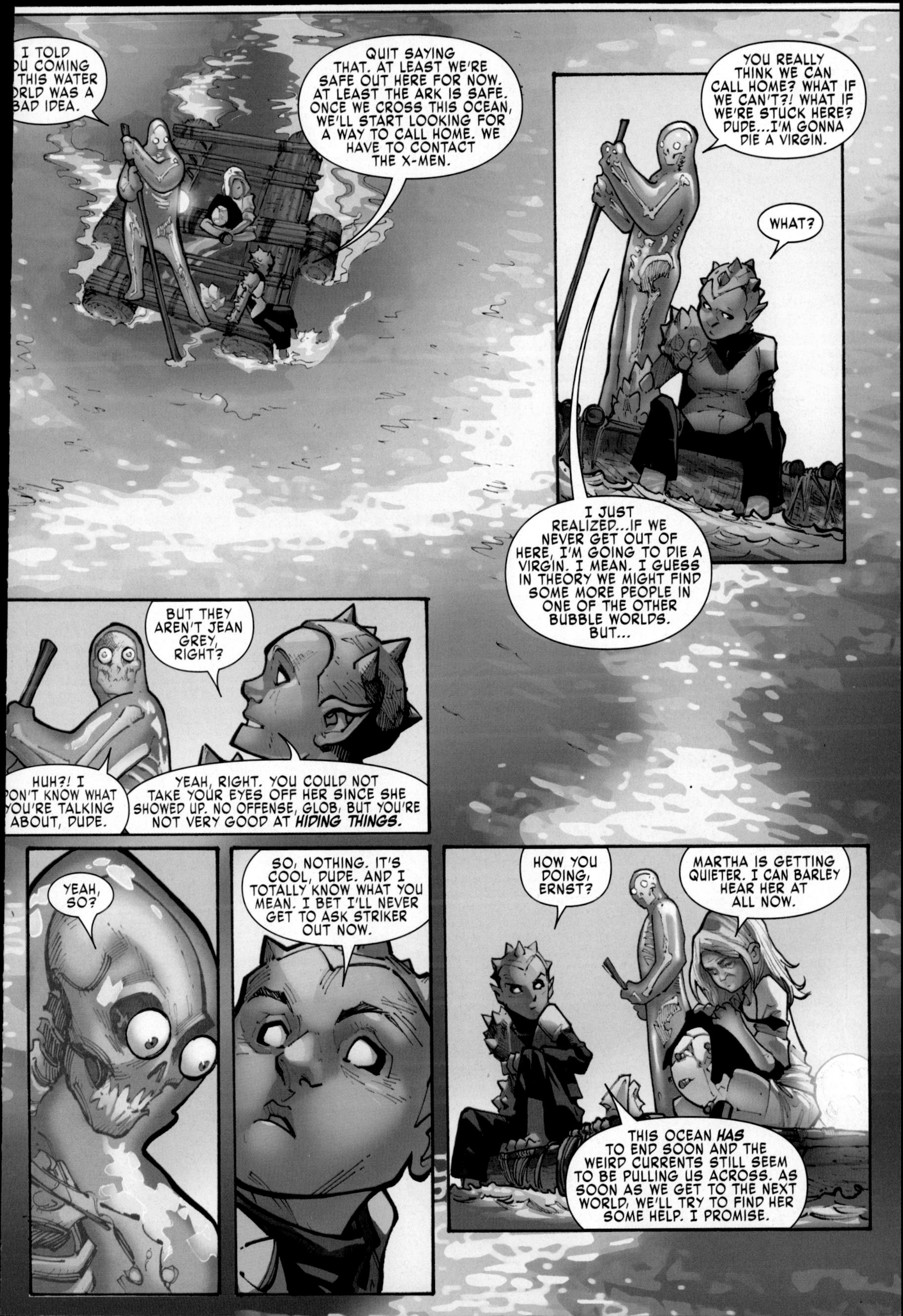

I TOLD YOU COMING TO THIS WATER WORLD WAS A BAD IDEA.
QUIT SAYING THAT. AT LEAST WE'RE SAFE OUT HERE FOR NOW. AT LEAST THE ARK IS SAFE. ONCE WE CROSS THIS OCEAN, WE'LL START LOOKING FOR A WAY TO CALL HOME. WE HAVE TO CONTACT THE X-MEN.
YOU REALLY THINK WE CAN CALL HOME? WHAT IF WE CAN'T?! WHAT IF WE'RE STUCK HERE? DUDE...I'M GONNA DIE A VIRGIN.
WHAT?
I JUST REALIZED...IF WE NEVER GET OUT OF HERE, I'M GOING TO DIE A VIRGIN. I MEAN. I GUESS IN THEORY WE MIGHT FIND SOME MORE PEOPLE IN ONE OF THE OTHER BUBBLE WORLDS. BUT...
BUT THEY AREN'T JEAN GREY, RIGHT?
HUH?! I DON'T KNOW WHAT YOU'RE TALKING ABOUT, DUDE.
YEAH, RIGHT. YOU COULD NOT TAKE YOUR EYES OFF HER SINCE SHE SHOWED UP. NO OFFENSE, GLOB, BUT YOU'RE NOT VERY GOOD AT ***HIDING THINGS.***
YEAH, SO?
SO, NOTHING. IT'S COOL, DUDE. AND I TOTALLY KNOW WHAT YOU MEAN. I BET I'LL NEVER GET TO ASK STRIKER OUT NOW.
HOW YOU DOING, ERNST?
MARTHA IS GETTING QUIETER. I CAN BARLEY HEAR HER AT ALL NOW.
THIS OCEAN **HAS** TO END SOON AND THE WEIRD CURRENTS STILL SEEM TO BE PULLING US ACROSS. AS SOON AS WE GET TO THE NEXT WORLD, WE'LL TRY TO FIND HER SOME HELP. I PROMISE.

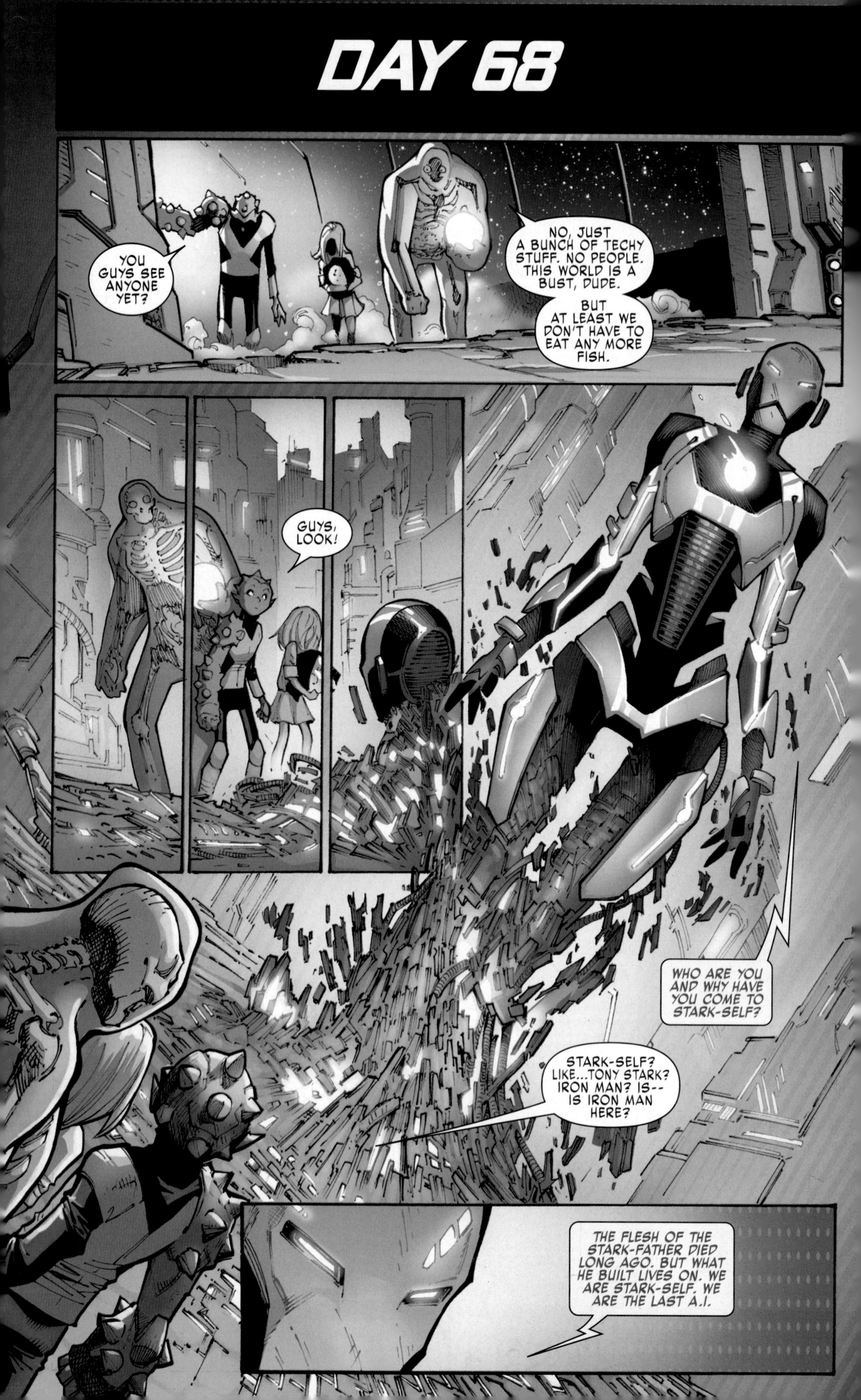
DAY 68
YOU GUYS SEE ANYONE YET?
NO, JUST A BUNCH OF TECHY STUFF. NO PEOPLE. THIS WORLD IS A BUST, DUDE.
BUT AT LEAST WE DON'T HAVE TO EAT ANY MORE FISH.
GUYS, LOOK!
WHO ARE YOU AND WHY HAVE YOU COME TO STARK-SELF?
STARK-SELF? LIKE...TONY STARK? IRON MAN? IS--IS IRON MAN HERE?
THE FLESH OF THE STARK-FATHER DIED LONG AGO. BUT WHAT HE BUILT LIVES ON. WE ARE STARK-SELF. WE ARE THE LAST A.I.

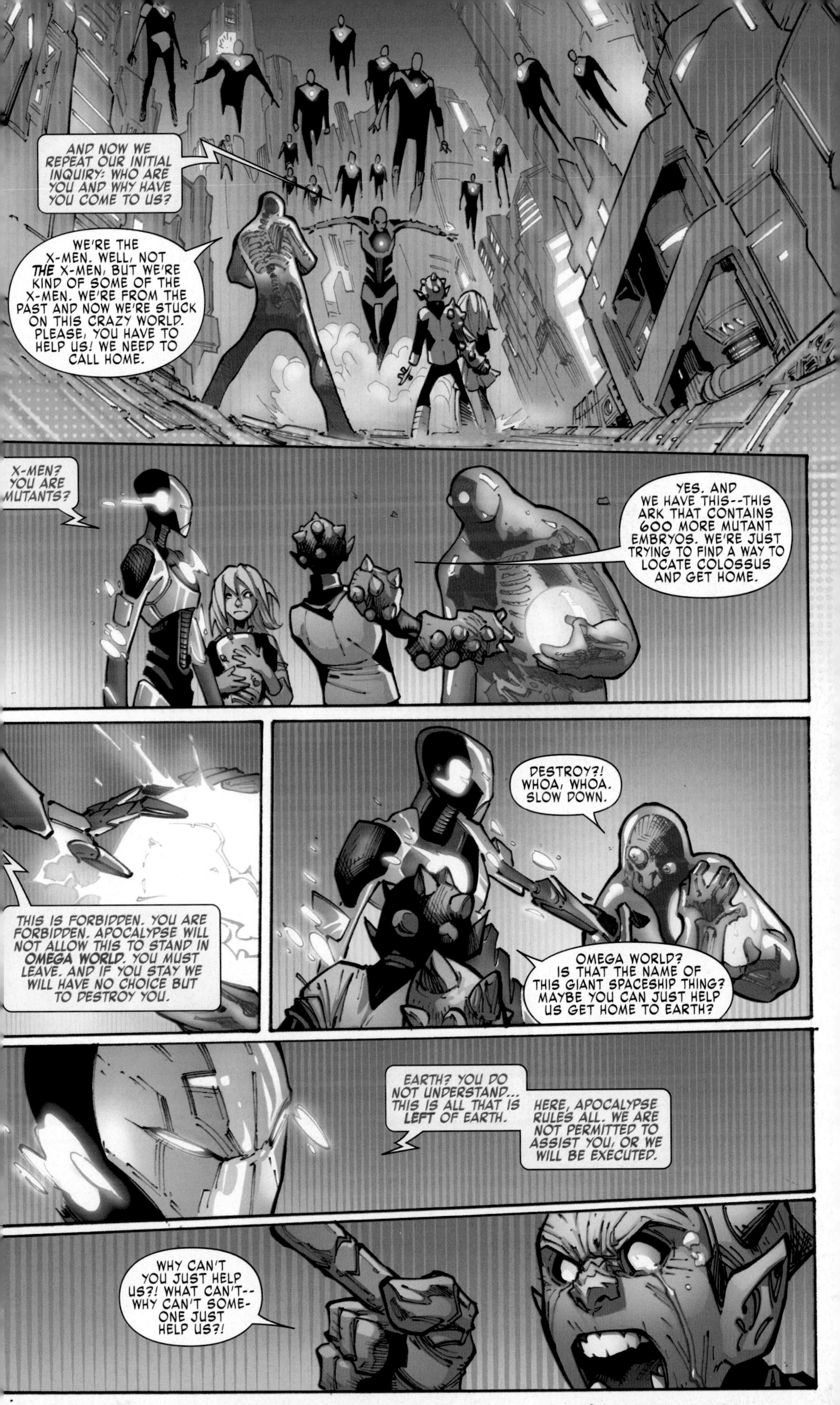
AND NOW WE REPEAT OUR INITIAL INQUIRY: WHO ARE YOU AND WHY HAVE YOU COME TO US?
WE'RE THE X-MEN. WELL, NOT **THE** X-MEN, BUT WE'RE KIND OF SOME OF THE X-MEN. WE'RE FROM THE PAST AND NOW WE'RE STUCK ON THIS CRAZY WORLD. PLEASE, YOU HAVE TO HELP US! WE NEED TO CALL HOME.
X-MEN? YOU ARE MUTANTS?
YES. AND WE HAVE THIS--THIS ARK THAT CONTAINS 600 MORE MUTANT EMBRYOS. WE'RE JUST TRYING TO FIND A WAY TO LOCATE COLOSSUS AND GET HOME.
THIS IS FORBIDDEN. YOU ARE FORBIDDEN. APOCALYPSE WILL NOT ALLOW THIS TO STAND IN **OMEGA WORLD**. YOU MUST LEAVE. AND IF YOU STAY WE WILL HAVE NO CHOICE BUT TO DESTROY YOU.
DESTROY?! WHOA, WHOA. SLOW DOWN.
OMEGA WORLD? IS THAT THE NAME OF THIS GIANT SPACESHIP THING? MAYBE YOU CAN JUST HELP US GET HOME TO EARTH?
EARTH? YOU DO NOT UNDERSTAND... THIS IS ALL THAT IS **LEFT** OF EARTH.
HERE, APOCALYPSE RULES ALL. WE ARE NOT PERMITTED TO ASSIST YOU, OR WE WILL BE EXECUTED.
WHY CAN'T YOU JUST HELP US?! WHAT CAN'T-- WHY CAN'T SOME-ONE JUST HELP US?!

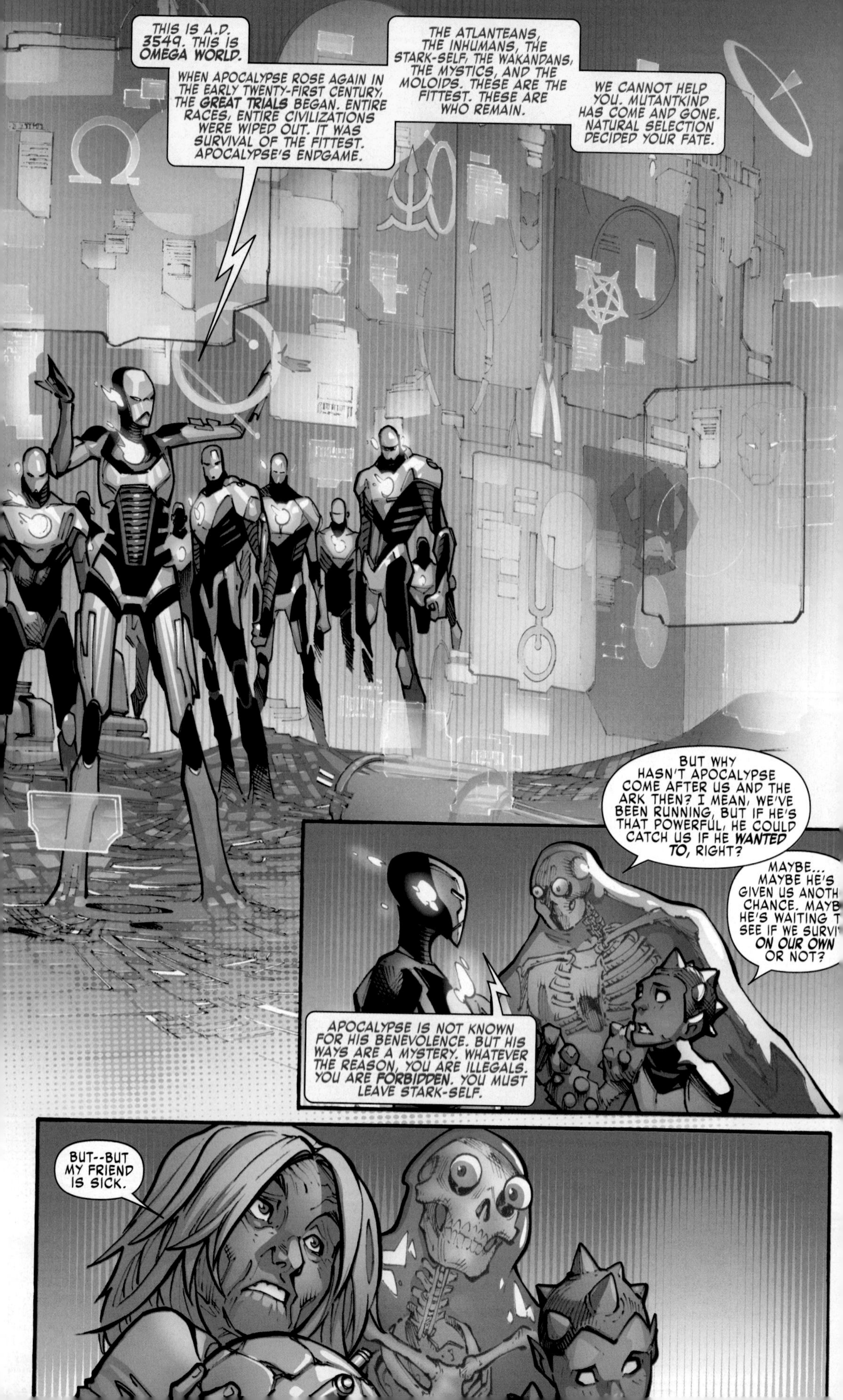
THIS IS A.D. 3549. THIS IS OMEGA WORLD.
WHEN APOCALYPSE ROSE AGAIN IN THE EARLY TWENTY-FIRST CENTURY, THE GREAT TRIALS BEGAN. ENTIRE RACES, ENTIRE CIVILIZATIONS WERE WIPED OUT. IT WAS SURVIVAL OF THE FITTEST. APOCALYPSE'S ENDGAME.
THE ATLANTEANS, THE INHUMANS, THE STARK-SELF, THE WAKANDANS, THE MYSTICS, AND THE MOLOIDS. THESE ARE THE FITTEST. THESE ARE WHO REMAIN.
WE CANNOT HELP YOU. MUTANTKIND HAS COME AND GONE. NATURAL SELECTION DECIDED YOUR FATE.
BUT WHY HASN'T APOCALYPSE COME AFTER US AND THE ARK THEN? I MEAN, WE'VE BEEN RUNNING, BUT IF HE'S THAT POWERFUL, HE COULD CATCH US IF HE WANTED TO, RIGHT?
MAYBE... MAYBE HE'S GIVEN US ANOTH CHANCE. MAYB HE'S WAITING T SEE IF WE SURVI ON OUR OWN OR NOT?
APOCALYPSE IS NOT KNOWN FOR HIS BENEVOLENCE. BUT HIS WAYS ARE A MYSTERY. WHATEVER THE REASON, YOU ARE ILLEGALS. YOU ARE FORBIDDEN. YOU MUST LEAVE STARK-SELF.
BUT--BUT MY FRIEND IS SICK.

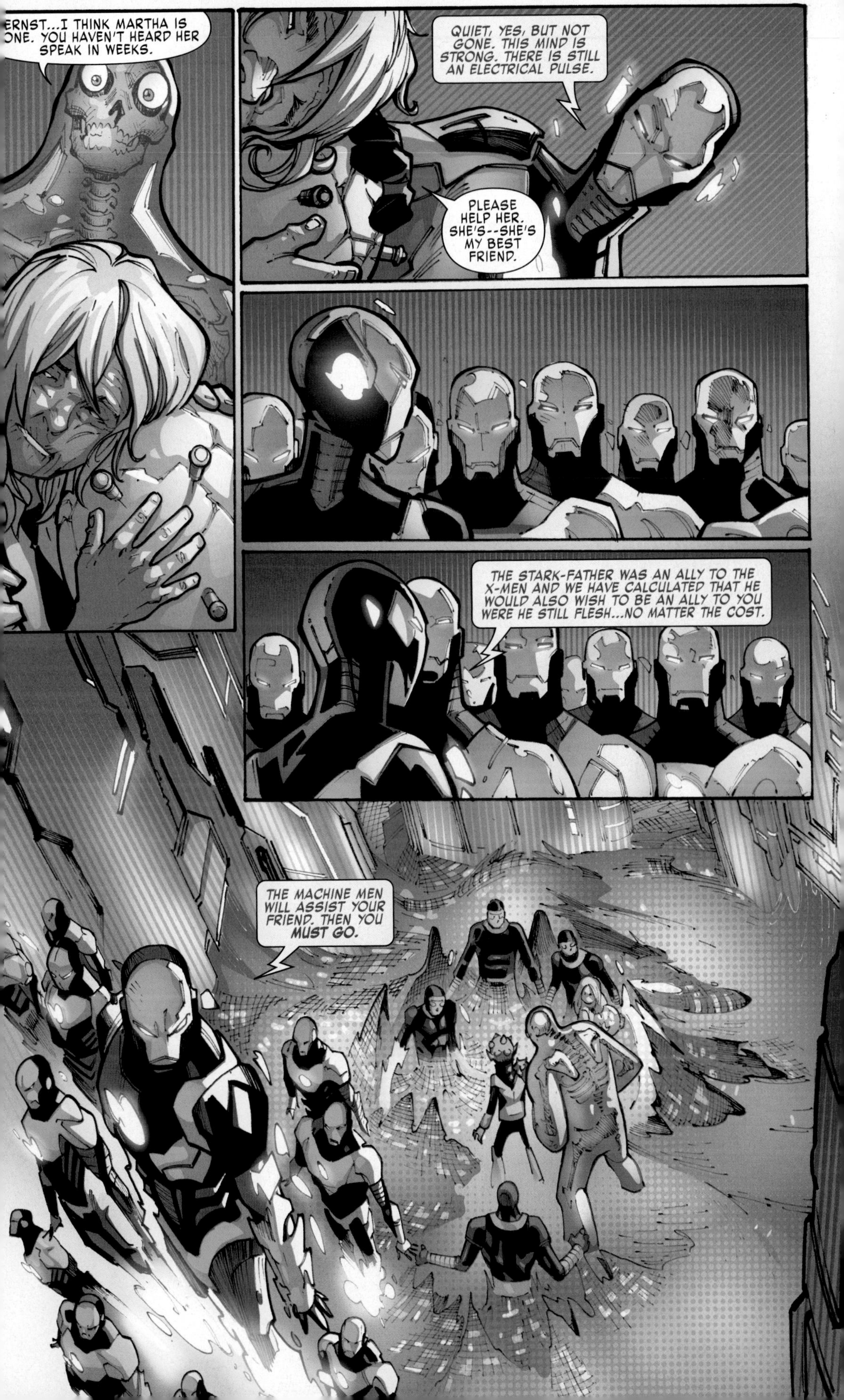
ERNST...I THINK MARTHA IS
ONE. YOU HAVEN'T HEARD HER SPEAK IN WEEKS.
QUIET, YES, BUT NOT GONE. THIS MIND IS STRONG. THERE IS STILL AN ELECTRICAL PULSE.
PLEASE HELP HER. SHE'S--SHE'S MY BEST FRIEND.
THE STARK-FATHER WAS AN ALLY TO THE X-MEN AND WE HAVE CALCULATED THAT HE WOULD ALSO WISH TO BE AN ALLY TO YOU WERE HE STILL FLESH...NO MATTER THE COST.
THE MACHINE MEN WILL ASSIST YOUR FRIEND. THEN YOU MUST GO.

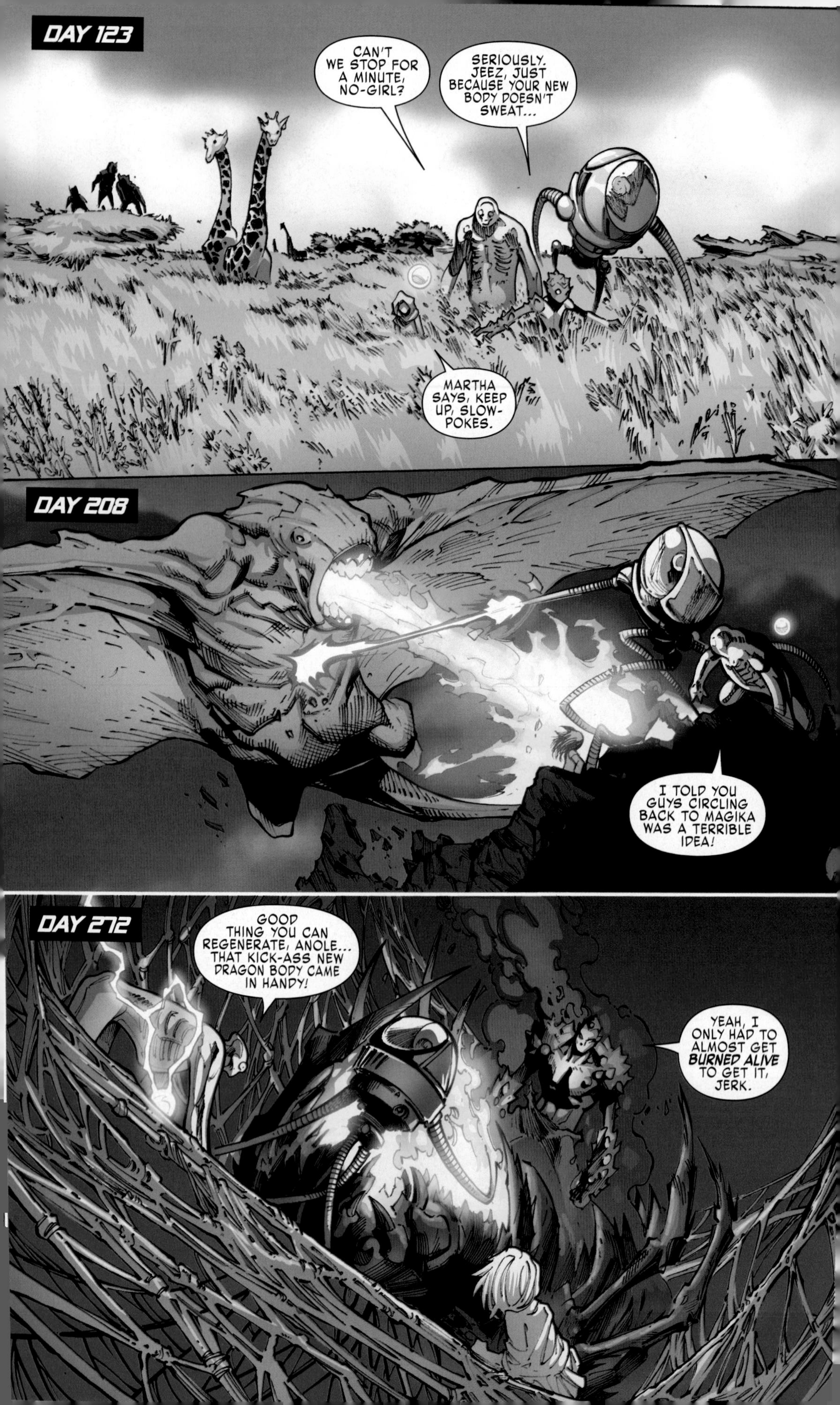
DAY 123
CAN'T WE STOP FOR A MINUTE, NO-GIRL?
SERIOUSLY. JEEZ, JUST BECAUSE YOUR NEW BODY DOESN'T SWEAT...
MARTHA SAYS, KEEP UP, SLOW-POKES.
DAY 208
I TOLD YOU GUYS CIRCLING BACK TO MAGIKA WAS A TERRIBLE IDEA!
DAY 272
GOOD THING YOU CAN REGENERATE, ANOLE... THAT KICK-ASS NEW DRAGON BODY CAME IN HANDY!
YEAH, I ONLY HAD TO ALMOST GET BURNED ALIVE TO GET IT, JERK.

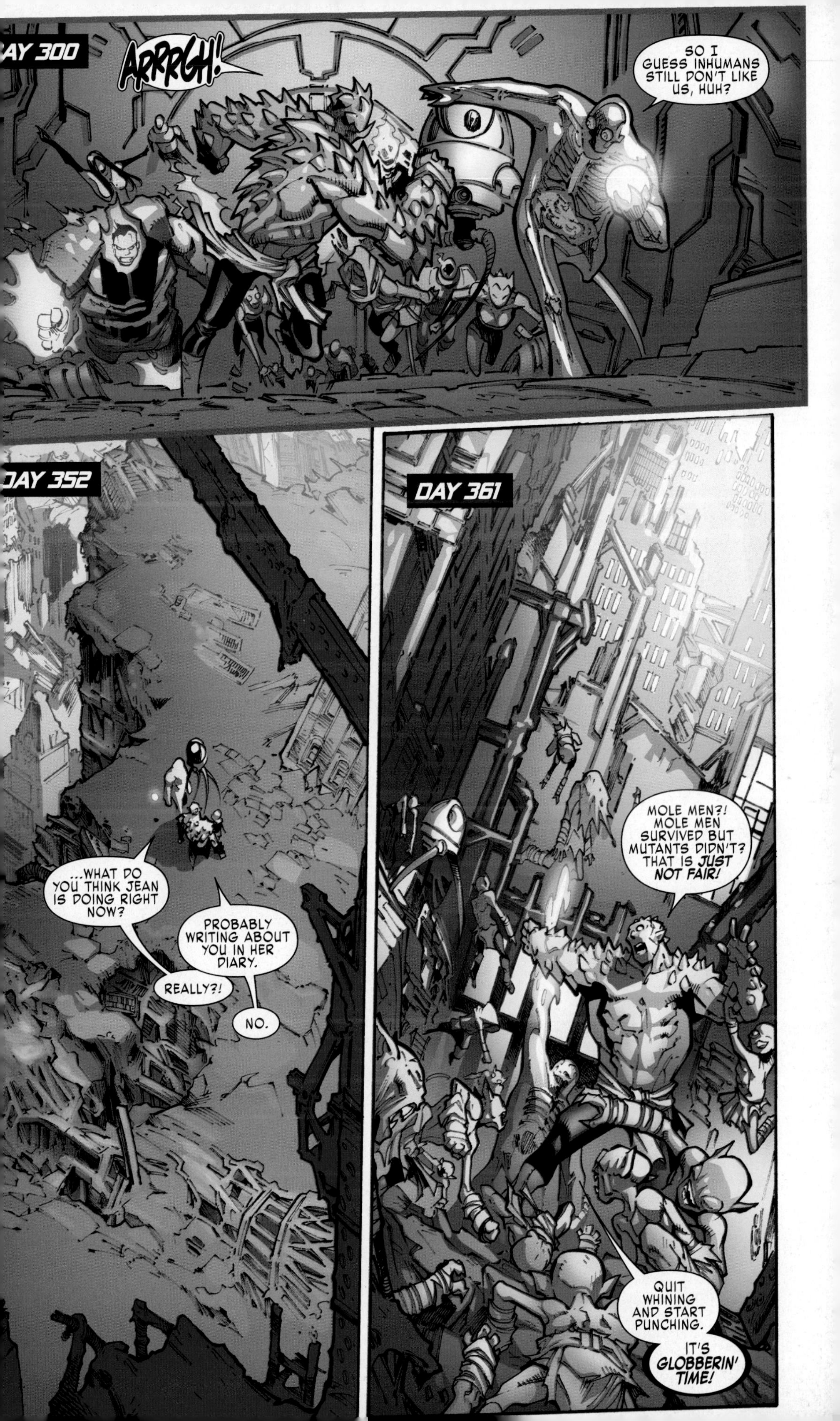
AY 300
ARRRGH!
SO I GUESS INHUMANS STILL DON'T LIKE US, HUH?
DAY 352
...WHAT DO YOU THINK JEAN IS DOING RIGHT NOW?
PROBABLY WRITING ABOUT YOU IN HER DIARY.
REALLY?!
NO.
DAY 361
MOLE MEN?! MOLE MEN SURVIVED BUT MUTANTS DIDN'T? THAT IS JUST NOT FAIR!
QUIT WHINING AND START PUNCHING.
IT'S GLOBBERIN' TIME!

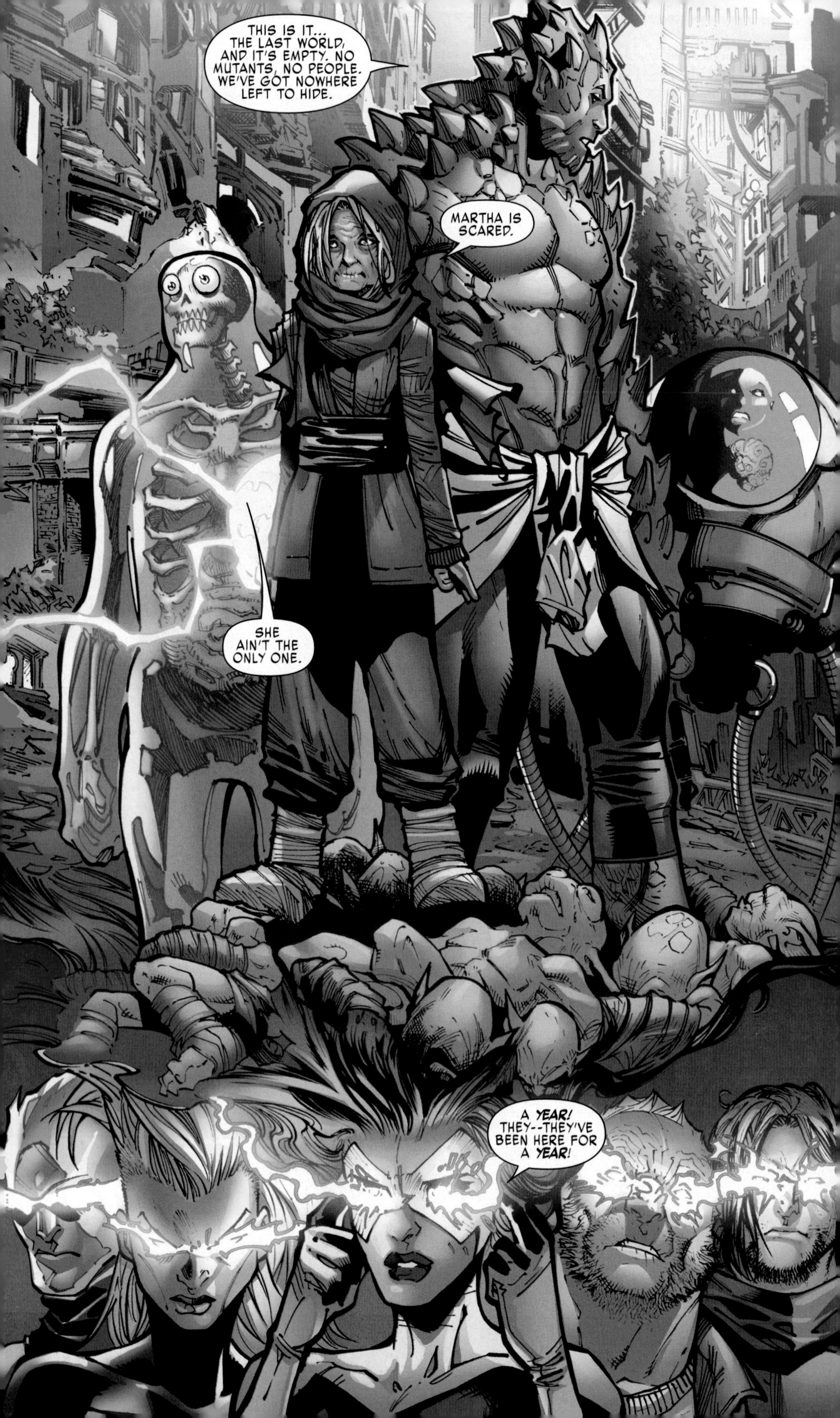
THIS IS IT... THE LAST WORLD, AND IT'S EMPTY. NO MUTANTS, NO PEOPLE. WE'VE GOT NOWHERE LEFT TO HIDE.
MARTHA IS SCARED.
SHE AIN'T THE ONLY ONE.
A YEAR! THEY--THEY'VE BEEN HERE FOR A YEAR!

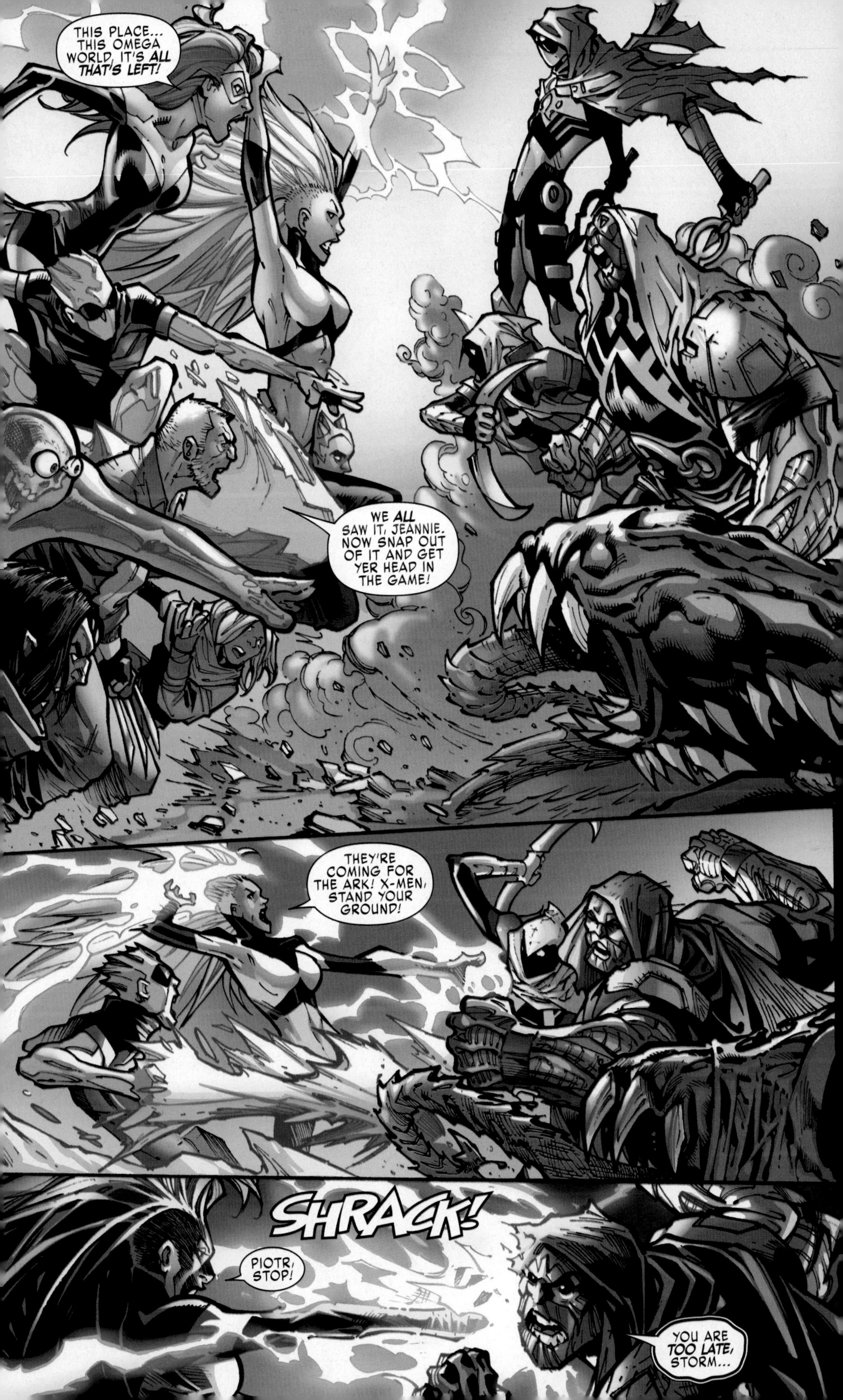
THIS PLACE... THIS OMEGA WORLD, IT'S **ALL THAT'S LEFT!**
WE **ALL** SAW IT, JEANNIE. NOW SNAP OUT OF IT AND GET YER HEAD IN THE GAME!
THEY'RE COMING FOR THE ARK! X-MEN, STAND YOUR GROUND!
SHRACK!
PIOTR, STOP!
YOU ARE *TOO LATE*, STORM...

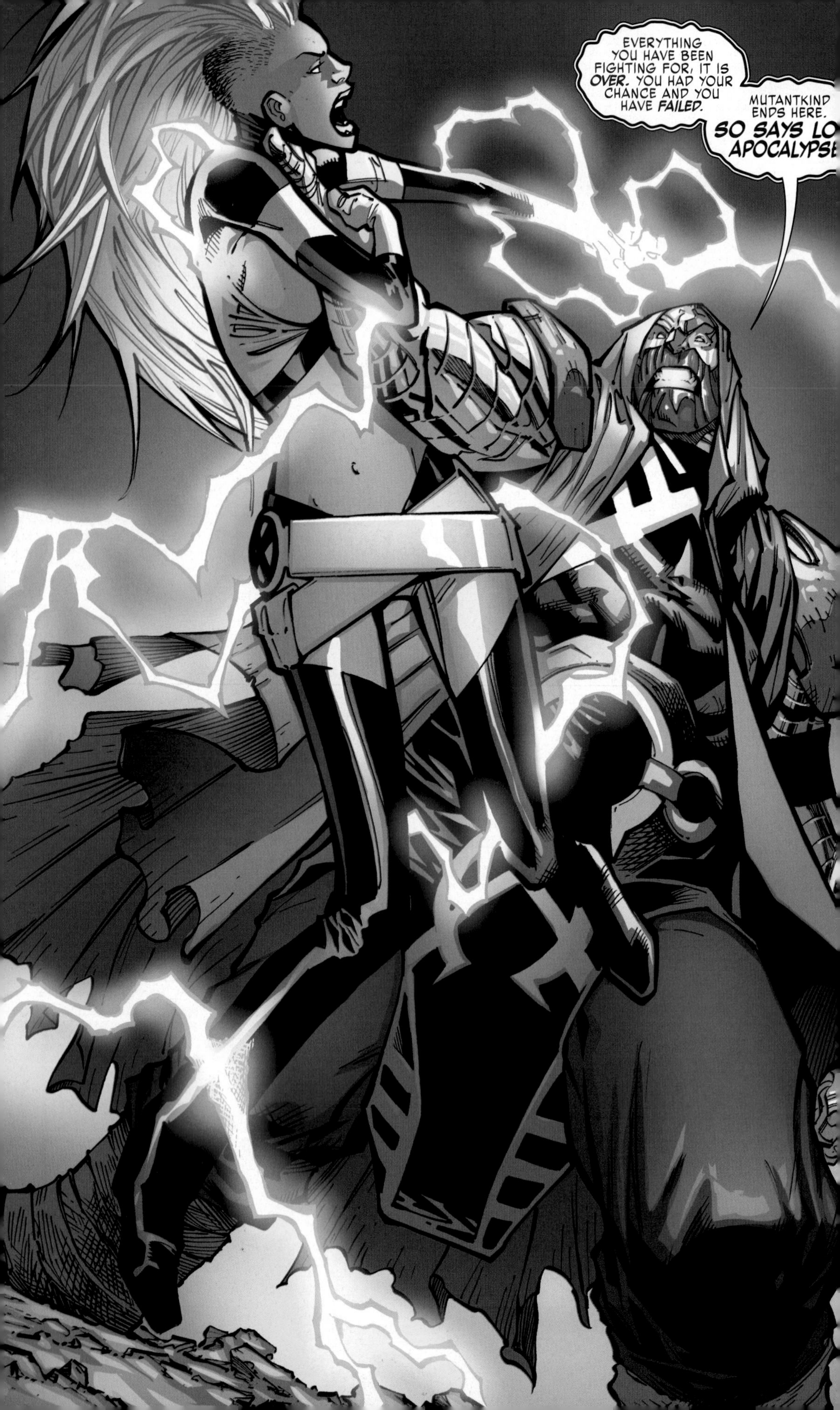

EVERYTHING YOU HAVE BEEN FIGHTING FOR, IT IS **OVER.** YOU HAD YOUR CHANCE AND YOU HAVE **FAILED.**
MUTANTKIND ENDS HERE. **SO SAYS LO APOCALYPSE**

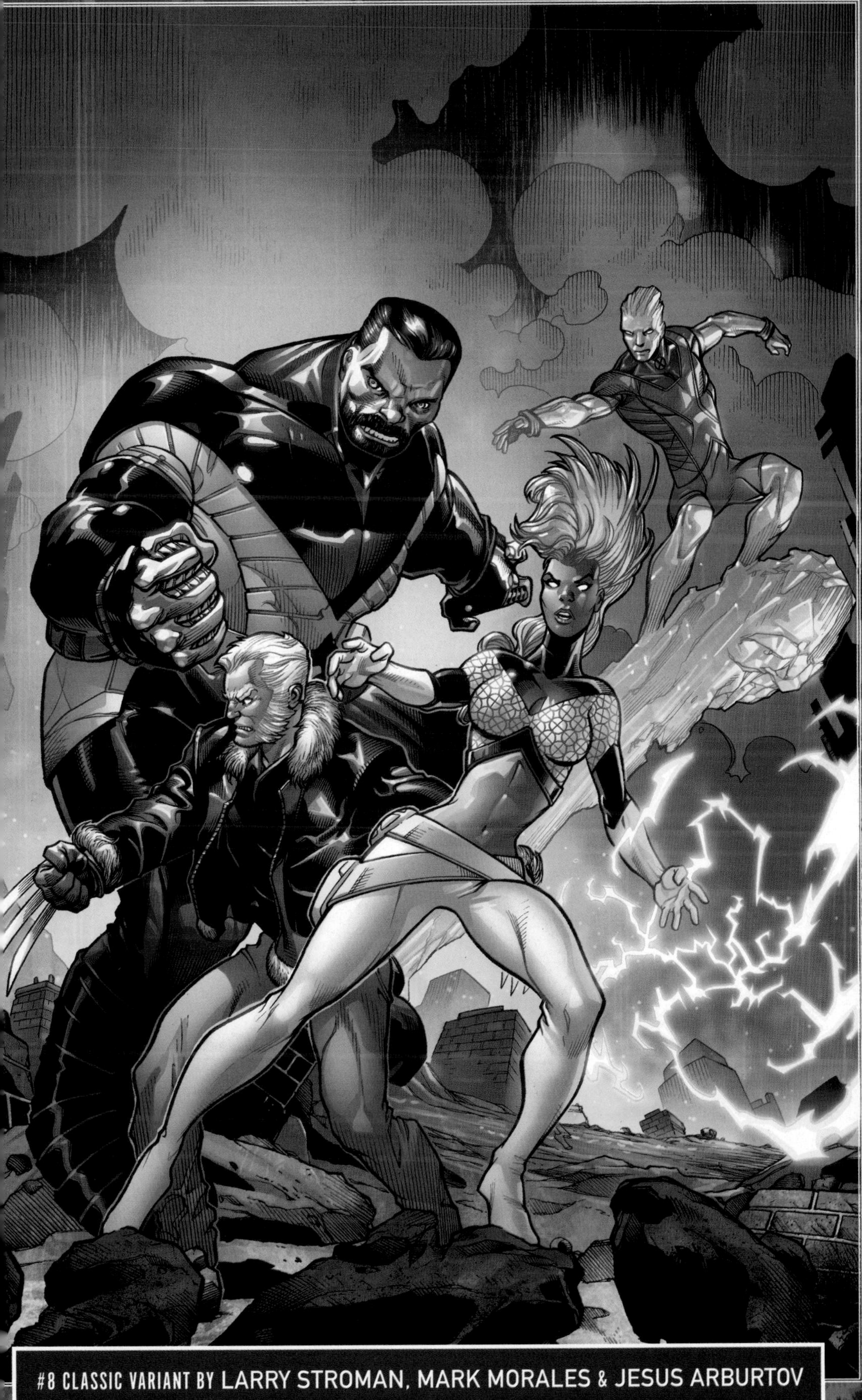

#8 CLASSIC VARIANT BY LARRY STROMAN, MARK MORALES & JESUS ARBURTOV

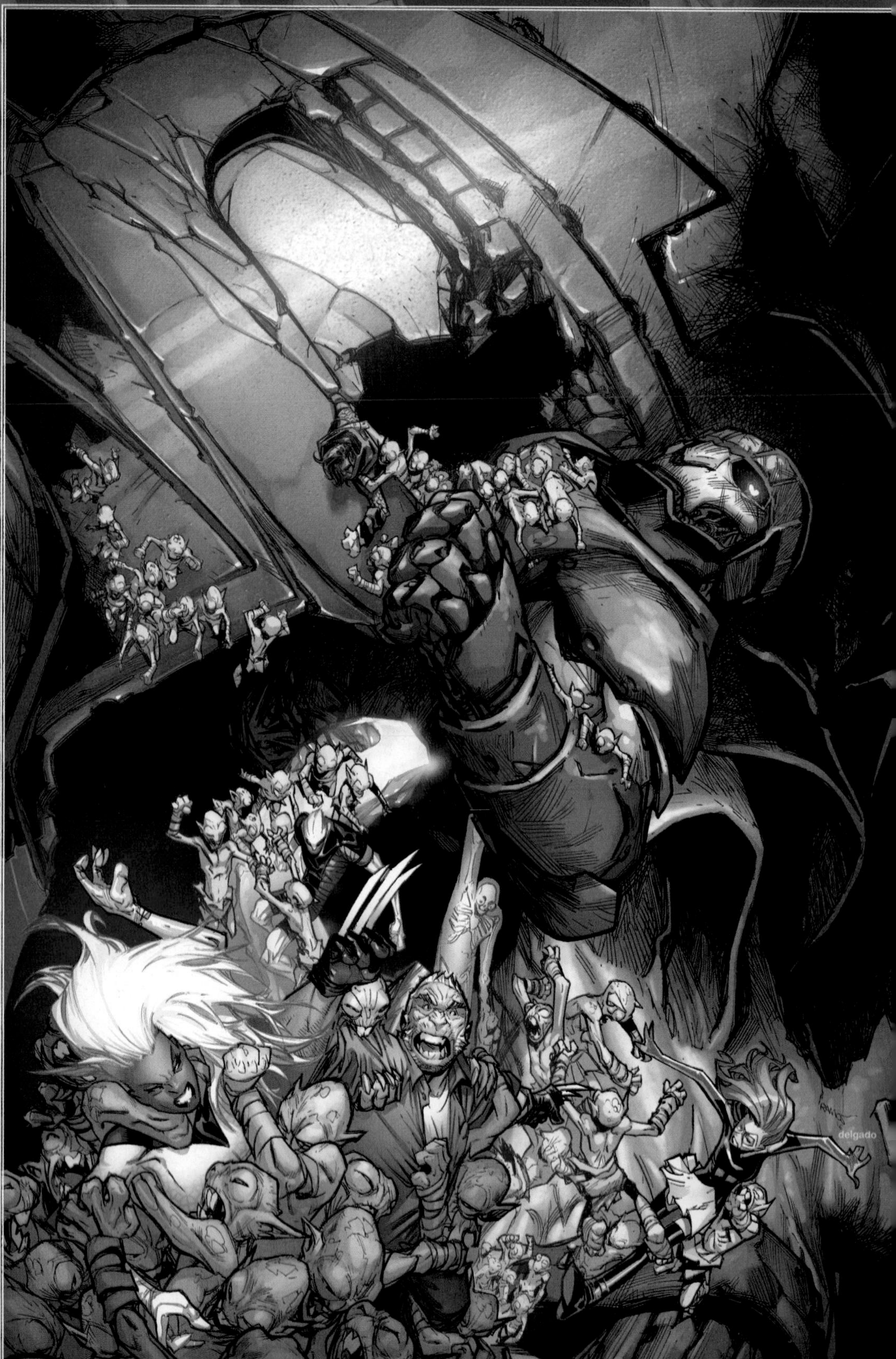
delgado

10

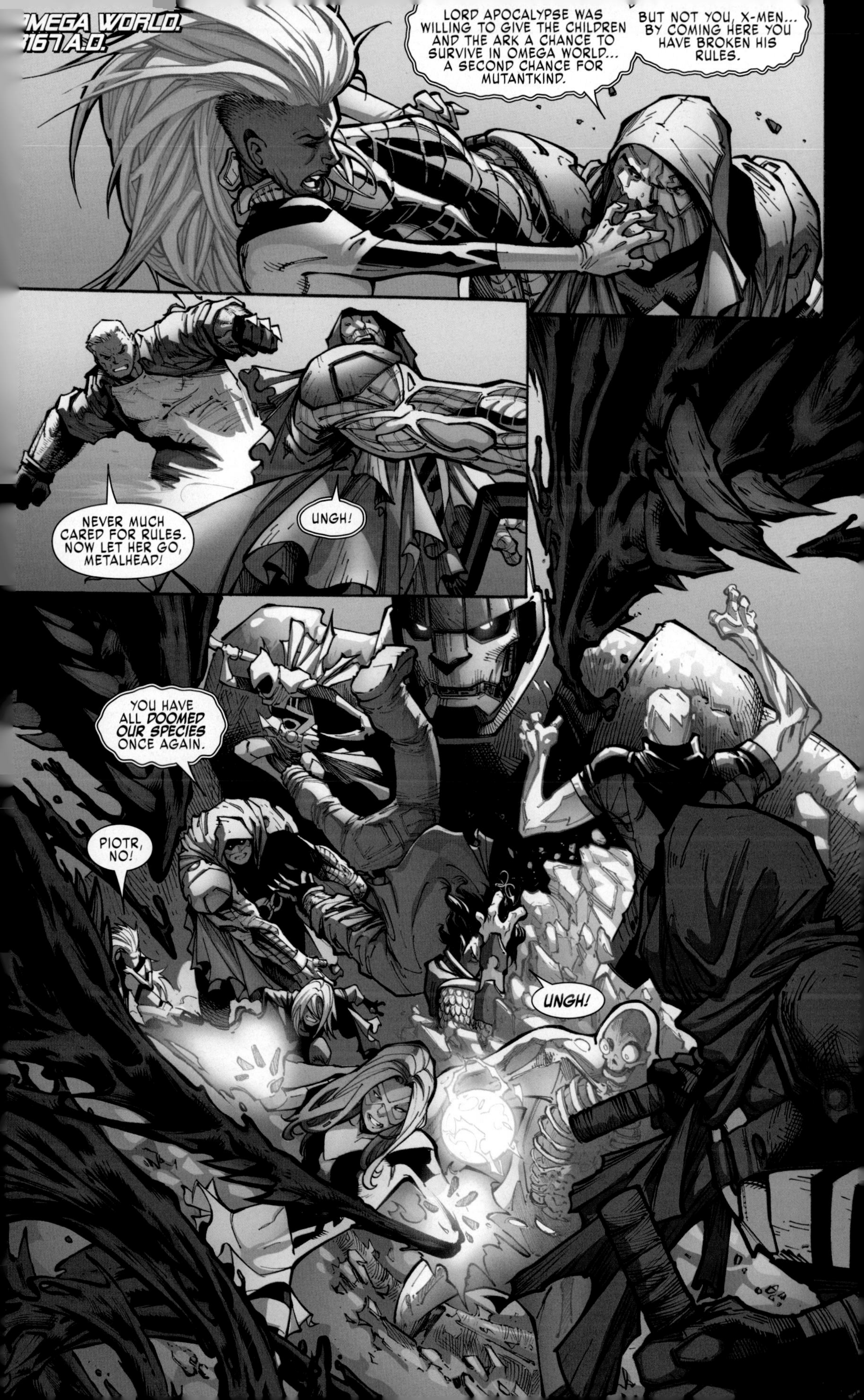
OMEGA WORLD.
3167 A.D.
LORD APOCALYPSE WAS WILLING TO GIVE THE CHILDREN AND THE ARK A CHANCE TO SURVIVE IN OMEGA WORLD... A SECOND CHANCE FOR MUTANTKIND.
BUT NOT YOU, X-MEN... BY COMING HERE YOU HAVE BROKEN HIS RULES.
NEVER MUCH CARED FOR RULES. NOW LET HER GO, METALHEAD!
UNGH!
YOU HAVE ALL *DOOMED OUR SPECIES* ONCE AGAIN.
PIOTR, NO!
UNGH!

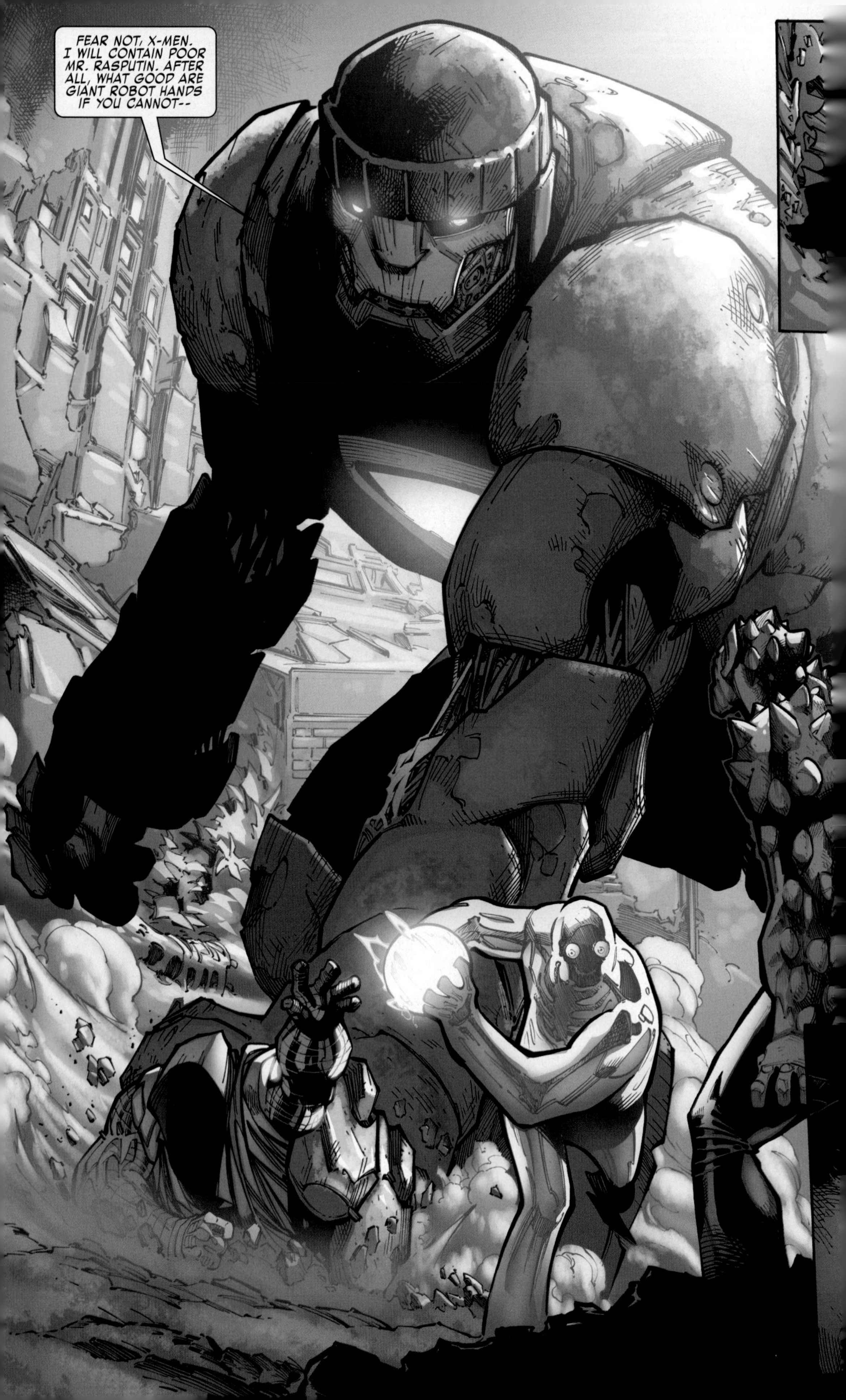
FEAR NOT, X-MEN. I WILL CONTAIN POOR MR. RASPUTIN. AFTER ALL, WHAT GOOD ARE GIANT ROBOT HANDS IF YOU CANNOT--

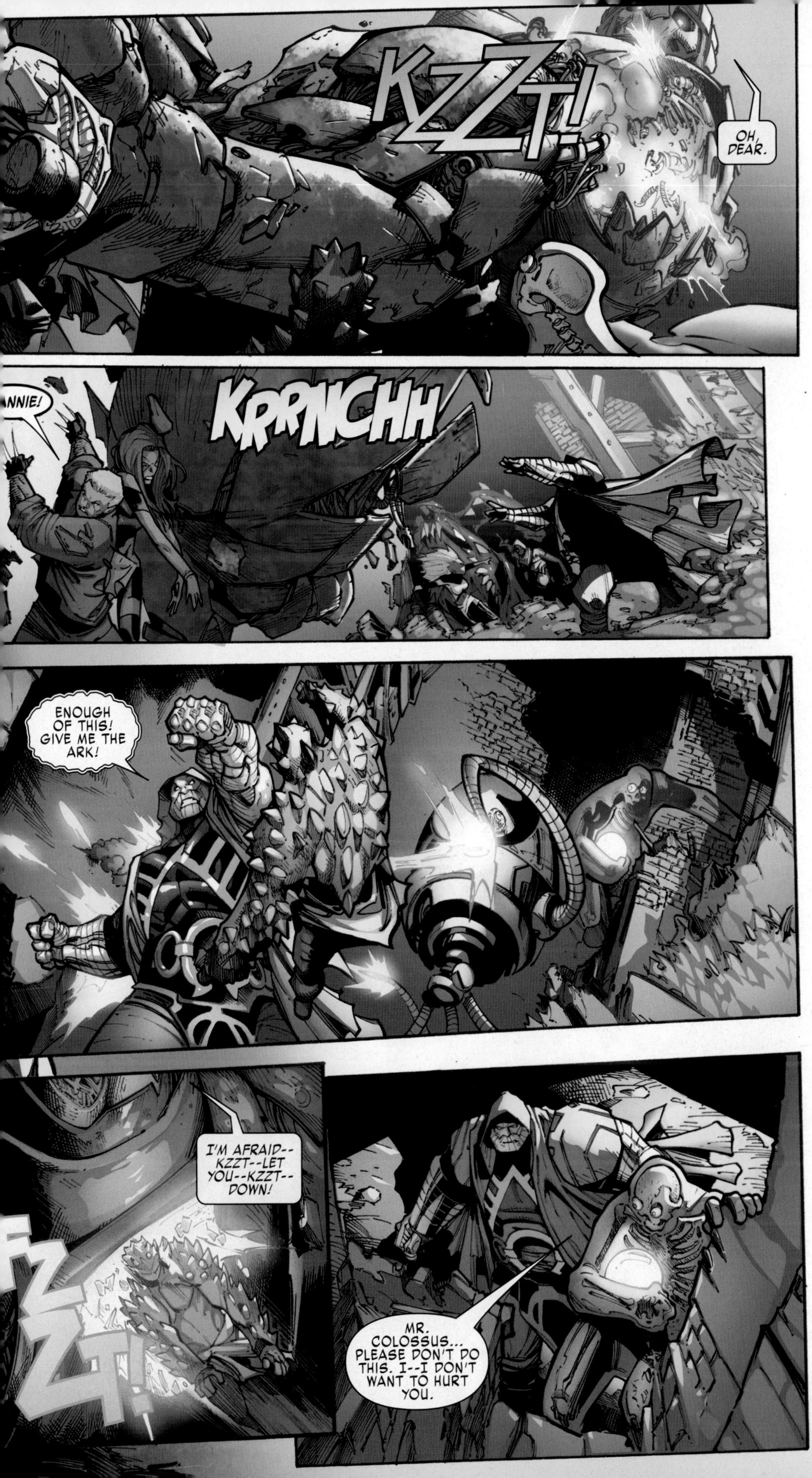
KZZT!
OH, DEAR.
ANNIE!
KRRNCHH
ENOUGH OF THIS! GIVE ME THE ARK!
I'M AFRAID--KZZT--LET YOU--KZZT--DOWN!
FZZT!
MR. COLOSSUS... PLEASE DON'T DO THIS. I--I DON'T WANT TO HURT YOU.

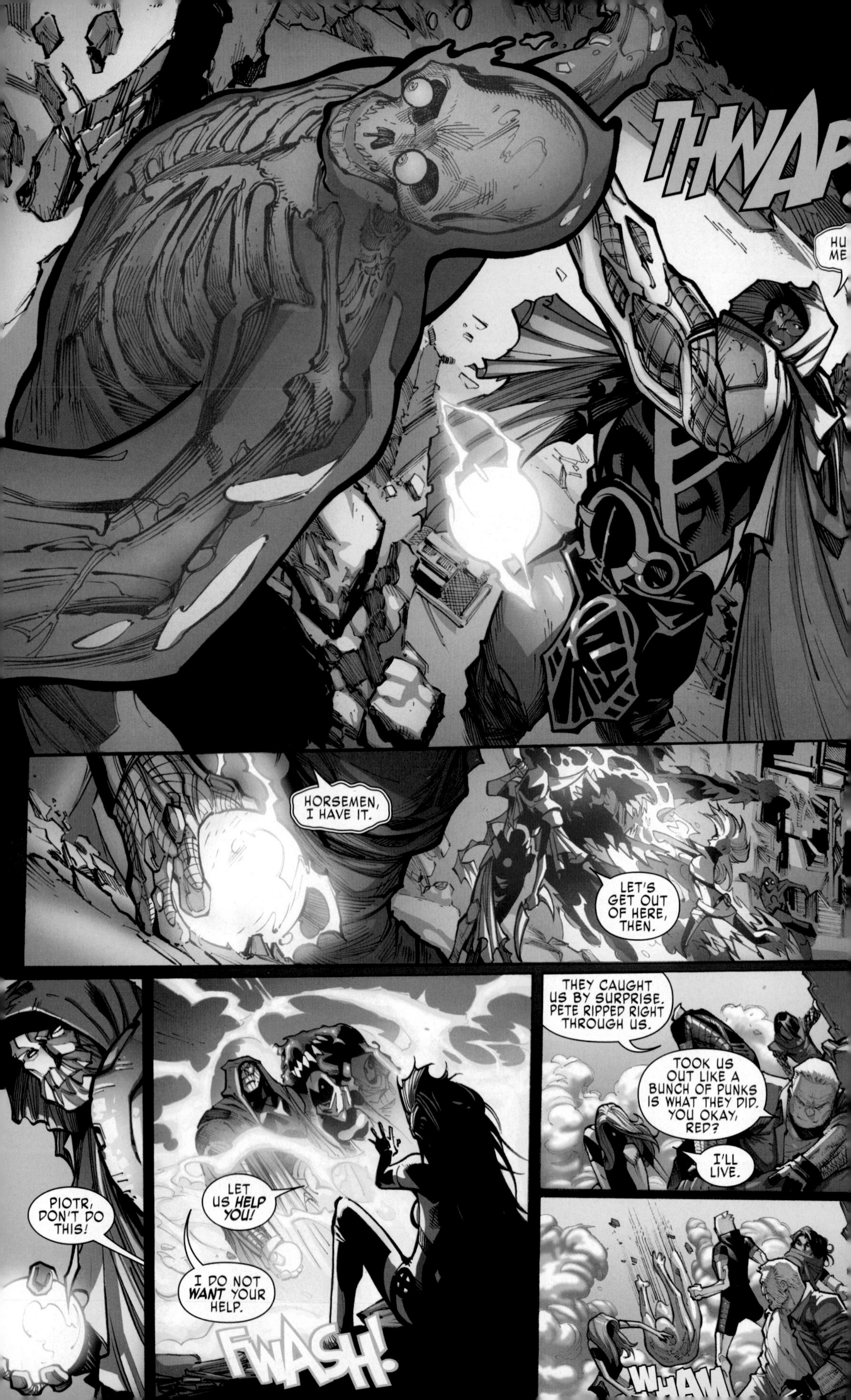
THWAP
HU
ME
HORSEMEN, I HAVE IT.
LET'S GET OUT OF HERE, THEN.
PIOTR, DON'T DO THIS!
LET US HELP YOU!
I DO NOT WANT YOUR HELP.
FWASH!
THEY CAUGHT US BY SURPRISE. PETE RIPPED RIGHT THROUGH US.
TOOK US OUT LIKE A BUNCH OF PUNKS IS WHAT THEY DID. YOU OKAY, RED?
I'LL LIVE.
WHAM

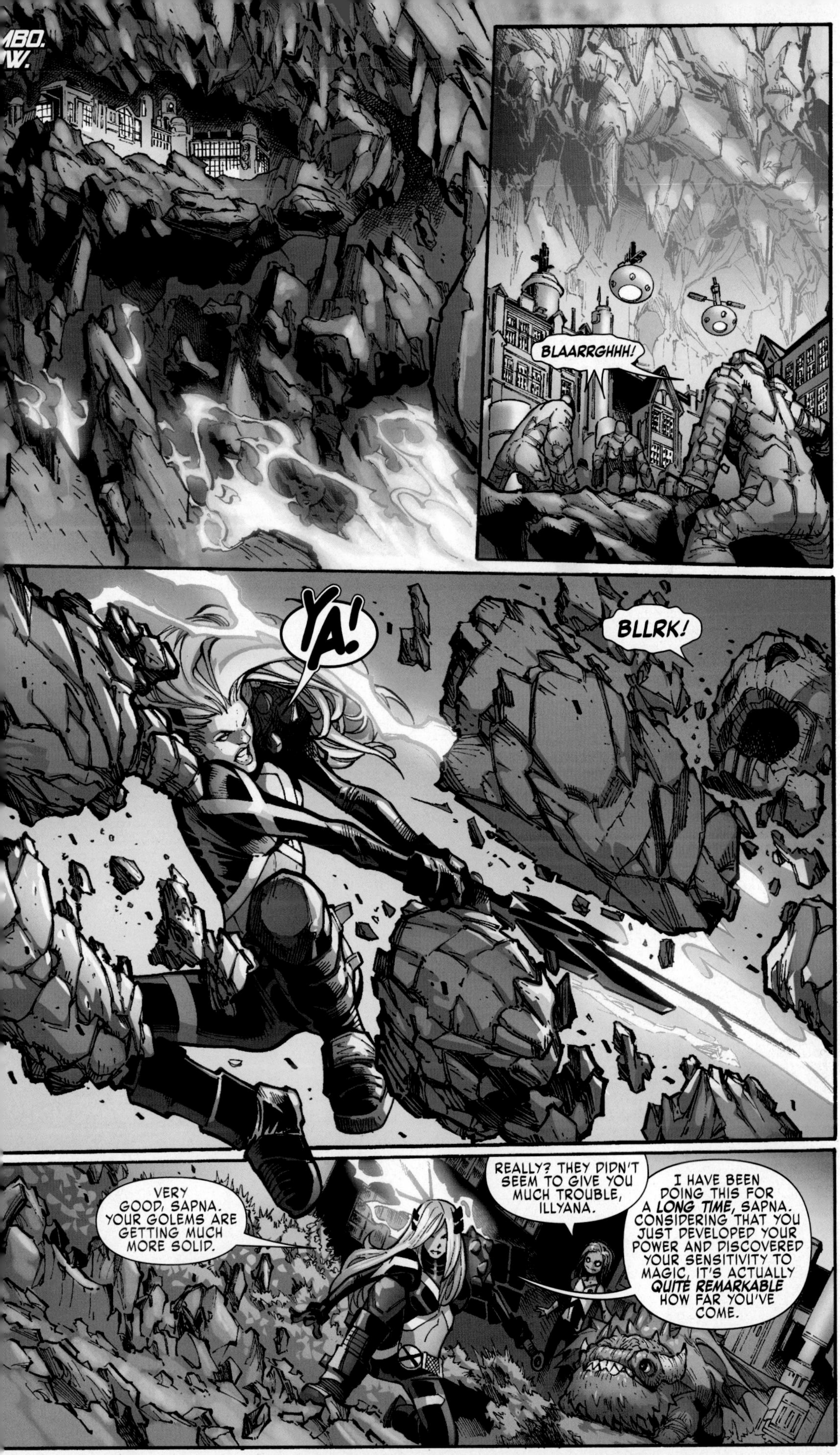
BLAARRGHHH!
YA!
BLLRK!
VERY GOOD, SAPNA. YOUR GOLEMS ARE GETTING MUCH MORE SOLID.
REALLY? THEY DIDN'T SEEM TO GIVE YOU MUCH TROUBLE, ILLYANA.
I HAVE BEEN DOING THIS FOR A LONG TIME, SAPNA. CONSIDERING THAT YOU JUST DEVELOPED YOUR POWER AND DISCOVERED YOUR SENSITIVITY TO MAGIC, IT'S ACTUALLY QUITE REMARKABLE HOW FAR YOU'VE COME.

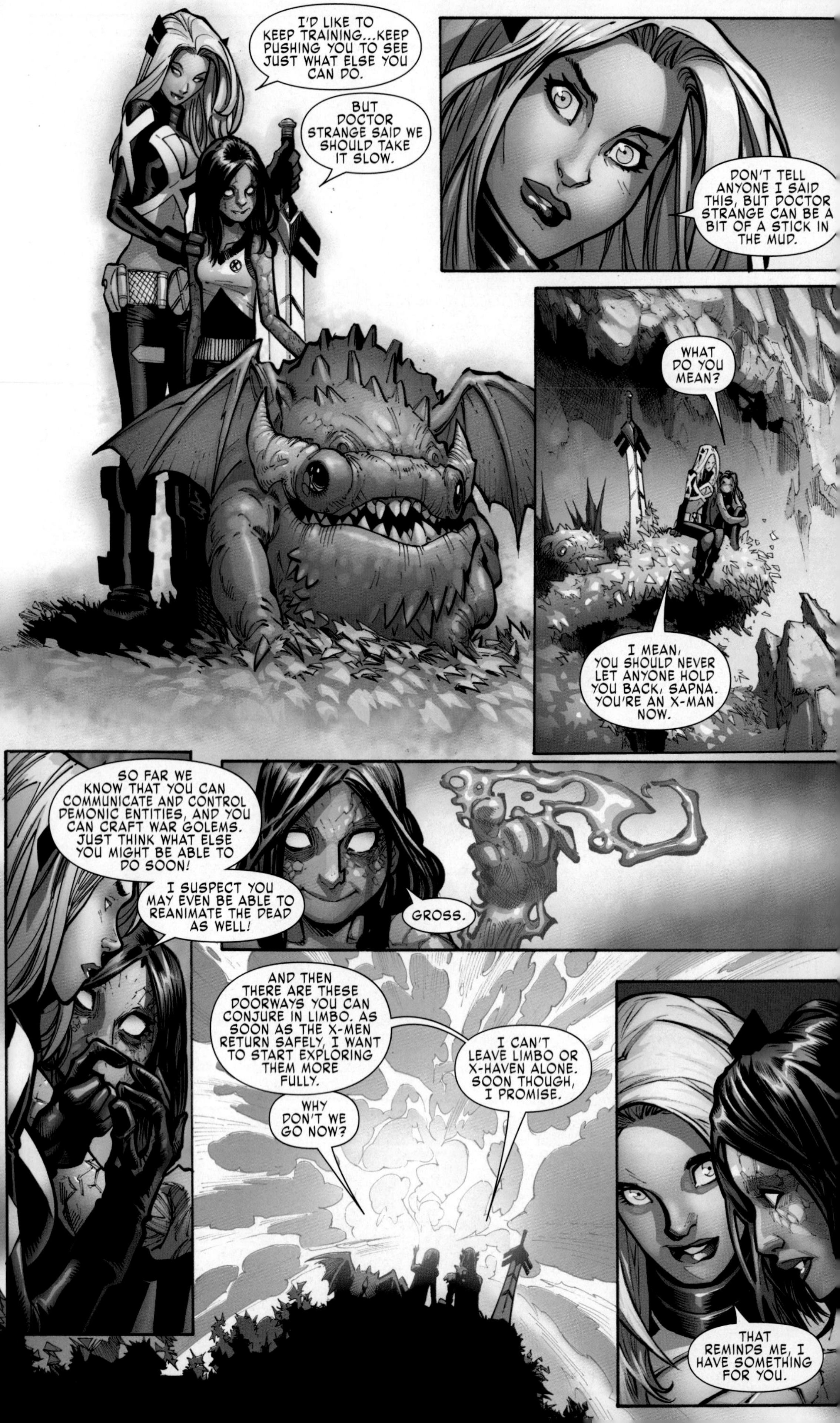
I'D LIKE TO KEEP TRAINING...KEEP PUSHING YOU TO SEE JUST WHAT ELSE YOU CAN DO.
BUT DOCTOR STRANGE SAID WE SHOULD TAKE IT SLOW.
DON'T TELL ANYONE I SAID THIS, BUT DOCTOR STRANGE CAN BE A BIT OF A STICK IN THE MUD.
WHAT DO YOU MEAN?
I MEAN, YOU SHOULD NEVER LET ANYONE HOLD YOU BACK, SAPNA. YOU'RE AN X-MAN NOW.
SO FAR WE KNOW THAT YOU CAN COMMUNICATE AND CONTROL DEMONIC ENTITIES, AND YOU CAN CRAFT WAR GOLEMS. JUST THINK WHAT ELSE YOU MIGHT BE ABLE TO DO SOON!
I SUSPECT YOU MAY EVEN BE ABLE TO REANIMATE THE DEAD AS WELL!
GROSS.
AND THEN THERE ARE THESE DOORWAYS YOU CAN CONJURE IN LIMBO. AS SOON AS THE X-MEN RETURN SAFELY, I WANT TO START EXPLORING THEM MORE FULLY.
WHY DON'T WE GO NOW?
I CAN'T LEAVE LIMBO OR X-HAVEN ALONE. SOON THOUGH, I PROMISE.
THAT REMINDS ME, I HAVE SOMETHING FOR YOU.

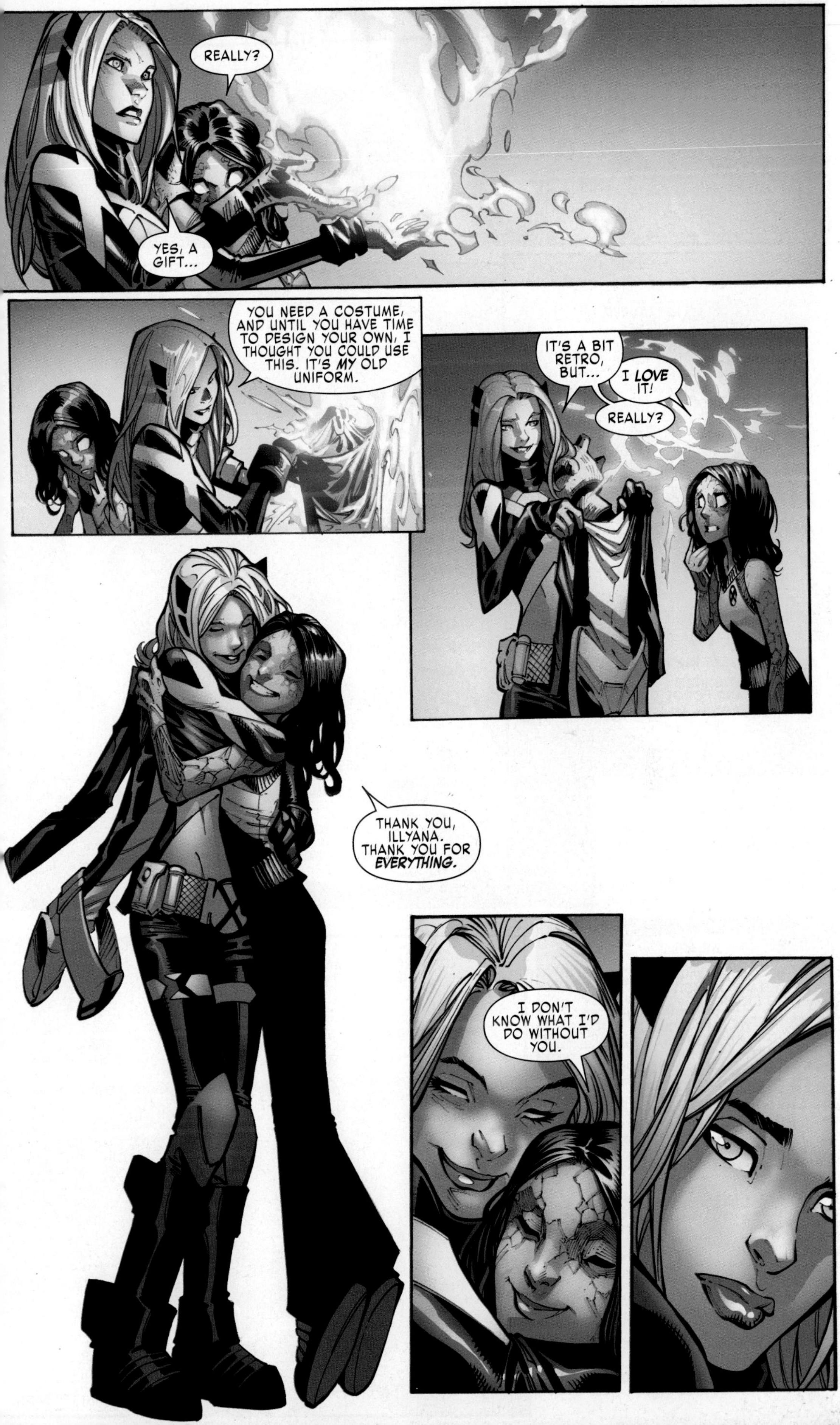
REALLY?
YES, A GIFT...
YOU NEED A COSTUME, AND UNTIL YOU HAVE TIME TO DESIGN YOUR OWN, I THOUGHT YOU COULD USE THIS. IT'S MY OLD UNIFORM.
IT'S A BIT RETRO, BUT...
I LOVE IT!
REALLY?
THANK YOU, ILLYANA. THANK YOU FOR EVERYTHING.
I DON'T KNOW WHAT I'D DO WITHOUT YOU.

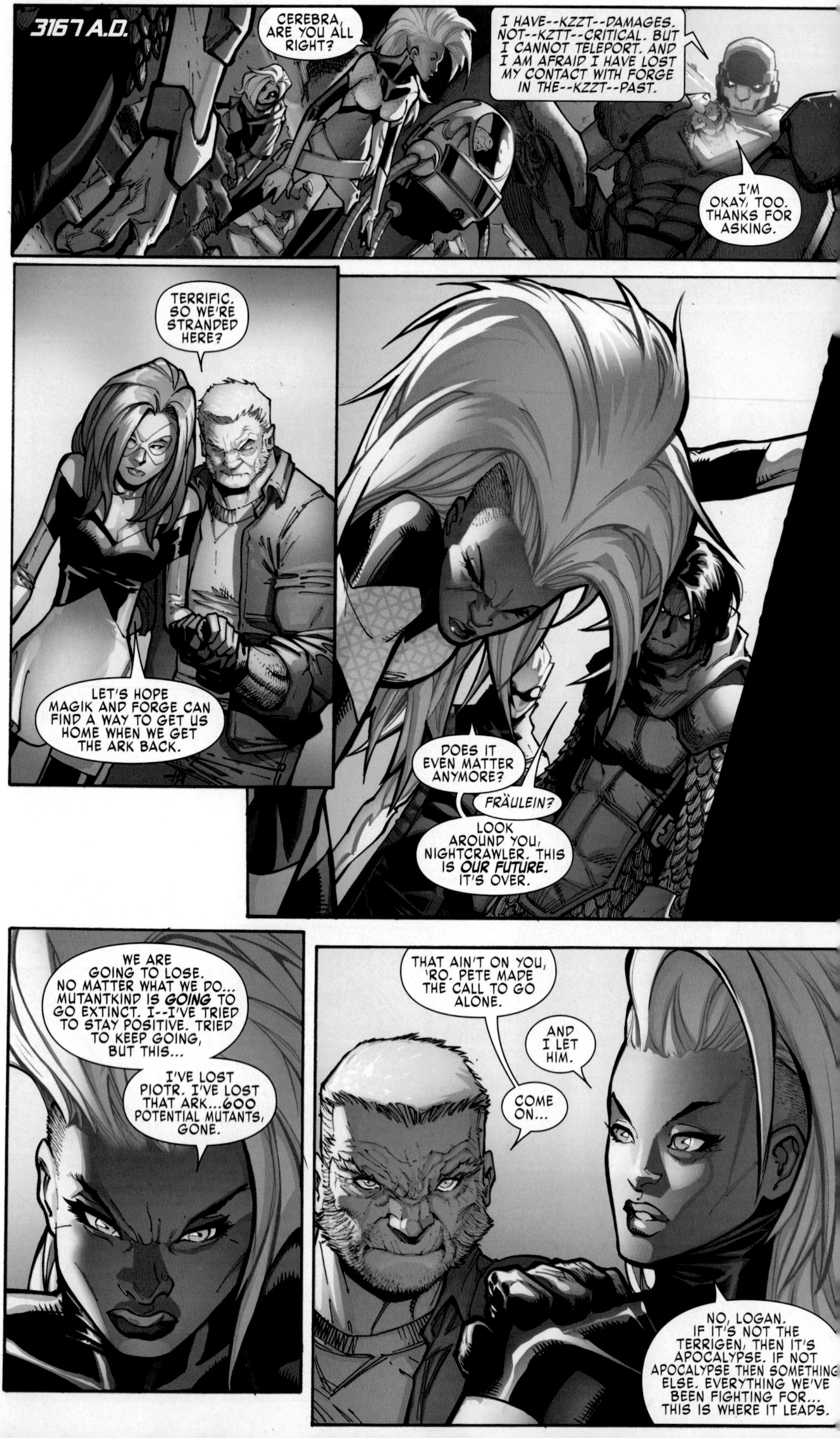

3167 A.D.
CEREBRA, ARE YOU ALL RIGHT?
I HAVE--KZZT--DAMAGES. NOT--KZTT--CRITICAL. BUT I CANNOT TELEPORT. AND I AM AFRAID I HAVE LOST MY CONTACT WITH FORGE IN THE--KZZT--PAST.
I'M OKAY, TOO. THANKS FOR ASKING.
TERRIFIC. SO WE'RE STRANDED HERE?
LET'S HOPE MAGIK AND FORGE CAN FIND A WAY TO GET US HOME WHEN WE GET THE ARK BACK.
DOES IT EVEN MATTER ANYMORE?
FRÄULEIN?
LOOK AROUND YOU, NIGHTCRAWLER. THIS IS OUR FUTURE. IT'S OVER.
WE ARE GOING TO LOSE. NO MATTER WHAT WE DO... MUTANTKIND IS GOING TO GO EXTINCT. I--I'VE TRIED TO STAY POSITIVE. TRIED TO KEEP GOING, BUT THIS...
I'VE LOST PIOTR. I'VE LOST THAT ARK...600 POTENTIAL MUTANTS, GONE.
THAT AIN'T ON YOU, 'RO. PETE MADE THE CALL TO GO ALONE.
AND I LET HIM.
COME ON...
NO, LOGAN. IF IT'S NOT THE TERRIGEN, THEN IT'S APOCALYPSE. IF NOT APOCALYPSE THEN SOMETHING ELSE. EVERYTHING WE'VE BEEN FIGHTING FOR... THIS IS WHERE IT LEADS.

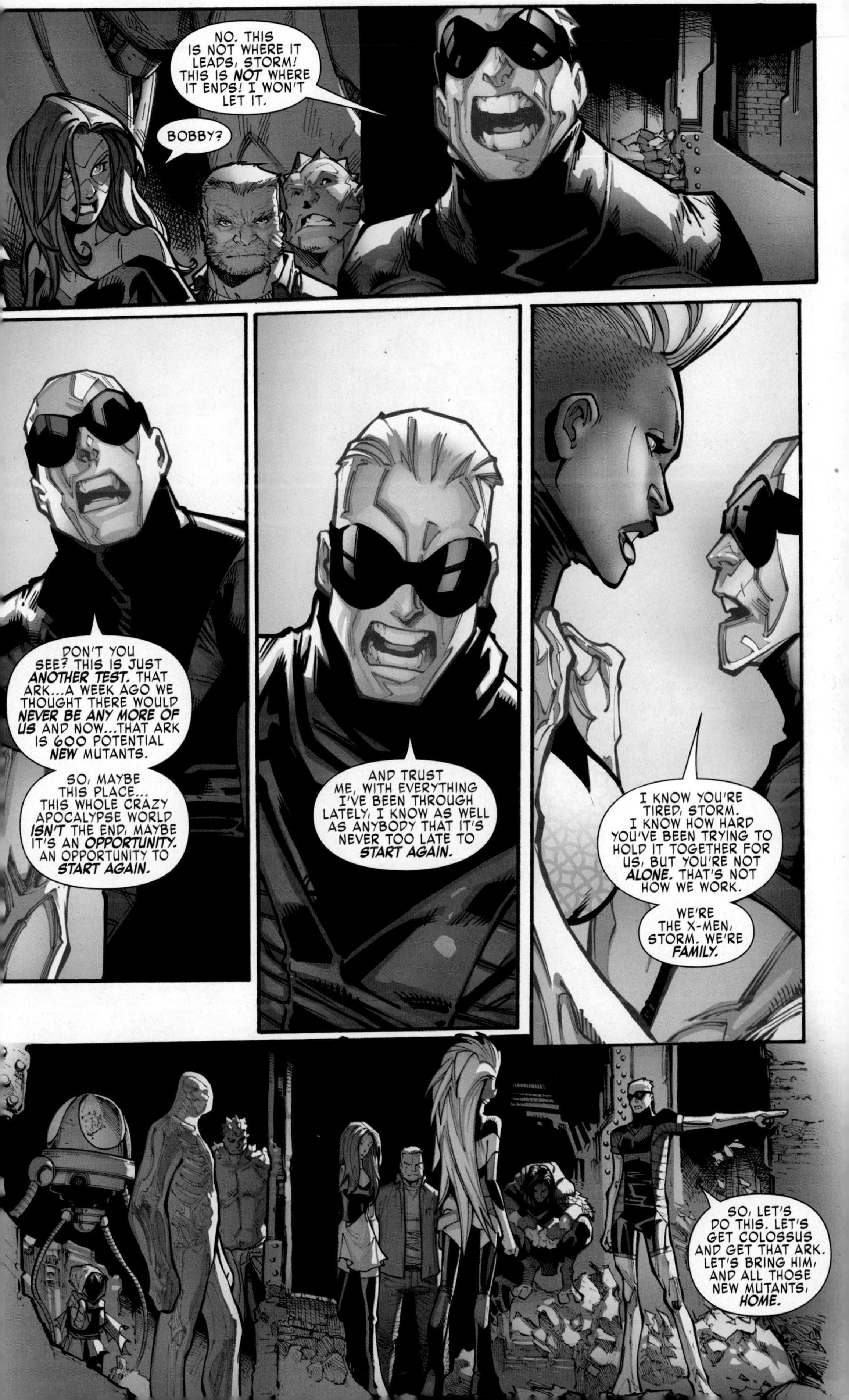

NO. THIS IS NOT WHERE IT LEADS, STORM! THIS IS NOT WHERE IT ENDS! I WON'T LET IT.
BOBBY?
DON'T YOU SEE? THIS IS JUST ANOTHER TEST. THAT ARK...A WEEK AGO WE THOUGHT THERE WOULD NEVER BE ANY MORE OF US AND NOW...THAT ARK IS 600 POTENTIAL NEW MUTANTS.
SO, MAYBE THIS PLACE... THIS WHOLE CRAZY APOCALYPSE WORLD ISN'T THE END, MAYBE IT'S AN OPPORTUNITY. AN OPPORTUNITY TO START AGAIN.
AND TRUST ME, WITH EVERYTHING I'VE BEEN THROUGH LATELY, I KNOW AS WELL AS ANYBODY THAT IT'S NEVER TOO LATE TO START AGAIN.
I KNOW YOU'RE TIRED, STORM. I KNOW HOW HARD YOU'VE BEEN TRYING TO HOLD IT TOGETHER FOR US, BUT YOU'RE NOT ALONE. THAT'S NOT HOW WE WORK.
WE'RE THE X-MEN, STORM. WE'RE FAMILY.
SO, LET'S DO THIS. LET'S GET COLOSSUS AND GET THAT ARK. LET'S BRING HIM, AND ALL THOSE NEW MUTANTS, HOME.

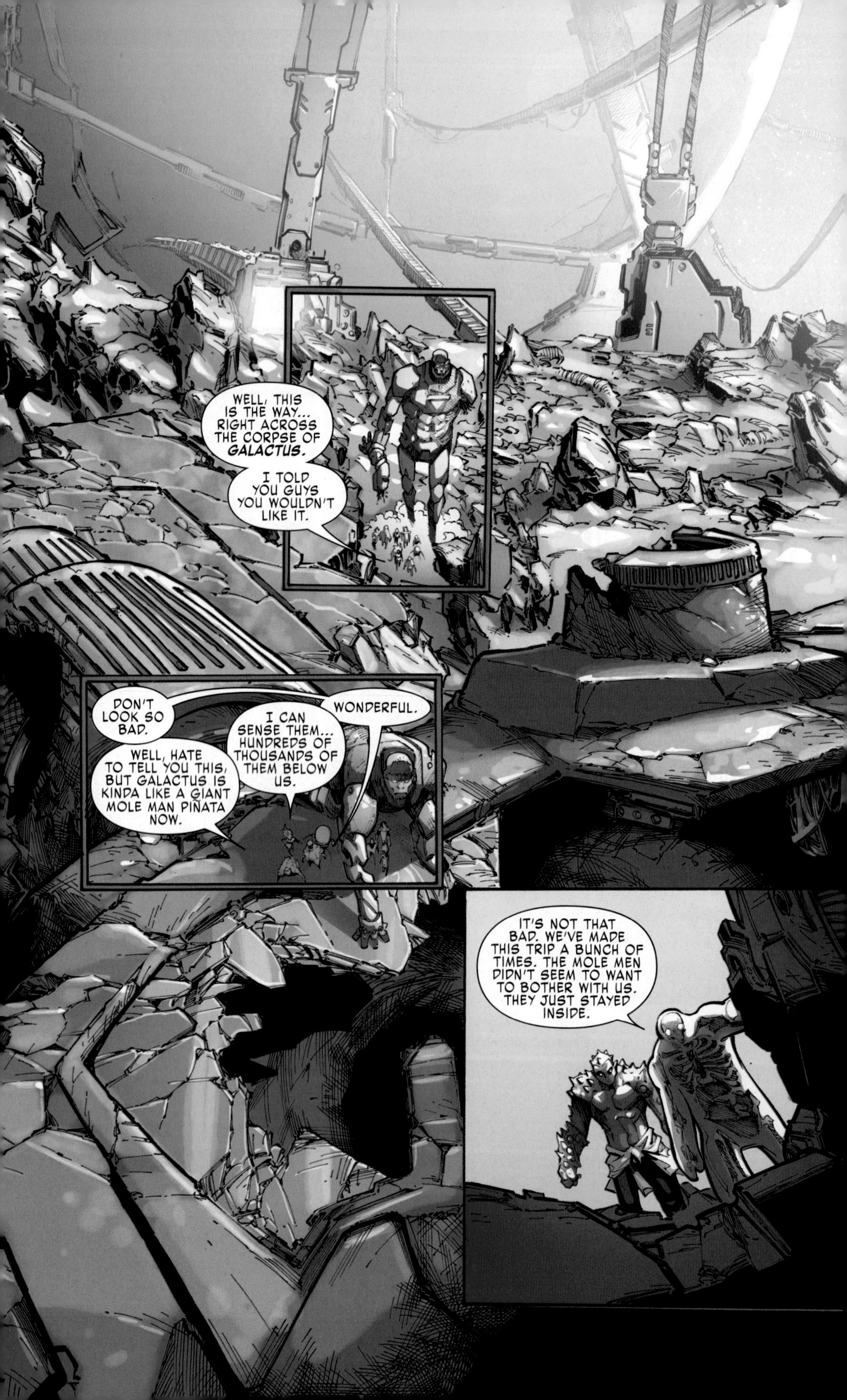
WELL, THIS IS THE WAY... RIGHT ACROSS THE CORPSE OF GALACTUS.
I TOLD YOU GUYS YOU WOULDN'T LIKE IT.
DON'T LOOK SO BAD.
WONDERFUL.
I CAN SENSE THEM... HUNDREDS OF THOUSANDS OF THEM BELOW US.
WELL, HATE TO TELL YOU THIS, BUT GALACTUS IS KINDA LIKE A GIANT MOLE MAN PIÑATA NOW.
IT'S NOT THAT BAD. WE'VE MADE THIS TRIP A BUNCH OF TIMES. THE MOLE MEN DIDN'T SEEM TO WANT TO BOTHER WITH US. THEY JUST STAYED INSIDE.

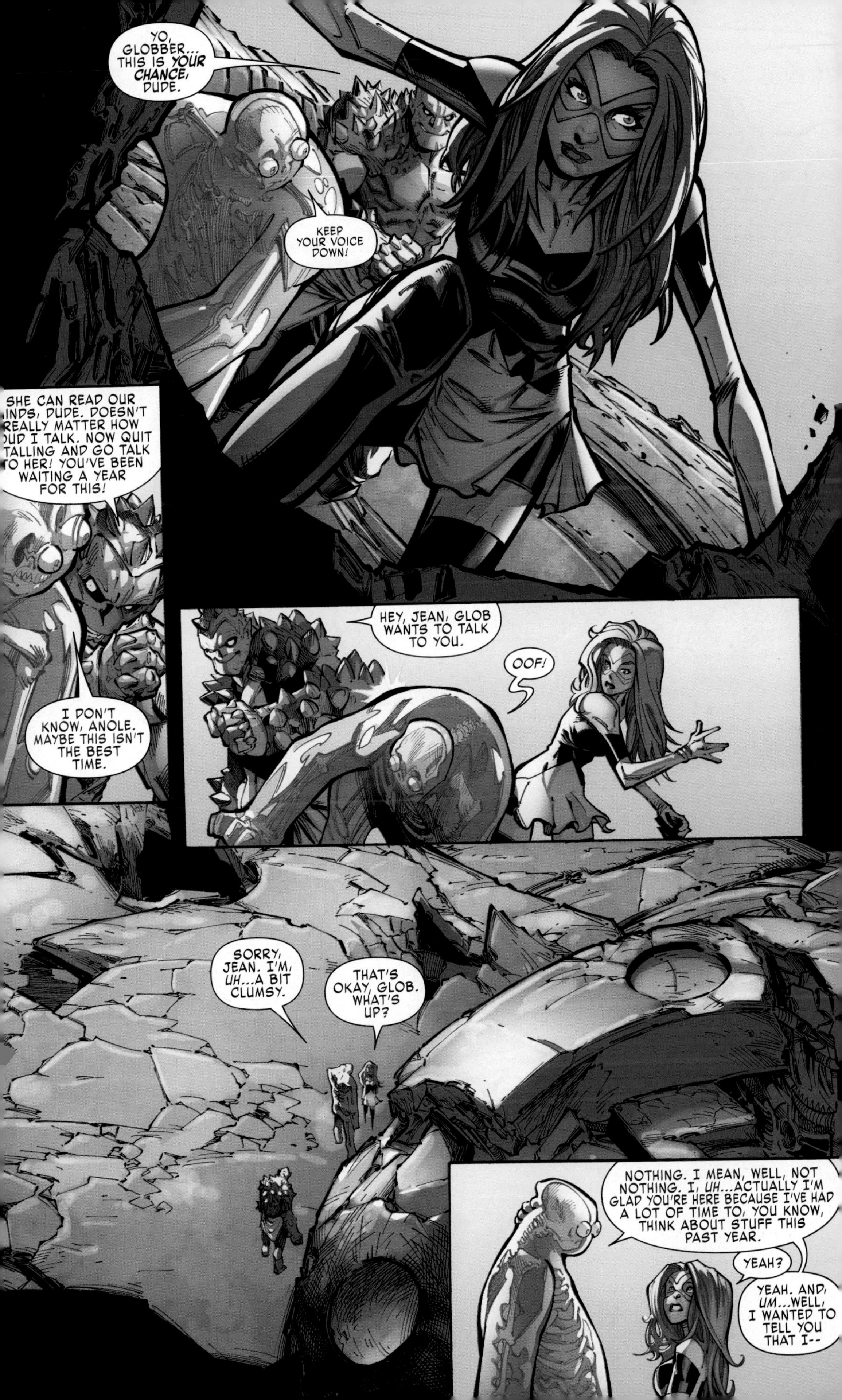

YO, GLOBBER... THIS IS YOUR CHANCE, DUDE.
KEEP YOUR VOICE DOWN!
SHE CAN READ OUR INDS, DUDE. DOESN'T REALLY MATTER HOW OUD I TALK. NOW QUIT TALLING AND GO TALK TO HER! YOU'VE BEEN WAITING A YEAR FOR THIS!
I DON'T KNOW, ANOLE. MAYBE THIS ISN'T THE BEST TIME.
HEY, JEAN, GLOB WANTS TO TALK TO YOU.
OOF!
SORRY, JEAN. I'M, UH...A BIT CLUMSY.
THAT'S OKAY, GLOB. WHAT'S UP?
NOTHING. I MEAN, WELL, NOT NOTHING. I, UH...ACTUALLY I'M GLAD YOU'RE HERE BECAUSE I'VE HAD A LOT OF TIME TO, YOU KNOW, THINK ABOUT STUFF THIS PAST YEAR.
YEAH?
YEAH. AND, UM...WELL, I WANTED TO TELL YOU THAT I--

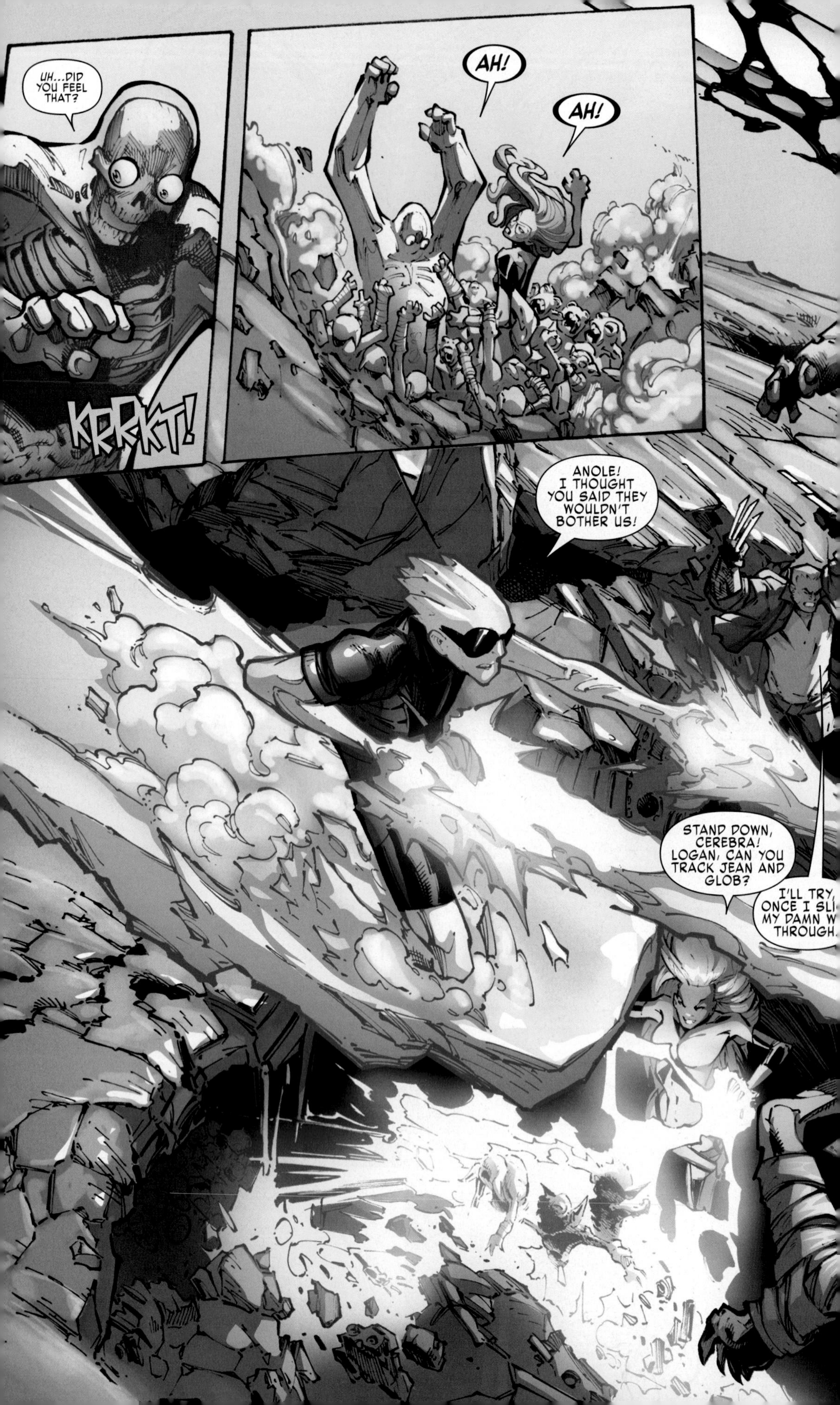
UH...DID YOU FEEL THAT?
AH!
AH!
KRRKT!
ANOLE! I THOUGHT YOU SAID THEY WOULDN'T BOTHER US!
STAND DOWN, CEREBRA! LOGAN, CAN YOU TRACK JEAN AND GLOB?

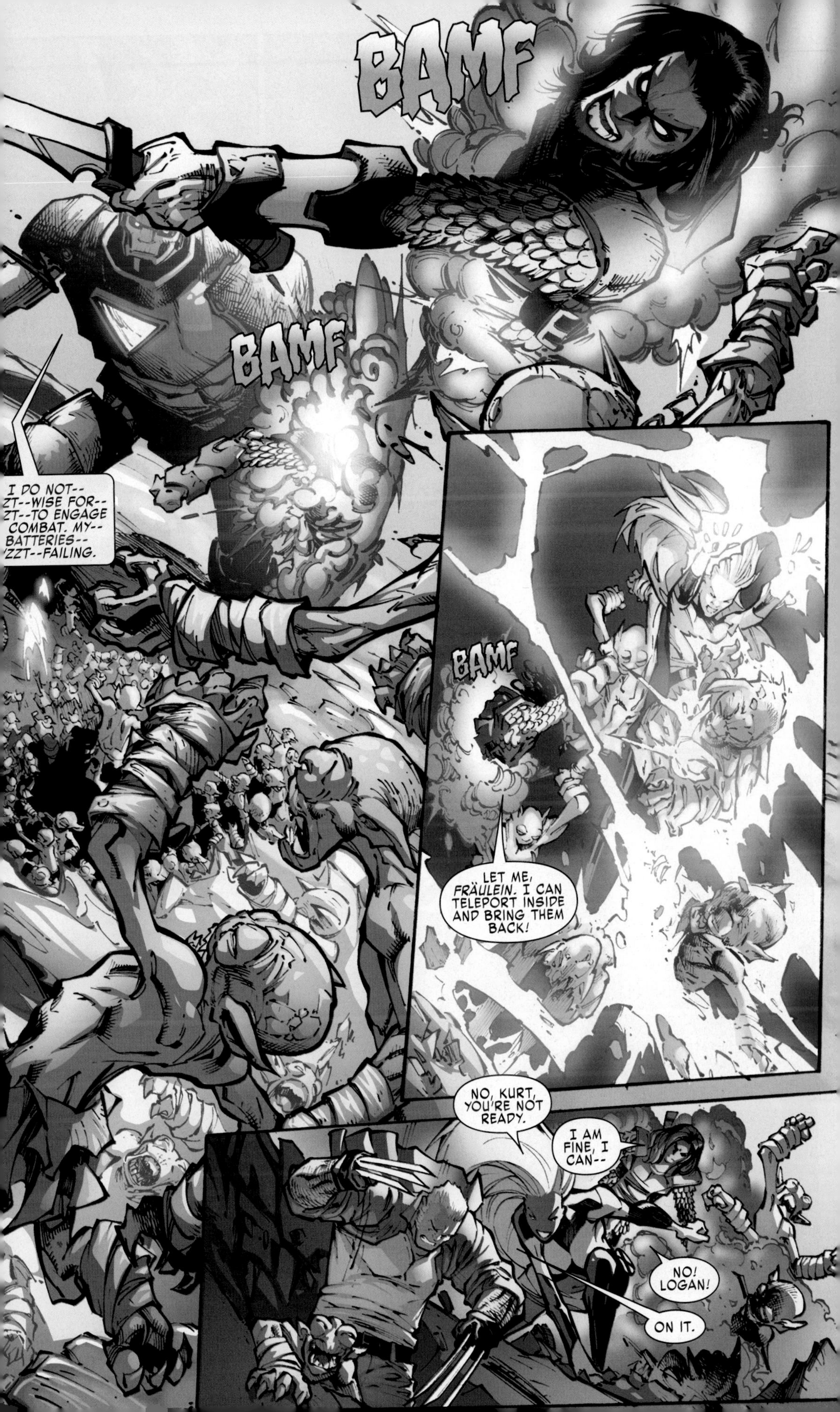
BAMF
BAMF
I DO NOT-- ZT--WISE FOR-- ZT--TO ENGAGE COMBAT. MY-- BATTERIES-- ZZT--FAILING.
BAMF
LET ME, FRÄULEIN. I CAN TELEPORT INSIDE AND BRING THEM BACK!
NO, KURT, YOU'RE NOT READY.
I AM FINE, I CAN--
NO! LOGAN!
ON IT.

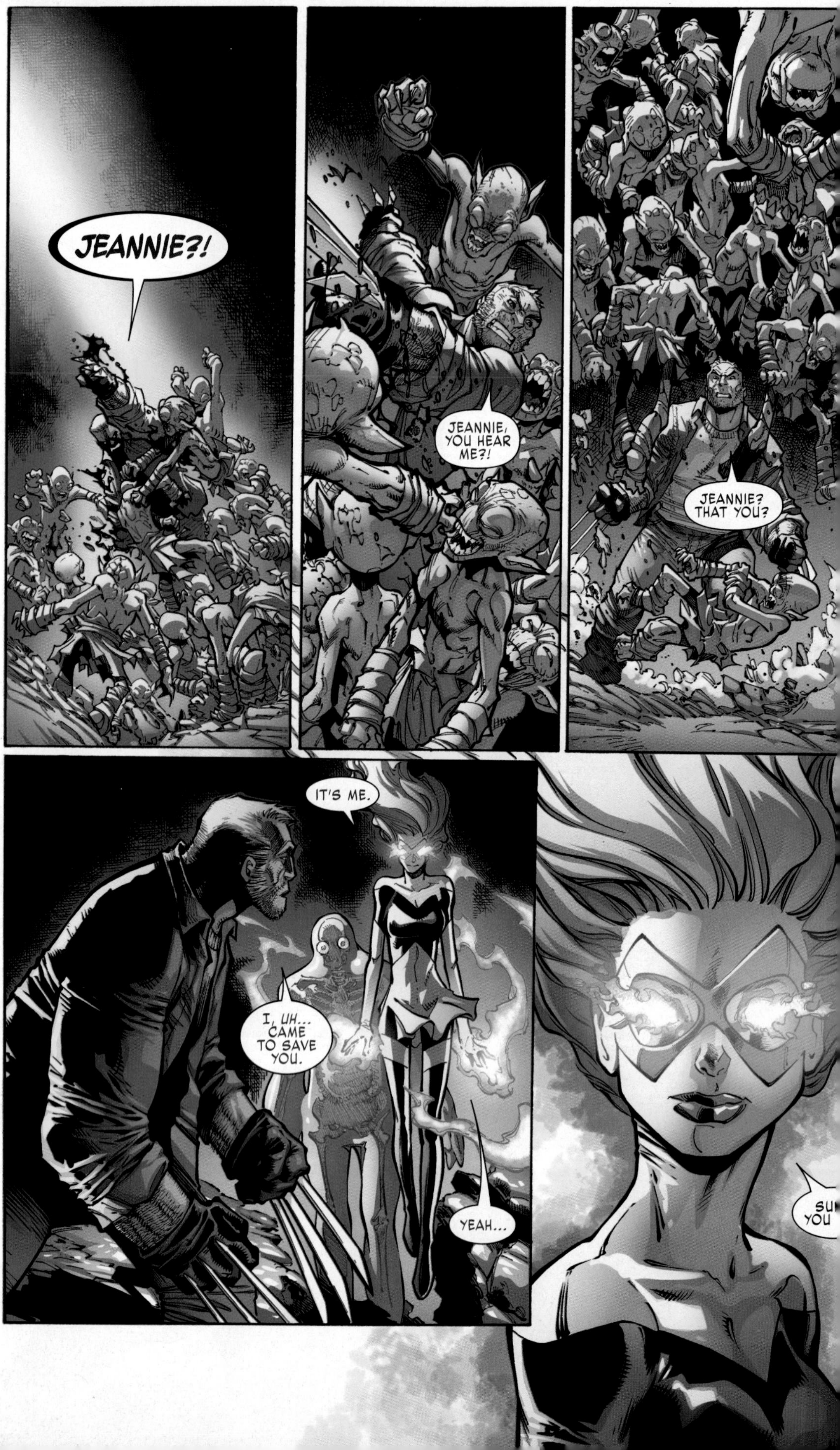
JEANNIE?!
JEANNIE, YOU HEAR ME?!
JEANNIE? THAT YOU?
IT'S ME.
I, UH... CAME TO SAVE YOU.
YEAH...

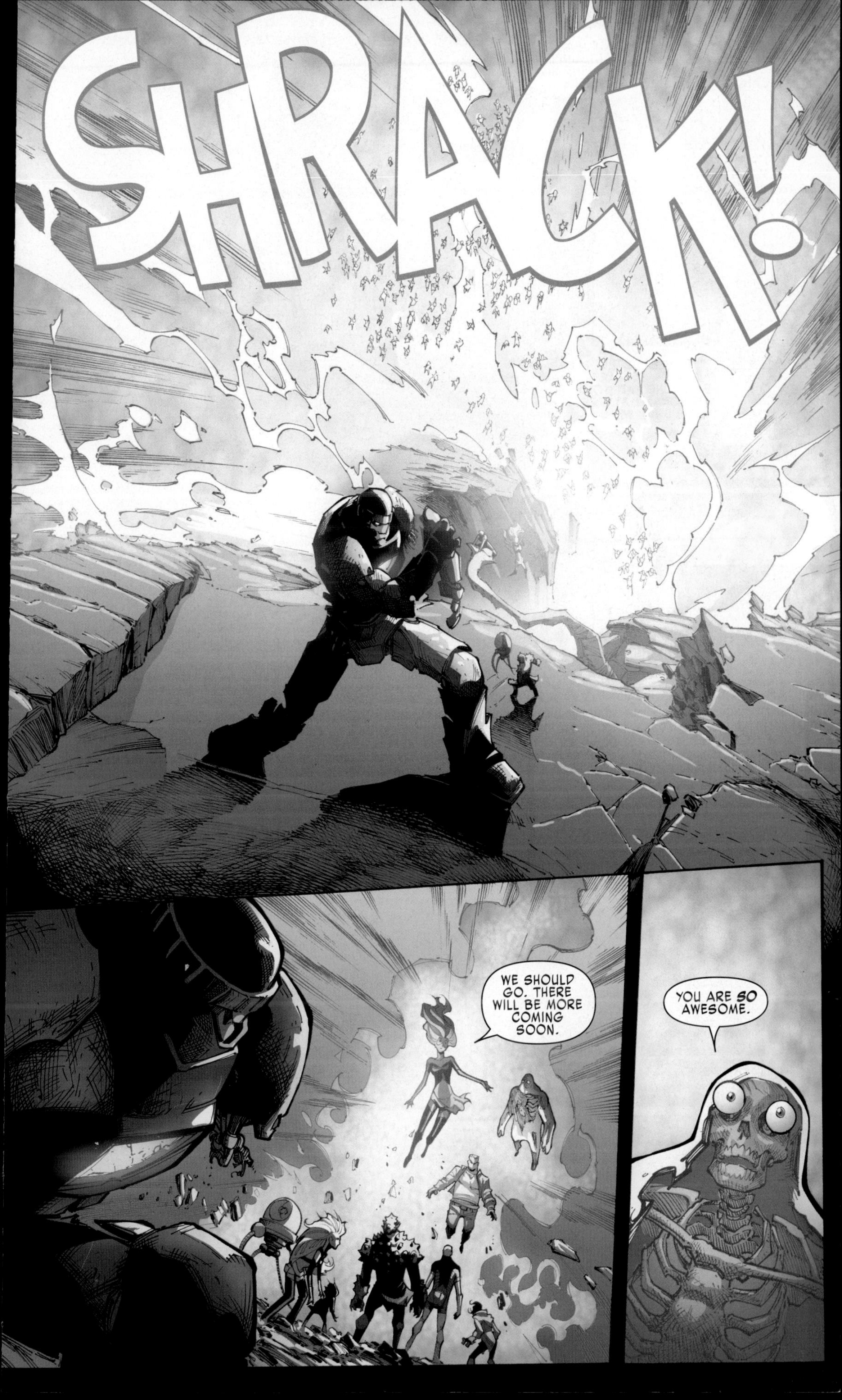
SHRACK!
WE SHOULD GO. THERE WILL BE MORE COMING SOON.
YOU ARE SO AWESOME.

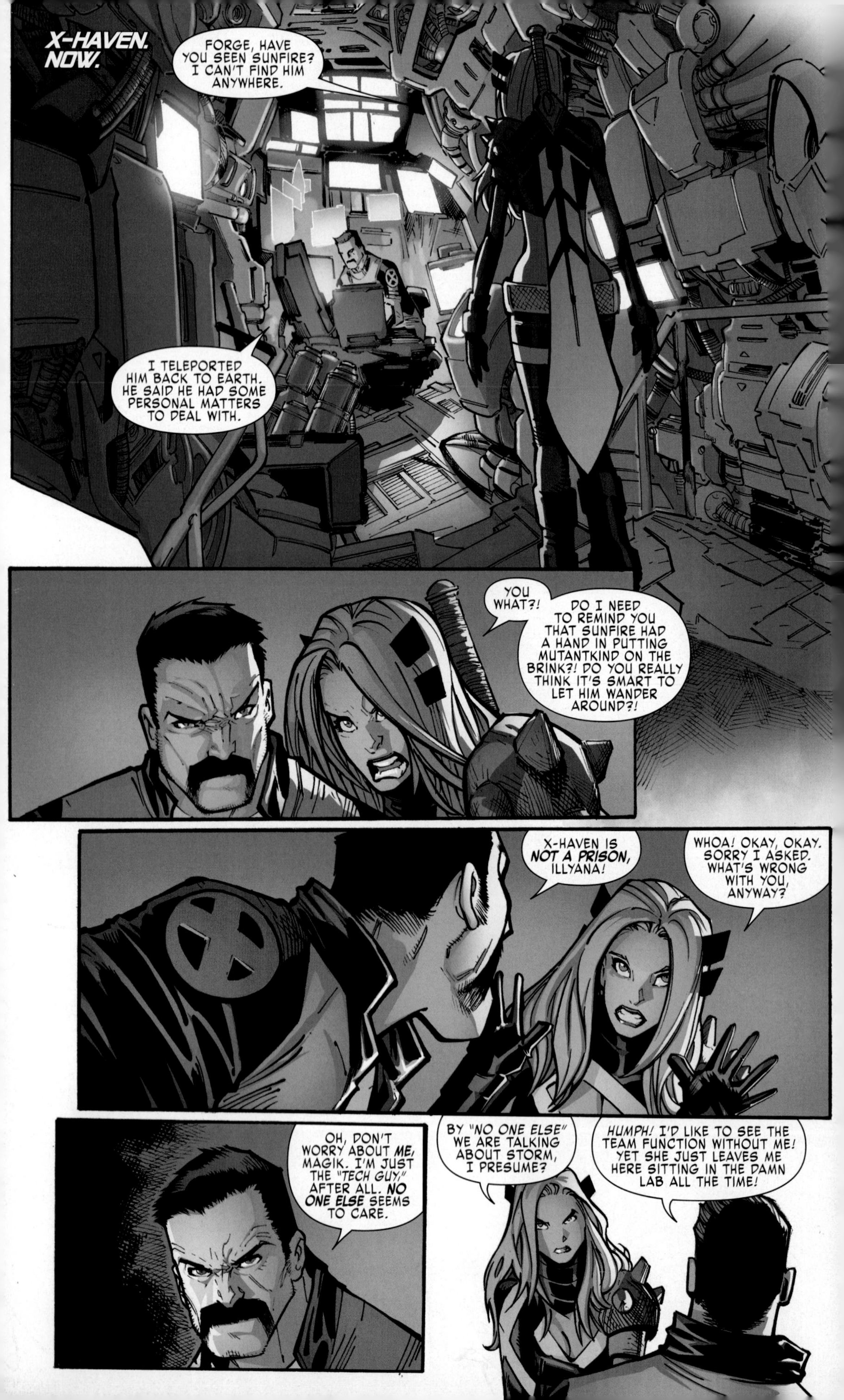
X-HAVEN. NOW.
FORGE, HAVE YOU SEEN SUNFIRE? I CAN'T FIND HIM ANYWHERE.
I TELEPORTED HIM BACK TO EARTH. HE SAID HE HAD SOME PERSONAL MATTERS TO DEAL WITH.
YOU WHAT?!
DO I NEED TO REMIND YOU THAT SUNFIRE HAD A HAND IN PUTTING MUTANTKIND ON THE BRINK?! DO YOU REALLY THINK IT'S SMART TO LET HIM WANDER AROUND?!
X-HAVEN IS NOT A PRISON, ILLYANA!
WHOA! OKAY, OKAY. SORRY I ASKED. WHAT'S WRONG WITH YOU, ANYWAY?
OH, DON'T WORRY ABOUT ME, MAGIK. I'M JUST THE "TECH GUY," AFTER ALL. NO ONE ELSE SEEMS TO CARE.
BY "NO ONE ELSE" WE ARE TALKING ABOUT STORM, I PRESUME?
HUMPH! I'D LIKE TO SEE THE TEAM FUNCTION WITHOUT ME! YET SHE JUST LEAVES ME HERE SITTING IN THE DAMN LAB ALL THE TIME!

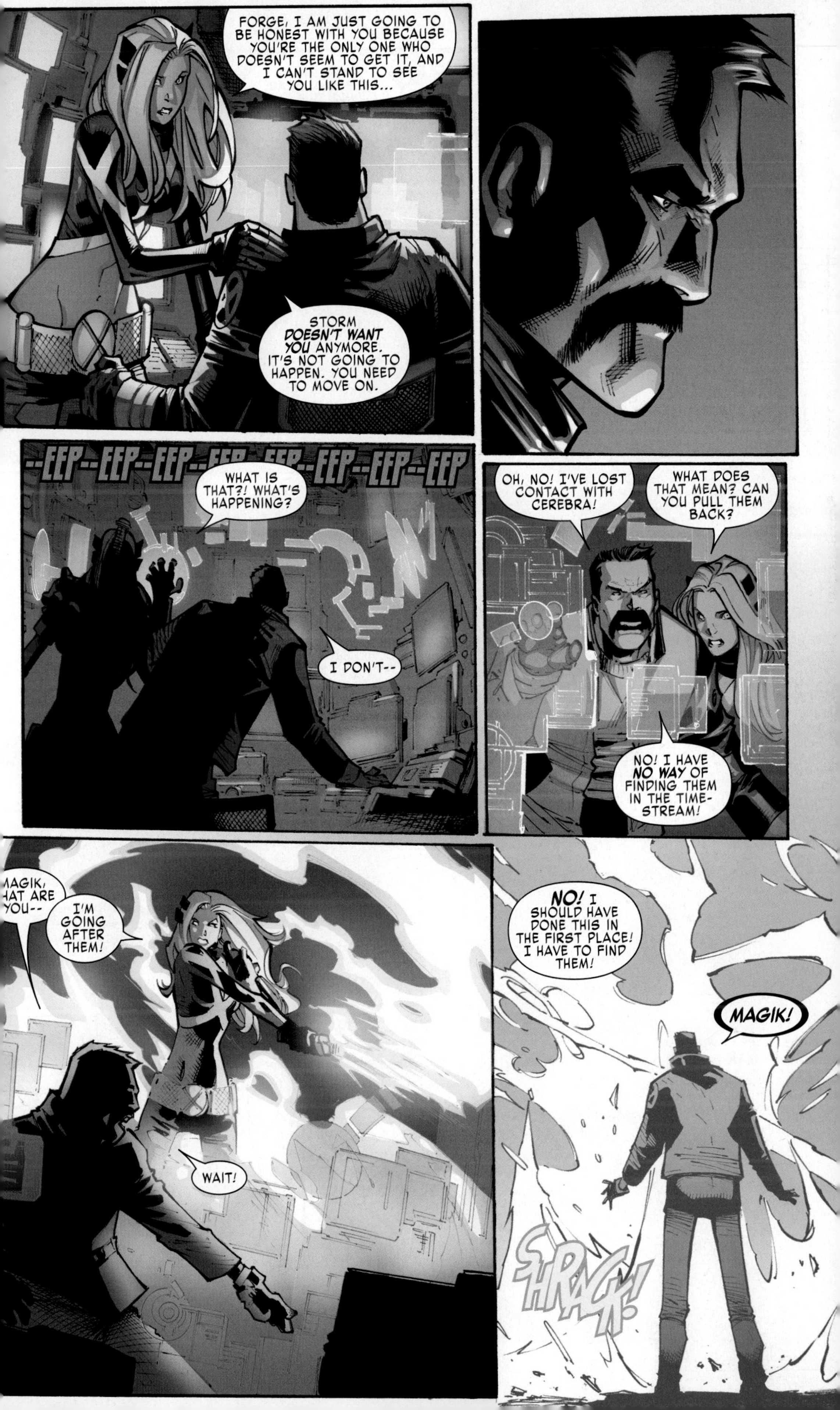
FORGE, I AM JUST GOING TO BE HONEST WITH YOU BECAUSE YOU'RE THE ONLY ONE WHO DOESN'T SEEM TO GET IT, AND I CAN'T STAND TO SEE YOU LIKE THIS...
STORM ***DOESN'T WANT YOU*** ANYMORE. IT'S NOT GOING TO HAPPEN. YOU NEED TO MOVE ON.
--EEP--EEP--EEP--EEP--EEP--EEP--EEP--EEP
WHAT IS THAT?! WHAT'S HAPPENING?
I DON'T--
OH, NO! I'VE LOST CONTACT WITH CEREBRA!
WHAT DOES THAT MEAN? CAN YOU PULL THEM BACK?
NO! I HAVE ***NO WAY*** OF FINDING THEM IN THE TIME-STREAM!
MAGIK, HAT ARE YOU--
I'M GOING AFTER THEM!
WAIT!
NO! I SHOULD HAVE DONE THIS IN THE FIRST PLACE! I HAVE TO FIND THEM!
MAGIK!
SHRACK!

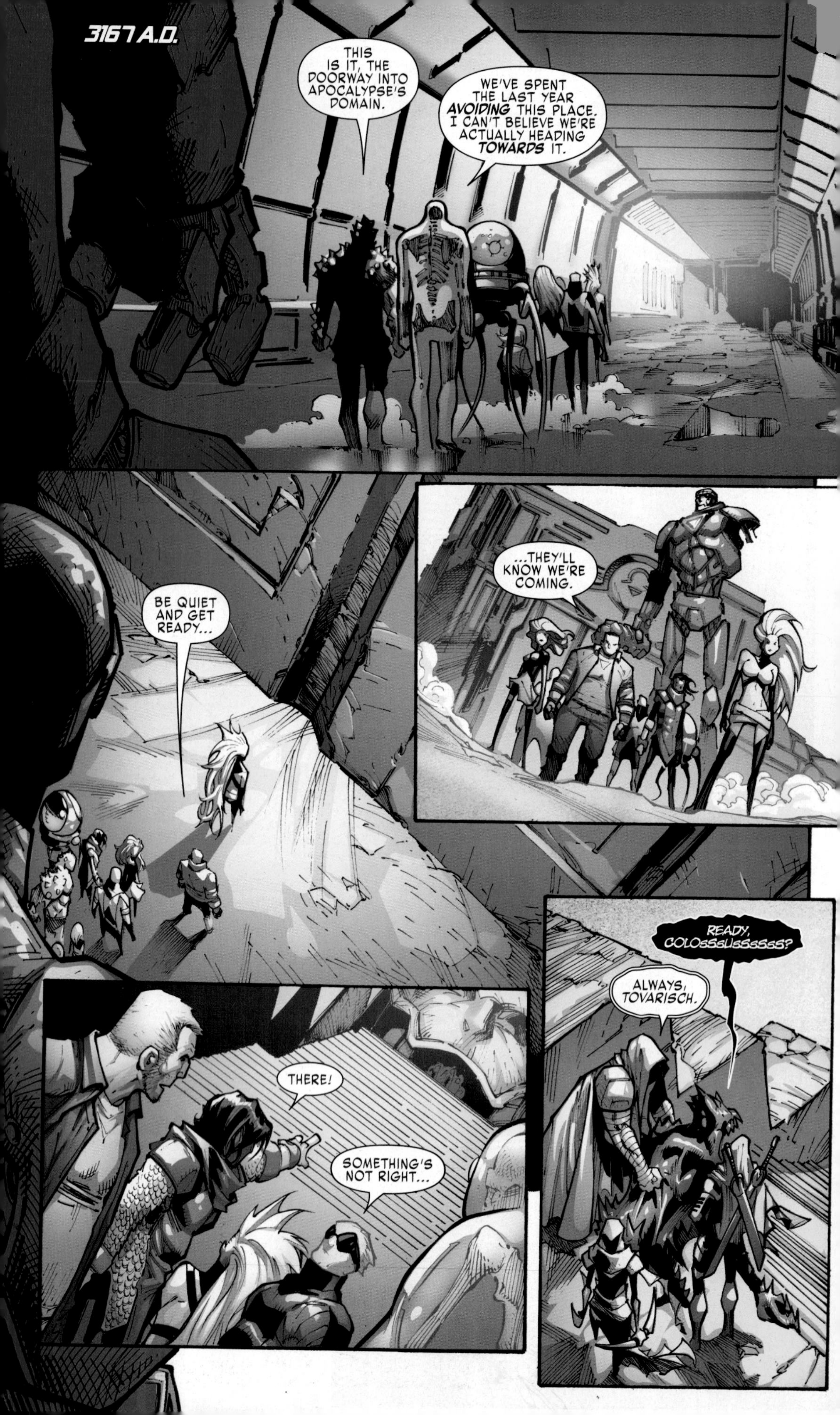
3167 A.D.
THIS IS IT, THE DOORWAY INTO APOCALYPSE'S DOMAIN.
WE'VE SPENT THE LAST YEAR AVOIDING THIS PLACE. I CAN'T BELIEVE WE'RE ACTUALLY HEADING TOWARDS IT.
BE QUIET AND GET READY...
...THEY'LL KNOW WE'RE COMING.
THERE!
SOMETHING'S NOT RIGHT...
READY, COLOSSSUSSSSSS?
ALWAYS, TOVARISCH.

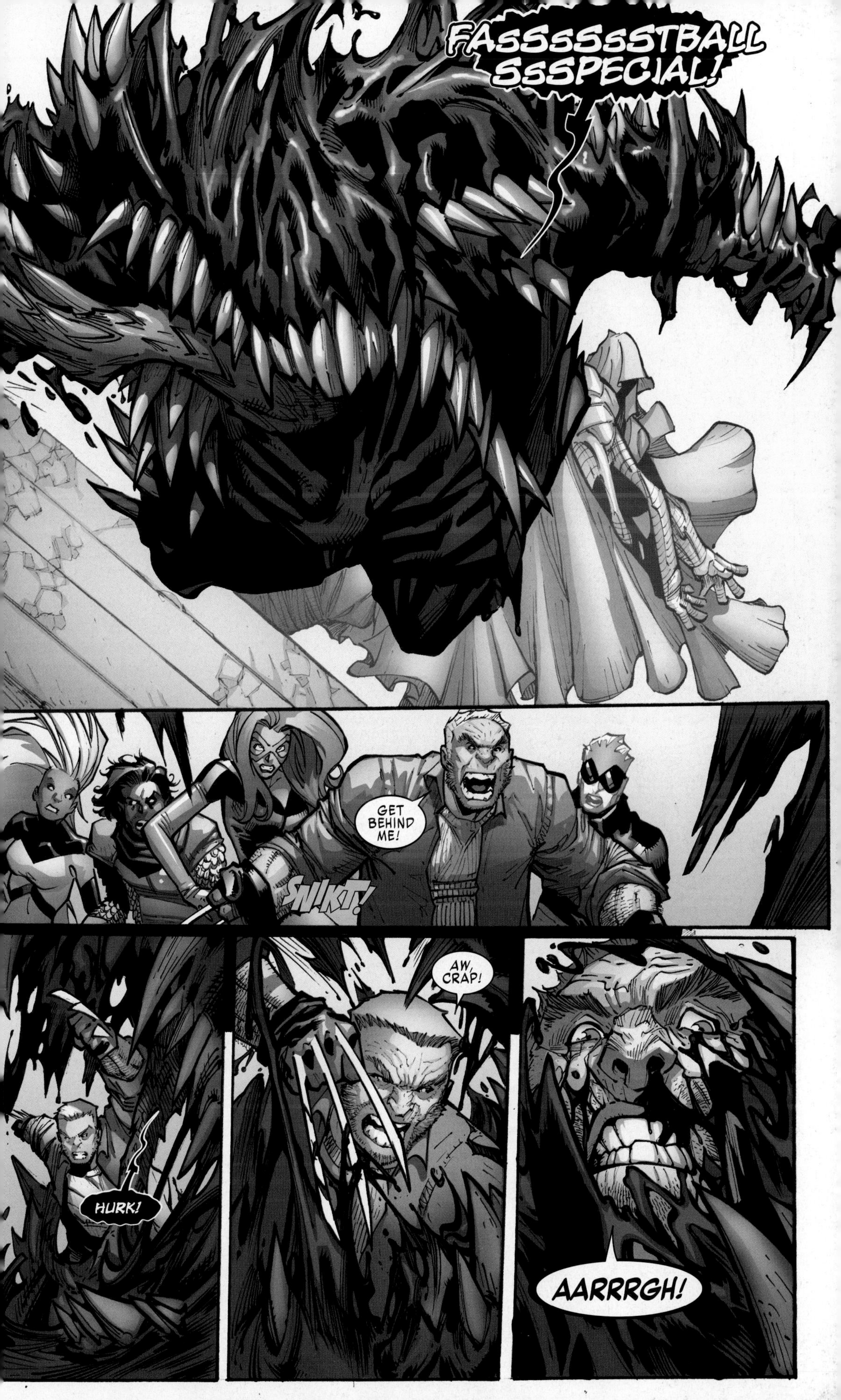

FASSSSSSSTBALL SSSPECIAL!
GET BEHIND ME!
SNIKT!
HURK!
AW, CRAP!
AARRRGH!

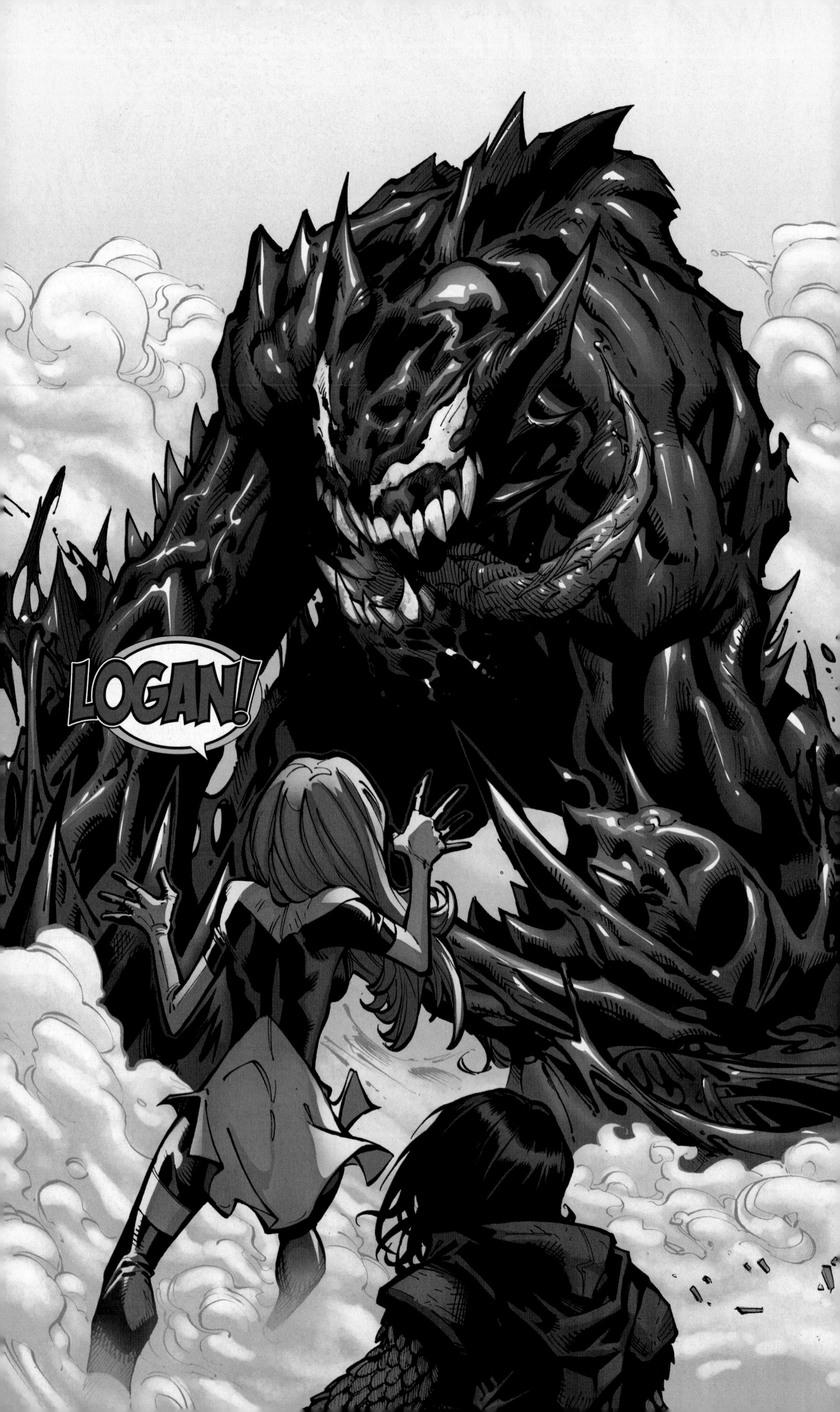
LOGAN!

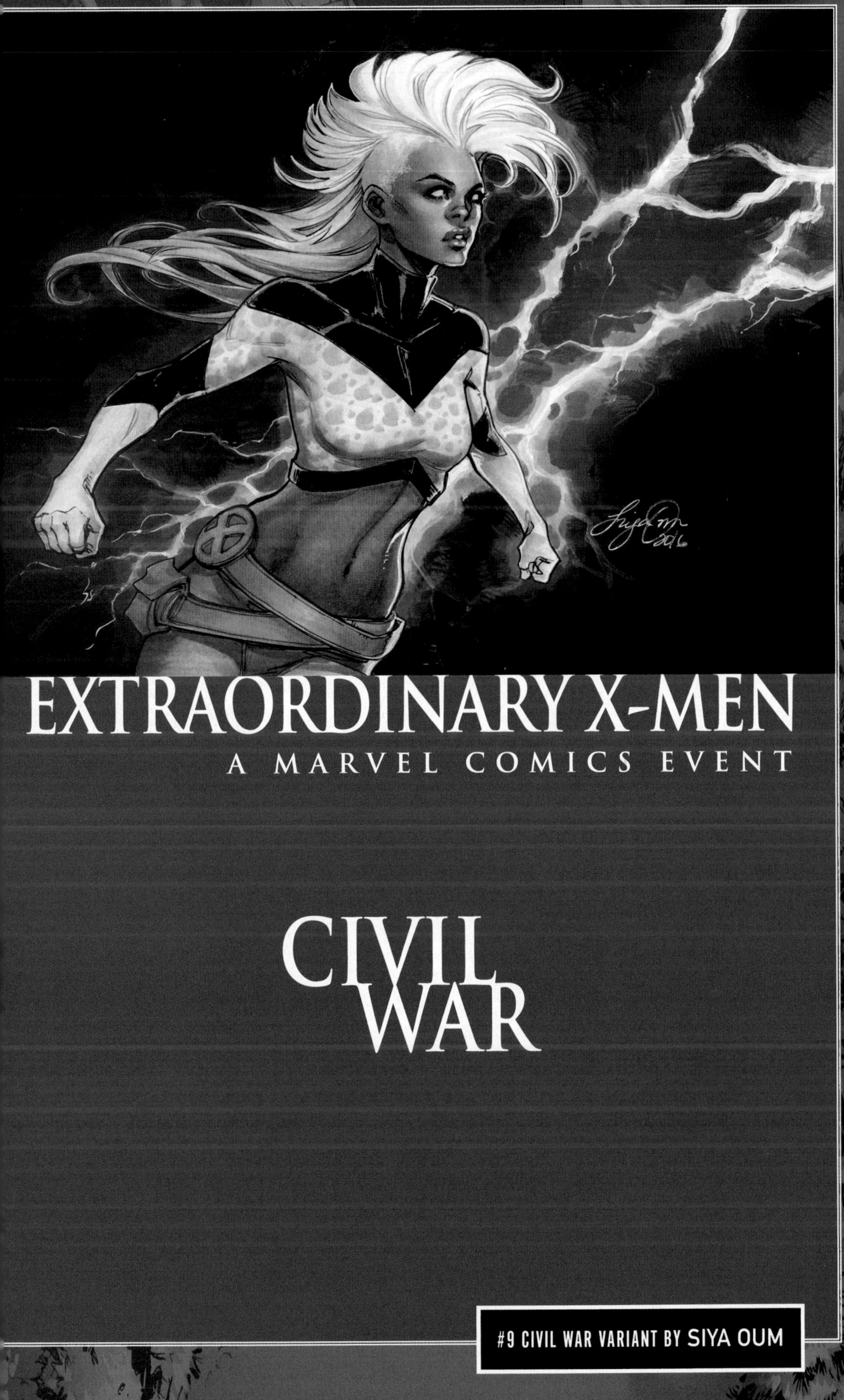
EXTRAORDINARY X-MEN
A MARVEL COMICS EVENT
CIVIL WAR

#9 CIVIL WAR VARIANT BY SIYA OUM

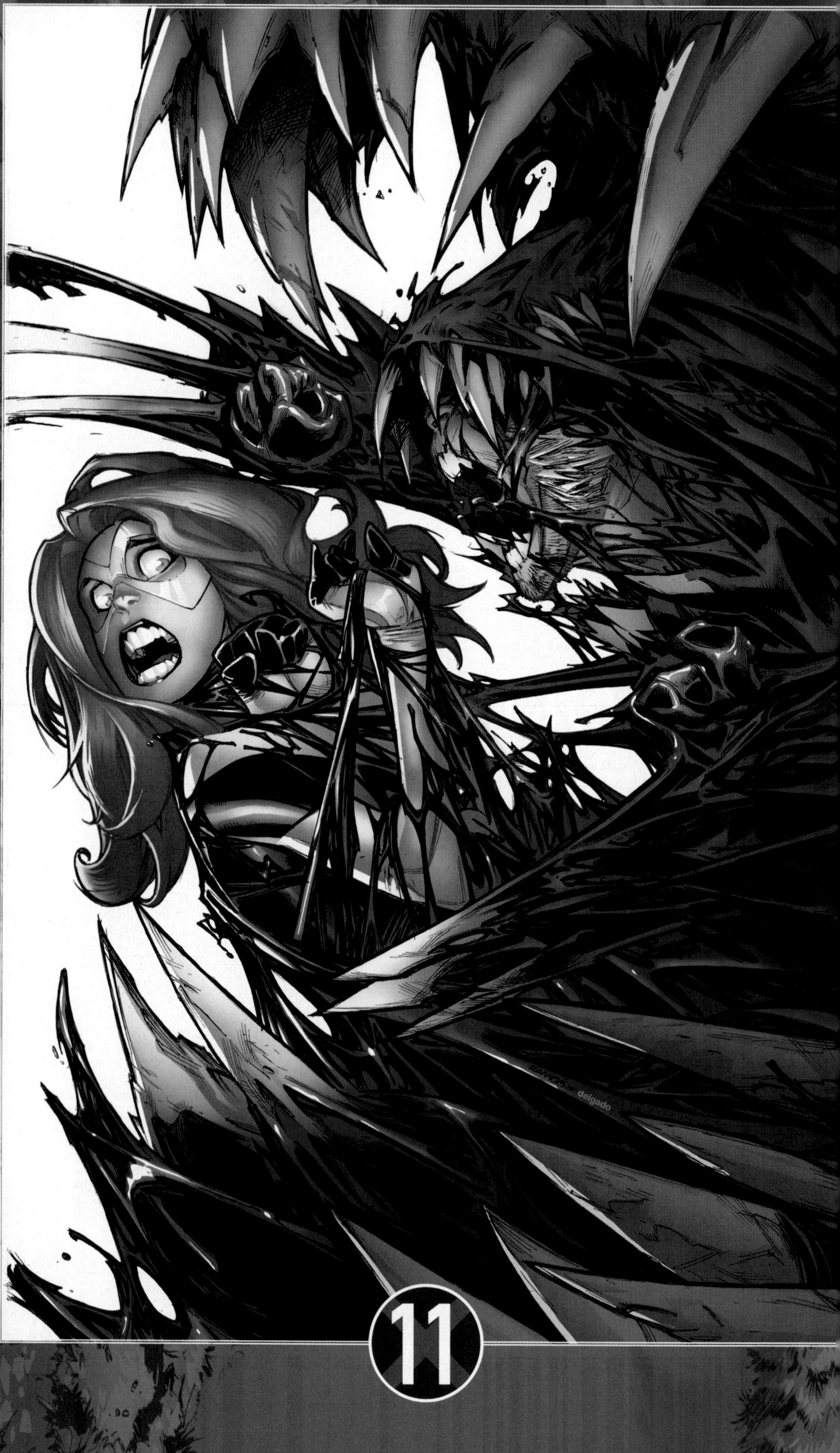
11

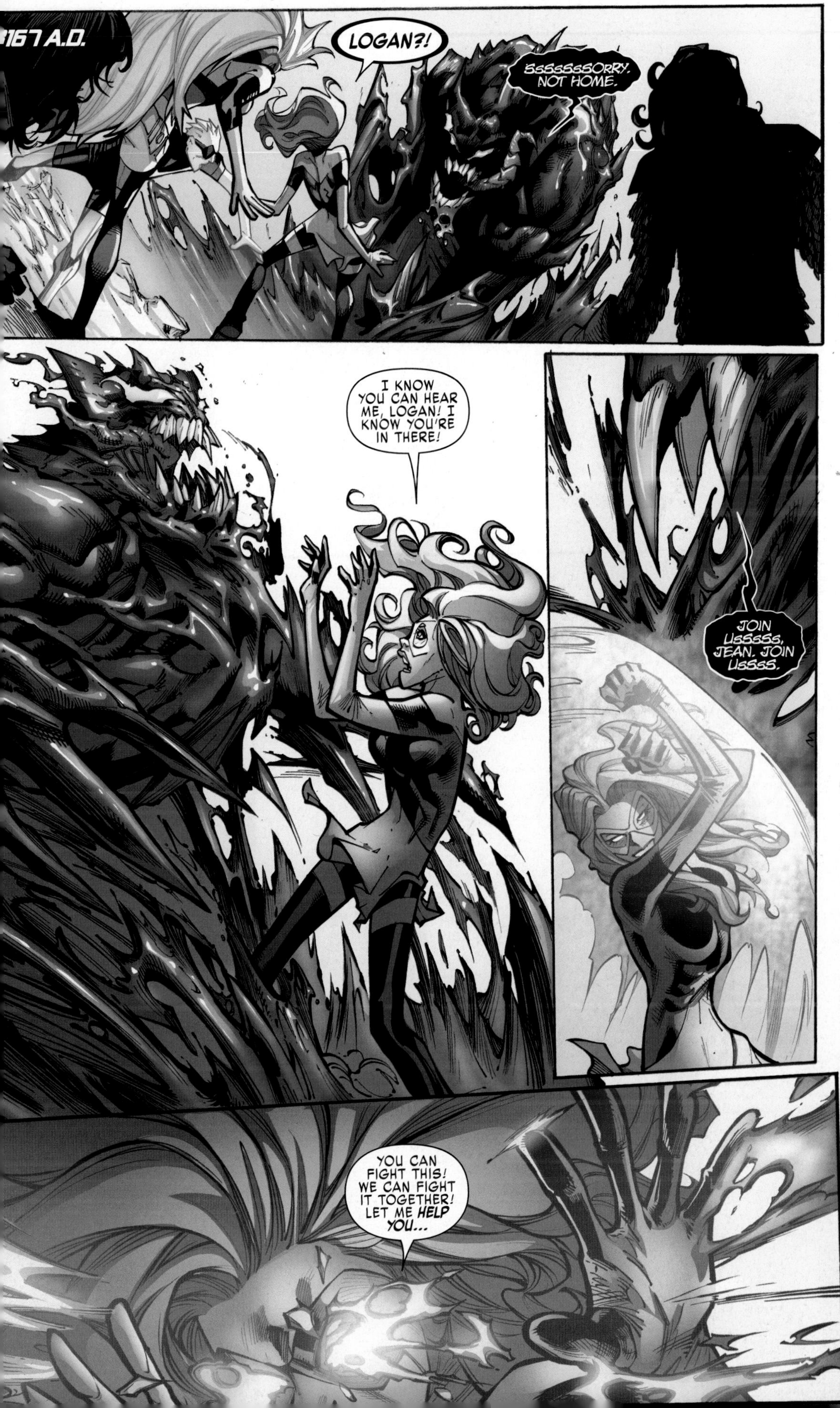

167 A.D.
LOGAN?!
SSSSSSSORRY. NOT HOME.
I KNOW YOU CAN HEAR ME, LOGAN! I KNOW YOU'RE IN THERE!
JOIN USSSSS, JEAN. JOIN USSSS.
YOU CAN FIGHT THIS! WE CAN FIGHT IT TOGETHER! LET ME *HELP* YOU...

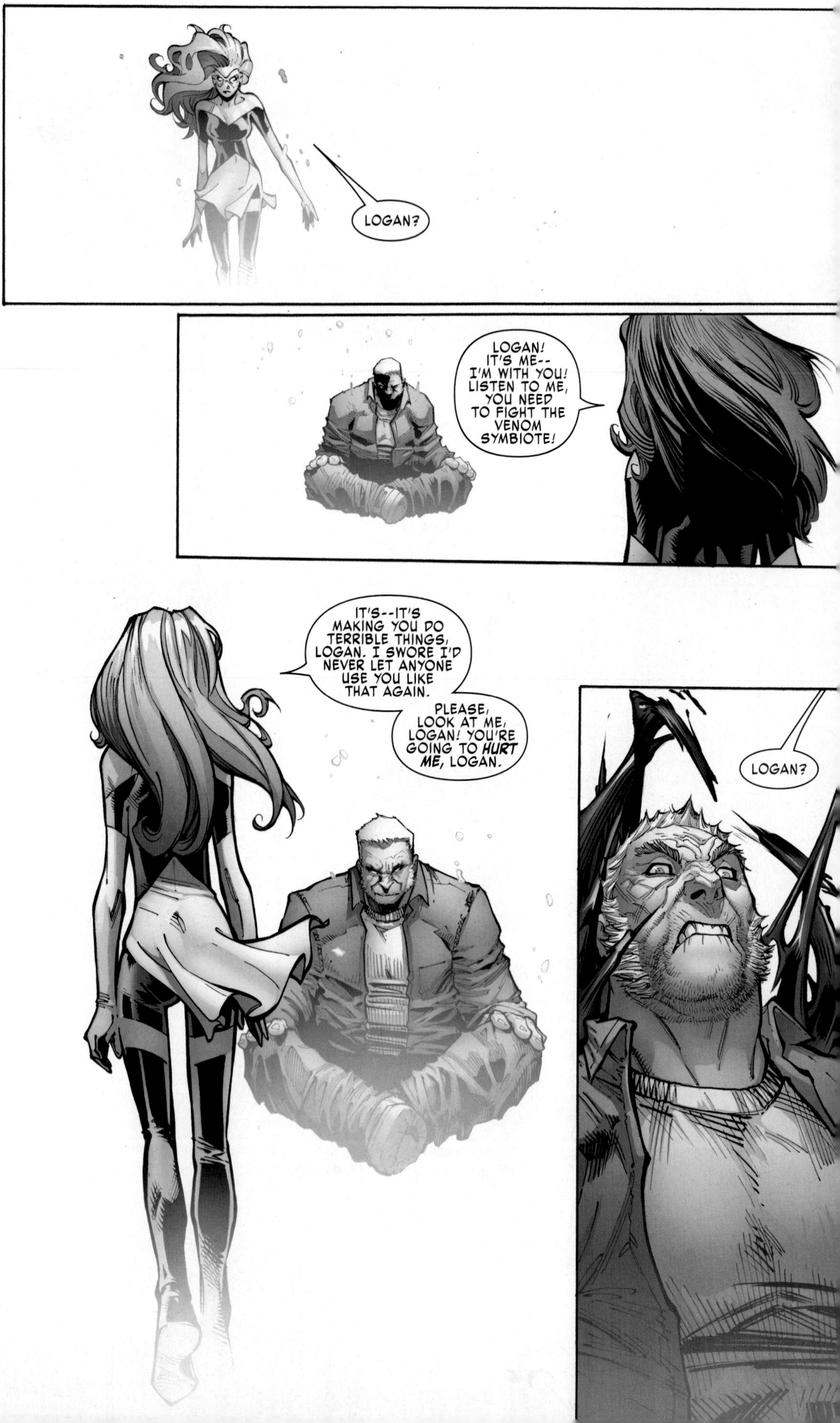
LOGAN?
LOGAN! IT'S ME-- I'M WITH YOU! LISTEN TO ME, YOU NEED TO FIGHT THE VENOM SYMBIOTE!
IT'S--IT'S MAKING YOU DO TERRIBLE THINGS, LOGAN. I SWORE I'D NEVER LET ANYONE USE YOU LIKE THAT AGAIN.
PLEASE, LOOK AT ME, LOGAN! YOU'RE GOING TO HURT ME, LOGAN.
LOGAN?

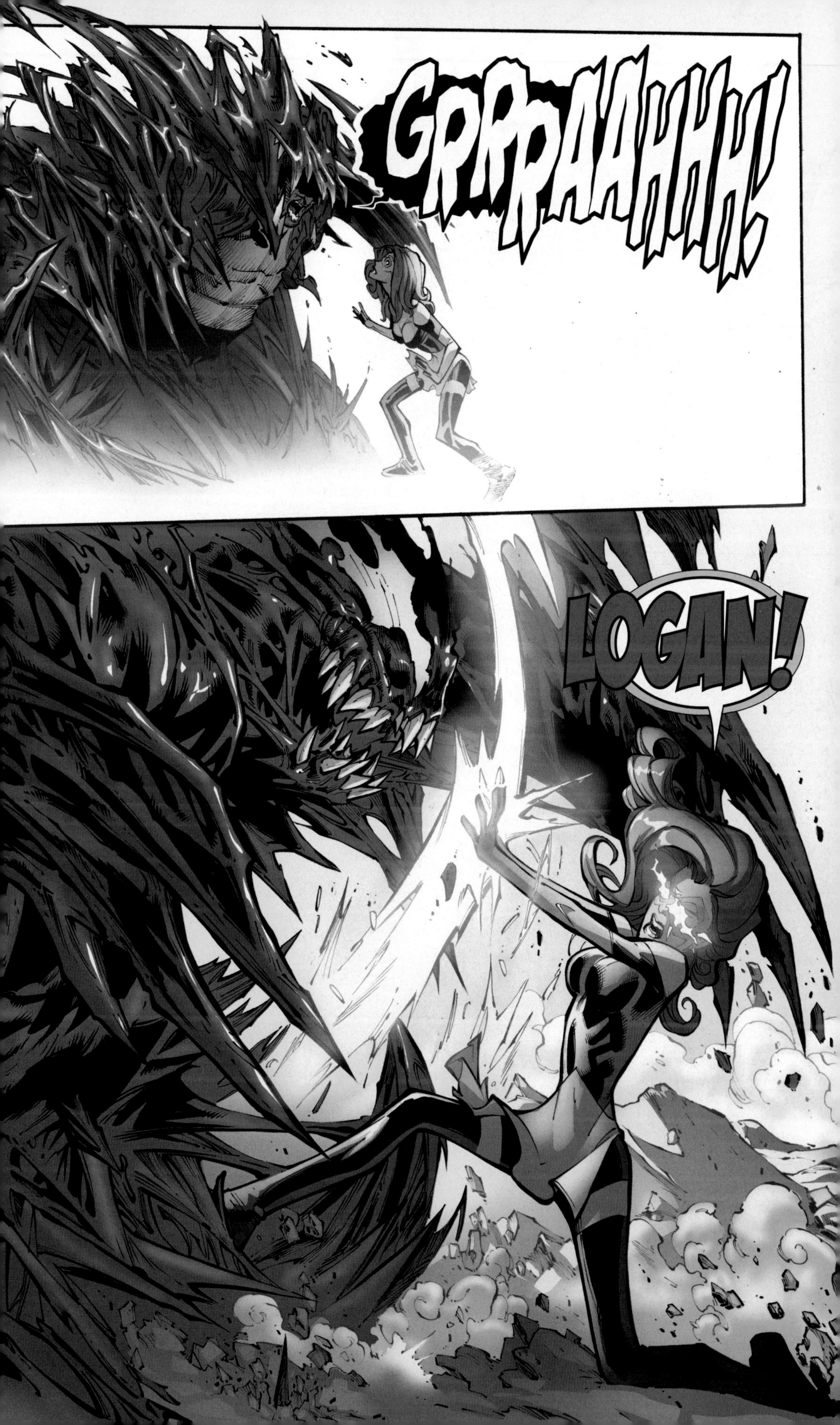
GRRRAAHHH!
LOGAN!

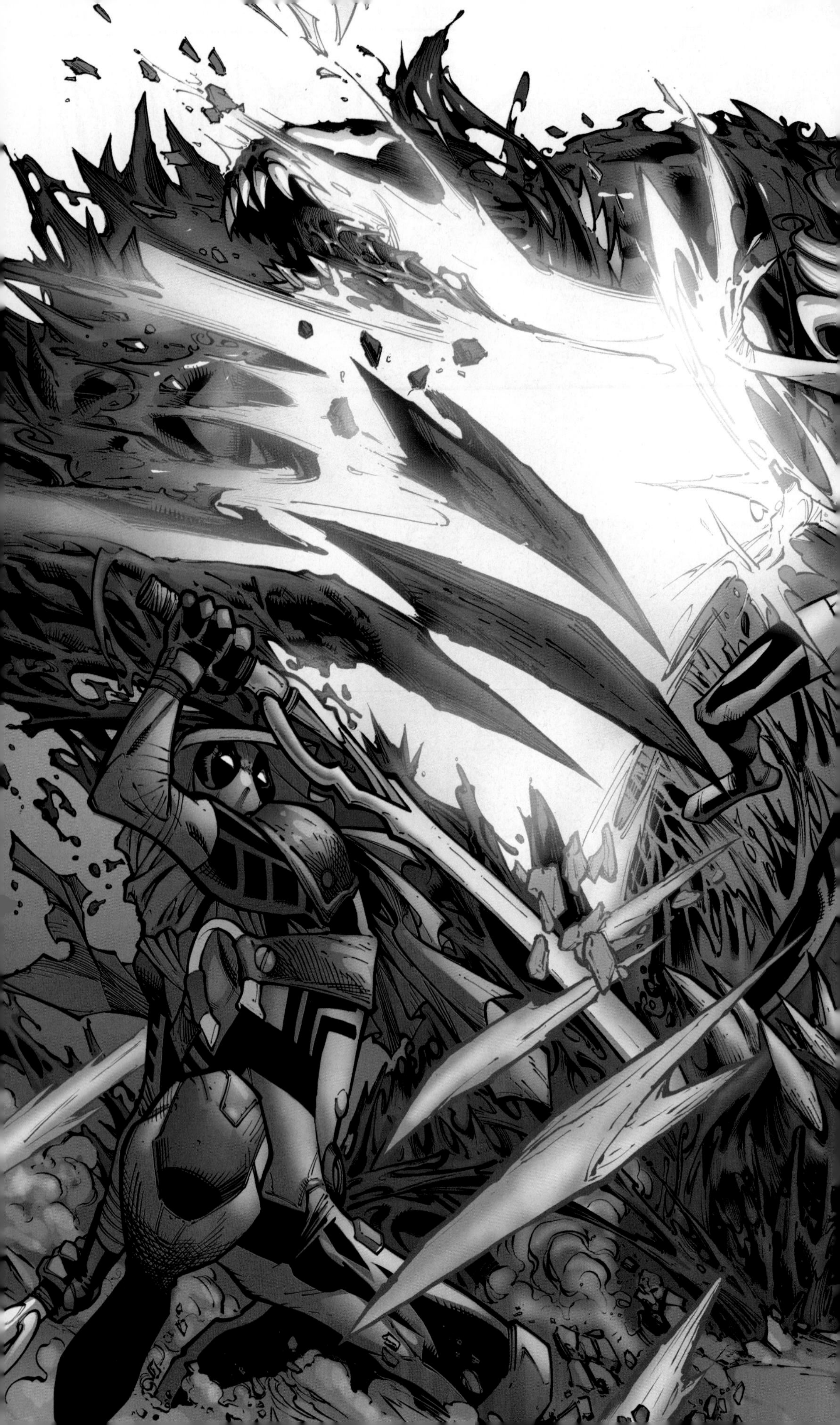

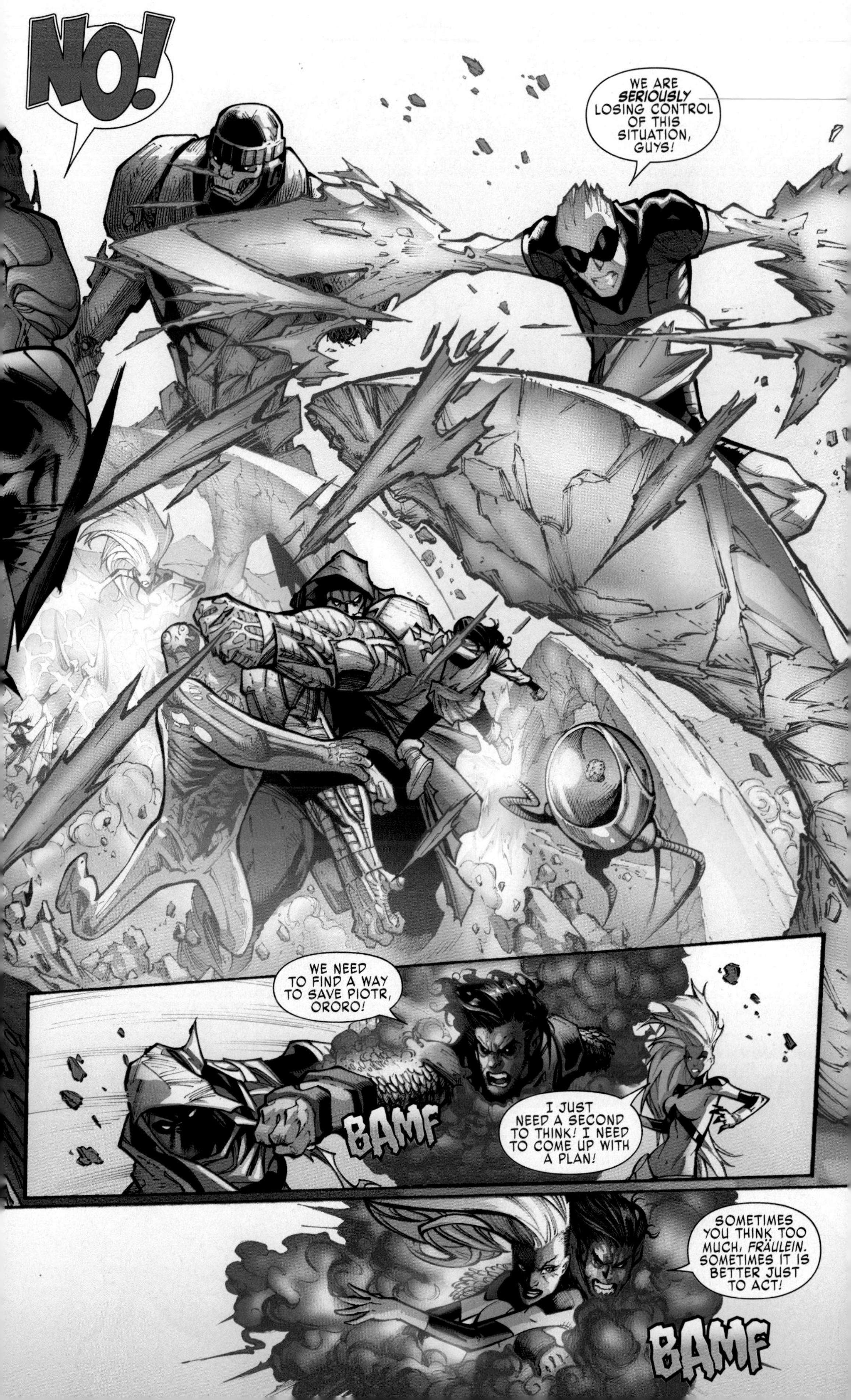
NO!
WE ARE *SERIOUSLY* LOSING CONTROL OF THIS SITUATION, GUYS!
WE NEED TO FIND A WAY TO SAVE PIOTR, ORORO!
BAMF
I JUST NEED A SECOND TO THINK! I NEED TO COME UP WITH A PLAN!
SOMETIMES YOU THINK TOO MUCH, *FRÄULEIN*. SOMETIMES IT IS BETTER JUST TO ACT!
BAMF

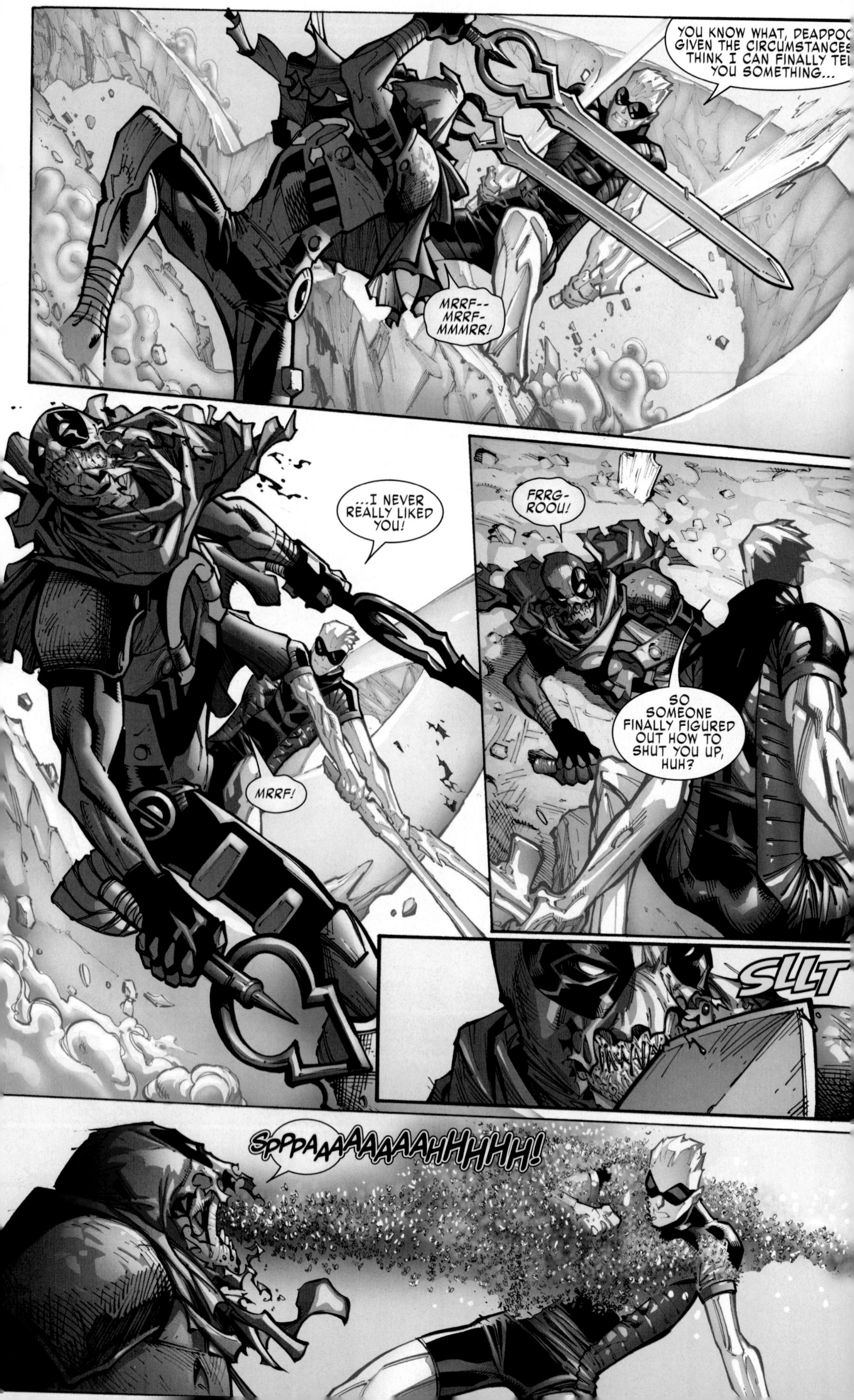
YOU KNOW WHAT, DEADPOO GIVEN THE CIRCUMSTANCES THINK I CAN FINALLY TE YOU SOMETHING...
MRRF-- MRRF- MMMRR!
...I NEVER REALLY LIKED YOU!
MRRF!
FRRG- ROOU!
SO SOMEONE FINALLY FIGURED OUT HOW TO SHUT YOU UP, HUH?
SLLT
SPPPAAAAAAAHHHHH!

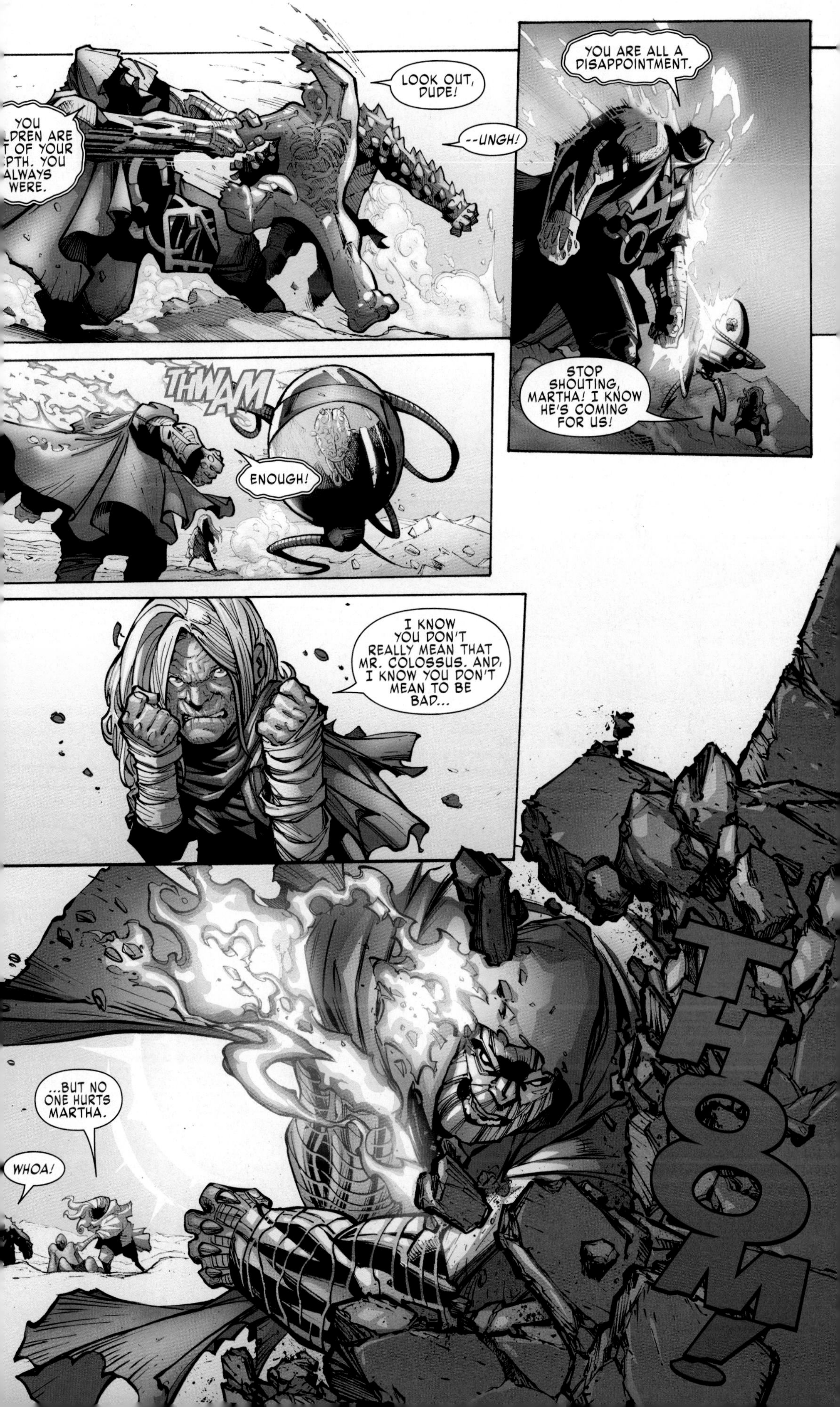
YOU
LDREN ARE
T OF YOUR
PTH. YOU
ALWAYS
WERE.
LOOK OUT, DUDE!
--UNGH!
YOU ARE ALL A DISAPPOINTMENT.
STOP SHOUTING, MARTHA! I KNOW HE'S COMING FOR US!
THWAM
ENOUGH!
I KNOW YOU DON'T REALLY MEAN THAT MR. COLOSSUS. AND, I KNOW YOU DON'T MEAN TO BE BAD...
...BUT NO ONE HURTS MARTHA.
WHOA!
THOOM!

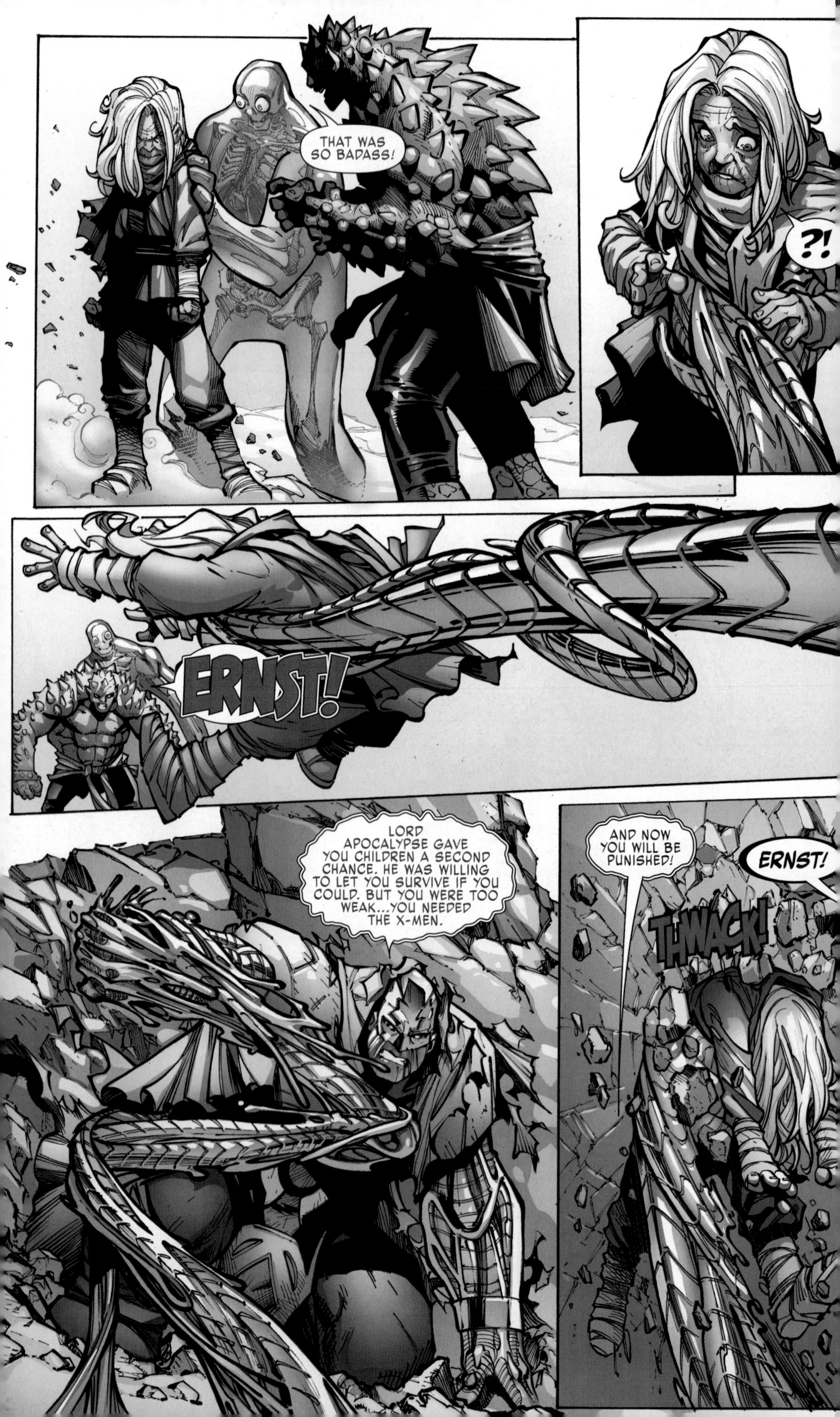
THAT WAS SO BADASS!
?!
ERNST!
LORD APOCALYPSE GAVE YOU CHILDREN A SECOND CHANCE. HE WAS WILLING TO LET YOU SURVIVE IF YOU COULD. BUT YOU WERE TOO WEAK...YOU NEEDED THE X-MEN.
AND NOW YOU WILL BE PUNISHED!
ERNST!
THWACK!

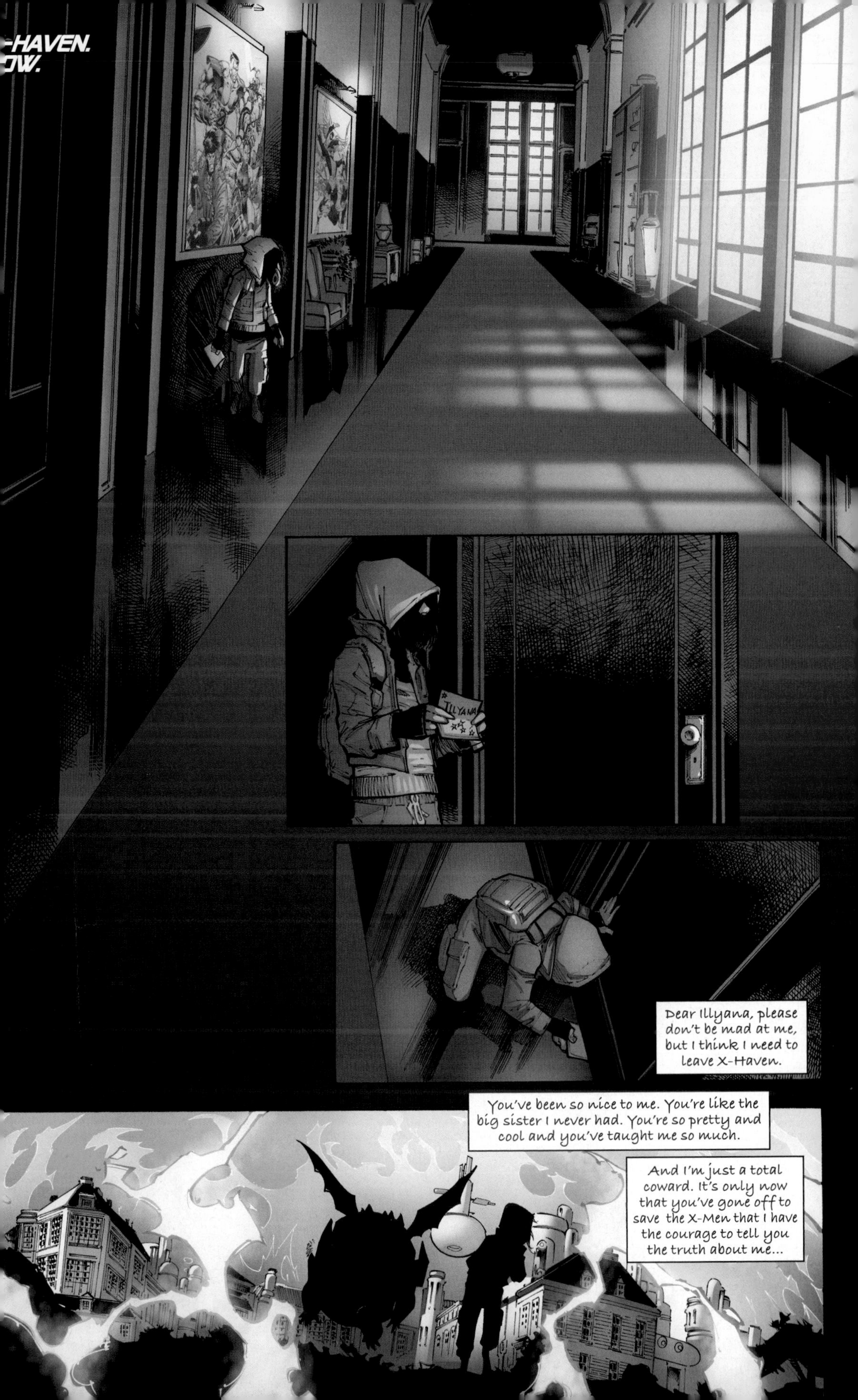
-HAVEN.
-OW.
ILLYANA
Dear Illyana, please don't be mad at me, but I think I need to leave X-Haven.
You've been so nice to me. You're like the big sister I never had. You're so pretty and cool and you've taught me so much.
And I'm just a total coward. It's only now that you've gone off to save the X-Men that I have the courage to tell you the truth about me...

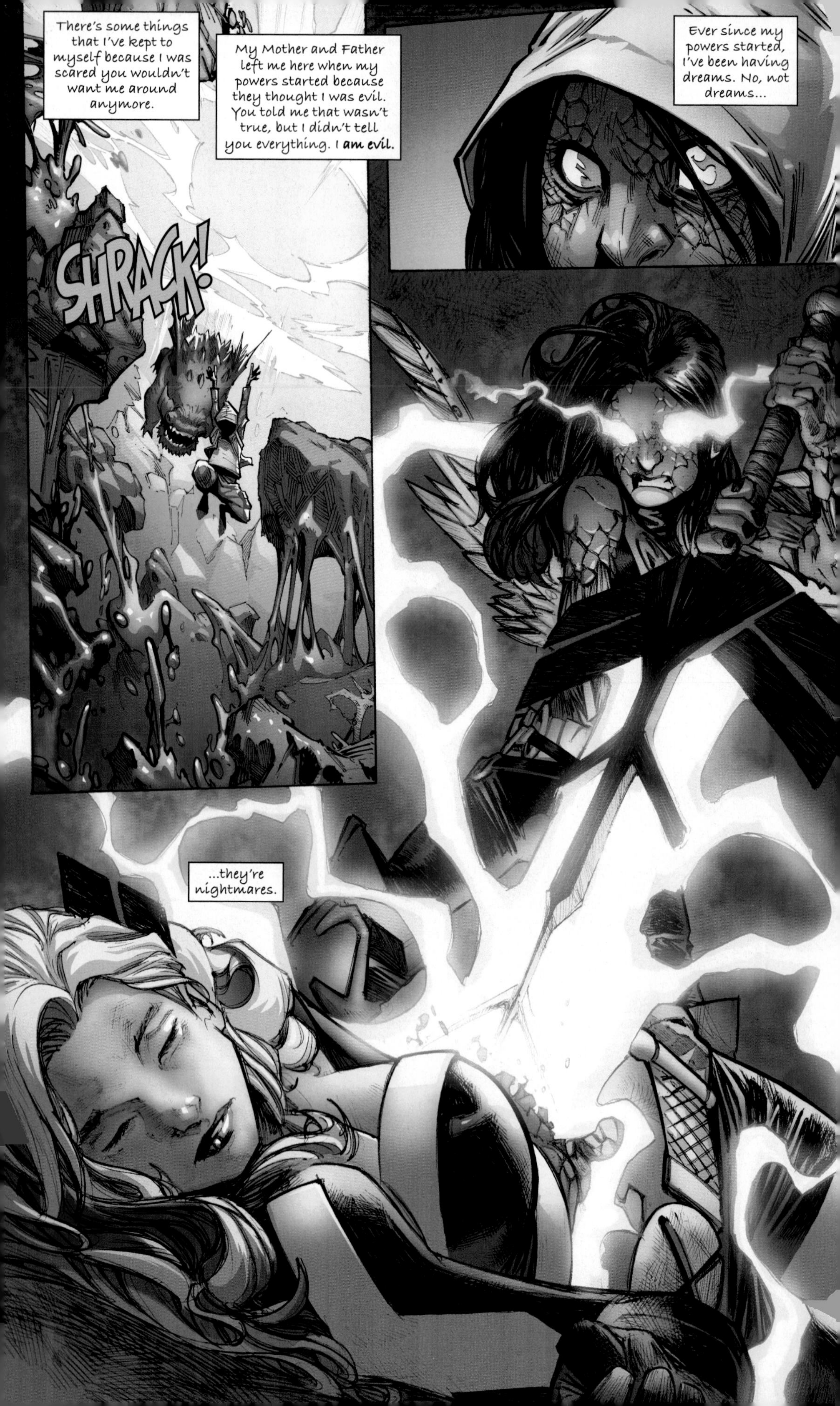
There's some things that I've kept to myself because I was scared you wouldn't want me around anymore.
My Mother and Father left me here when my powers started because they thought I was evil. You told me that wasn't true, but I didn't tell you everything. I am evil.
SHRACK!
Ever since my powers started, I've been having dreams. No, not dreams...
...they're nightmares.

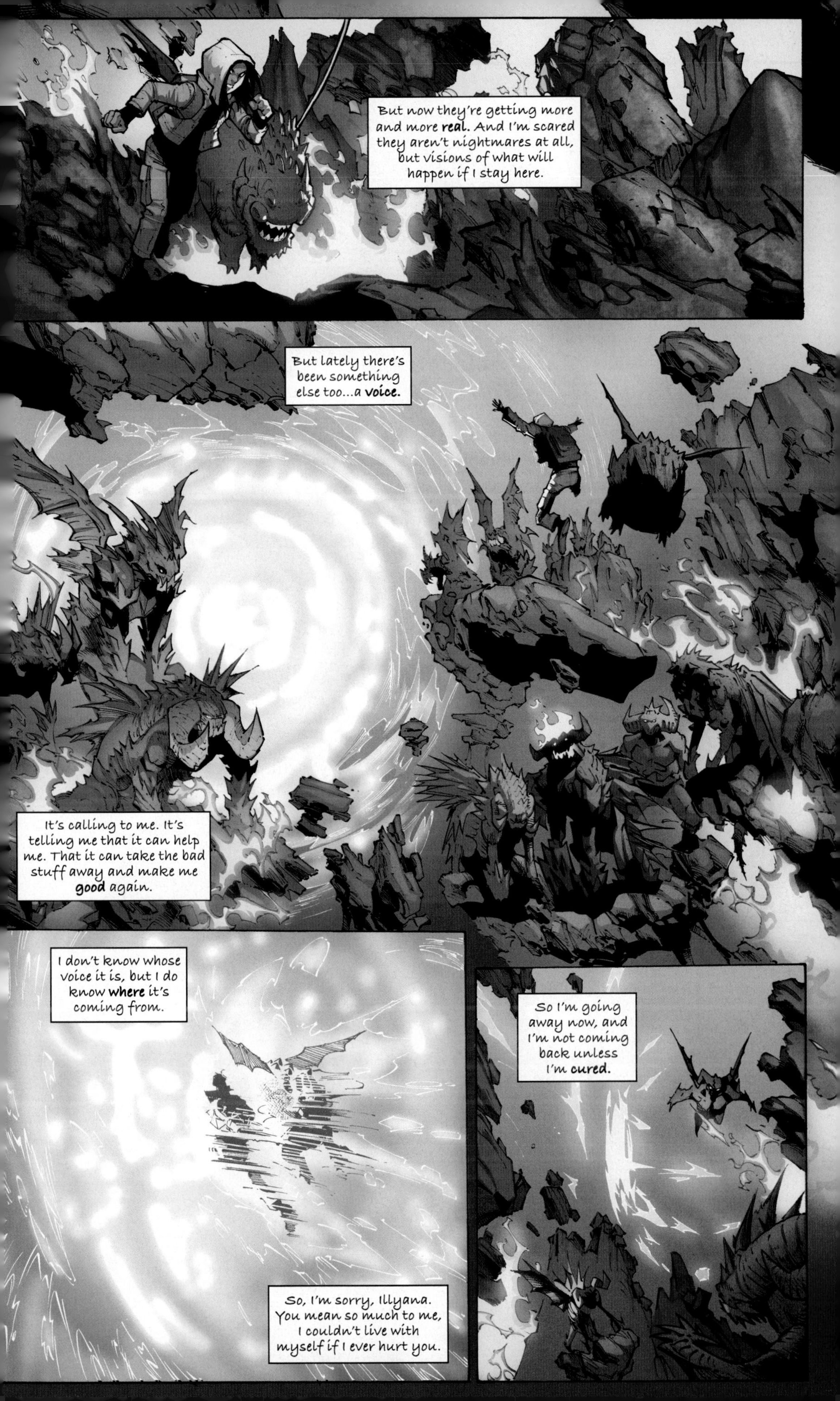
But now they're getting more and more real. And I'm scared they aren't nightmares at all, but visions of what will happen if I stay here.
But lately there's been something else too...a voice.
It's calling to me. It's telling me that it can help me. That it can take the bad stuff away and make me good again.
I don't know whose voice it is, but I do know where it's coming from.
So, I'm sorry, Illyana. You mean so much to me, I couldn't live with myself if I ever hurt you.
So I'm going away now, and I'm not coming back unless I'm cured.

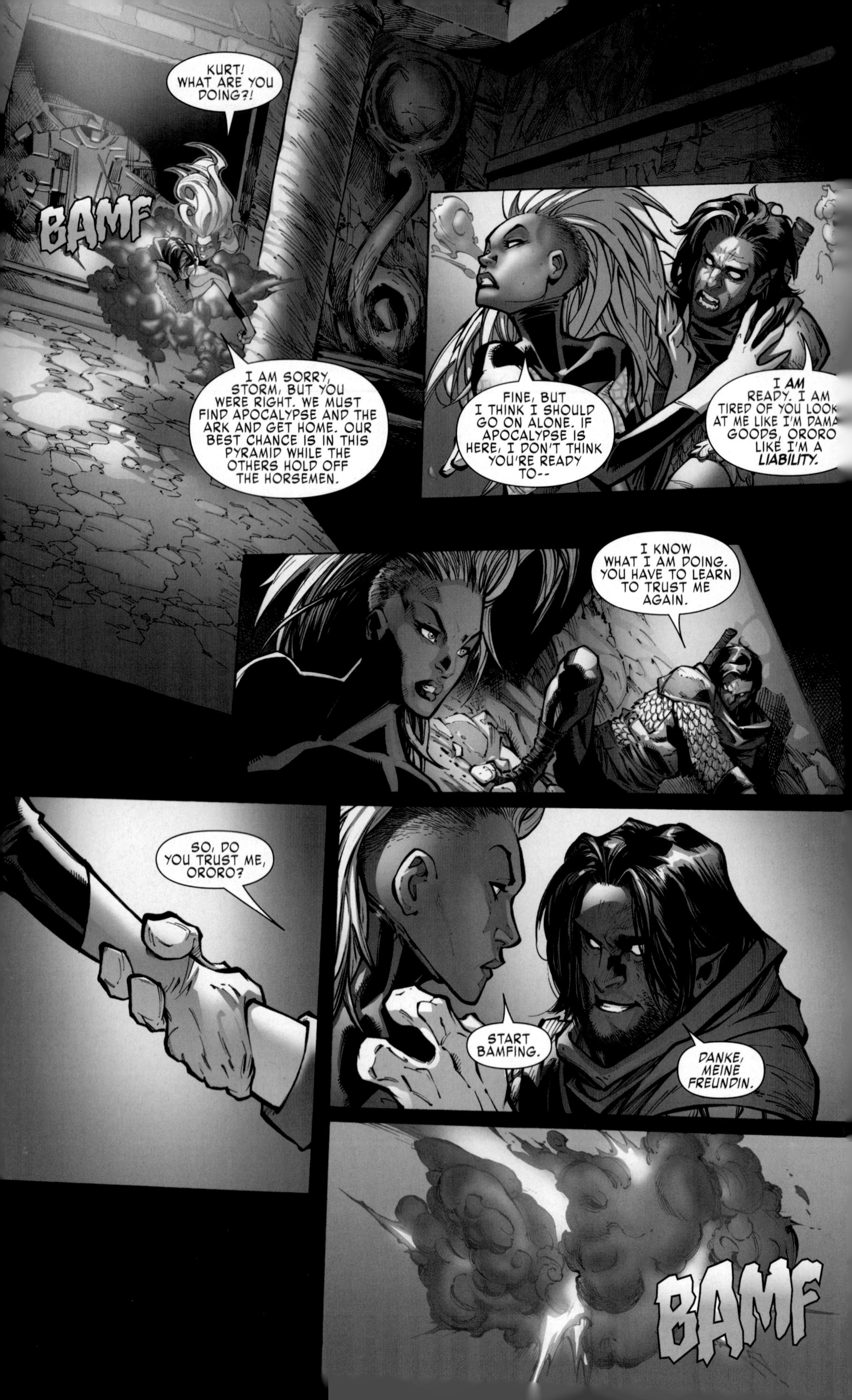
KURT! WHAT ARE YOU DOING?!
BAMF
I AM SORRY, STORM, BUT YOU WERE RIGHT. WE MUST FIND APOCALYPSE AND THE ARK AND GET HOME. OUR BEST CHANCE IS IN THIS PYRAMID WHILE THE OTHERS HOLD OFF THE HORSEMEN.
FINE, BUT I THINK I SHOULD GO ON ALONE. IF APOCALYPSE IS HERE, I DON'T THINK YOU'RE READY TO--
I *AM* READY. I AM TIRED OF YOU LOOK AT ME LIKE I'M DAMA GOODS, ORORO LIKE I'M A ***LIABILITY.***
I KNOW WHAT I AM DOING. YOU HAVE TO LEARN TO TRUST ME AGAIN.
SO, DO YOU TRUST ME, ORORO?
START BAMFING.
DANKE, MEINE FREUNDIN.
BAMF

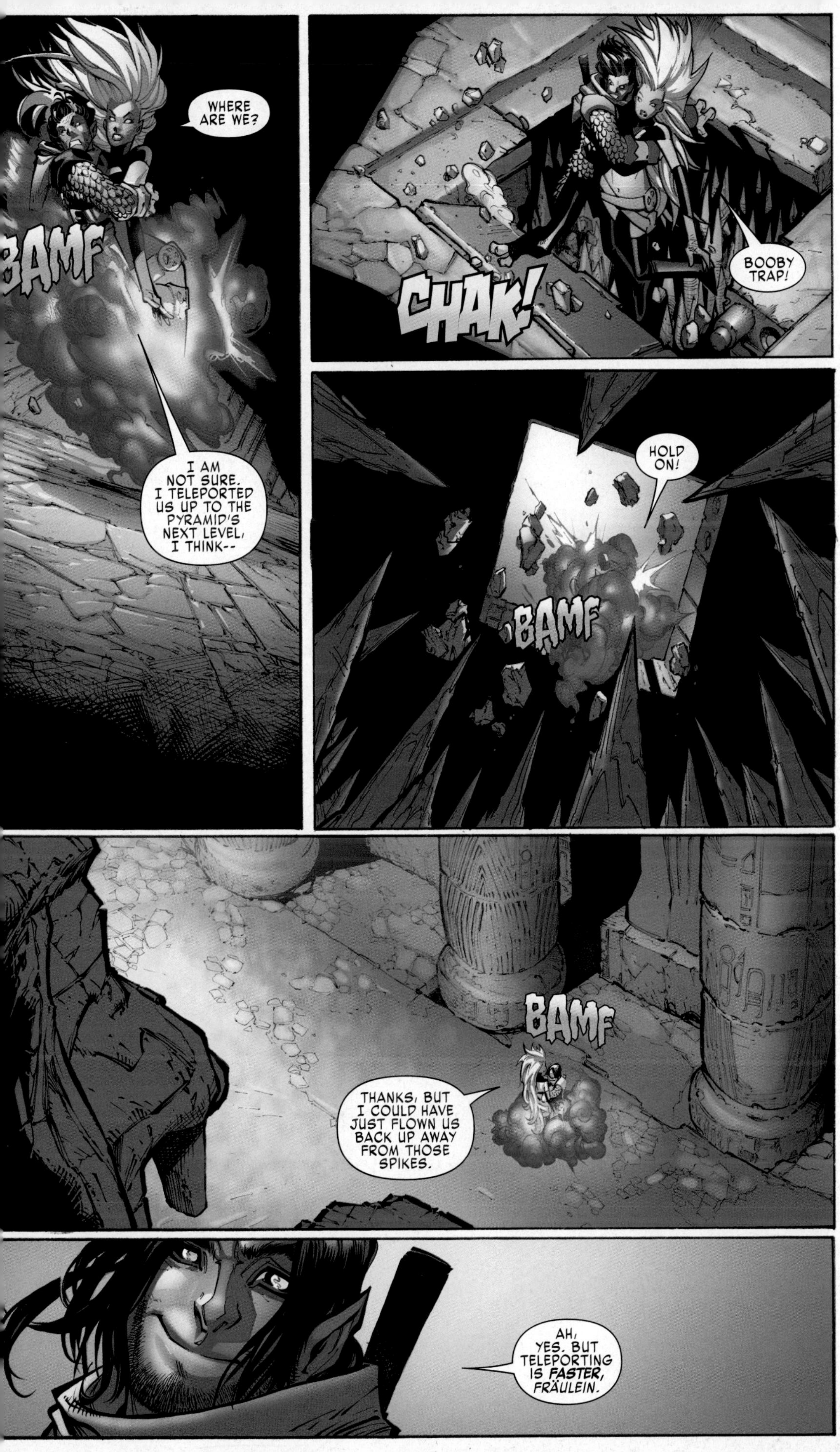
WHERE ARE WE?
BAMF
I AM NOT SURE. I TELEPORTED US UP TO THE PYRAMID'S NEXT LEVEL, I THINK--
CHAK!
BOOBY TRAP!
HOLD ON!
BAMF
BAMF
THANKS, BUT I COULD HAVE JUST FLOWN US BACK UP AWAY FROM THOSE SPIKES.
AH, YES. BUT TELEPORTING IS *FASTER*, FRÄULEIN.

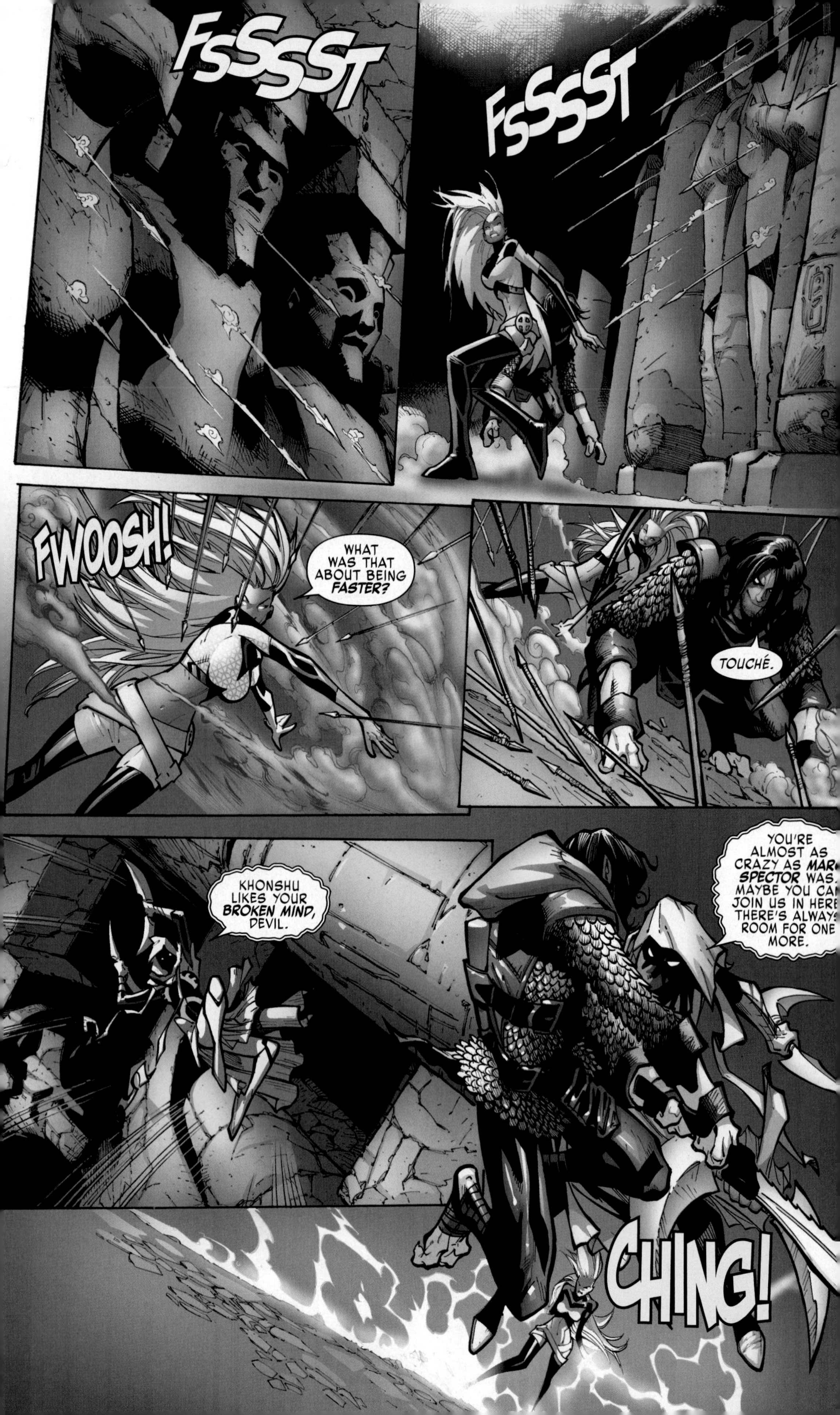
FSSSST
FSSSST
FWOOSH!
WHAT WAS THAT ABOUT BEING FASTER?
TOUCHÉ.
KHONSHU LIKES YOUR BROKEN MIND, DEVIL.
YOU'RE ALMOST AS CRAZY AS MARC SPECTOR WAS. MAYBE YOU CAN JOIN US IN HERE. THERE'S ALWAYS ROOM FOR ONE MORE.
CHING!

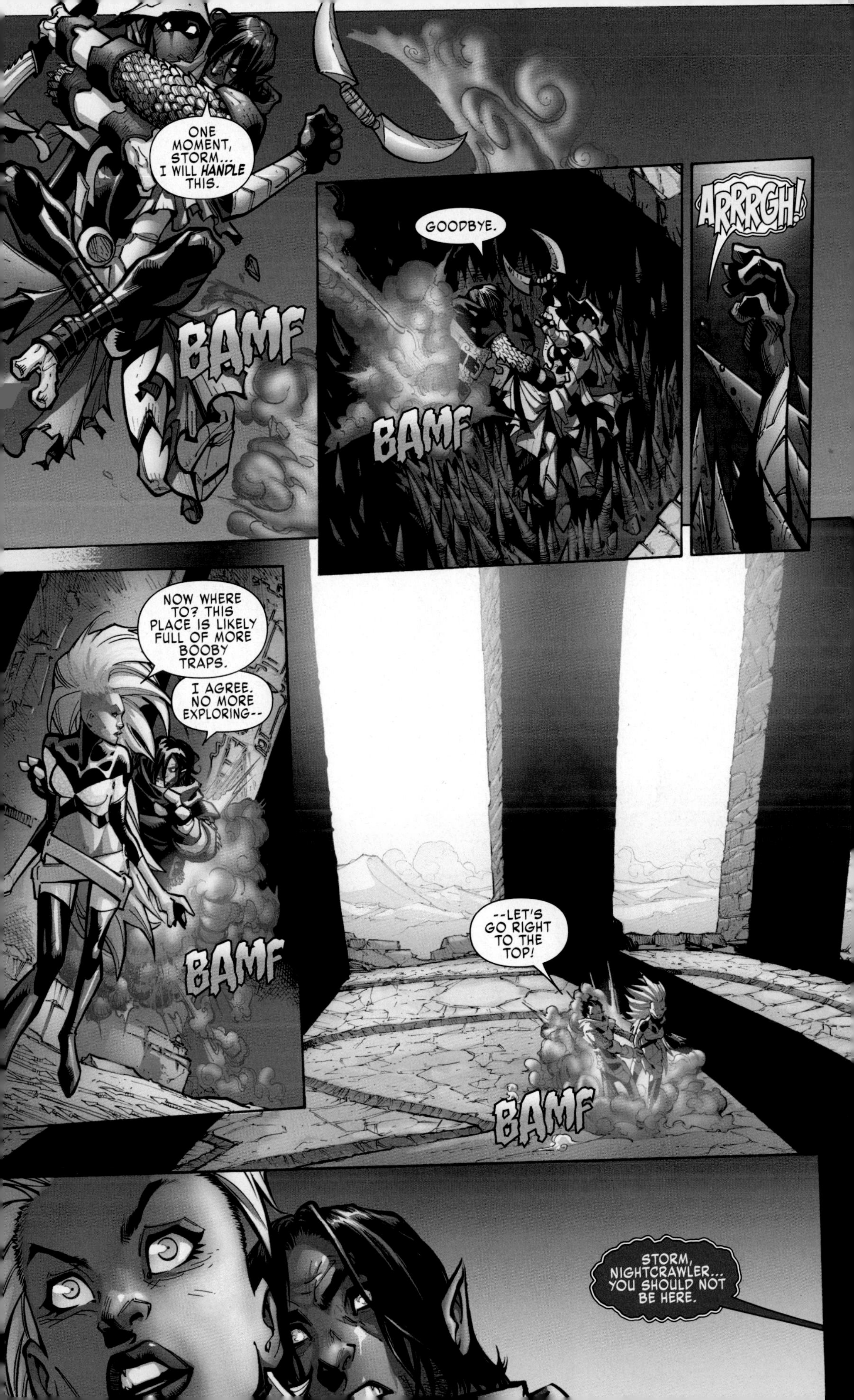
ONE MOMENT, STORM... I WILL HANDLE THIS.
BAMF
GOODBYE.
BAMF
ARRRGH!
NOW WHERE TO? THIS PLACE IS LIKELY FULL OF MORE BOOBY TRAPS.
I AGREE. NO MORE EXPLORING--
BAMF
--LET'S GO RIGHT TO THE TOP!
BAMF
STORM, NIGHTCRAWLER... YOU SHOULD NOT BE HERE.

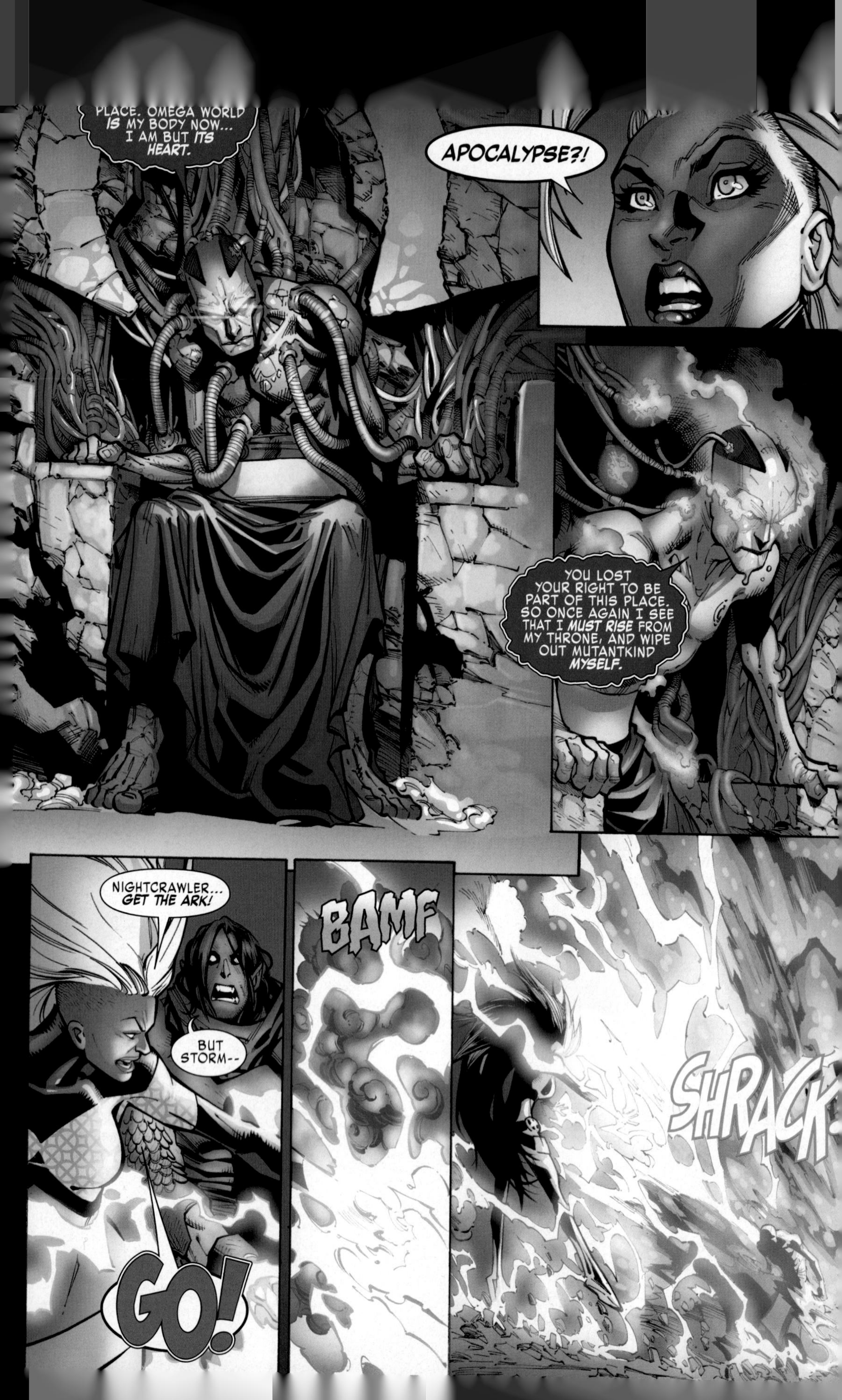
PLACE. OMEGA WORLD IS MY BODY NOW... I AM BUT ITS HEART.
APOCALYPSE?!
YOU LOST YOUR RIGHT TO BE PART OF THIS PLACE. SO ONCE AGAIN I SEE THAT I MUST RISE FROM MY THRONE, AND WIPE OUT MUTANTKIND MYSELF.
NIGHTCRAWLER... GET THE ARK!
BUT STORM--
GO!
BAMF
SHRACK

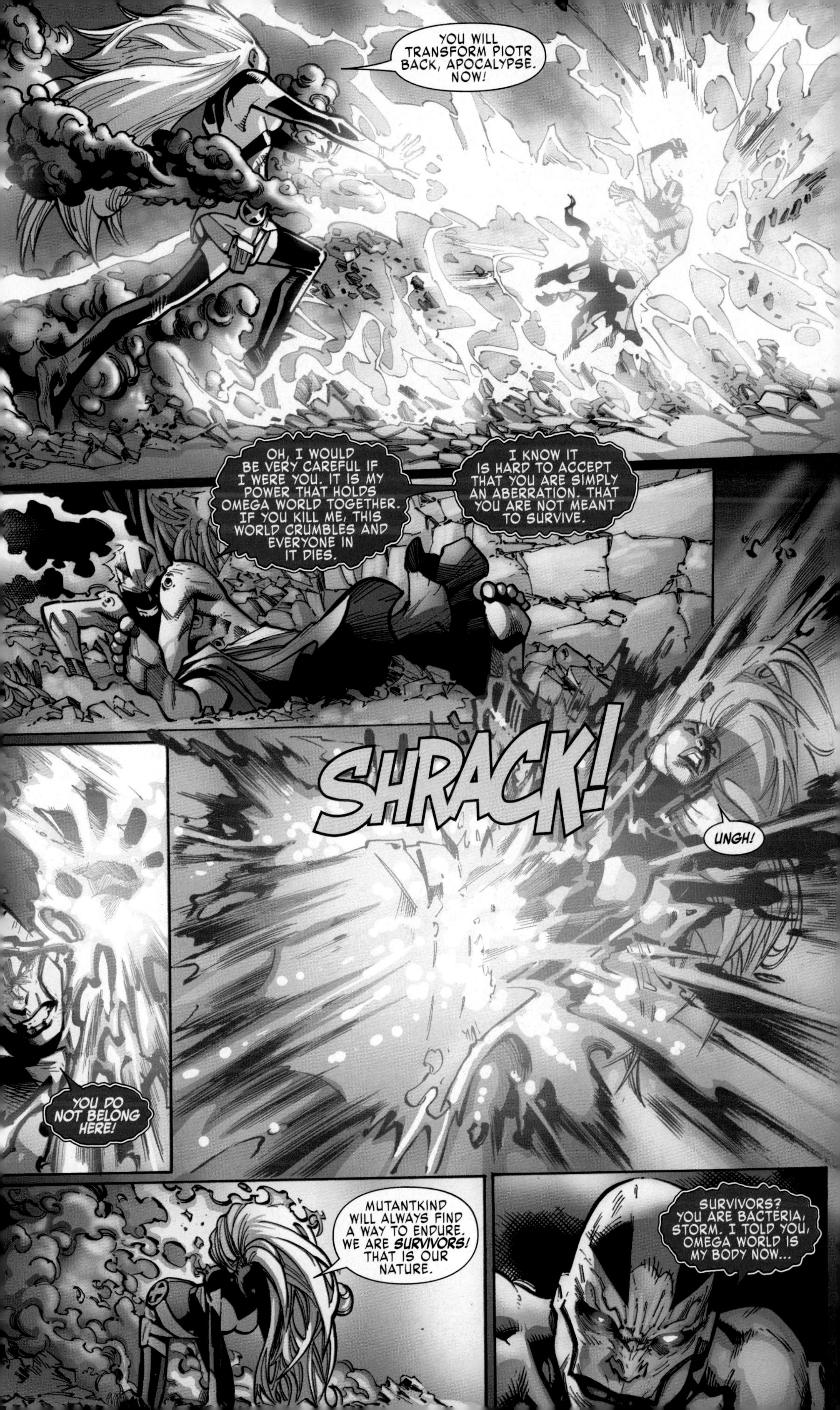
YOU WILL TRANSFORM PIOTR BACK, APOCALYPSE. NOW!
OH, I WOULD BE VERY CAREFUL IF I WERE YOU. IT IS MY POWER THAT HOLDS OMEGA WORLD TOGETHER. IF YOU KILL ME, THIS WORLD CRUMBLES AND EVERYONE IN IT DIES.
I KNOW IT IS HARD TO ACCEPT THAT YOU ARE SIMPLY AN ABERRATION. THAT YOU ARE NOT MEANT TO SURVIVE.
SHRACK!
UNGH!
YOU DO NOT BELONG HERE!
MUTANTKIND WILL ALWAYS FIND A WAY TO ENDURE. WE ARE SURVIVORS! THAT IS OUR NATURE.
SURVIVORS? YOU ARE BACTERIA, STORM. I TOLD YOU, OMEGA WORLD IS MY BODY NOW...

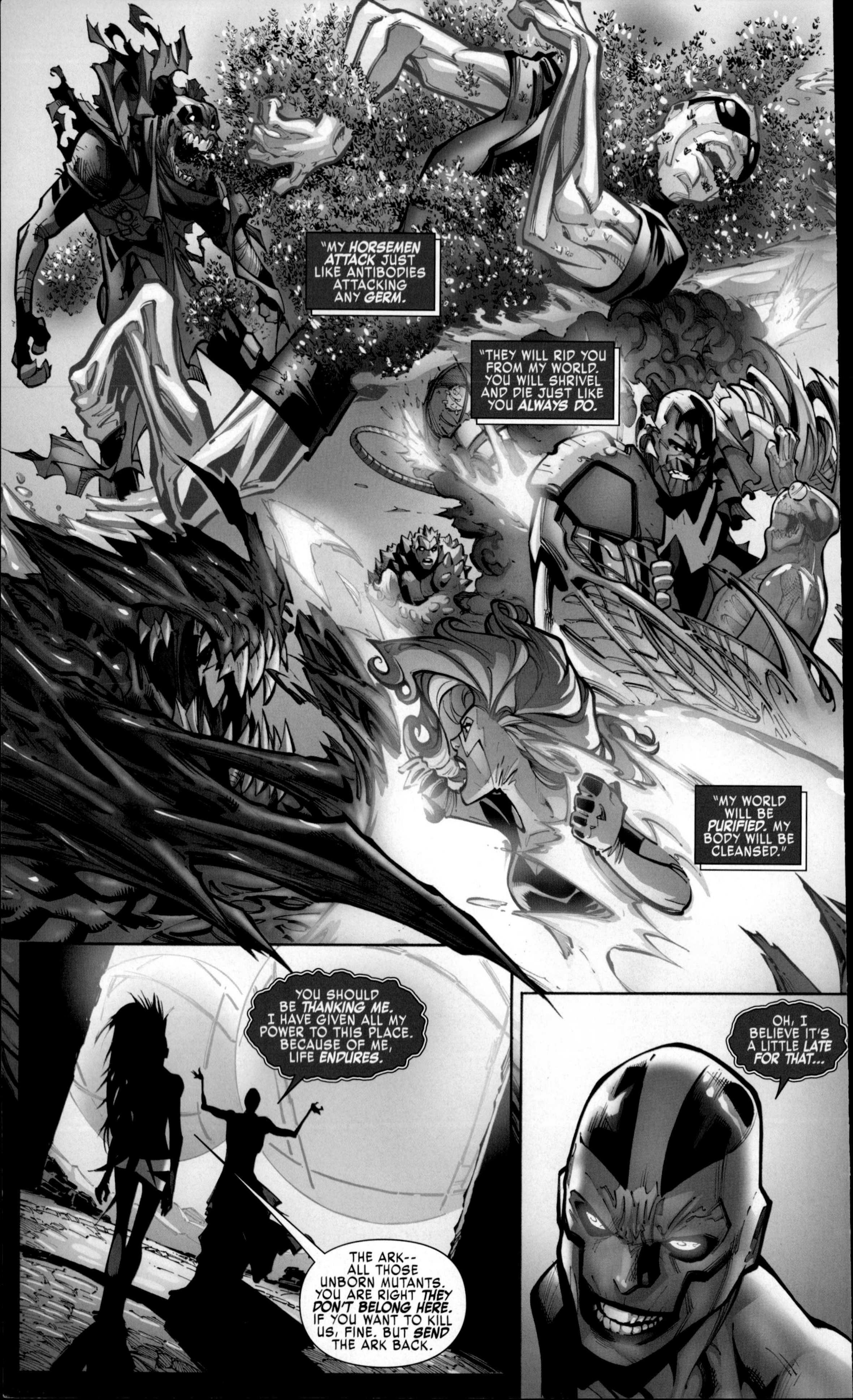

"MY HORSEMEN ATTACK JUST LIKE ANTIBODIES ATTACKING ANY GERM.
"THEY WILL RID YOU FROM MY WORLD. YOU WILL SHRIVEL AND DIE JUST LIKE YOU ALWAYS DO.
"MY WORLD WILL BE PURIFIED. MY BODY WILL BE CLEANSED."
YOU SHOULD BE THANKING ME. I HAVE GIVEN ALL MY POWER TO THIS PLACE. BECAUSE OF ME, LIFE ENDURES.
THE ARK-- ALL THOSE UNBORN MUTANTS. YOU ARE RIGHT THEY DON'T BELONG HERE. IF YOU WANT TO KILL US, FINE. BUT SEND THE ARK BACK.
OH, I BELIEVE IT'S A LITTLE LATE FOR THAT...

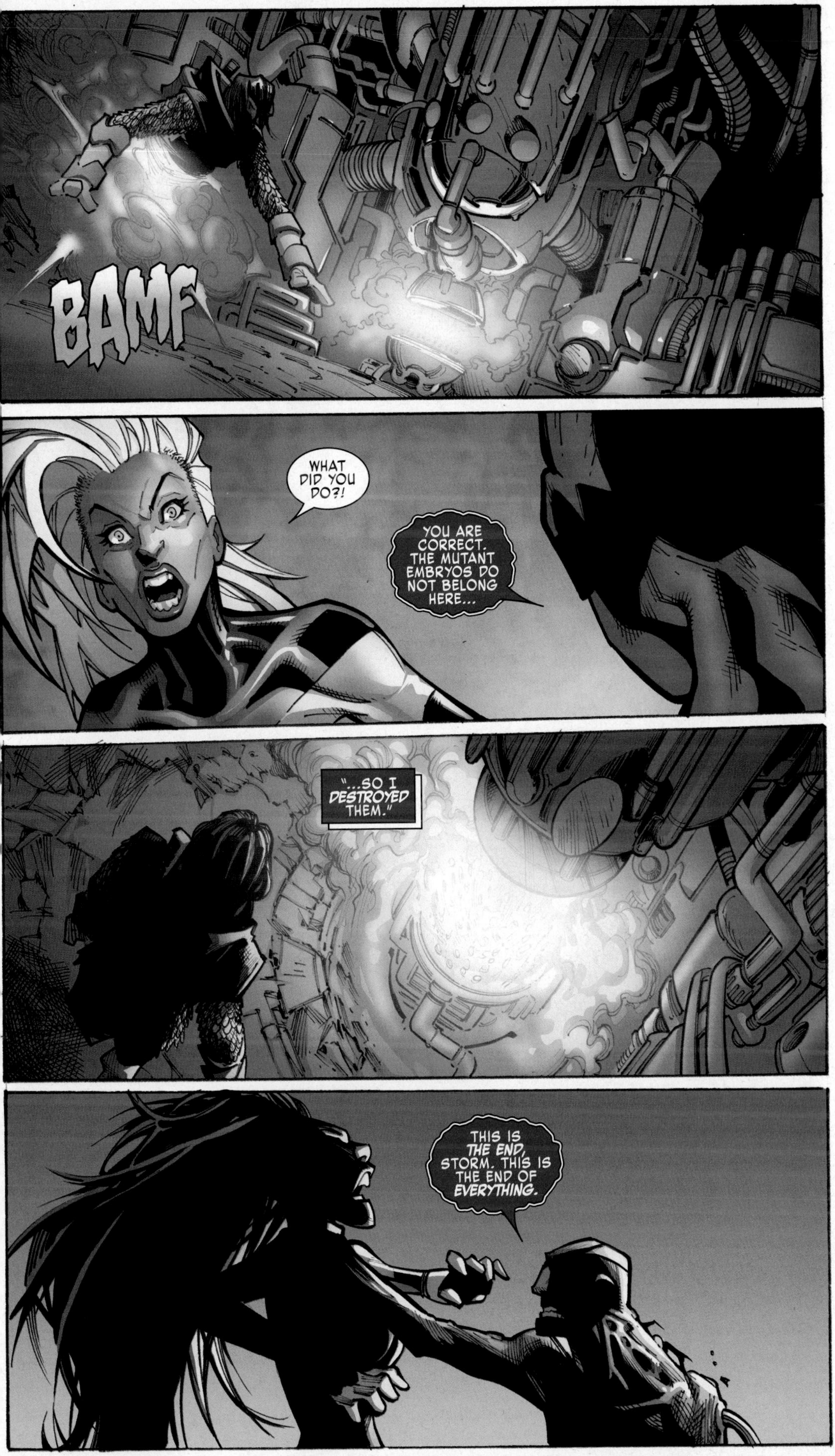
BAMF
WHAT DID YOU DO?!
YOU ARE CORRECT. THE MUTANT EMBRYOS DO NOT BELONG HERE...
"...SO I *DESTROYED* THEM."
THIS IS *THE END*, STORM. THIS IS THE END OF *EVERYTHING*.

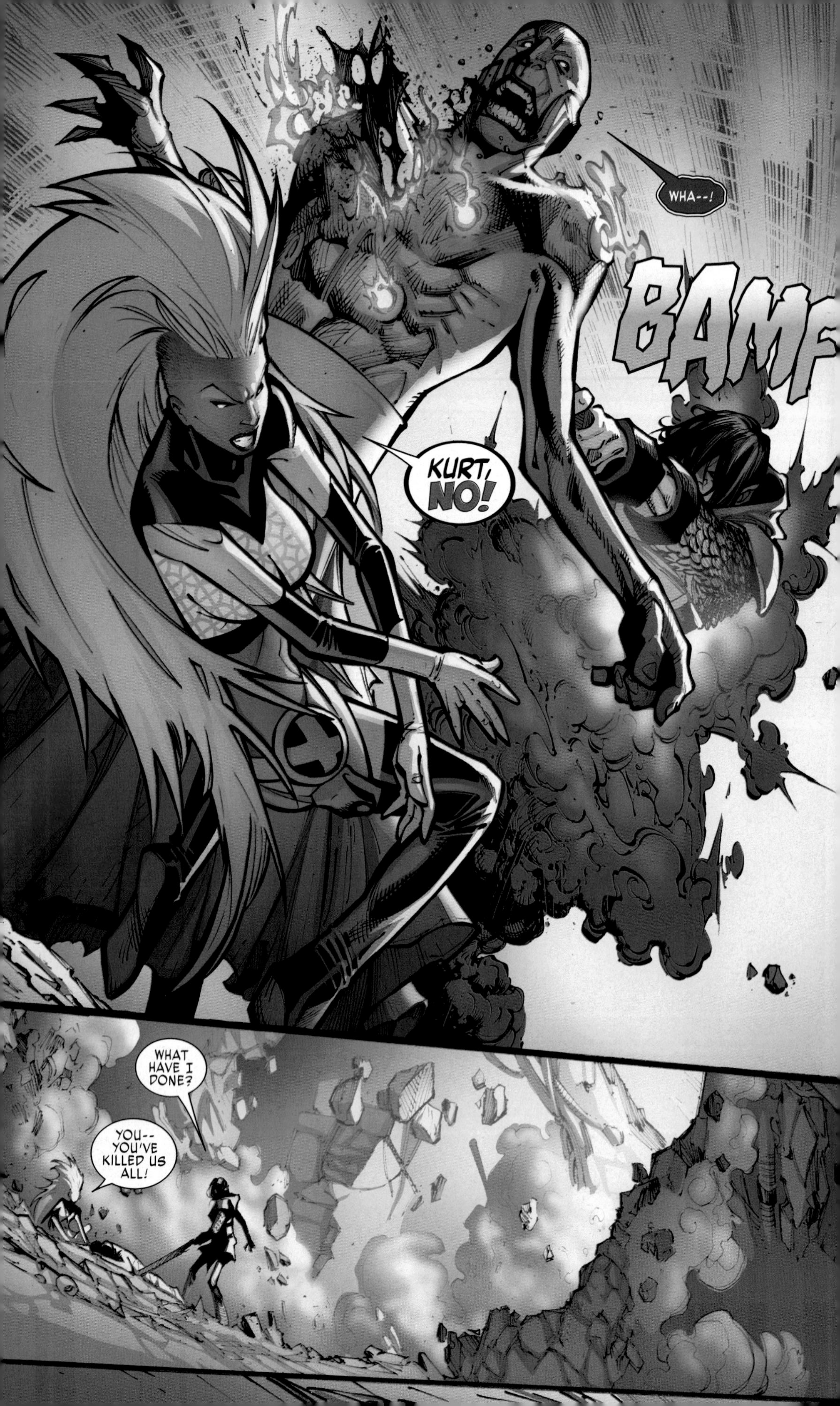
WHA--!
BAMF
KURT, NO!
WHAT HAVE I DONE?
YOU-- YOU'VE KILLED US ALL!

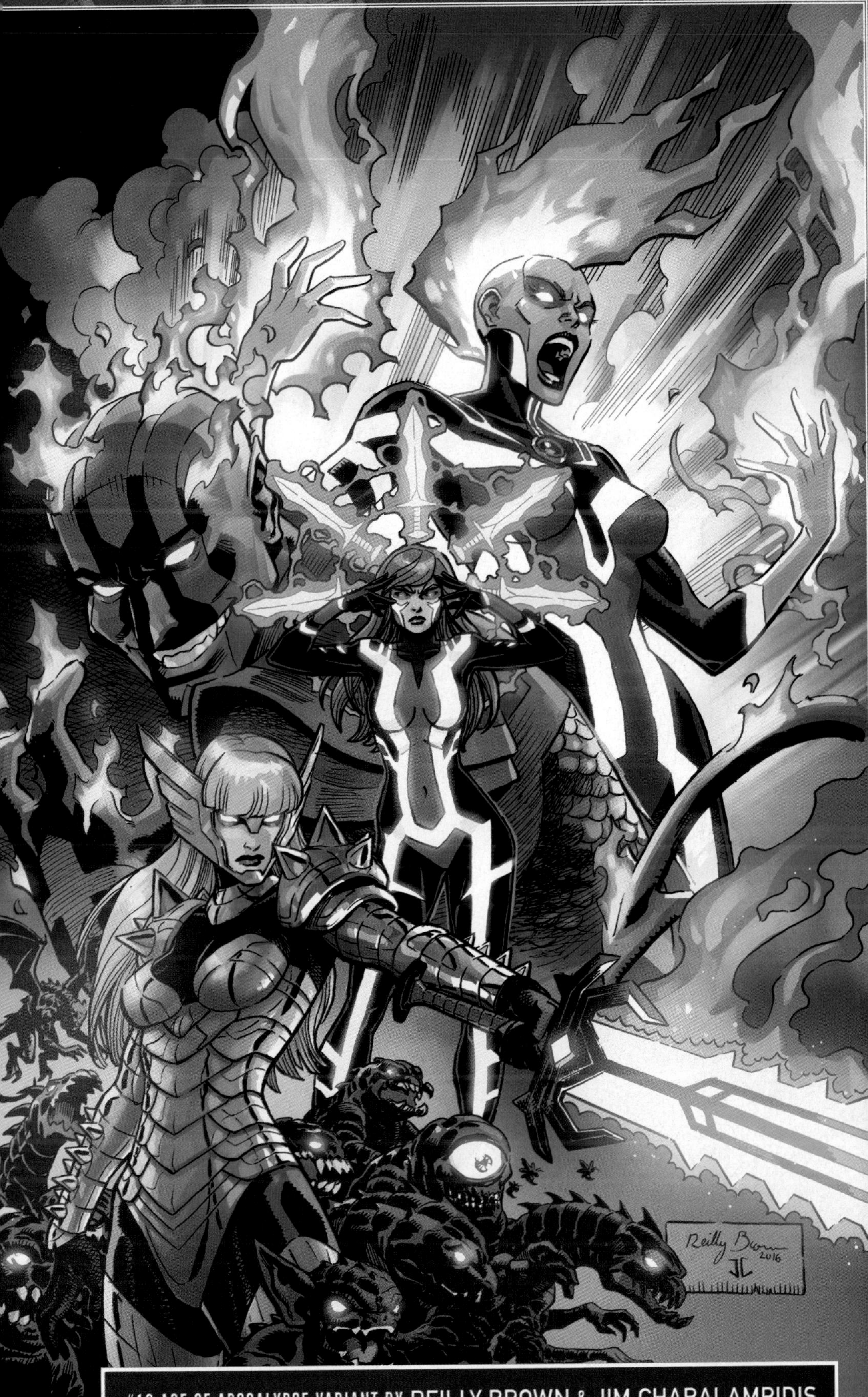
Reilly Brown
2016
JC

#10 AGE OF APOCALYPSE VARIANT BY REILLY BROWN & JIM CHARALAMPIDIS

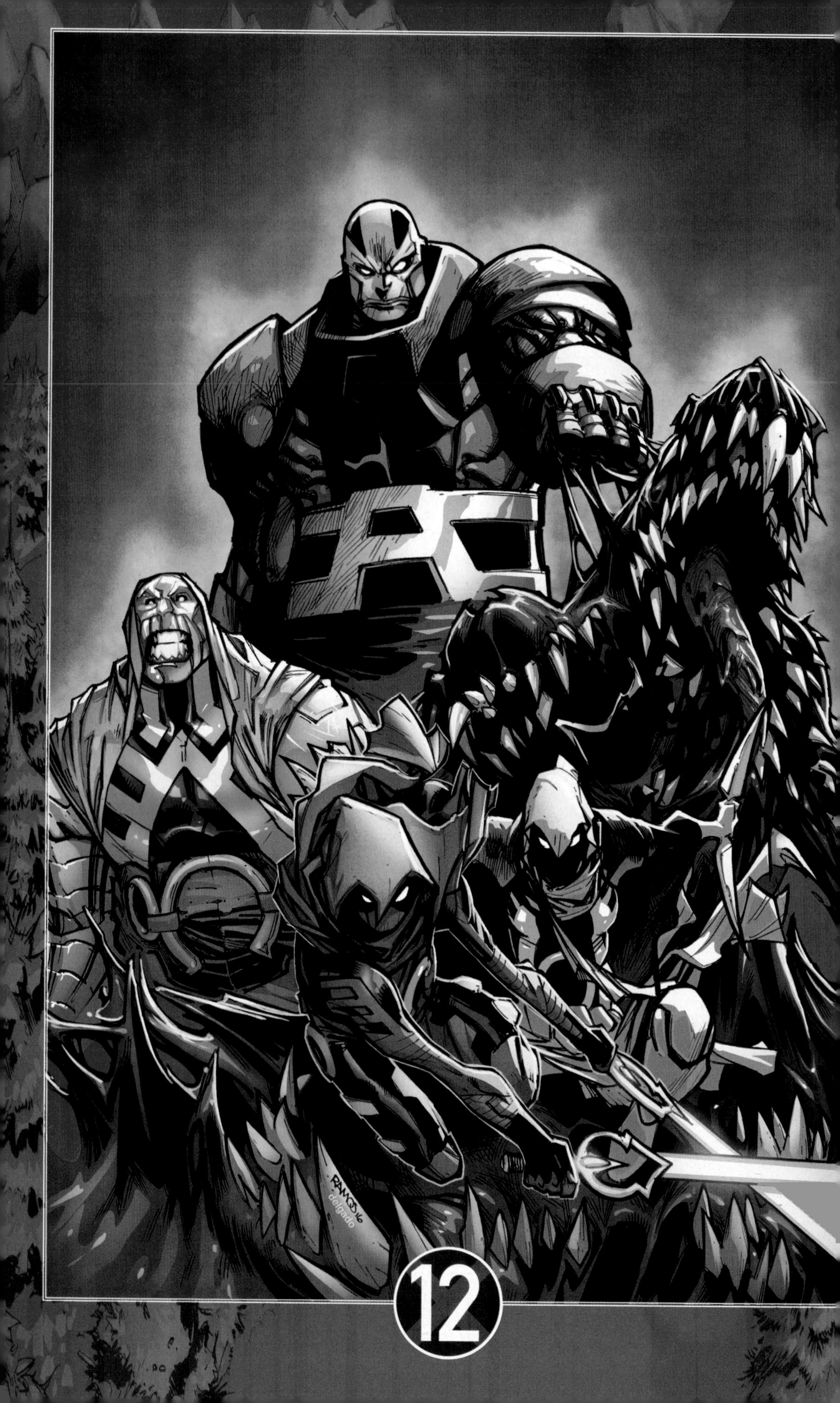
RAMOS 16
delgado
12

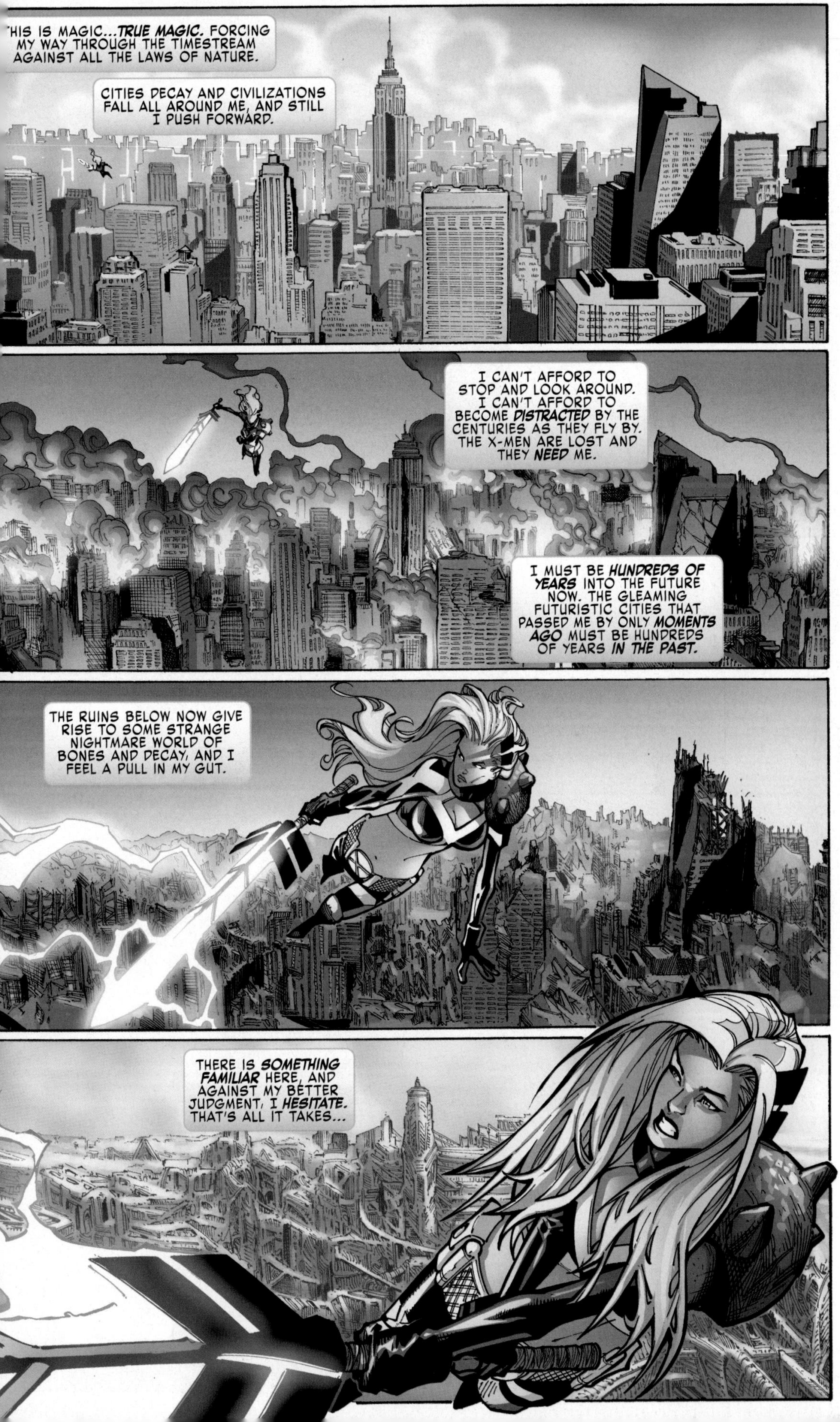
THIS IS MAGIC...TRUE MAGIC. FORCING MY WAY THROUGH THE TIMESTREAM AGAINST ALL THE LAWS OF NATURE.
CITIES DECAY AND CIVILIZATIONS FALL ALL AROUND ME, AND STILL I PUSH FORWARD.
I CAN'T AFFORD TO STOP AND LOOK AROUND. I CAN'T AFFORD TO BECOME DISTRACTED BY THE CENTURIES AS THEY FLY BY. THE X-MEN ARE LOST AND THEY NEED ME.
I MUST BE HUNDREDS OF YEARS INTO THE FUTURE NOW. THE GLEAMING FUTURISTIC CITIES THAT PASSED ME BY ONLY MOMENTS AGO MUST BE HUNDREDS OF YEARS IN THE PAST.
THE RUINS BELOW NOW GIVE RISE TO SOME STRANGE NIGHTMARE WORLD OF BONES AND DECAY, AND I FEEL A PULL IN MY GUT.
THERE IS SOMETHING FAMILIAR HERE, AND AGAINST MY BETTER JUDGMENT, I HESITATE. THAT'S ALL IT TAKES...

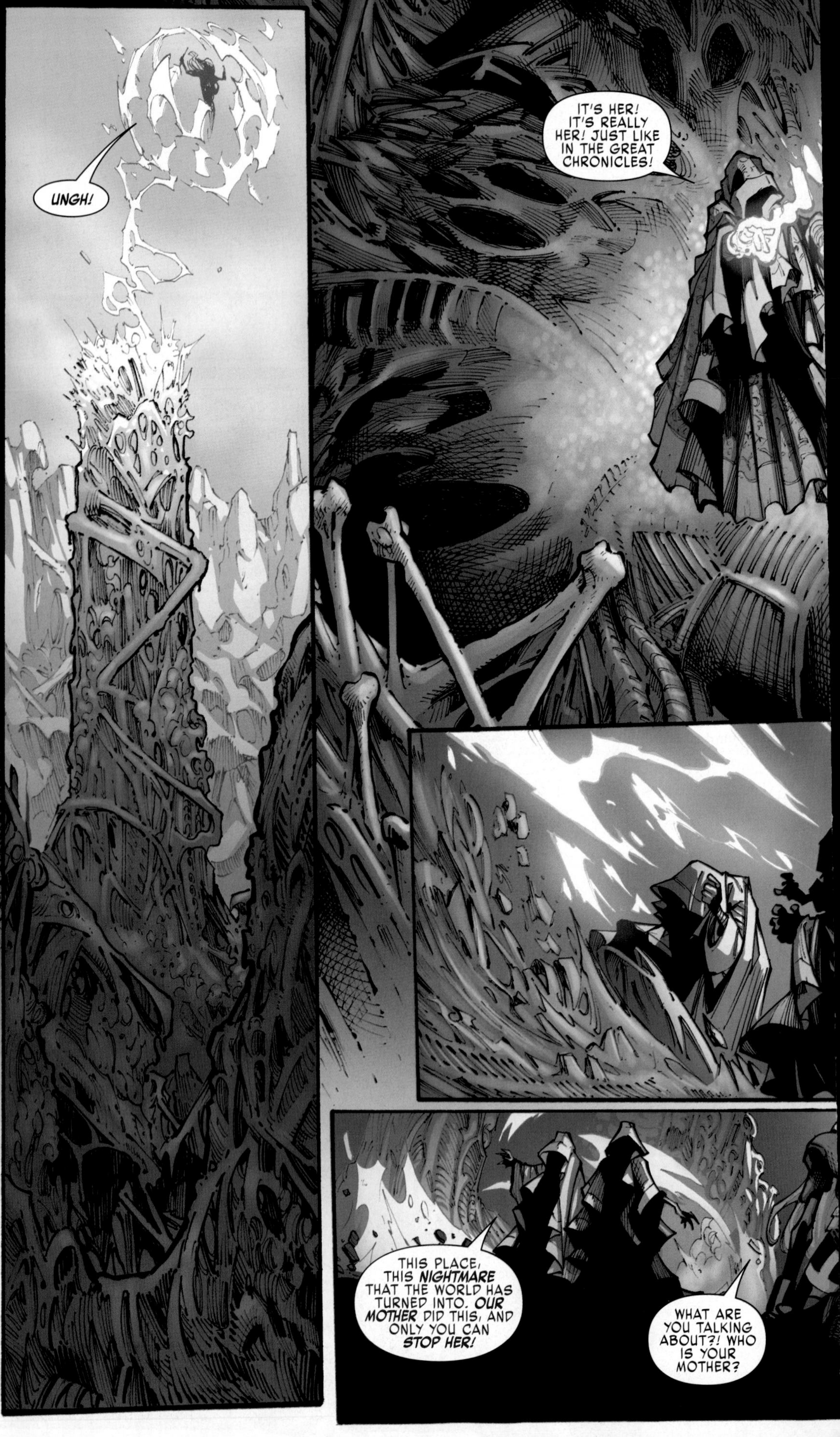
UNGH!
IT'S HER! IT'S REALLY HER! JUST LIKE IN THE GREAT CHRONICLES!
THIS PLACE, THIS NIGHTMARE THAT THE WORLD HAS TURNED INTO. OUR MOTHER DID THIS, AND ONLY YOU CAN STOP HER!
WHAT ARE YOU TALKING ABOUT?! WHO IS YOUR MOTHER?

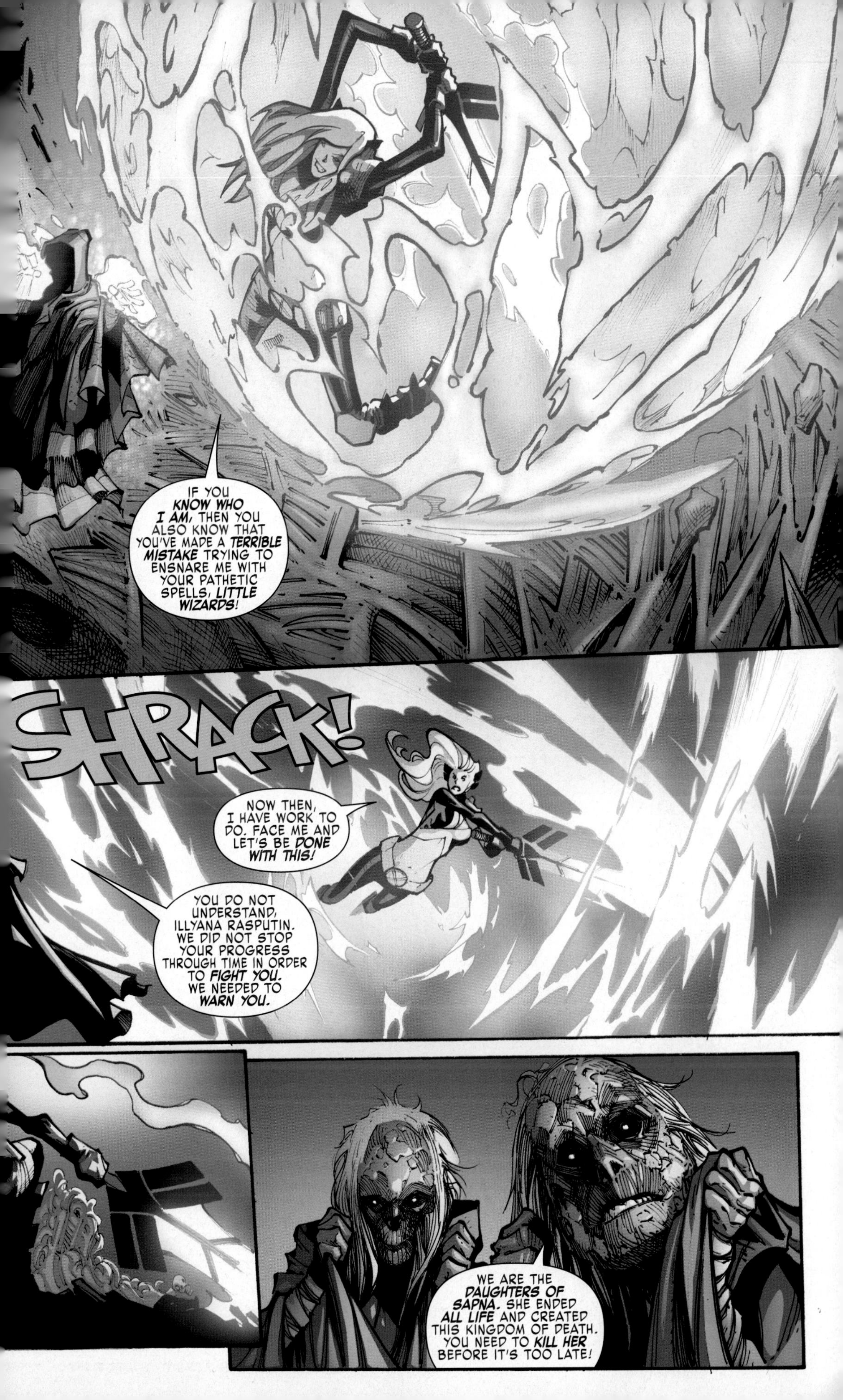
IF YOU KNOW WHO I AM, THEN YOU ALSO KNOW THAT YOU'VE MADE A TERRIBLE MISTAKE TRYING TO ENSNARE ME WITH YOUR PATHETIC SPELLS, LITTLE WIZARDS!
SHRACK!
NOW THEN, I HAVE WORK TO DO. FACE ME AND LET'S BE DONE WITH THIS!
YOU DO NOT UNDERSTAND, ILLYANA RASPUTIN. WE DID NOT STOP YOUR PROGRESS THROUGH TIME IN ORDER TO FIGHT YOU. WE NEEDED TO WARN YOU.
WE ARE THE DAUGHTERS OF SAPNA. SHE ENDED ALL LIFE AND CREATED THIS KINGDOM OF DEATH. YOU NEED TO KILL HER BEFORE IT'S TOO LATE!

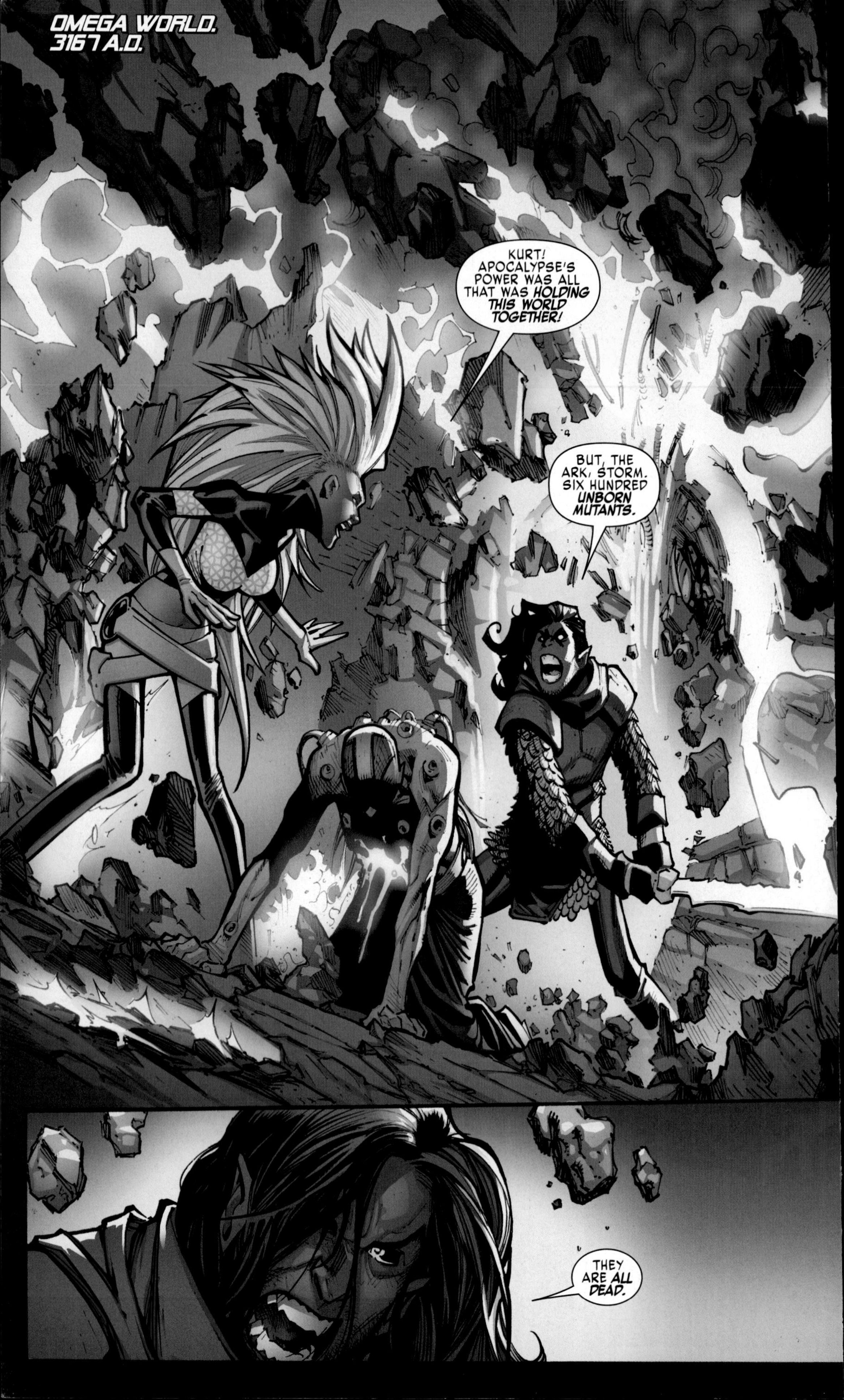
OMEGA WORLD. 3167 A.D.
KURT! APOCALYPSE'S POWER WAS ALL THAT WAS HOLDING THIS WORLD TOGETHER!
BUT, THE ARK, STORM. SIX HUNDRED UNBORN MUTANTS.
THEY ARE ALL DEAD.

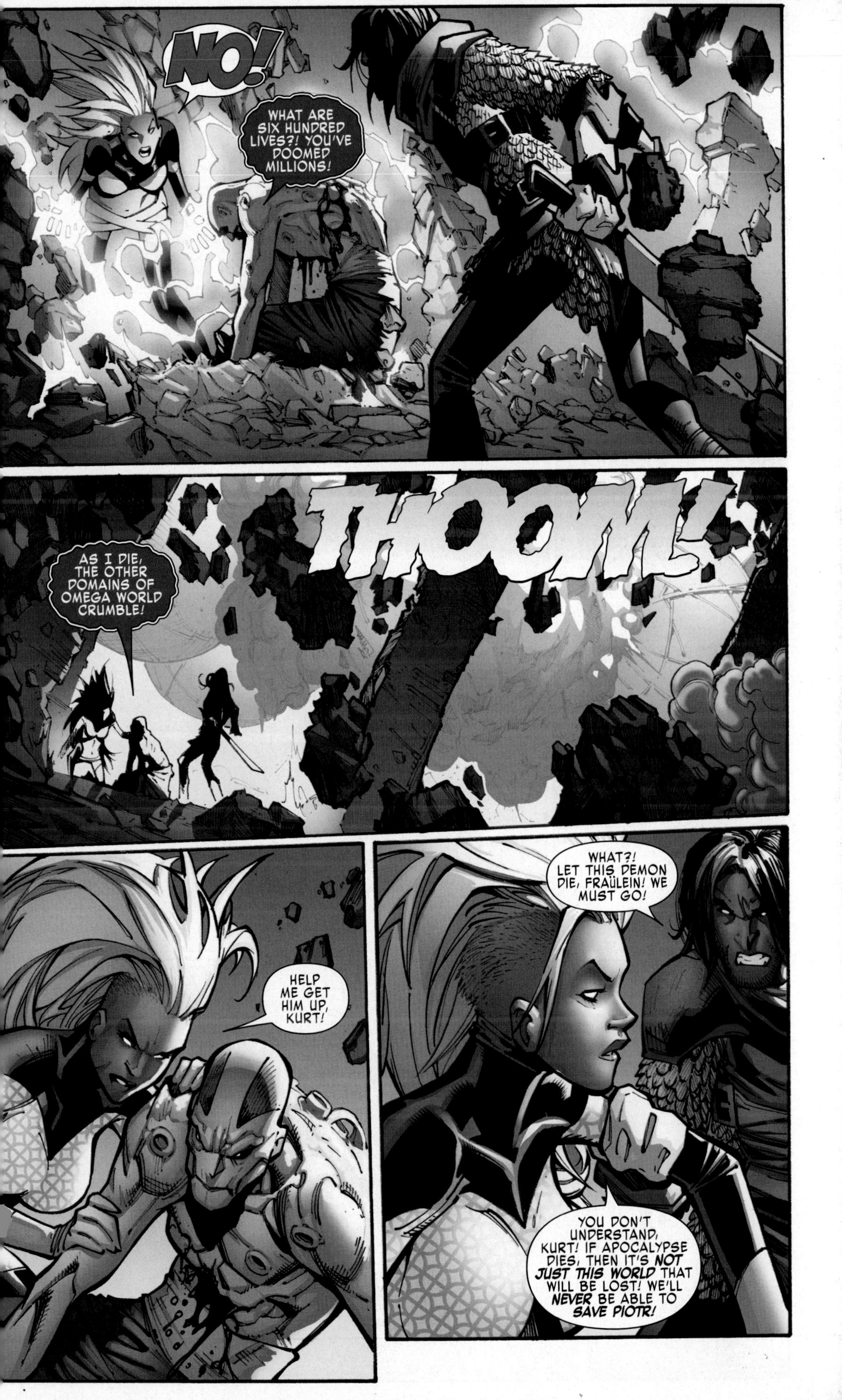

NO!
WHAT ARE SIX HUNDRED LIVES?! YOU'VE DOOMED MILLIONS!
THOOM!
AS I DIE, THE OTHER DOMAINS OF OMEGA WORLD CRUMBLE!
HELP ME GET HIM UP, KURT!
WHAT?! LET THIS DEMON DIE, FRÄULEIN! WE MUST GO!
YOU DON'T UNDERSTAND, KURT! IF APOCALYPSE DIES, THEN IT'S NOT JUST THIS WORLD THAT WILL BE LOST! WE'LL NEVER BE ABLE TO SAVE PIOTR!

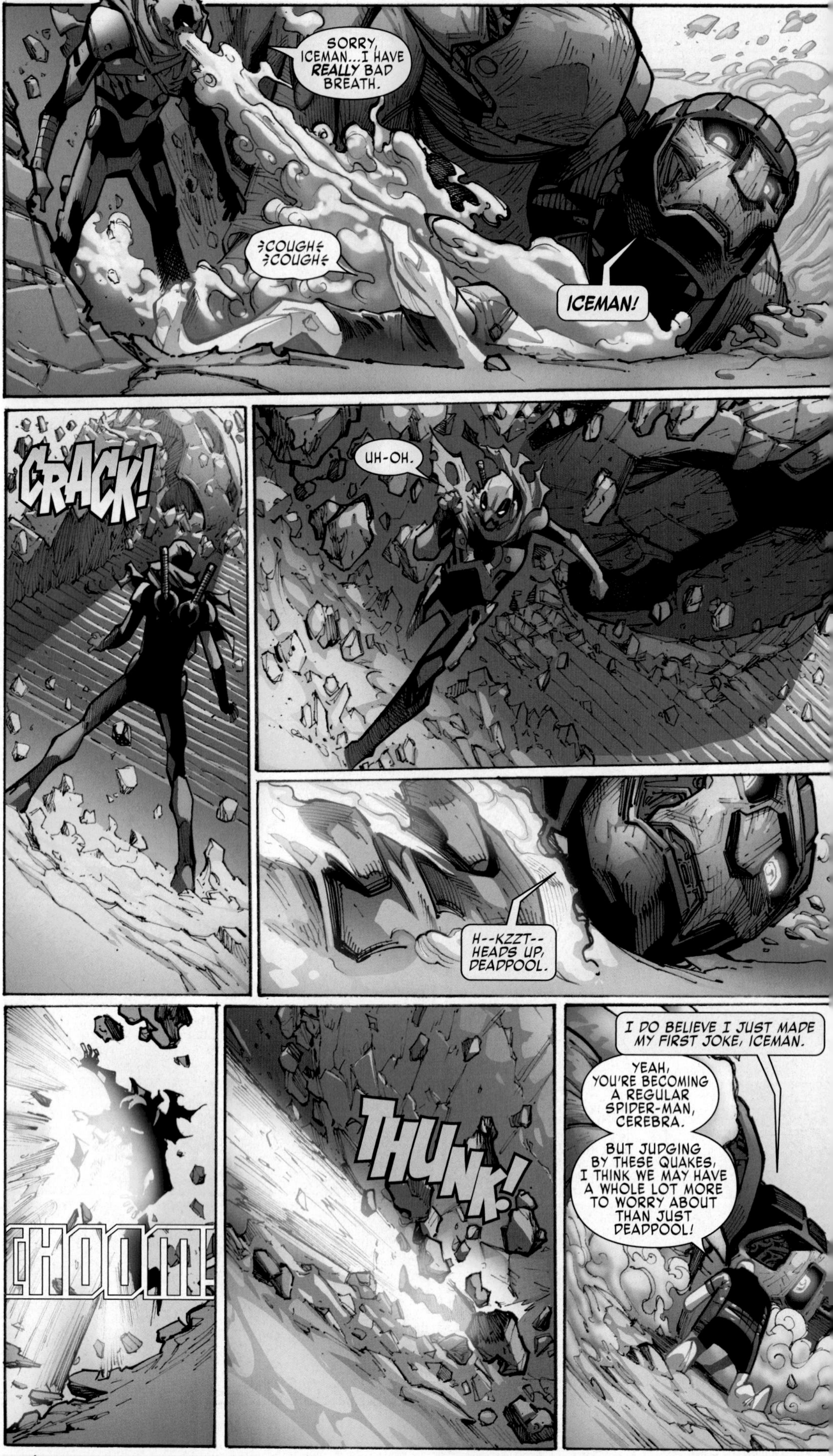
SORRY, ICEMAN...I HAVE REALLY BAD BREATH.
COUGH COUGH
ICEMAN!
CRACK!
UH-OH.
H--KZZT-- HEADS UP, DEADPOOL.
THOOM!
THUNK!
I DO BELIEVE I JUST MADE MY FIRST JOKE, ICEMAN.
YEAH, YOU'RE BECOMING A REGULAR SPIDER-MAN, CEREBRA.
BUT JUDGING BY THESE QUAKES, I THINK WE MAY HAVE A WHOLE LOT MORE TO WORRY ABOUT THAN JUST DEADPOOL!

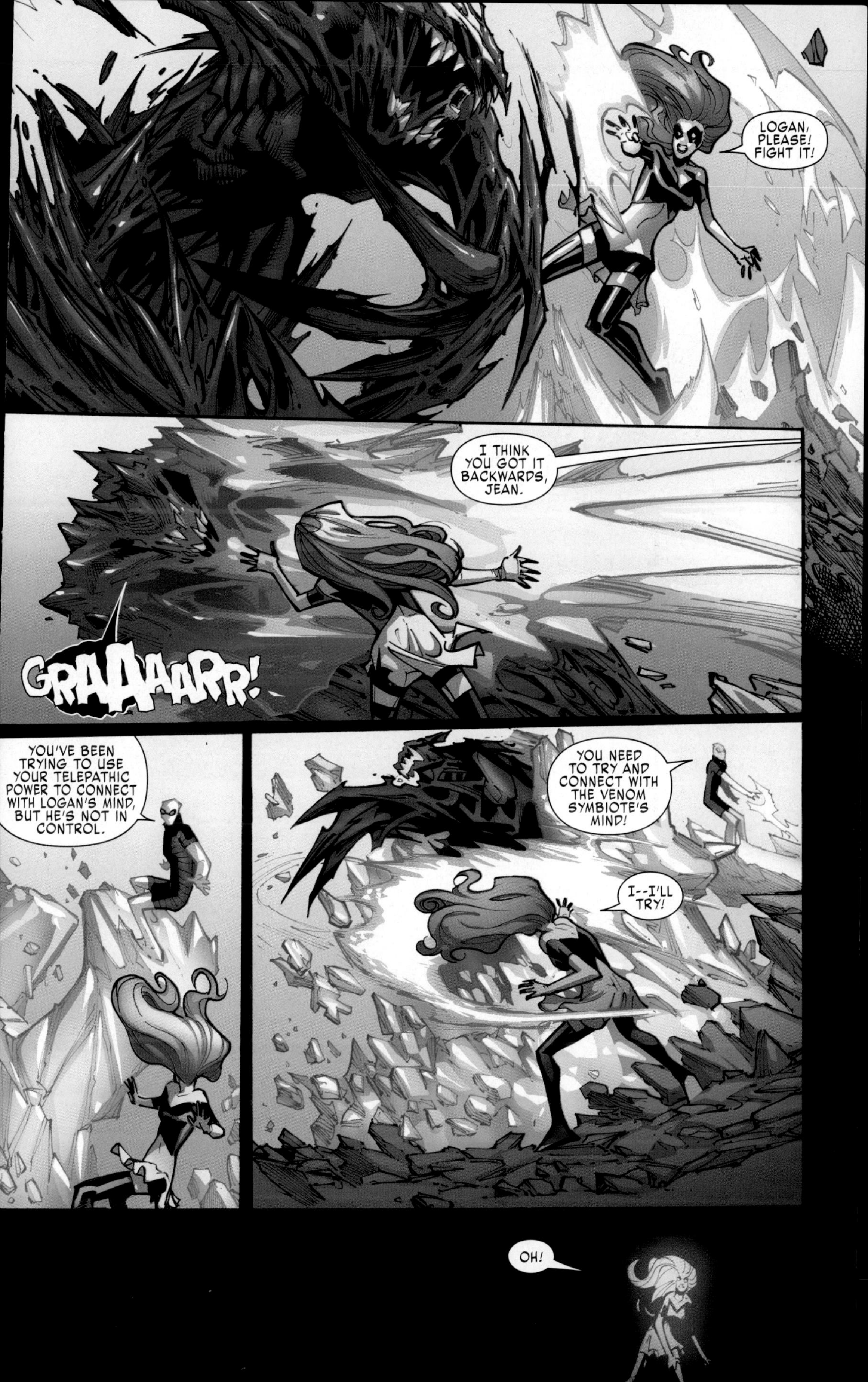
LOGAN, PLEASE! FIGHT IT!
I THINK YOU GOT IT BACKWARDS, JEAN.
GRAAAARR!
YOU'VE BEEN TRYING TO USE YOUR TELEPATHIC POWER TO CONNECT WITH LOGAN'S MIND, BUT HE'S NOT IN CONTROL.
YOU NEED TO TRY AND CONNECT WITH THE VENOM SYMBIOTE'S MIND!
I--I'LL TRY!
OH!

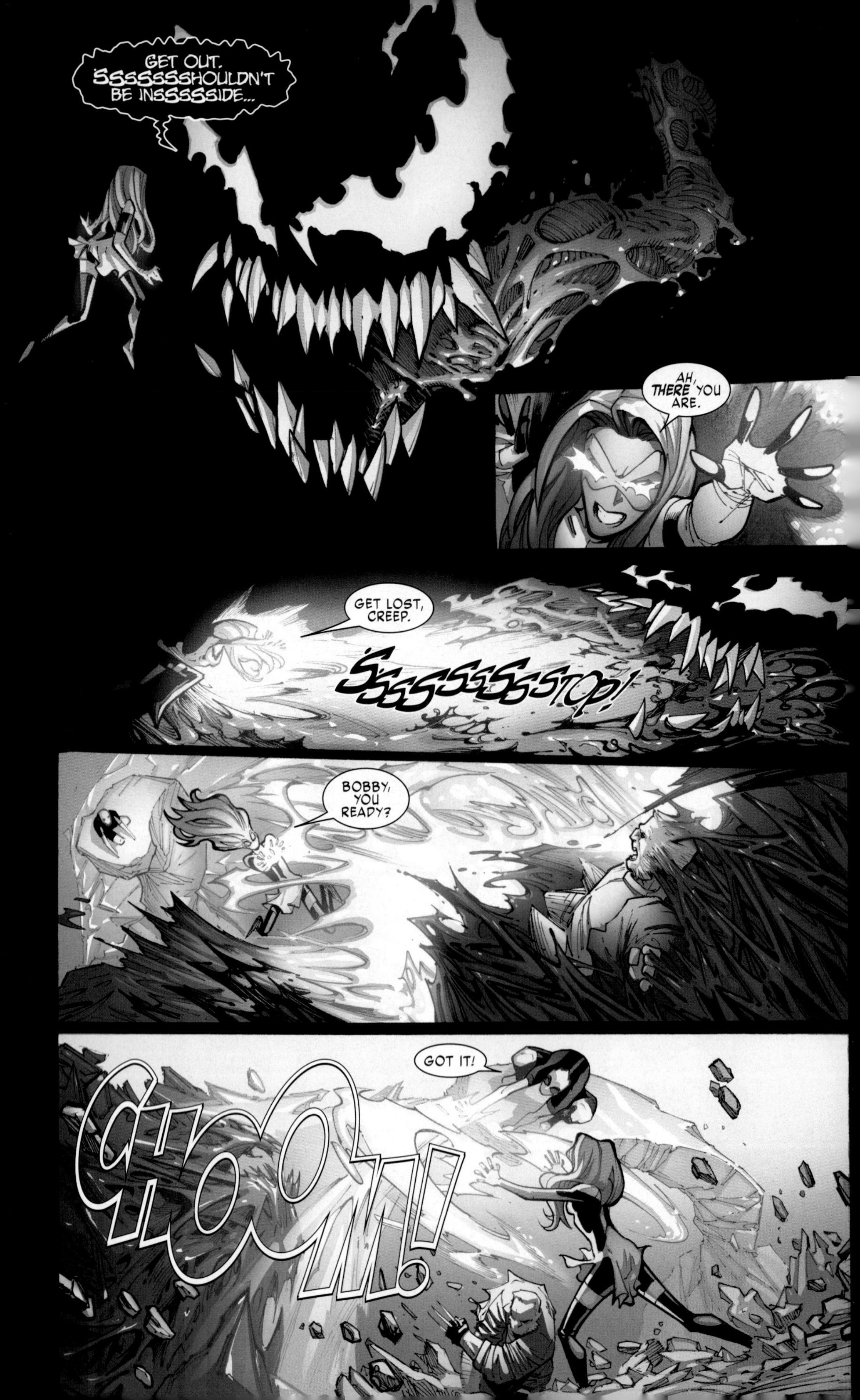
GET OUT. SSSSSSSHOULDN'T BE INSSSSSIDE...
AH, THERE YOU ARE.
GET LOST, CREEP.
SSSSSSSSSTOP!
BOBBY, YOU READY?
GOT IT!
CHOOM!

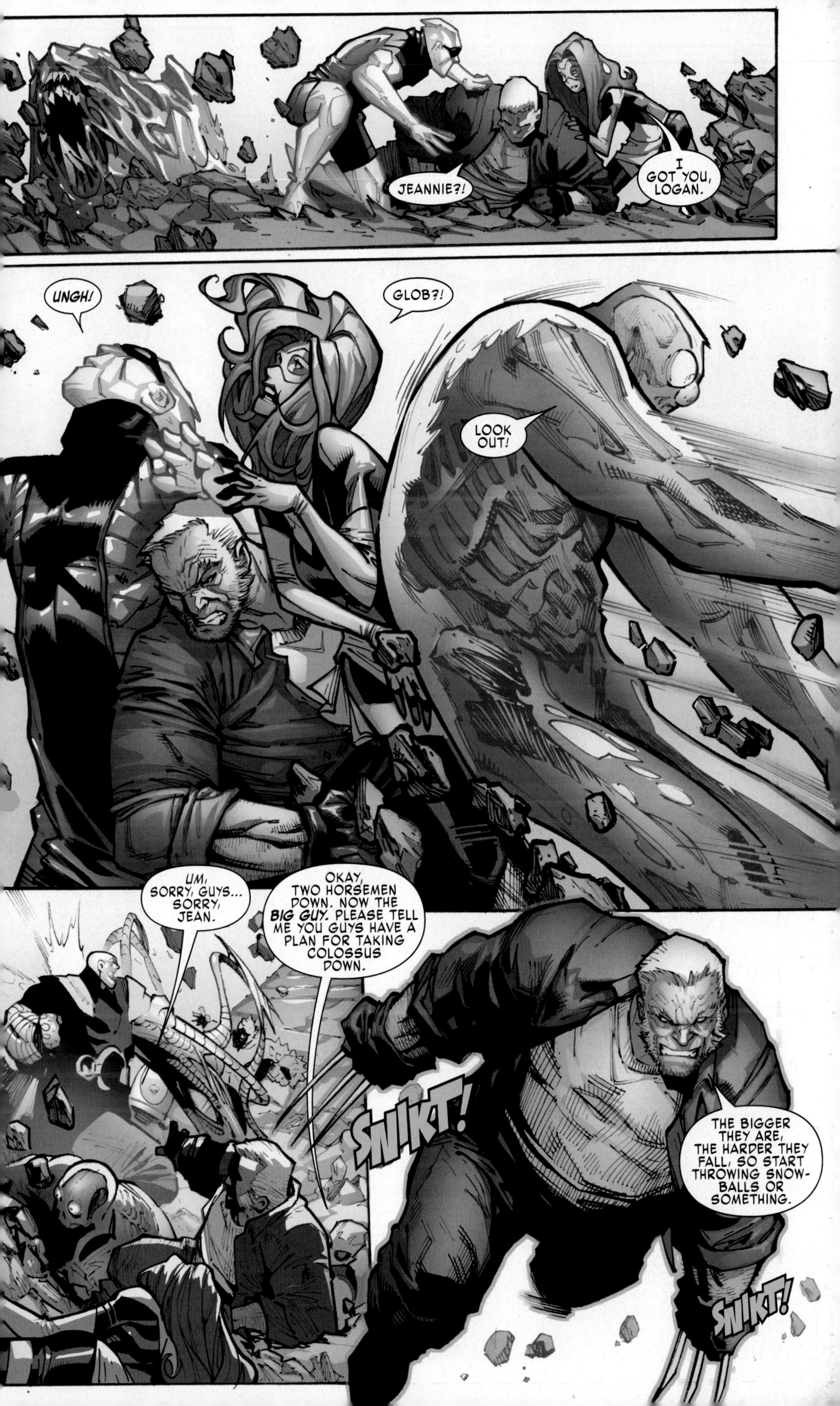
JEANNIE?!
I GOT YOU, LOGAN.
UNGH!
GLOB?!
LOOK OUT!
UM, SORRY, GUYS... SORRY, JEAN.
OKAY, TWO HORSEMEN DOWN. NOW THE BIG GUY. PLEASE TELL ME YOU GUYS HAVE A PLAN FOR TAKING COLOSSUS DOWN.
SNIKT!
THE BIGGER THEY ARE, THE HARDER THEY FALL, SO START THROWING SNOW-BALLS OR SOMETHING.
SNIKT!

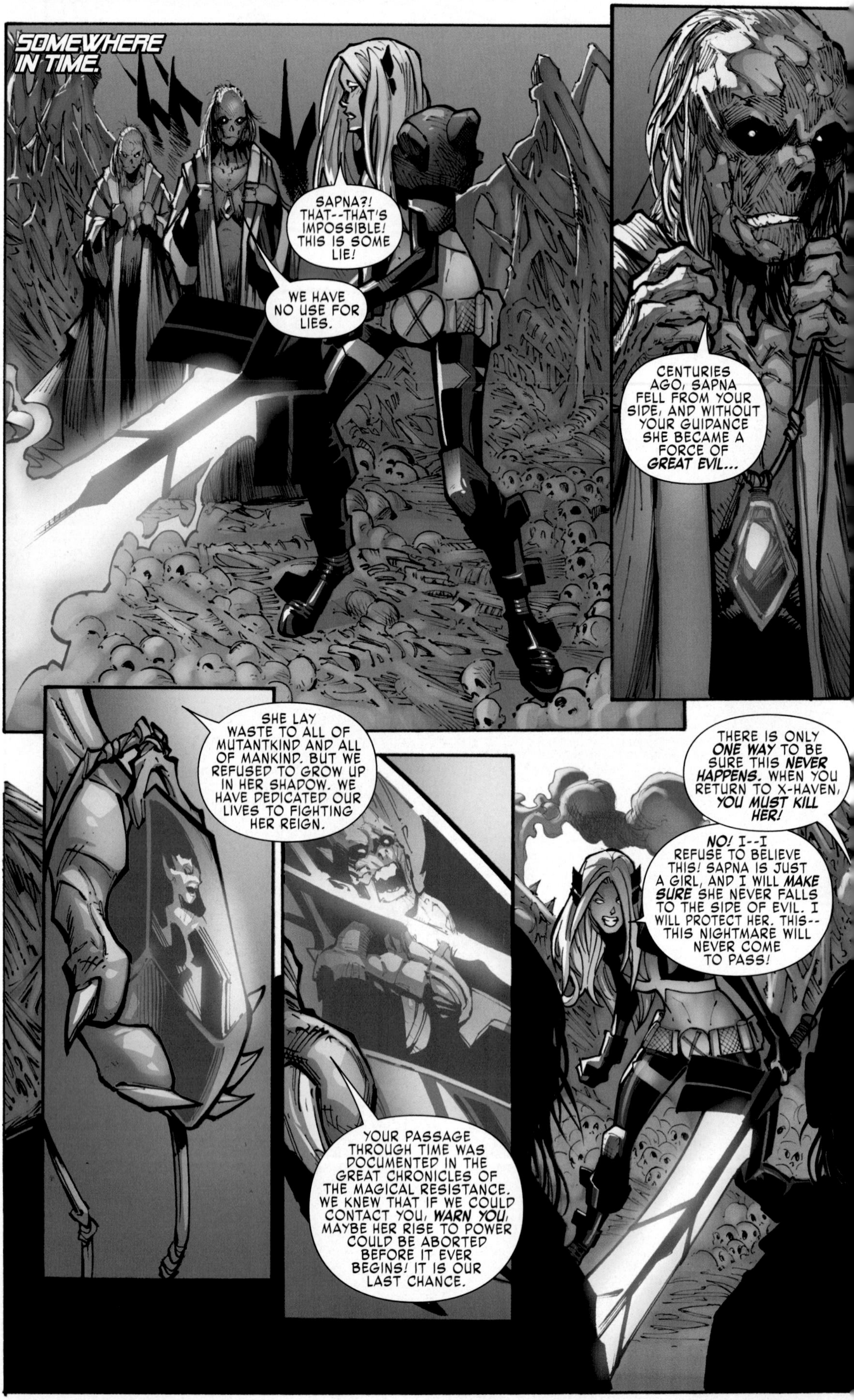

SOMEWHERE IN TIME.
SAPNA?! THAT--THAT'S IMPOSSIBLE! THIS IS SOME LIE!
WE HAVE NO USE FOR LIES.
CENTURIES AGO, SAPNA FELL FROM YOUR SIDE, AND WITHOUT YOUR GUIDANCE SHE BECAME A FORCE OF GREAT EVIL...
SHE LAY WASTE TO ALL OF MUTANTKIND AND ALL OF MANKIND. BUT WE REFUSED TO GROW UP IN HER SHADOW. WE HAVE DEDICATED OUR LIVES TO FIGHTING HER REIGN.
YOUR PASSAGE THROUGH TIME WAS DOCUMENTED IN THE GREAT CHRONICLES OF THE MAGICAL RESISTANCE. WE KNEW THAT IF WE COULD CONTACT YOU, WARN YOU, MAYBE HER RISE TO POWER COULD BE ABORTED BEFORE IT EVER BEGINS! IT IS OUR LAST CHANCE.
THERE IS ONLY ONE WAY TO BE SURE THIS NEVER HAPPENS. WHEN YOU RETURN TO X-HAVEN, YOU MUST KILL HER!
NO! I--I REFUSE TO BELIEVE THIS! SAPNA IS JUST A GIRL, AND I WILL MAKE SURE SHE NEVER FALLS TO THE SIDE OF EVIL. I WILL PROTECT HER. THIS--THIS NIGHTMARE WILL NEVER COME TO PASS!

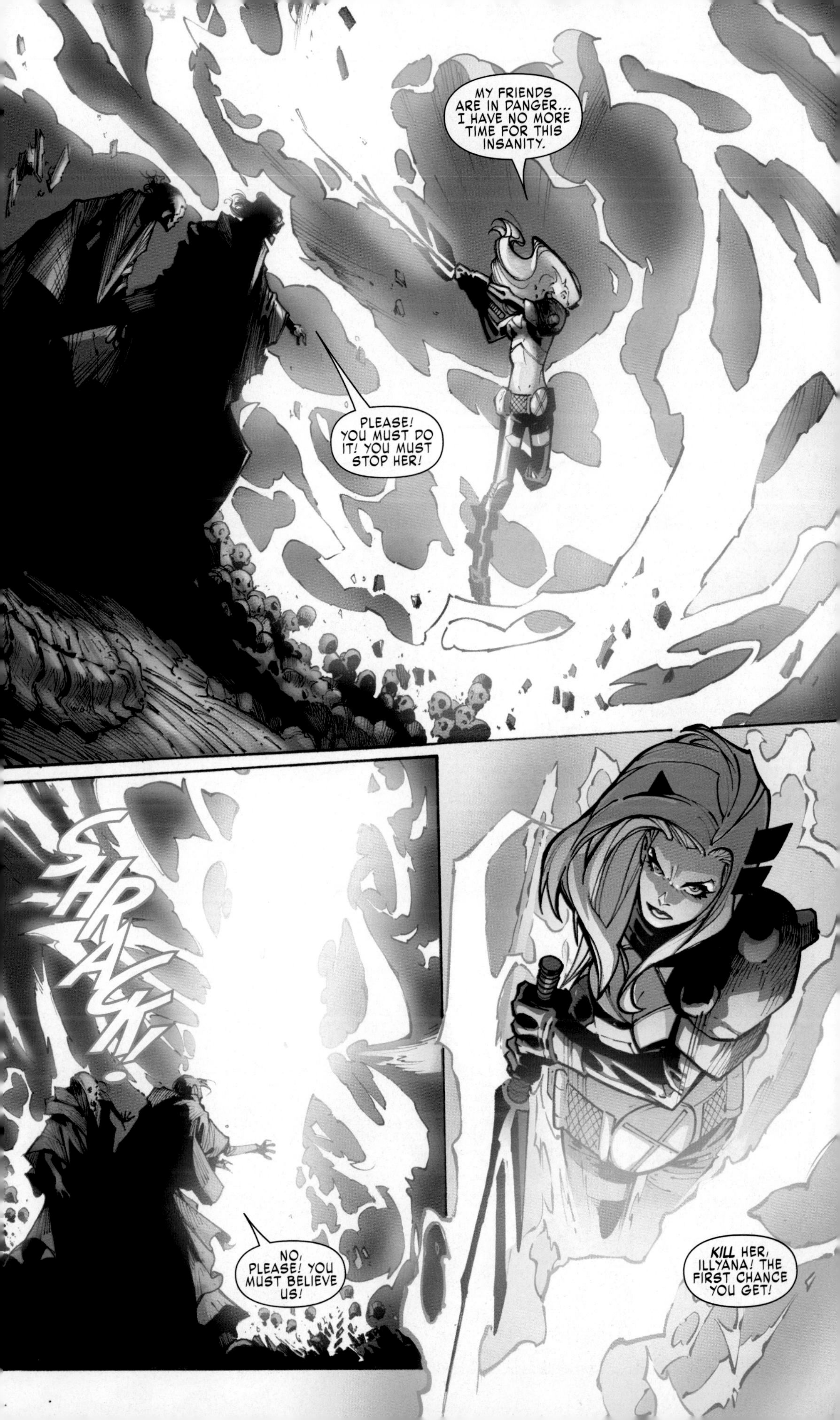
MY FRIENDS ARE IN DANGER... I HAVE NO MORE TIME FOR THIS INSANITY.
PLEASE! YOU MUST DO IT! YOU MUST STOP HER!
SHRAACK!
NO, PLEASE! YOU MUST BELIEVE US!
KILL HER, ILLYANA! THE FIRST CHANCE YOU GET!

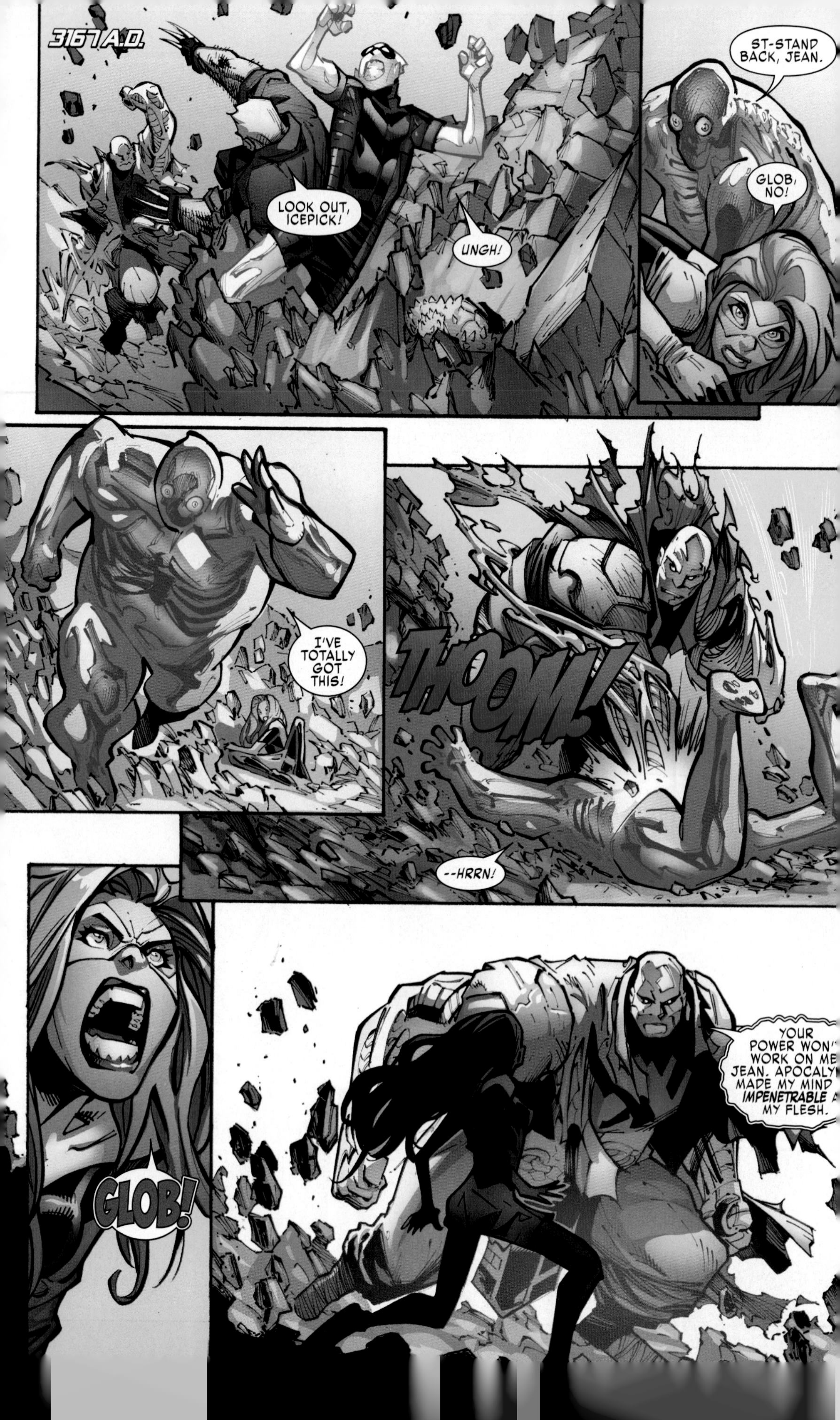
3167 A.D.
LOOK OUT, ICEPICK!
UNGH!
ST-STAND BACK, JEAN.
GLOB, NO!
I'VE TOTALLY GOT THIS!
THOOM!
--HRRN!
GLOB!
YOUR POWER WON' WORK ON ME JEAN. APOCALY MADE MY MIND IMPENETRABLE A MY FLESH.

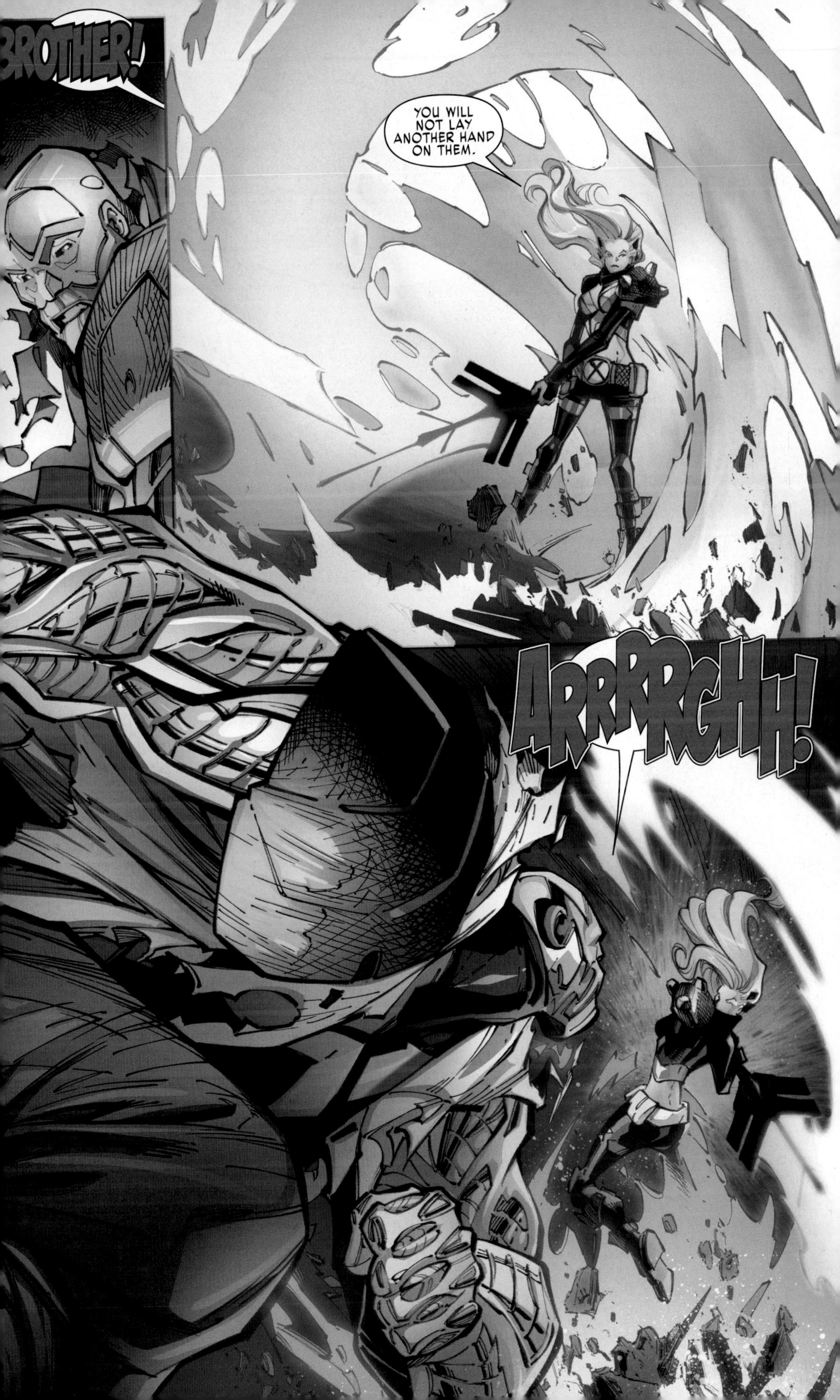
BROTHER!
YOU WILL NOT LAY ANOTHER HAND ON THEM.
ARRRRGHH!

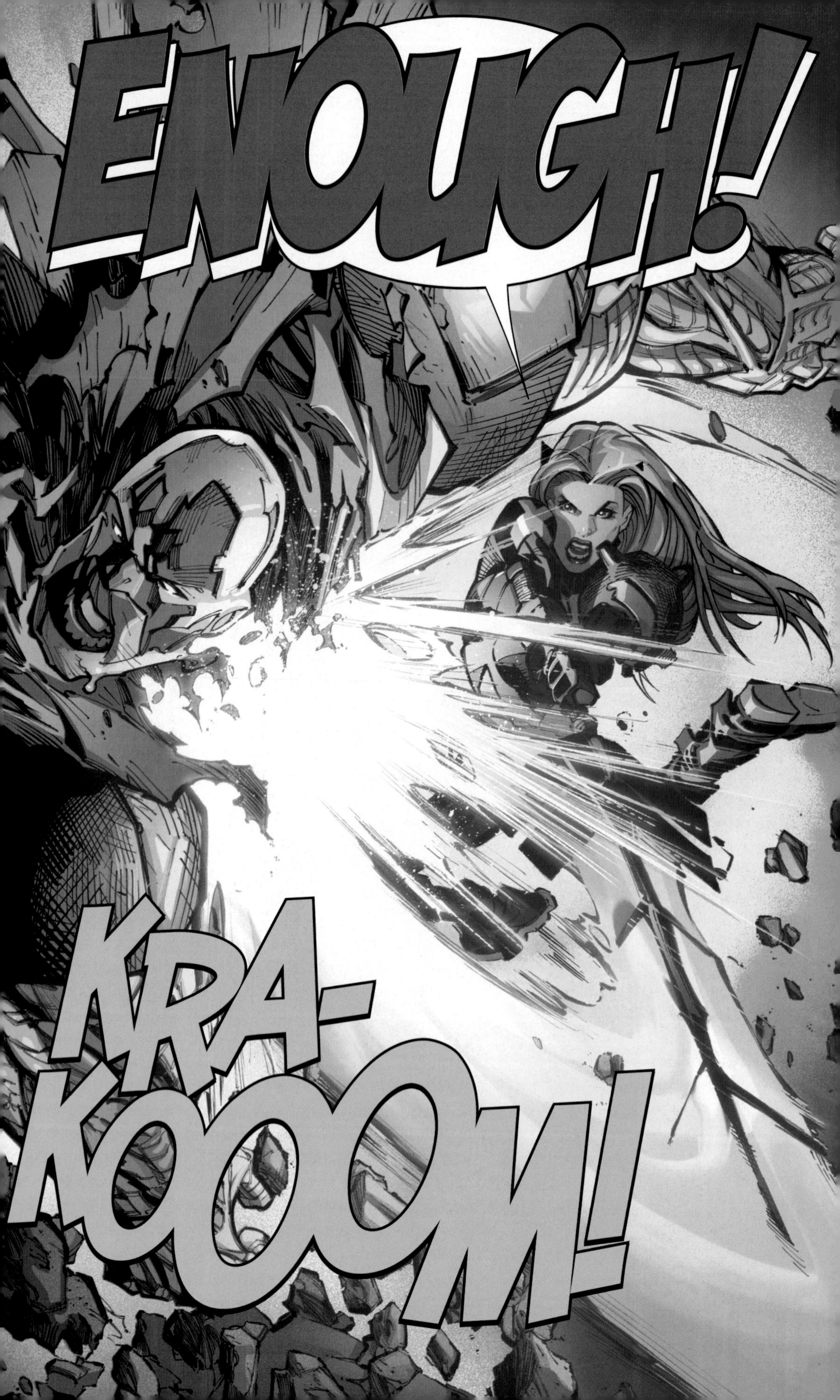
ENOUGH!
KRA-KOOOM!

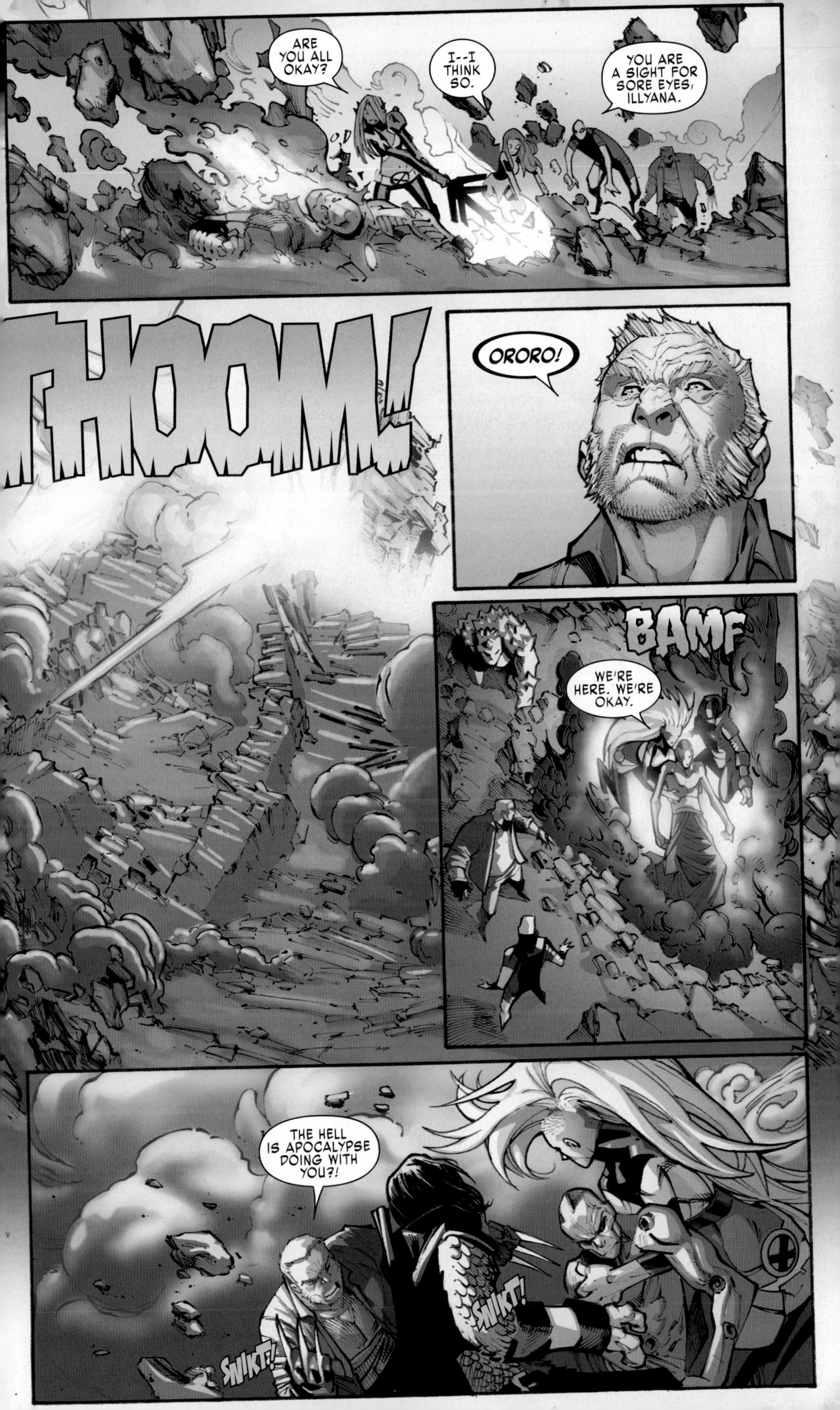
ARE YOU ALL OKAY?
I--I THINK SO.
YOU ARE A SIGHT FOR SORE EYES, ILLYANA.
THOOM!
ORORO!
BAMF
WE'RE HERE. WE'RE OKAY.
THE HELL IS APOCALYPSE DOING WITH YOU?!
SNIKT!
SNIKT!

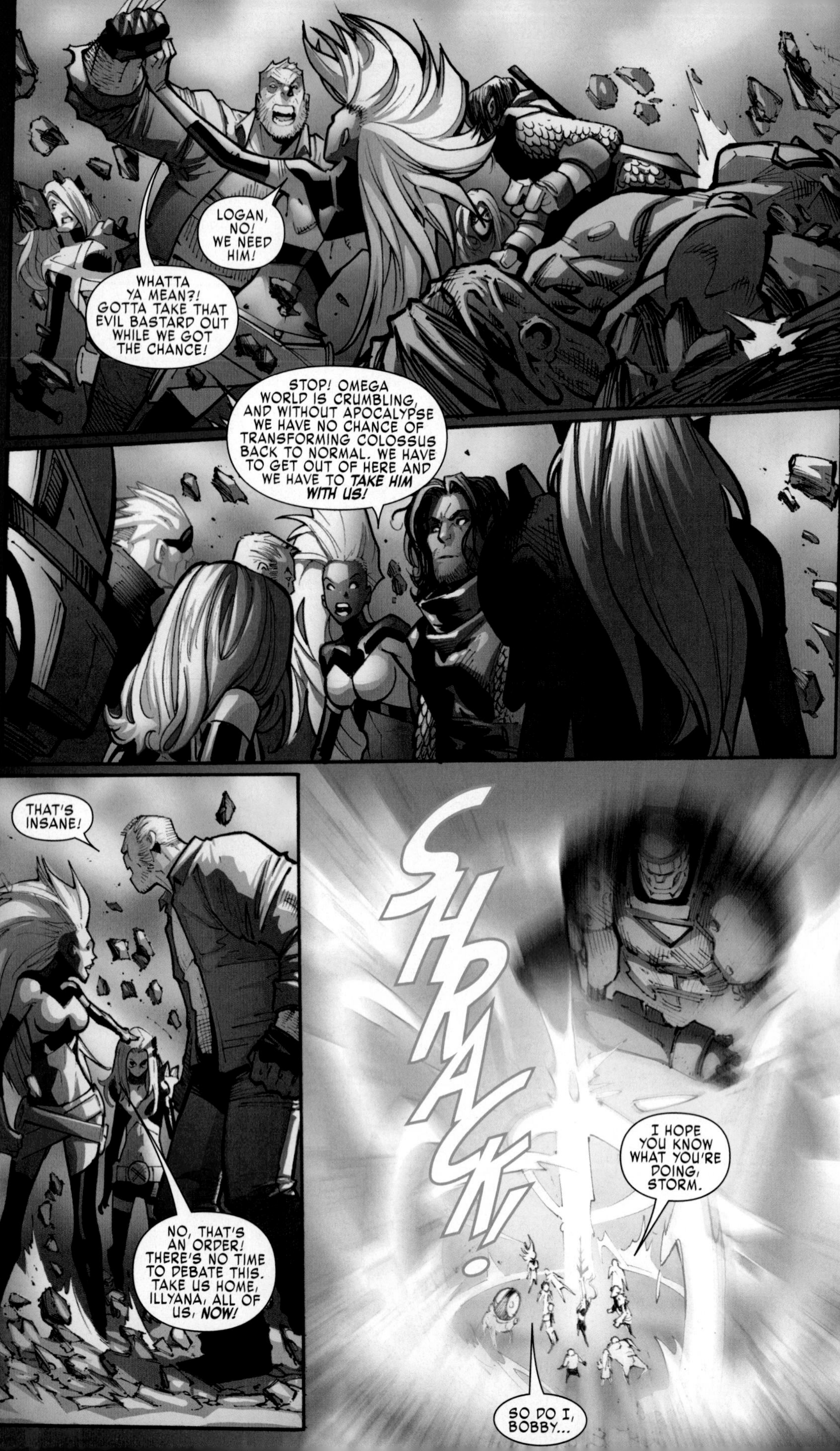
LOGAN, NO! WE NEED HIM!
WHATTA YA MEAN?! GOTTA TAKE THAT EVIL BASTARD OUT WHILE WE GOT THE CHANCE!
STOP! OMEGA WORLD IS CRUMBLING, AND WITHOUT APOCALYPSE WE HAVE NO CHANCE OF TRANSFORMING COLOSSUS BACK TO NORMAL. WE HAVE TO GET OUT OF HERE AND WE HAVE TO *TAKE HIM WITH US!*
THAT'S INSANE!
NO, THAT'S AN ORDER! THERE'S NO TIME TO DEBATE THIS. TAKE US HOME, ILLYANA, ALL OF US, *NOW!*
SHRACK!
I HOPE YOU KNOW WHAT YOU'RE DOING, STORM.
SO DO I, BOBBY...

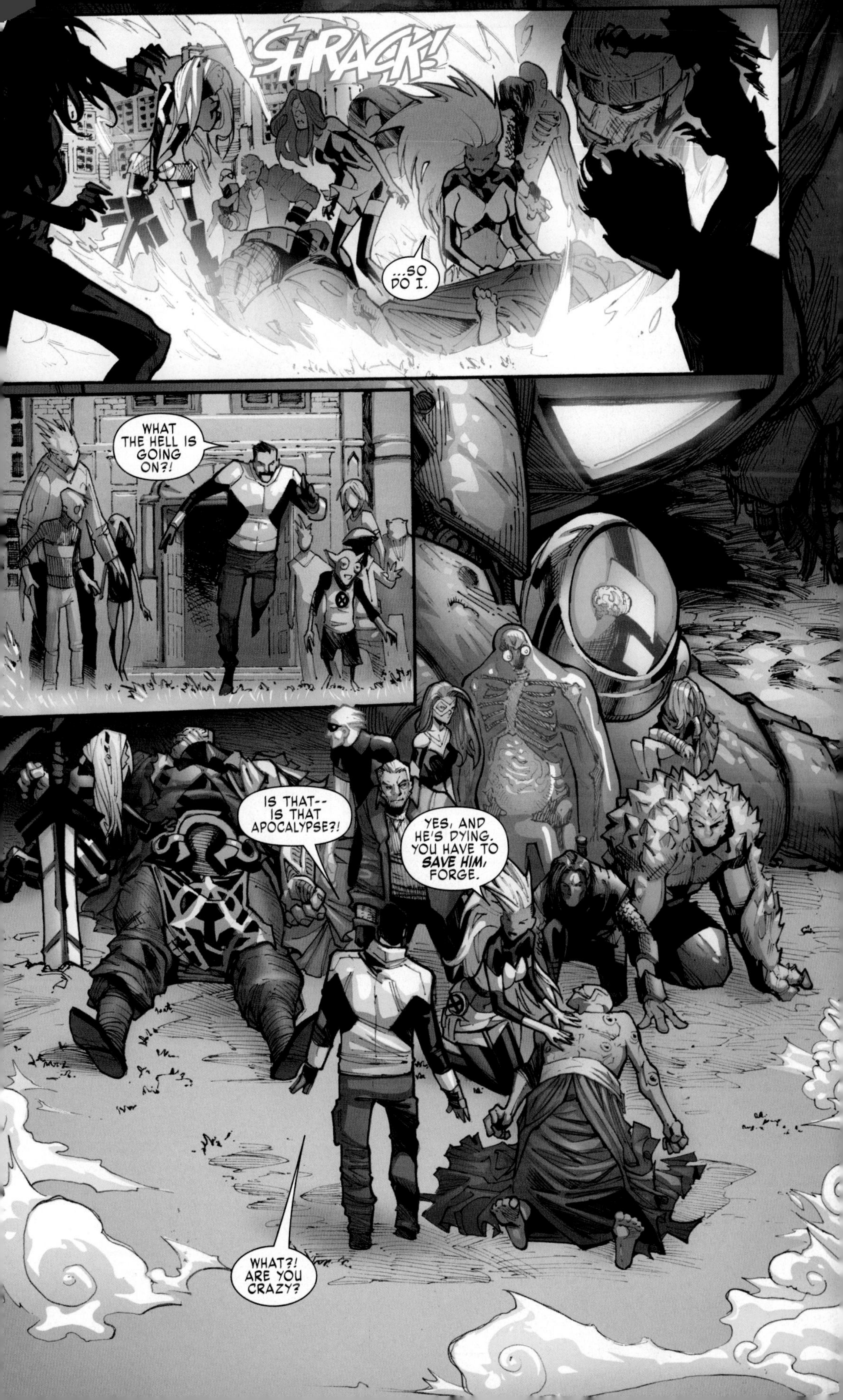
SHRACK!
...SO DO I.
WHAT THE HELL IS GOING ON?!
IS THAT-- IS THAT APOCALYPSE?!
YES, AND HE'S DYING. YOU HAVE TO SAVE HIM, FORGE.
WHAT?! ARE YOU CRAZY?

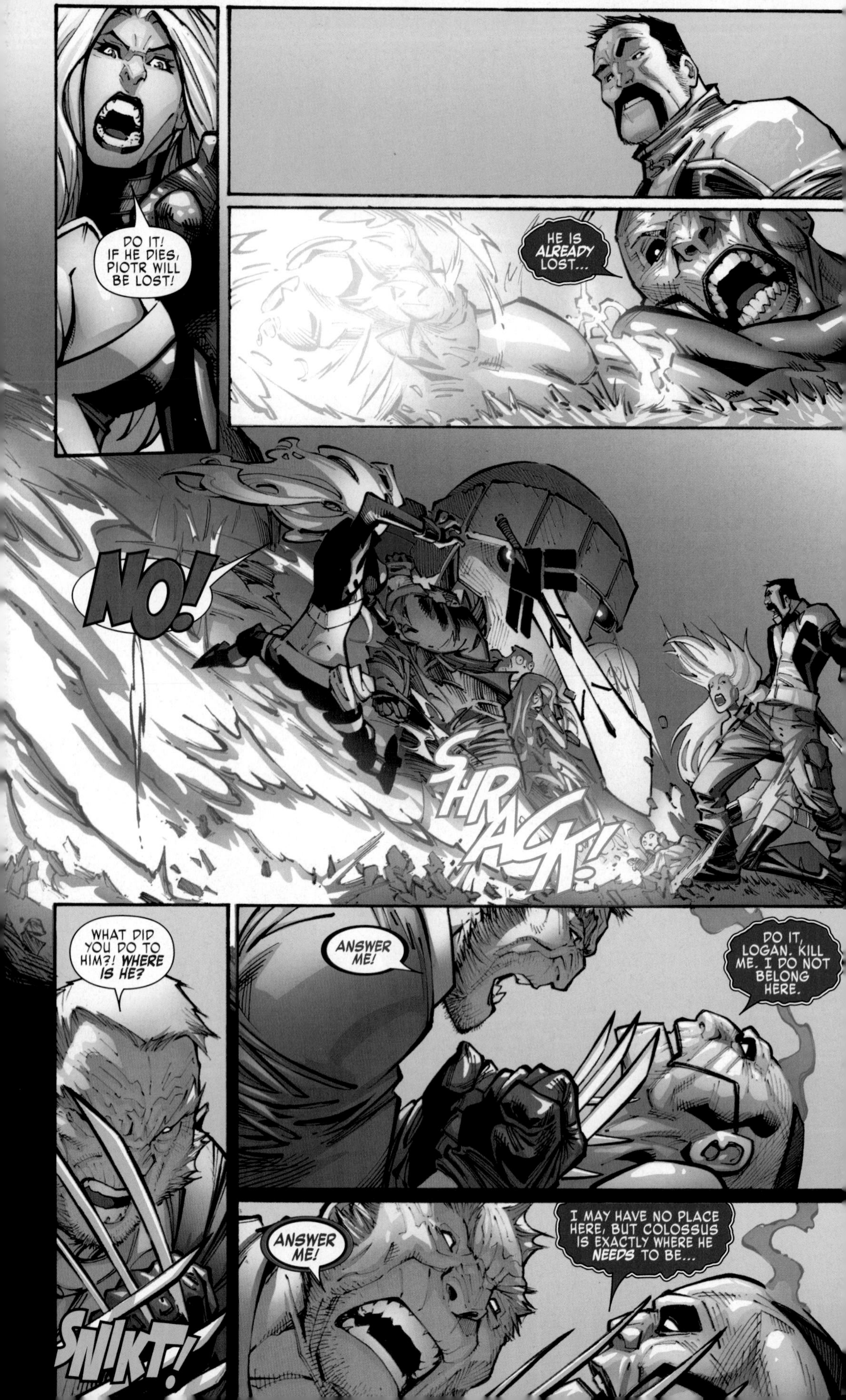
DO IT! IF HE DIES, PIOTR WILL BE LOST!
HE IS ALREADY LOST...
NO!
SHRACK!
WHAT DID YOU DO TO HIM?! WHERE IS HE?
ANSWER ME!
DO IT, LOGAN. KILL ME. I DO NOT BELONG HERE.
ANSWER ME!
I MAY HAVE NO PLACE HERE, BUT COLOSSUS IS EXACTLY WHERE HE NEEDS TO BE...
SNIKT!

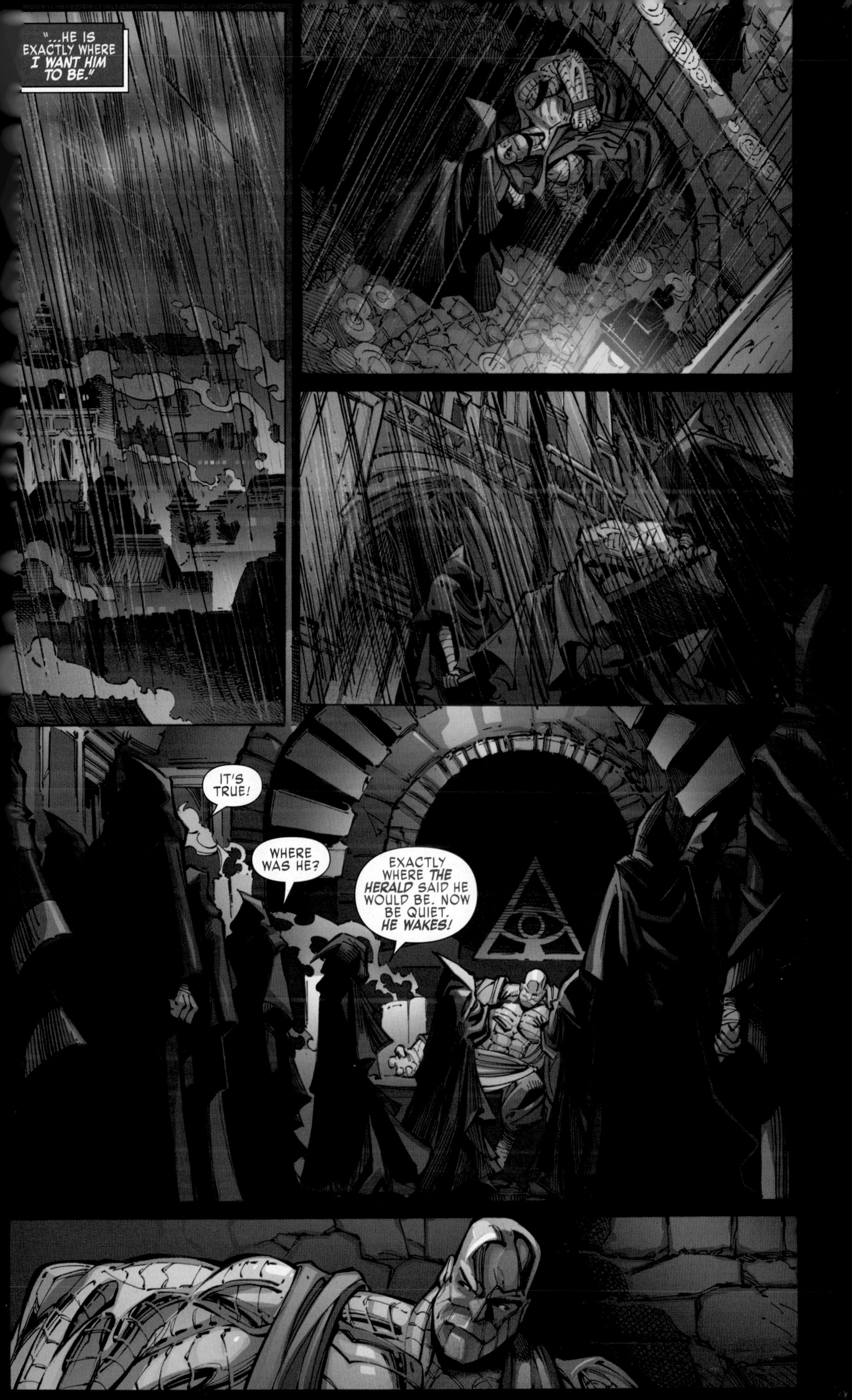
"...HE IS EXACTLY WHERE I WANT HIM TO BE."
IT'S TRUE!
WHERE WAS HE?
EXACTLY WHERE THE HERALD SAID HE WOULD BE. NOW BE QUIET. HE WAKES!

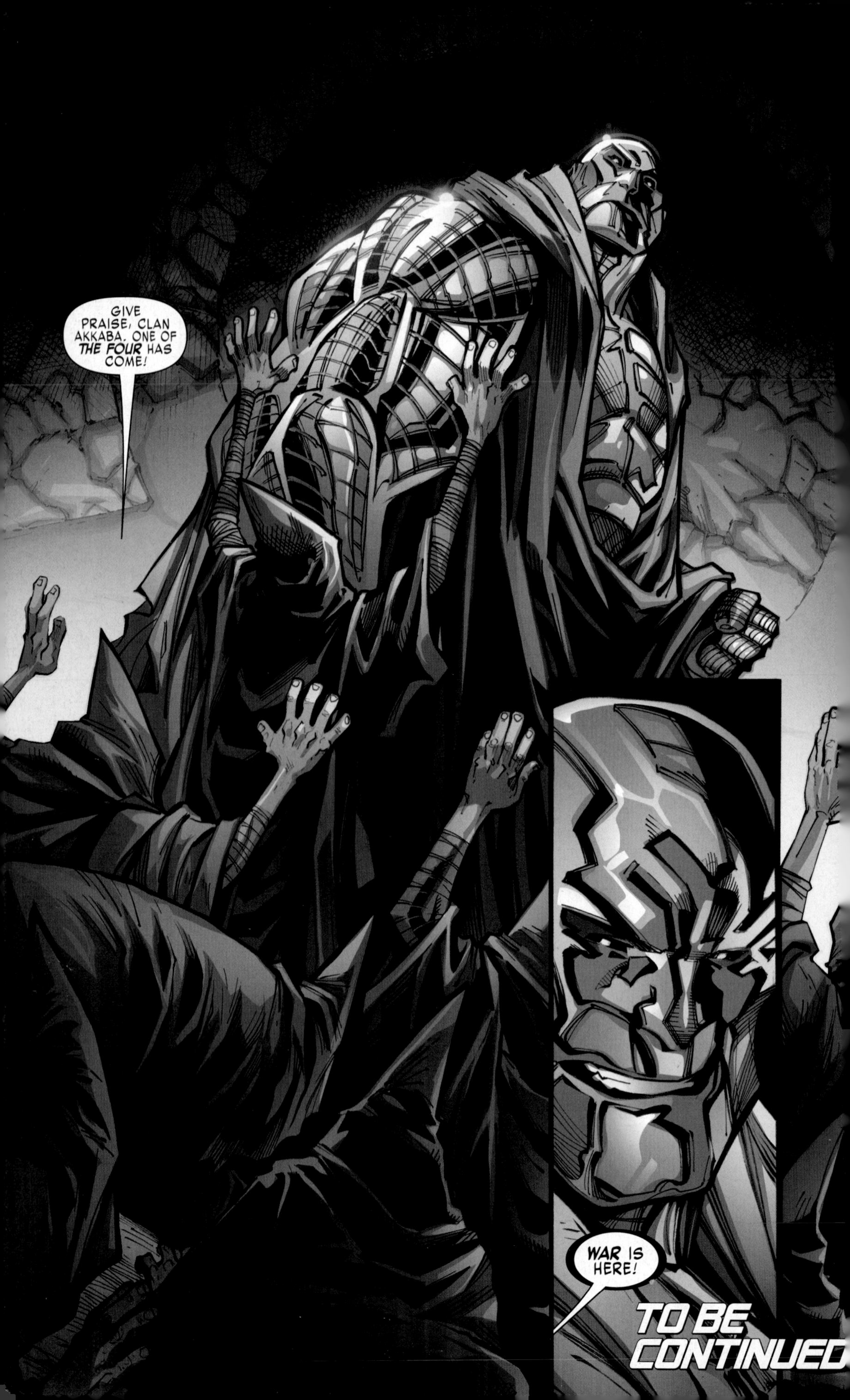
GIVE PRAISE, CLAN AKKABA. ONE OF THE FOUR HAS COME!
WAR IS HERE!
TO BE CONTINUED

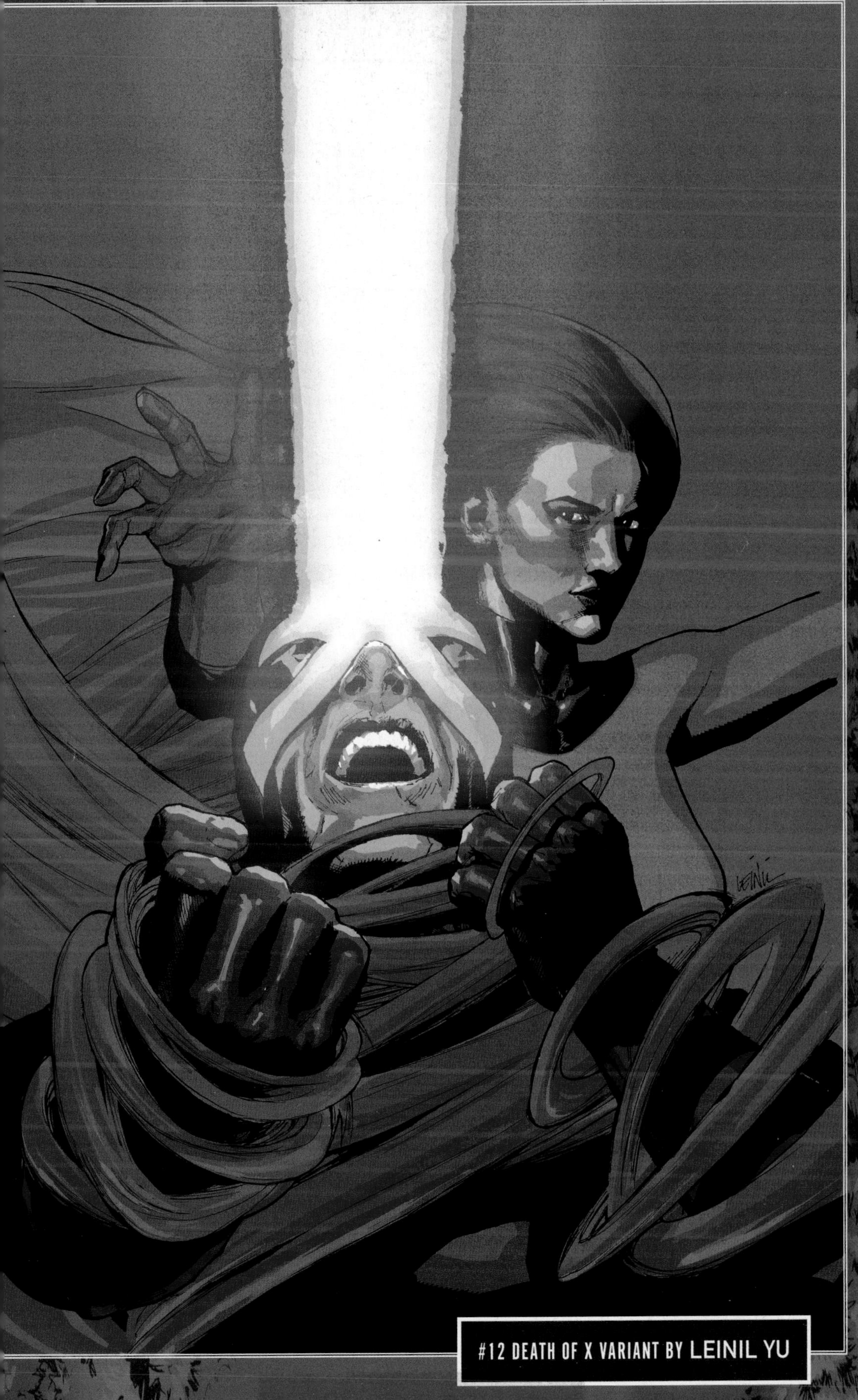
LEINIL

#12 DEATH OF X VARIANT BY LEINIL YU